# MOTOR LEARNING

# MOTOR LEARNING

## CONCEPTS AND APPLICATIONS

*Fifth Edition*

*Richard A. Magill*

Louisiana State University

WCB
McGraw-Hill

Boston, Massachusetts   Burr Ridge, Illinois   Dubuque, Iowa
Madison, Wisconsin   New York, New York   San Francisco, California   St. Louis, Missouri

*McGraw-Hill*

*A Division of The McGraw-Hill Companies*

**MOTOR LEARNING: CONCEPTS AND APPLICATIONS**
**International Editions 1998**

Exclusive rights by McGraw-Hill Book Co – Singapore for manufacture and export. This book cannot be re-exported from the country to which it is consigned by McGraw-Hill.

4  5  6  7  8  9  0  BJE  PMP  0

**Library of Congress Cataloging-in-Publication Data**

Magill, Richard A.
    Motor learning : concepts and applications / Richard A. Magill.–5th ed.
        p.    cm.
    Includes bibliographical references and indexes.
    ISBN 0-0697-24652-3
    1.  Motor learning.
    BF295.M36     1997
    152.3'34–dc21                                            97-16623

http://www.mhcollege.com

**When ordering this title, use ISBN 0-07-115821-9**

Printed in Singapore

# CONTENTS

■

# Unit III

## The Learning Environment 124

■

# Unit IV

## Individual Differences 272

# PREFACE

It is both exciting and challenging to prepare the fifth edition of this book. The excitement is due to knowing that there is continued interest in this book and in motor learning as subject matter for the development of students who aspire to professions involving skill acquisition and/or rehabilitation. Preparing this edition is a challenge because the increase in the amount of research done since the fourth edition makes updating the text without expanding it to unrealistic proportions a difficult task. An additional challenge is created by the increased interest by rehabilitation professions to include motor learning as part of the programs of study for students. This means that the text must be amended to establish its relevance for these professions but without diminishing its relevance to teaching and coaching professions, which in the past have been the primary users of motor learning courses.

To achieve the goals established by these challenges, several features of this text have been kept the same as in previous editions while several have been changed and added. Primary among the features that remain unchanged is the "concepts approach" taken to present the content of the text.

Again, each chapter presents a different general area of study in motor learning. Each chapter is subdivided into several essential concepts that represent the key points of our present knowledge about the area of study. Then an application section describes motor skill examples of relevance to each concept, adapted to the everyday environment in which we live and work. Finally, a discussion section presents research, theory, and issues that establish how the concept was derived. Within this framework, a special effort has been made to keep the text appropriate for undergraduate students, for whom this book is prepared.

As in every new edition, several changes and additions are included. One important change is that there is a reduction in the number of references cited in text. The purpose of this change is to keep the book focused more on discussing the concept and applying it to the needs of the professional. Reviews of the last edition indicated a drift toward becoming too focused on motor learning research issues and controversies. It is important, however, to keep in mind that the motor learning concepts presented in this text have a research evidence basis and are not derived from weight of unsubstantiated opinion. Thus, the need is to find the right balance of discussing relevant research while not allowing the research issues to overwhelm the point of the discussion of a concept. Accordingly, research studies included in this edition serve two purposes: to present an example of research done about an issue to substantiate a point and to provide research references for the student and/or instructor who wants more information about a topic.

Another notable change in this edition is the expansion of motor skill learning and performance examples that involve everyday skills and rehabilitative clinical environments. Although the fourth edition began providing these examples, the present edition gives them more prominence and increases the amount of them. Adding these types of skill examples increases awareness of the relevance of motor learning concepts to a broad range of skills and performance situations.

An important change to this edition is the restructuring of some of the content from the previous edition. In some cases, topics have been deleted or integrated with other topics. For example, two chapters from the fourth edition on memory and motivation are deleted. This will help to keep the amount of information appropriate for a one-semester course. Also, some topics included in chapters of past editions are minimally relevant to the undergraduate's needs in acquiring a basic knowledge of motor learning. However, material from those chapters considered essential to that knowledge base has been incorporated into other chapters.

The chapters from the fourth edition on the control of movement and attention have been restructured in this edition to reduce the quantity of information in each. The goal of this restructuring is to maintain a focus on content that is most relevant for understanding of motor skill learning. As undergraduate courses in motor control become more numerous, the need to have an expansive discussion of motor control topics diminishes. However, in keeping with the need to provide a contemporary view of issues, this edition presents a more developed discussion of the dynamical systems theory of the control of coordinated movement.

To provide a better working organization of topics, the three Units in the previous edition have been restructured into four. This new structure allows for a better presentation of the study of motor learning. Now, the book engages the student first in understanding the characteristics and measurement of motor skills, which are essential components of the foundation of knowledge for all professions related to motor skill learning and rehabilitation. In the second unit, the student studies theoretical aspects of how the nervous system controls coordinated movement and limitations built into the system. In Unit Three, the focus shifts to the acquisition of motor skills and the influence on acquisition of a variety of instructional and practice conditions. Finally, the potential caveat in many of the generalizations presented in the preceding chapters is discussed in Unit Four: individual differences. Certainly noteworthy here is that by moving this subject matter to the last chapter, the presentation of topics in Units 2 and 3 now flow with less interruption.

Finally, it is important to point out a prominent new pedagogical feature added to this edition. Several shaded boxes entitled "A Closer Look" are now included in each Concept discussion. The title for each box indicates its content. These boxes typically serve one of two purposes: to provide more detail about a research study to illustrate a point made in text, or to describe situation(s) to apply a discussion point to a context relevant to professional practice. The boxes are included to enhance or enrich the information presented in the discussion of a Concept. Thus, the student can acquire basic knowledge about the Concept without reading the boxed information. But, he or she can enrich that knowledge by reading it.

No edition of a textbook can be developed without sage advice and direction from a number of people. This edition is no exception. I am especially thankful to the many users of the previous editions who have contacted me with feedback on what they like about the book or with suggestions for changes. Howie Zelaznik, Sally White, Tim Lee, and Kellie Hall deserve special recognition and thanks in this regard. Also, the reviewers selected by my editor to critique the fourth edition provided many useful suggestions for developing this new edition. I also thank my LSU colleagues for their support and patience as I went through this process. Don Franks, as my department chair, has been a constant source of encouragement and bad jokes to keep things from getting bogged down. As I have done in previous editions, I want to emphasize the importance of the contributions to this book from the undergraduate and graduate students I teach at LSU. They continue to remind me why they enroll in and what they need from a motor learning course. Finally, thinks again to the editorial and production staffs at WCB/McGraw-Hill. They and the company have experienced numerous changes during the development of this edition. I appreciate how well they have maintained their focus, encouragement, and sense of humor to enable me to get the job done.

**Richard A. Magill**
Baton Rouge, Louisiana

———— ■ ————

*For Straley and Jeff*

———— ■ ————

# MOTOR LEARNING

© Jean-Claude Lejeune

# UNIT

# I

# INTRODUCTION TO MOTOR LEARNING

CHAPTER

1

# INTRODUCTION TO MOTOR SKILLS

## CONCEPT 1.1

Motor skills can be classified into general categories

## CONCEPT 1.2

The measurement of motor performance is critical to understanding motor learning

# CONCEPT 1.1

## Motor skills can be classified into general categories

## Key Terms

skill

motor skill

movements

actions

gross motor
  skills

fine motor
  skills

discrete motor
  skill

serial motor
  skill

continuous
  motor skills

closed motor
  skill

open motor
  skill

regulatory
  conditions

intertrial
  variability

## Application

When a person runs, walks with an artificial limb, throws a baseball, hits a tennis ball, plays the piano, dances, or operates a wood lathe, that person is using one or more of the human skills called *motor skills*. In this book, we focus on helping you understand how people learn, and how you can help people learn, motor skills such as these.

As you engage in this study, you will find it useful to draw general conclusions, applying what you learn to a broad range of motor skills, rather than making many specific statements about many skills.

In the Discussion section of this Concept, we provide a starting point for making these kinds of general statements. That starting point is the classification of motor skills into broad categories that emphasize the similarities rather than the differences among skills.

For example, the skill of maneuvering a wheelchair through a crowded hallway and that of hitting a pitched baseball seem quite distinct. However, both these skills have one characteristic in common. People must perform both skills in what we will call an "open" environment. This means that to perform the skill successfully, a person must adapt certain aspects of his or her movements to changing characteristics in the performance environment. For the wheelchair skill, this means that the person must be able to maneuver successfully through a crowded hallway in which people are standing or walking around. For the baseball-hitting skill, the changing environment includes the ball itself as it moves toward the person. For both of these skills, performance success requires the performer to adapt quickly and accurately to changing conditions. When we view them in terms of this common characteristic, we can see that these two seemingly diverse skills are related.

## Discussion

To begin your study of motor learning, you should understand some things about the skills that are at the heart of this study. To enhance this understanding, we will discuss two important points about motor skills. First, we will define motor skills, considering what distinguishes them from other skills; as we do so, we will define some other commonly used terms related to the term *motor skill*. Second, we will discuss four different approaches to classi-

fying motor skills into categories that identify common characteristics of various skills. The benefit of classifying skills is that it can provide us with an appropriate basis for establishing generalizations, or principles, about how we perform and learn motor skills. These generalizations enable us in turn to develop theories about skill performance and learning. Additionally, they help us to establish guidelines for instructors and therapists who must develop effective strategies that will enhance motor skill learning and rehabilitation.

## Skills, Movements, and Actions

Several terms in the motor learning literature are related to the term *motor skills*. These are *skills, movements,* and *actions*. Each term is used in a specific way; we should understand and use each one correctly.

*Skills.* The term **skill** is a commonly used word that we will use in this text to denote *a task that has a specific goal to achieve.* For example, we say that "multiplication is a fundamental skill of mathematics," or "playing the piano is a skill that takes practice." Of these two examples, the skill of piano playing includes a **motor skill** because it is *a skill that requires voluntary body and/or limb movement to achieve the goal.* Looked at this way, the skill of piano playing involves the goal of striking the correct keys in the proper sequence and at the appropriate time, and it requires finger and hand movement to achieve that goal.

Note several characteristics in this definition that are common to motor skills. First, there is *a goal to achieve.* This means that motor skills have a purpose. Some theorists use the term *action goal* in motor learning and control literature to refer to the goal of a motor skill. Second, motor skills of interest in this text are *performed voluntarily;* in other words, we are not considering reflexes as skills. Although an eye blink may have a purpose and involve movement, it occurs involuntarily and is therefore not a skill in the sense in which we are using the term. Third, a motor skill *requires body and/or limb movement* to accomplish the goal of the task. This characteristic indicates that when we use the term *skill,* we are referring to a specific type of skill. Although calculating math problems is a skill, it does not require body and/or limb movement to achieve its goal. We commonly refer to the type of skill used for math problems as a cognitive skill.

One additional characteristic further identifies the types of motor skills of interest in this text: they *need to be learned* in order for a person to achieve the goal of the skill successfully. The piano-playing example clearly has this characteristic. But consider a skill like walking. While walking may seem to be something that humans do "naturally," it must be learned by the infant who is attempting to move in his or her environment by this new and exciting means of locomotion. And walking is a skill some people may need to relearn. Examples are people who have had strokes, or hip or knee joint replacements, as well as people who must learn to walk with artificial legs.

*Movements.* In the motor learning and control literature, the term **movements** indicates *behavior characteristics of a specific limb or a combination of limbs.* In this sense, movements are component parts of skills. A variety of different limb behavior characteristics can occur that still enable a person to walk successfully. For example, our limbs move differently in distinct ways when we walk on a concrete sidewalk and when we walk on an icy sidewalk—or on a sandy beach. However, while the actual movements may differ, the skill we perform in each of these different situations is walking.

*Actions.* A term that has become increasingly more common and more important in the motor learning and control literature is the term *actions.* For our purposes, we will use this term as synonymous with *skills* and distinct from *movements.* That is, **actions** are *goal-directed responses that consist of body and/or limb movements.* Another way of defining an action is to say that it is *a family of movements.* Some have referred to an action as *an equivalence class of movements* (see Schmidt and Turvey 1992).

The important point here is that a variety of movements can produce the same action and thereby accomplish the same goal. For example, walking up a set of stairs is an action. The goal is to get to the top of the stairs. However, to achieve this goal a person can use a variety of different movements. A person can take one step at a time very slowly, or take each step very quickly, or take two steps at a time, and so on. In each situation, the action is the same but the movements the person produces to achieve the goal of the action are different.

## One-Dimension Classification Systems

Theorists base the process of classifying motor skills on determining which skill characteristics are similar to those of other skills. The most prevalent approach has been to categorize skills according to one common characteristic. The first three of the four skill classification systems we discuss in this section use this approach.

For each system, the common characteristic is divided into two categories, which represent extreme ends of a continuum rather than dichotomous categories. This continuum approach allows a skill to be classified in terms of which category the skill characteristic is more like, rather than requiring that the characteristic fit one category exclusively. Consider an analogy. The concepts "hot" and "cold" represent two categories of temperatures. While we typically consider them as distinct categories, we also can view hot and cold as words describing opposite ends of a temperature continuum, because there are degrees of hot or cold that do not fit exclusively into one or the other category. By considering hot and cold as anchor points on a continuum, we can maintain the category distinctions while at the same time more accurately classify various temperature levels that do not fit into only one or the other category.

*Size of musculature required.*   One characteristic describing most motor skills is the type of muscle groups required to perform the skill. Skills like walking and hopping do not require as the prime movers muscle groups of the same size as the muscle groups used for skills like piano playing and sewing. By distinguishing skills based on the size of the muscle groups required to accomplish the actions, researchers have established a motor skill classification system in which there are two categories, known as gross and fine motor skills.

To achieve the goals of **gross motor skills,** people need to use *large musculature* to produce the actions. These skills need less movement precision than fine motor skills do. We classify skills such as the so-called *fundamental motor skills*—walking, jumping, throwing, leaping, etc.—as gross motor skills.

**Fine motor skills** fall at the other end of this classification continuum. Fine motor skills require greater control of the *small muscles,* especially those involved in hand-eye coordination, and require a high degree of precision in hand and finger movement. Handwriting, typing, drawing, sewing, and fastening a button are examples of motor skills that are on the fine-motor-skill end of the continuum in the muscle size classification system. Note that while large muscles may be involved in the action of a fine motor skill, the small muscles are the primary muscles involved to achieve the goal of the skill.

The use of the gross/fine distinction for motor skills is popular in a number of settings. In education settings, special education and adapted physical education curricula and tests commonly distinguish skills on this basis. We also find this classification system in rehabilitation environments. Physical therapists typically work with patients who need to rehabilitate gross motor skills such as walking, whereas occupational therapists more commonly deal with patients who need to learn fine motor skills. People who are involved in early childhood development also find the gross/fine categorization useful and have developed tests of motor development along the gross/fine dimension. Also, industrial and military aptitude tests commonly are developed using the gross and fine motor skill distinction.

*The distinctiveness of the movements.*   Researchers also classify motor skills on the basis of how distinct the movements are as a person performs the skill. If a skill requires one distinct movement having an identifiable beginning and end point, we categorize the skill as a **discrete motor skill.** Discrete skills include flipping a light switch, depressing the clutch of an automobile, and hitting a piano key. Each of these skills requires one distinct movement that begins and ends at clearly defined points.

Sometimes an individual puts several discrete movements together in a series or sequence. When this occurs, we consider the skill a **serial motor skill.** Starting a standard shift automobile is a good example, because the driver must perform a series of distinct movements. First, the driver depresses the clutch. Next, he or she turns the key to start the engine. Then the person must put the gear shift into first gear, and depress the accelerator properly as he or she lets out the clutch and the car finally begins to move. Each movement in this series is distinct, with a specific beginning and end point. We also can consider playing the piano as a serial motor skill, because the pianist must accomplish discrete movements of striking the piano keys in a definite, serial order.

At the opposite end of this classification system continuum fall **continuous motor skills,** which contain movements that are always repetitive. We can classify skills such as steering an automobile, tracking a moving cursor on a computer monitor with a joystick, swimming, and walking as continuous skills.

This classification system has been especially prevalent in motor skills research literature when authors are focusing on the control of movement. Researchers have found, for example, that certain phenomena about how we control movement are applicable to discrete skills but not to continuous skills, and vice versa. The distinction between discrete and continuous skills is especially popular in the research literature of those who view the motor skill performance from the perspectives of human engineering and human factors.

***The stability of the environment.*** One classification system has its roots in industrial as well as educational and rehabilitation settings. Researchers base this system on the stability of the environment in which the skill is performed (Gentile 1972; Poulton 1957). For this classification system, the term *environment* refers specifically to the object the person is acting on or to the characteristics of the context in which the person performs the skill. For example, if a person is hitting a ball, the critical component of the environment is the ball itself. For the skill of walking, however, the critical environment features are the surface on which the person must walk and the characteristics of the environmental context in which the person must walk.

According to this classification scheme, if the environment is stable, that is, if it does not change

while the person is performing the skill, then we classify the skill as a **closed motor skill.** For these skills, *the object to be acted on does not change during the performance of a skill*. In effect, the object waits to be acted on by the performer. For example, picking up a cup from a table is a closed motor skill, because the cup does not move between the time you decide to pick it up until you pick it up. Walking in an uncluttered room is also a closed motor skill, because the environmental context does not change while you are walking. Other examples of closed motor skills are shooting an arrow at a stationary target, buttoning a shirt, stair climbing, and hitting a ball off a tee. For each of these skills, the performer can initiate action when he or she is ready to do so and perform the skill according to his or her own wishes.

Conversely, an **open motor skill** is *a skill that a person performs in a non-stable environment, where the object or context changes during the performance of the skill*. To perform such a skill successfully, the performer must act according to the action of the object or the changing characteristics of the environment. For example, skills such as driving a car, stepping onto a moving escalator, walking through the woods, striking a moving tennis ball, and catching a ball are all open motor skills. People perform each of these skills in a temporally and/or spatially changing environment. For example, during a rally a tennis player cannot stand in one spot and decide when and how he or she will respond to the ball. To be successful, the player must move and act in accordance with the ball's spatial location and speed characteristics. Similarly, walking through the woods is an open motor skill, because the person's walking characteristics vary depending on the locations of the trees, stumps, stones, and holes in the ground.

Notice that in the last two paragraphs, we have classified the skill of walking as *both an open and a closed skill*. The distinguishing feature is the situation in which the walker performs the skill. When walking occurs in an uncluttered environment, it is a closed skill. But when a person must walk in a cluttered environment, walking is an open skill. We can make the same distinction for several skills. For example, hitting a ball from a tee is a closed skill, whereas hitting a pitched ball is an open skill.

Consider how closed and open skills differ in terms of the performance demands placed on the person. A person can initiate his or her movements at will when performing a closed skill. In addition, the person does not need to adjust the movements to changing conditions while the performance is in progress. For example, to climb a set of stairs, a person can initiate his or her first step at will. However, quite the opposite is the case when someone performs open skills. To perform an open skill successfully, a person must time the initiation of movement to conform to the movement of the object he or she is acting on. If, for example, the person must step onto a moving escalator, the moment when the first step can be initiated must conform to the speed and position of the escalator. And for many open skills, changes can occur while an action is in progress that will require the person to make movement adjustments to conform to these environmental changes. For example, the spin of a tennis ball will influence the direction and height of its bounce, which may require the tennis player to adjust his or her planned movements to return a serve after the ball hits the ground.

The open/closed classification system has achieved a large degree of popularity in instructional methodology contexts and increasing popularity in rehabilitation contexts. A likely reason for this is that the professionals involved can adapt the closed and open skill categories readily to the types of motor skills involved in these settings. Skills in each of these categories follow common principles of instruction that instructors and therapists can apply easily to specific situations. The closed and open distinction between motor skills also has become increasingly common in the motor learning research literature, undoubtedly because of its simplicity and its ability to accommodate both complex "real-world" skills and laboratory skills.

## Gentile's Two-Dimensions Taxonomy

While the simplicity of the classification scheme is an advantage of classifying motor skills based on one common characteristic, this advantage also can be a disadvantage. The problem is that the one-characteristic approach does not capture the complexity of many skills that a professional must take into account when making decisions about instruction or practice routines. To overcome this limitation, Gentile (1987) broadened the one-dimension approach by considering two general characteristics of all skills: the *environmental context* in which the person performs the skill and the *function of the action* characterizing the skill. She then subdivided these two characteristics to create an expansive taxonomy that yields sixteen skill categories, depicted in table 1.1–1.

Gentile proposed this taxonomy as a functional guide for physical therapists, in carrying out their clinical activities. The various skill categories in the taxonomy place distinct demands on the performer and demand different practice conditions. Gentile saw this taxonomy as having two practical purposes for the therapist. First, it provides a *systematic and comprehensive evaluation guide* to direct the therapist in the clinical process of determining the movement problems characterizing patients. Second, the taxonomy provides the *basis on which the therapist can select functionally appropriate activities* for the patient after having made the evaluation.

Although Gentile developed the taxonomy with physical therapy in mind, it is not limited to that context. The taxonomy provides an excellent basis for understanding the performer demands for a wide variety of motor skills. Everyone who is involved in teaching motor skills should appreciate this taxonomy. It is an excellent means of becoming aware of the skill characteristics that make skills distinct from, as well as related to, other skills, and is an excellent guide for establishing practice or training routines.

***Environmental context.*** The first dimension of Gentile's taxonomy can be seen in the first column of table 1.1–1. This dimension relates to the *environmental context* in which a person performs a skill. Two context characteristics are involved in this dimension. We see these in the category labels in the first column in table 1.1–1.

The first environmental characteristic concerns **regulatory conditions,** which are those characteristics of the environmental context that control

**TABLE 1.1–1** Gentile's Taxonomy of Motor Skills

| Action Function ⇒ / Environmental Context ⇓ | Body transport: None / Object manipulation: None | Body transport: None / Object manipulation: Yes | Body transport: Yes / Object manipulation: None | Body transport: Yes / Object manipulation: Yes |
|---|---|---|---|---|
| | **1** | **2** | **3** | **4** |
| *Regulatory conditions:* Stationary *Intertrial variability:* None | Regulatory cond. stationary No intertrial variability No body transport No object manipulation | Regulatory cond. stationary No intertrial variability No body transport Object manipulation | Regulatory cond. stationary No intertrial variability Body transport No object manipulation | Regulatory cond. stationary No intertrial variability Body transport Object manipulation |
| | **5** | **6** | **7** | **8** |
| *Regulatory conditions:* Stationary *Intertrial variability:* Yes | Regulatory cond. stationary Intertrial variability No body transport No object manipulation | Regulatory cond. stationary Intertrial variability No body transport Object manipulation | Regulatory cond. stationary Intertrial variability Body transport No object manipulation | Regulatory cond. stationary Intertrial variability Body transport Object manipulation |
| | **9** | **10** | **11** | **12** |
| *Regulatory conditions:* In motion *Intertrial variability:* None | Regulatory cond. in motion No intertrial variability No body transport No object manipulation | Regulatory cond. in motion No intertrial variability No body transport Object manipulation | Regulatory cond. in motion No intertrial variability Body transport No object manipulation | Regulatory cond. in motion No intertrial variability Body transport Object manipulation |
| | **13** | **14** | **15** | **16** |
| *Regulatory conditions:* In motion *Intertrial variability:* Yes | Regulatory cond. in motion Intertrial variability No body transport No object manipulation | Regulatory cond. in motion Intertrial variability No body transport Object manipulation | Regulatory cond. in motion Intertrial variability Body transport No object manipulation | Regulatory cond. in motion Intertrial variability Body transport Object manipulation |

(i.e., regulate) the movement characteristics of an action. This means that a person's movements must conform to these specific environmental features to be successful. For example, the surface on which a person walks influences the movements a person uses to walk on that surface. Also, for the action of hitting a ball, the size, shape, and weight of the ball as well as its speed and spatial location in flight influence when a person can initiate hitting the ball and what the movement characteristics of the swing must be like.

An important distinction for differentiating motor skills is whether the regulatory conditions during performance are *stationary* or *in motion*. Sometimes the regulatory conditions are stationary; this is the case when you walk on a sidewalk or hit

---

**A CLOSER LOOK**

### Skill Control Influences of Stationary and In-Motion Regulatory Conditions

**STATIONARY ENVIRONMENTAL CONTEXT**

*spatial features* of the environment control spatial features of the action; the timing of the action is controlled by the performer

*e.g.*   picking up a cup

walking up a flight of stairs

hitting a ball from a tee

throwing a dart at a target

**IN-MOTION ENVIRONMENTAL CONTEXT**

*spatial and timing features* of the environment control spatial and timing features of the action

*e.g.*   stepping onto an escalator

standing in a moving bus

hitting a pitched ball

catching a batted ball

---

a ball off a tee. Sometimes the regulatory conditions are in motion; this occurs when you must step onto an escalator or hit a pitched ball. In this part of Gentile's taxonomy, we can see the application of the closed and open motor skills categories. Skills for which the regulatory conditions are stationary are closed skills, whereas those for which they are in motion are open skills. However, this closed/open distinction is too limiting to capture the wide range of skills that people perform every day. Because of this limitation, Gentile added another environmental context characteristic.

The second environmental characteristic in the taxonomy is *intertrial variability,* which refers to whether the regulatory conditions during performance are the same or different from one performance of the skill to another. We can distinguish motor skills according to whether intertrial variability is *absent* or *present*. For example, when a person walks across an uncluttered room, intertrial variability is absent because the regulatory conditions do not change from one step to another. On the other hand, intertrial variability is present when someone walks across a floor crowded with people, because each step may need to have different characteristics for the walker to avoid colliding with other people.

***The function of the action.***   Notice in table 1.1–1 that for each of the four categories in the first column, which are created by combining the two envi-

ronmental context characteristics, there are several other categories across the row associated with that category. Gentile created these additional categories by making the four environmental context characteristics interact with four characteristics related to the *function of the action,* which is the second dimension on which the taxonomy is based.

Gentile specified that we can determine the function of an action by deciding whether or not performing a given skill involves moving the body, and whether or not performance involves manipulating an object. She viewed these characteristics as parts of two broad action functions: body orientation and manipulation. *Body orientation* refers to the changing or maintaining of body position. Two types of body orientation are important for classifying skills. Some skills, such as standing, sitting, or shooting an arrow in archery, require *body stability*. Other skills require *body transport,* which means moving from one place to another. Skills such as walking, running, and swimming involve body transport.

The second type of action function concerns *object manipulation*. Some motor skills require us to *change or maintain the position of an object,* such as a ball, a tool, or another person. We perform other skills with *no object manipulation*. It is important to note that when a person must manipulate an object, the skill increases in complexity and difficulty, because the person must do two things at once. First, the person must manipulate the object correctly, and

---

| A CLOSER LOOK |

## A Practical Application of the Environmental Context Dimension of Gentile's Taxonomy to Organizing Instruction for Teaching Open Skills

Those who teach motor skills can apply Gentile's taxonomy to the teaching of open skills by placing the four components of the environmental context dimension of the taxonomy on a closed/open skills continuum. As shown in the figure below, we can develop a logical progression from totally closed to totally open skills from these components.

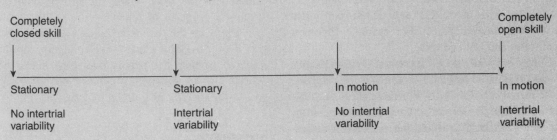

*Example:* Teaching goal = to teach a person to hit a baseball thrown by a pitcher under game conditions.

The following sequence of practice events would occur according to the progression in figure 1.1–1:

1. Practice begins with a closed version of the open skill; the instructor or coach keeps the regulatory conditions "stationary" and has intertrial variability "absent."

   ⇒ the learner bats the ball from a batting tee at the same height on each practice attempt

2. In the next version of the skill, the instructor or coach keeps the regulatory conditions "stationary" but has intertrial variability "present."

   ⇒ the learner bats the ball from a batting tee, but from different heights on each practice attempt

3. Next, practice proceeds to an open version of the skill; the instructor or coach has the regulatory conditions "in motion" but, intertrial variability "absent."

   ⇒ a pitching machine that can keep the speed and location of each pitch constant puts the ball in motion

4. Finally, the instructor or coach has the learner practice the completely open skill itself; the regulatory conditions are "in motion" and intertrial variability is "present."

   ⇒ a live pitcher pitches the ball using different speeds and locations on each practice attempt

*Note:* For research evidence supporting the effectiveness of this progression for helping people learn an open skill, see Hautala and Conn (1993).

---

second, he or she must adjust body posture to accommodate for the imbalance created by the object.

***The sixteen skill categories.*** The interaction of the four environmental context categories and the four action function categories creates sixteen skill categories. Table 1.1–1 shows the critical characteristics of these sixteen categories. Gentile specified that each skill category poses different demands on the performer, with *complexity of the skill increasing* from the top leftmost category to the bottom rightmost category. Note that in table 1.1–1, numbers have been added to this taxonomy to label each category.

The category containing the simplest skills, shown in box 1 of the table, includes skills in which the environmental context is stationary, there is no intertrial variability, and there is no body transport or object manipulation required. Some examples here are standing and sitting. Skills in this category are comparable to those at the extreme closed-skills end of the closed/open skills continuum we discussed earlier. The next step in complexity is for skills in box 2 of the table, where everything is the same as for skills in box 1, except that the performer must manipulate an object. For example, a person must stand and hold a box.

Complexity of skills increases systematically through box 16 of table 1.1–1 which is the category of the most complex skills. For these skills, the regulatory conditions are in motion and change from one performance to another, the person is manipulating an object, and the person is moving. Many sport skills fall into this category; one example is running to catch a hit ball in baseball. Skills in this category are comparable to those at the extreme open-skills end of the closed/open skills continuum.

*Practical application of the taxonomy.* Gentile proposed that the taxonomy has practical value for therapists and teachers because they can use it in two ways. First, it can be a useful guide for *evaluation of movement capabilities and limitations*. The therapist or teacher can evaluate deficits by systematically altering environmental contexts and/or action functions to identify skill performance characteristics that pose difficulty for an individual. Contextual versus action-function difficulties suggest different types of problems. By identifying the specific characteristics limiting performance, the therapist or teacher can determine what he or she needs to do to help the person improve his or her performance capabilities.

After the taxonomy provides the basis from which the professional assesses performance problems, it then becomes a valuable tool for *selecting functionally appropriate activities* to help the person overcome his or her deficits. This is an important feature of the taxonomy, because it emphasizes the complementary part of the rehabilitation or skill training process. To assess skill deficits is important, but the effectiveness of any rehabilitation or training protocol depends on the implementation of appropriate activities to achieve functional goals for the patient or student. In the activity selection process, the therapist or teacher begins selecting activities related to the taxonomy category in which the person is not capable at first of handling the demands of the skill. Then, the professional can develop a program of rehabilitation or instruction by working up the numbered categories. Each category then provides a guide for selecting appropriate activities to help the person overcome his or her deficits and systematically achieve the functional goal of the therapy or training experience.

## Summary

We have defined motor skills as skills that require voluntary body and/or limb movement to achieve their goal. There is a wide variety of motor skills, including grasping a cup, walking, dancing, throwing a ball, and playing the piano. We sometimes refer to skills such as these as *actions*. Movements are components of skills and actions. Because there are so many different motor skills, researchers have developed motor skill classification systems. These systems identify common characteristics of skills and place skills within distinct categories based on those characteristics. An important purpose of classification systems is to help teachers and therapists apply concepts and principles of motor skill learning to instruction and rehabilitation situations.

We have discussed three classification schemes that group motor skills into categories based on one common characteristic. One system is based on the size of the musculature required to perform the skill, and classifies skills as either gross or fine. The second is based on the distinctiveness of the beginning and end points of a skill, and classifies skills as either discrete or continuous. The third classification system is based on the stability of the environment in which the skill is performed. If this environment is stable, the system categorizes the skills as closed motor skills. If the environment is changeable, it categorizes the skills as open motor skills.

The fourth classification system is based on two common characteristics of skills. Gentile developed a taxonomy that presents sixteen categories of motor skills, created from the environmental context and the action function characteristics of skills. The taxonomy is useful in helping us gain an understanding of the unique requirements of the different motor skills that are placed on a person when he or she performs these skills. The practical benefit of this taxonomy is that it provides an effective guide by which therapists and teachers can evaluate the nature of motor skill performance deficits and then systematically select functionally appropriate activities to help people overcome those deficits.

## Related Readings

Gentile, A. M. 1987. Skill acquisition: Action, movement, and the neuromotor processes. In J. H. Carr, R. B. Shepherd, J. Gordon, A. M. Gentile, and J. M. Held (Eds.), *Movement science: Foundations for physical therapy in rehabilitation* (pp. 93–154). Rockville, MD: Aspen. (Read pp. 93–117.)

Mulder, T., and S. Geurts. 1991. The assessment of motor dysfunctions: Preliminaries to a disability-oriented approach. *Human Movement Science* 10: 565–74.

Newell, K. M. 1985. Coordination, control and skill. In D. Goodman, R. B. Wilberg, and I. M. Franks (Eds.), *Differing perspectives in motor learning, memory, and control* (pp. 295–317). Amsterdam: North-Holland.

# CONCEPT 1.2

The measurement of motor performance is critical to understanding motor learning

## Key Terms

performance outcome measures

performance production measures

reaction time (RT)

movement time (MT)

response time

absolute error (AE)

constant error (CE)

variable error (VE)

root-mean-squared error (RMSE)

kinematics

displacement

velocity

acceleration

kinetics

electromyography (EMG)

## Application

Suppose that you are a physical educator teaching your students a tennis serve. What characteristic of performance will you measure to assess students' progress? Consider a few possibilities. You could count the number of serves that land in and out of the proper service court. Or you could mark the service court in some way so that the "better" serves, in terms of where they land, are scored higher than others. Or you could establish a measure that is concerned with the students' serving form.

Now, imagine that you are a physical therapist helping a stroke patient learning to walk again. How will you measure your patient's progress to determine if what you are doing is facilitating his or her rehabilitation? You have several possible walking characteristics to choose from. For example, you could count the number of steps made or the distance walked on each walking attempt;

these measures could give you some general indicators of progress. If you wanted to know more specifically about certain walking-related characteristics, you could measure the balance and stability of the person as he or she walked. Or you could assess the biomechanical progress the person was making by analyzing the kinematic characteristics of the segments of the legs, trunk, and arms. Each of these measurements can be valuable and tells you something different about the person's walking performance.

In both of these performance assessment situations, your important concern as an educator or therapist is using a performance measure, or measures, appropriately to make an assessment. As a first step in addressing this problem, you must determine which aspects of performance you should measure to make a valid assessment of performance. Then, you must determine how to measure those aspects of performance. The following discussion will help you to know how to accomplish this two-step measurement process by describing a number of different motor skill performance measures. We will discuss each measure in terms of which feature of performance the measure assesses and how to obtain and interpret the measure.

In addition to helping you better understand the measurement of motor skill performance, this discussion of measuring skill performance should help you better understand the various concepts presented in this book. Throughout this text, we will refer to the various measures introduced in this section, especially as researchers use these measures to investigate various concepts.

## Discussion

There are a variety of ways to measure motor skill performance. A useful way to organize the many types of motor performance measures is by creating two categories related to different levels of performance observation. We will call the first category **performance outcome measures.** Included in this category are measures that indicate the outcome or result of performing a motor skill. For example, measures of how far a person walked, how fast a person ran a certain distance, and how many degrees a person flexed his or her knee all are based on the outcome of the person's performance.

Notice that performance outcome measures do not tell the researcher anything about the behavior of the limbs or body that led to the observed outcome. Nor do these measures provide any information about the activity of the various muscles involved in each action. To know something about these types of characteristics, researchers use measures in the category called **performance production measures.** These measures can tell the researcher a number of different things about how the nervous system is functioning, how the muscular system is operating, or how the limbs or joints are acting before, during, or after a person performs a skill.

Although additional categories of performance measures could exist, these two represent the motor skill performance measures found in this text. Table 1.2–1 presents examples of these two categories of measures. For the remainder of this discussion, we will discuss several of the more common performance measures found in the motor learning research literature.

### Reaction Time

The common measure indicating how long it takes a person to initiate a movement is **reaction time (RT).** Figure 1.2–1 shows that RT is the interval of

---

**TABLE 1.2–1**    Two Categories of Motor Skill Performance Measures

| Category | Examples of Measures | Performance Examples |
|---|---|---|
| 1. **Performance outcome measures** | Time to complete a response, e.g., sec., min., hr. | Amount of time to: Run a mile; Type a word |
| | Reaction time (RT) | Time between starter's gun and beginning of movement |
| | Amount of error in performing criterion movement, e.g., AE, CE, VE | Number of cm away from the target in reproducing a criterion limb position |
| | Number or percentage of errors | Number of free throws missed |
| | Number of successful attempts | Number of times the beanbag hit the target |
| | Time on/off target | Number of seconds stylus in contact with target on pursuit rotor |
| | Time on/off balance | Number of seconds stood in stork stance |
| | Distance | Height of vertical jump |
| | Trials to completion | Number of trials it took until all responses correct |
| 2. **Performance production measures** | Displacement | Distance limb traveled to produce response |
| | Velocity | Speed limb moved while performing response |
| | Acceleration | Acceleration/deceleration pattern while moving |
| | Joint angle | Angle of each joint of arm at impact in hitting ball |
| | Joint torque | Net joint torque of the knee joint at takeoff on a vertical jump |
| | Electromyography (EMG) | Time at which the biceps initially fired during a rapid flexion movement |
| | Electroencephalogram (EEG) | Characteristic of the P300 for a choice RT response |

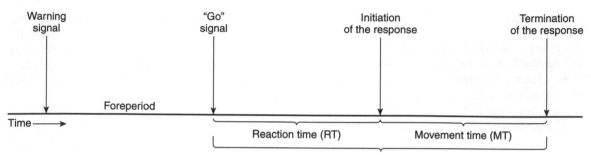

**FIGURE 1.2–1**   The events and time intervals related to the typical measurement of reaction time (RT) and movement time (MT).

**FIGURE 1.2–2**   Three different types of reaction time (RT) test situations: simple RT, choice RT, and discrimination RT.

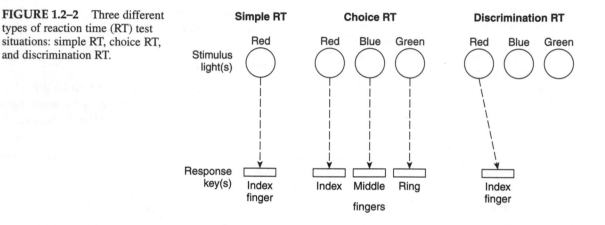

time between the onset of a signal (stimulus) and the *initiation* of a movement response. Note that RT includes not the movement itself, but only the time before the movement begins.

The stimulus (or "go") signal is the indication to respond. Researchers can use a variety of signals, such as a light, a buzzer, a shock, or a word on a screen. As such, the researcher may present the signal to any sensory system, i.e., vision, hearing, or touch. The response the person makes can be any type of movement. For example, the person might be required to lift a finger off a telegraph key, depress a keyboard key, speak a word, or kick a board. Finally, note that the experimenter may or may not use a warning signal, which can be any type of indicator, when measuring RT. However, if the researcher wants optimal RT, some type of warning signal should be given prior to the stimulus signal.

*Types of RT situations.*   Figure 1.2–2 depicts three of the most common types of RT situations. In each situation shown in this figure, a light is the stimulus signal and lifting a finger from a telegraph key is the required movement.

When an experiment uses only one signal and requires only one response, the RT situation is known as *simple* RT. In the example presented in figure 1.2–2, the person must lift a finger from the telegraph key when a light comes on. Another type of RT situation is *choice* RT, where there is more than one signal to which the person must respond, and each signal has a specified response. The example in figure 1.2–2 indicates that the person must respond to the red light by lifting the index finger from a telegraph key, to the blue light by lifting the middle finger, and to the green light by lifting the ring finger. If the person does not make the specified response, the researcher considers the attempt an error and typically redoes it. The third type of RT situation is *discrimination* RT, where there is also more than one signal, but only one response. In the figure 1.2–2 example, the person is required to lift his or her finger from the telegraph key only when the red light comes on. If the blue or green light is illuminated, the person should make no response.

***RT interval components.*** Through the use of electromyography (EMG) to measure the beginning of muscle activity in an RT situation, a researcher can *fractionate* RT into two component parts. The EMG recording will indicate the time at which the muscle shows increased activity after the stimulus signal has occurred. However, there is a period of time between the onset of the stimulus signal and the beginning of the muscle activity. This "quiet" interval of time is the first component part of RT and is called the *premotor time*. The second component is the period of time from the increase in muscle activity until the actual beginning of observable limb movement. This RT component is called the *motor time*.

By fractionating the RT interval into two parts, researchers interested in understanding the movement preparation process are able to obtain more specific insights into what occurs as a person prepares to move. Most researchers agree that the premotor time is a measure of the receipt and transmission of information from the environment, through the nervous system, to the muscle itself. This time interval seems to be an indicator of perceptual and cognitive decision-making activity in which the person is engaging while preparing a movement. The motor time interval indicates that there is muscle activity before observable limb movement occurs. Researchers commonly agree that this activity indicates a time lag in the muscle that it needs in order to overcome the inertia of the limb after the muscle receives the command to contract.

***The use of RT in research.*** Reaction time has a long history as a popular measure of human motor skill performance. Although RT is a performance measure, researchers commonly use it in the motor skills literature as a basis for inferring what a person does or what information a person uses while preparing to produce a required action. For example, if one performance situation yields a longer RT than another situation, the researcher can investigate the characteristics of the two situations to determine what may have led to the different RT lengths. Thus, in addition to indicating how fast a person responds to a signal, RT also provides a window for examining how a person interacts with the performance environment while preparing to produce a required action.

***Relating RT to movement time and response time.*** In any movement situation in which a person must make a movement response to a signal, researchers can assess two performance measures in addition to RT. These are shown in figure 1.2–1 as movement time (MT) and response time. **Movement time (MT)** begins when RT ends. It is the interval of time between the initiation and the completion of movement. **Response time** is the total time interval, involving both RT and MT.

An important characteristic of RT and MT is that they are relatively *independent* measures. This means that the correlation between them is typically low, indicating that researchers cannot use RT to predict MT, or vice versa. Franklin Henry (1961), considered by many to be the "father" of modern-day motor learning, first provided evidence supporting RT-MT independence many years ago. In a comprehensive experiment, he compared RT to MT for men and women of different ages and on tasks of various complexities. The experiment involved 402 subjects between eight and thirty years old. Henry used simple, discrimination, and two-choice RT situations, along with four different conditions of movement complexity. For all situations the RT-MT correlations were consistently close to zero. The significance of this result is that it establishes that RT and MT measure different aspects of human performance and that training to improve one will not help improve the other.

## Error Measures

The amount of error a person makes as a result of performing a skill has had a prominent place in human performance research. Error measures allow

---

| A CLOSER LOOK |
| :---: |

### An Example of How the Knowledge That RT and MT Are Independent Measures of Performance Can Benefit Instruction

Suppose that you are working with a person in a car driving simulator. You are trying to help this person improve the amount of time he or she takes to notice the sudden appearance of an obstacle in the street and stop the car. In this situation, RT is the time from the appearance of the obstacle until the person's foot begins to move from the accelerator; MT is the time it takes the foot to begin moving from the accelerator until it makes contact with the brake.

Suppose that the person's response time (RT + MT) changes across a variety of different situations. Based on the person's RT and MT for each situation,

you can determine if the person has a *decision-making problem or a motor problem*. If RT increases across the various situations while MT remains relatively constant, you know that the problem is primarily a decision-making one. This should lead you to work on problems related to identifying and becoming aware of situations requiring quick stopping of the car. If RT stays relatively constant but MT changes across these situations, you know that the problem is movement related, and you can begin working with the person at that level.

---

us to evaluate performance for skills for which *accuracy* is the action goal. Skills such as reaching to grasp a cup, throwing a ball at a target, walking along a prescribed path, and driving a car on a street require people to make movements that demand spatial and/or temporal accuracy. In assessing performance outcome for this type of skill, the researcher finds the amount of error a person makes in relation to the goal to be a meaningful performance measure.

Error measures not only provide indicators of performance accuracy; certain types of error measures also provide information about possible causes of performance problems. This is especially true if performance is assessed for more than one trial. For a series of trials (typical in a sport-skill-training or a rehabilitation setting), the instructor or therapist can determine whether the observed movement inaccuracy is due to problems associated with *consistency* or to those associated with *bias*. These important measures provide the professional with a basis for selecting the appropriate intervention to help the person overcome the inaccuracy. Consistency problems indicate a lack in acquiring the basic movement pattern, whereas bias problems indicate that the person has acquired the movement

pattern but is having difficulties adapting to the specific demands of the performance situation.

*Assessing error for one-dimension action goals.* When a person must move a limb a certain amount in one dimension, as when a patient attempts to achieve a certain knee extension, the resulting error will be a certain distance short of or past the goal. Similarly, if a pitcher in baseball is attempting to throw the ball at a certain rate of speed, the resulting error will be either too slow or too fast in relation to the goal. Measuring the amount of error in these situations simply involves subtracting the achieved performance value (e.g., 15 cm, 5°, 20 sec) from the target or goal amount.

We can calculate at least three error measures to assess the general accuracy characteristics of performance over repeated performances and to assess what may be causing the accuracy problems. To determine a general idea of how successfully the goal was achieved, we calculate **absolute error (AE).** AE is the absolute difference between the actual performance on each trial and the goal. Summing these differences and dividing by the number of trials will give us the average absolute error for the trials in the session. AE provides

---

## A CLOSER LOOK

### Using Performance Bias and Consistency Assessments

An example demonstrating the value of performance measures assessing bias and consistency occurs when a person is learning archery. In archery, overall performance on a trial is assessed by the total score of a series of six arrows shot at the target. This total score is based on the target rings in which the arrows are located. How the arrows are grouped on the target is not a part of this total score. However, if you are working to help a person improve his or her performance, the total score, which is a general performance score, is not as valuable as the indicators of bias and consistency. If the person's

shots are grouped in one portion of the target away from the center, the problem is one of bias. Correcting this problem is relatively simple, as it requires an aiming or release adjustment in a specific direction toward the target center. But a more complex correction problem occurs if the arrows are scattered all over the target. Here the problem is consistency. This characteristic suggests that the person has not acquired the fundamental movement pattern appropriate for performing this skill and needs continued work on this aspect of the skill.

---

useful information about the *magnitude of error* a person has made on a trial or over a series of trials. This score gives you *a general index of accuracy* for the session for this person. But a problem with evaluating performance solely on the basis of AE is that it hides important information about the source of this person's inaccurate performance. To assess these characteristics, we need two additional error measures.

A performance characteristic that we cannot determine from AE is the person's tendency to overshoot or to undershoot the goal, which is referred to as *performance bias*. To obtain this information, we must calculate **constant error (CE),** which is the signed (+/–) deviation from the goal. When calculated over a series of trials, CE provides a meaningful *index of the person's tendency to be directionally biased* when performing the skill. Calculating CE involves making the same calculations used to determine AE, except that the algebraic signs are kept for each trial's performance.

The error measure that assesses the *performance consistency* (or, conversely, variability) for a series of trials is known as **variable error (VE).** To determine this consistency index, calculate the standard deviation of the person's CE scores for the series of trials.

*Assessing error for two-dimension action goals.* When the outcome of performing a skill requires accuracy in the vertical and horizontal directions, the person assessing error must make modifications to the one-dimension assessment method. The general accuracy measure for the two-dimension situation is called *radial error (RE)*, which is the analog of AE in the one-dimension case. To calculate RE for one trial, measure the length of the error in both the horizontal (X-axis) and the vertical (Y-axis) directions. Square each of these values, add them together, and then take the square root of this total. For example, if the length of the X-direction error is 10mm, and the length of the Y-direction error is 5mm, the RE is 11.2 mm (i.e., $\sqrt{100 + 25}$). Another way to assess RE is to set the target as the 0 X- and 0 Y-coordinates. Then, determine the X and Y locations of the actual response, square each of these values, add them together, and then take the square root of this total. To determine the average RE for a series of trials, simply calculate the mean of the total RE for the series.

Performance bias and consistency are more difficult to assess for the two-dimension case than in one dimension, because the algebraic signs + and – have little meaning for the two-dimension case. Hancock, Butler, and Fischman (1995) have presented a detailed description of calculating measures of bias and consistency in the two-dimension situation. Rather than go into the details of this calculation, we will consider a general approach to the problem here. For a series of two-dimensional movements, a researcher can obtain a qualitative assessment of bias and consistency by looking at the actual grouping of the movement locations. If the grouping tends to be in one quadrant of the target, then a performance bias is evident, whereas responses scattered in all quadrants would indicate no apparent performance bias. In these two examples, consistency would be much better in the former than in the latter case. Again, as for the one-dimension situation, the practical utility of assessing these characteristics is that the strategies used to improve performance would differ for the bias and the consistency cases.

***Assessing error for continuous skills.*** The error measures described in the preceding two sections are based on skills that have discrete accuracy goals. However, continuous motor skills also require accuracy. For example, when a person must walk along a specified pathway, performance assessment can include measuring how well the person stayed on the pathway. Or, if a person is in a car simulator and must steer the car along the road as projected on a screen, a measure of performance can be based on how well the person kept the car on the road. Error measures for these types of skills must be different from those used to assess discrete skill performance.

A common error score for continuous skills is the **root-mean-squared error (RMSE),** which we can think of as AE for a continuous task. To illustrate how this error measure is determined and used, we will consider the following example taken from performing a continuous skill known as *pursuit tracking*. To perform this skill, subjects move a joystick, steering wheel, or lever to make an object, such as a cursor, follow a specified pathway. The criterion pathway can be described kinematically as a displacement curve. Figure 1.2–3 provides an example. A displacement curve also can represent the subject's tracking performance. To determine how accurately the subject tracked the criterion pathway, we would calculate an RMSE score.

We calculate RMSE by determining the amount of error between the displacement curve produced by the subject's tracking performance and the displacement curve of the criterion pathway (see figure 1.2-3). The actual calculation of RMSE is complex and requires a computer program that can sample and record the subject's position in relation to the criterion pathway at specified points of time, such as 100 times each second (100 Hz; note that 1 Hz = 1 time/sec). At each sampling point, the difference between the criterion pathway location and the subject's location is calculated. For the 100-Hz example, this yields 100 error scores each second. If the criterion pattern were 5 sec, there would be 500

**FIGURE 1.2–3** The difference between the subject's response and the stimulus at each specified time interval is used to calculate one root-mean-squared error (RMSE) score. (From I. M. Franks, et al., "The Generation of Movement Patterns During the Acquisition of a Pursuit Tracking Task," in *Human Movement Science,* 1982, 1:251–272. Copyright © 1982 Elsevier/North-Holland, Amsterdam, The Netherlands. Reprinted by permission.)

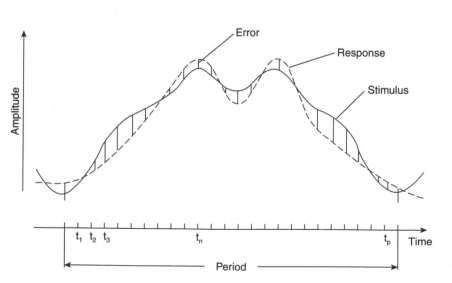

error scores for the trial. The computer then derives one score, RMSE, from these by calculating an average error score for the total pathway.

## Kinematic Measures

Kinematic measures, traditionally associated with biomechanics, have become important descriptors of performance in research on motor learning and control. The term **kinematics** refers to the description of motion without regard to force or mass. Three of the most common of such descriptors refer to an object's changes in position, its speed, and its changes in speed. The terms used to refer to these kinematic characteristics are *displacement, velocity,* and *acceleration.*

Kinematic measures are performance production measures that are based on recording the movement of specific body segments while a person is performing a skill. A typical procedure is first to mark the body segments of interest in a distinctive way with tape, a marking pen, special light-reflecting balls, or light-emitting diodes (LEDs). The researcher then records the person's performance of the skill on videotape, or using special LED-reading cameras. Computer software developed to calculate kinematic measures then analyzes the recordings. This approach is used in commercially available movement analysis systems such as those produced by Peak Performance®, Motion Analysis Systems®, Optitrack®, and WATSMART®.

Another way to obtain kinematic measures is to use the pursuit tracking task described earlier and depicted in figure 1.2–3. Here, a computer samples and records the movements of the tracking device. In this example, a horizontal lever on a tabletop was the movement device. A potentiometer attached to the axle of the lever provided movement-related information that the computer could sample. We can take similar samplings of movement from the movement of a joystick, a mouse, or a rollerball.

*Displacement.* The first kinematic measure of interest is **displacement,** which is the spatial position of a limb or joint during the time period of the movement. Displacement describes changes in spatial locations as a person carries out a movement. We calculate displacement by using a movement analysis system to identify where the movement device, marked limb, or joint is in space (in terms of its X-Y coordinate in two-dimensional analysis or its X-Y-Z coordinate in three-dimensional analysis) at a given time. The system then determines the location of that entity in that position for the next sampled time. The analysis system samples (observes) these spatial positions at specific rates, which vary according to the analysis system used. For example, a common videotape sampling rate is 60 Hz. Faster sampling rates are possible, depending on the analysis system used. Thus, the spatial location of a movement device or limb can be plotted for each sampled time as a displacement curve. Examples of displacement curves are in figures 1.2–3 and 1.2–4.

*Velocity.* The second kinematic measure of interest is **velocity,** which is a time-based derivative of displacement. *Velocity* refers to the rate of change in an object position with respect to time. That is, how rapidly did this change in position occur and in what direction was this change (faster or slower than its previous rate)? Velocity is typically derived in movement analysis systems from displacement. The calculation involves dividing a change in position (between time 1 and time 2) by the change in time (from time 1 to time 2). Velocity is always presented on a graph as a position-by-time curve. Note that in figure 1.2–4 the velocity curve is based on the same movement as the displacement curve. Scientists always refer to velocity in terms of an amount of distance per an amount of time. The tracking example in figure 1.2–4 shows velocity as the number of degrees per second. As the slope of this curve steepens, it represents increasing velocity, while negative velocity is represented by a slope that goes downward. Zero velocity is indicated by no change in positive or negative position of the curve.

*Acceleration.* The third kinematic measure to be discussed is **acceleration,** which describes change in velocity during movement. We derive

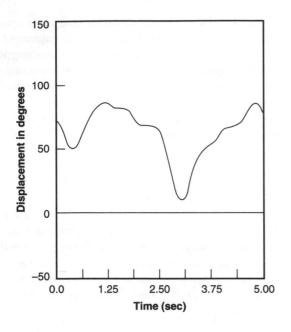

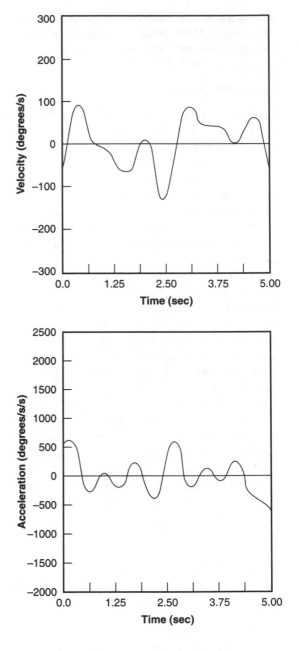

**FIGURE 1.2–4** Recordings of displacement, velocity, and acceleration for a tracking task. (From R. G. Marteniuk and S. K. E. Romanow, "Human Movement Organization and Learning as Revealed by Variability of Movement, Use of Kinematic Information, and Fourier Analysis," in R. A. Magill, (Ed.) *Memory and Control of Action.* Copyright © 1983 Elsevier/North-Holland, Amsterdam, The Netherlands. Reprinted by permission.)

acceleration from velocity by dividing change in velocity by change in time. We also depict acceleration curves as a function of time, as you can see in the acceleration graph in figure 1.2–4, which is based on the displacement and velocity graphs also in that figure. The acceleration curve depicts the speeding up and slowing down of the movements as the subject moves. Rapid acceleration means that a velocity change occurred quickly.

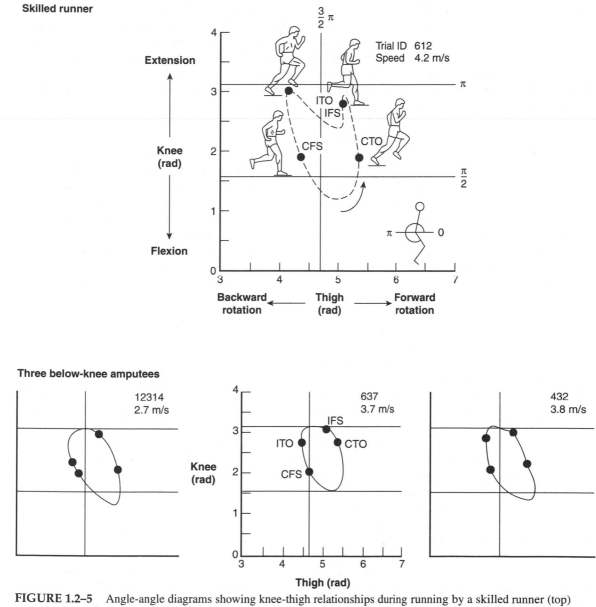

**FIGURE 1.2–5** Angle-angle diagrams showing knee-thigh relationships during running by a skilled runner (top) and three below-knee amputees (bottom). The abbreviations indicate ipsilateral (left) footstrike (IFS), ipsilateral takeoff (ITO), contralateral (right) footstrike (CFS), and contralateral takeoff (CTO), which are the four components of a running stride. (From R. M. Enoka, et al., "Below Knee Amputee Running Gait," in *American Journal of Physical Medicine and Rehabilitation,* 61, 1978:70–78. Copyright © 1982 Williams & Wilkins Company, Baltimore, Maryland. Reprinted by permission.)

*Linear and angular motion.* In kinematic descriptions of movement, the measures of displacement, velocity, and acceleration can refer to either linear or angular motion. The distinction between these types of motion is important to understand and is a critical distinction in the analysis of movement. *Linear motion* describes the movement of all parts of the moving object, while *angular motion* refers to movement that occurred for some parts of the object but not for other parts. If you want to describe the kinematics of walking, for example, linear motion descriptions are appropriate for movement from one location to another; the whole body is moving linearly. However, if you want to describe the foot movement characteristics during walking, angular motion descriptions are more appropriate, because the foot rotates about the ankle joint during walking.

The most common way researchers describe angular motion is by comparing the motion of one joint to the limb segment it rotates about while a movement is occurring. Two examples are shown in figure 1.2–5. The top part of this figure shows an angle-angle diagram for a skilled runner, where the displacement of the knee joint is compared to the thigh during the four phases of a running stride: toe-off, opposite footstrike, opposite foot toeoff, and opposite footstrike. Note that this angle-angle diagram produces a heart-shaped pattern, which is the classic knee-thigh relationship pattern during gait. The bottom part of the figure shows similar diagrams for three persons who have had amputation below the knee. What is noticeable here is that the amputee does not flex the knee joint at the beginning of the stance as a skilled runner does. These examples demonstrate that an important benefit of kinematic measures is that they allow us to describe the characteristics of critical components of a skill during movement.

## Kinetics

The term **kinetics** refers to the consideration of force in the study of motion. Whereas *kinematics* refers to descriptors of motion without concern for the cause of that motion, *kinetics* refers to force as a cause of motion. Force has both magnitude and direction, which we need to take into account when we study kinetics. Newton's laws of motion all refer to the role of force in motion. Force is needed for motion to be started, changed, or stopped; it influences the rate of change in momentum of an object; and it is involved in the action and reaction that occur in the interaction between two objects.

Researchers can investigate various types of forces in the study of human motor skill performance. These include ground reaction force, joint reaction force, muscle force, fluid resistance, elastic force, and inertial force. In addition, an important force-related characteristic of human movement is that human motion involves rotation of body segments around their joint axes. The effect of a force on this rotation is called *joint torque,* or rotary force (see figure 1.2–6 for an example of how to graphically present joint torque). Because of the range of influence of different types of force on human movement, researchers studying motor skill learning and control are increasingly including the measurement of forces as part of their research.

Researchers can measure certain forces directly using devices such as force plates, force transducers, and strain gauges. They use force plates to measure ground reaction forces, which are involved in the interaction between an object, such as a person, and the ground. Force plates are popular force measurement devices in laboratories and clinics in which locomotion research and rehabilitation take place. Researchers use force transducers and strain gauges to measure force that is muscle produced; these are popular in laboratory and clinical settings to determine the magnitude of force generated while a subject is performing limb movement tasks.

Force also can be measured indirectly: we can calculate it on the basis of its relationship to velocity or acceleration and to the mass of the object. Force involves a lawful relationship: force = mass × acceleration. Because of this, we can calculate force without needing to use mechanical and electronic force measurement instruments, if acceleration can be assessed from a kinematic analysis of the movement.

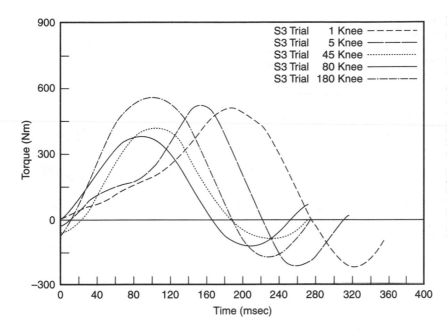

**FIGURE 1.2–6**   Results of an experiment by Sanders and Allen showing knee torques for one subject during contact with a surface after the subject drop-jumped from a platform and immediately initiated a vertical jump for maximum height. Each line on the graph represents performance for the trial noted in the key on the graph. (Reprinted from *Human Movement Science,* Volume 12, R. H. Sanders and J. B. Allen, pp. 299–326, 1993 with kind permission of Elsevier Science-NL, Sara Burgerharstraat 25, 1055 KV Amsterdam, The Netherlands.)

## EMG Measures

Movement involves electrical activity in the muscles, which can be measured by **electromyography (EMG).** Researchers commonly accomplish this by attaching surface electrodes to the skin over muscles. These electrodes detect muscle electrical activity, which then can be recorded by a computer or polygraph recorder. Figure 1.2–7 shows some EMG recordings of electrical activity in the ipsilateral biceps femoris (BFi) and contralateral biceps femoris (BFc) of the legs and the anterior deltoid (AD) of the shoulder girdle for a task that required the person to move his or her arm, on a signal, from the reaction-time key to a position directly in front of the shoulder. The EMG signals presented for these muscles show when electrical activity began in the muscles; we can identify this activity by the increase in the frequency and height of the traces for each muscle. The actual beginning of movement off the RT key is designated in the diagram by the vertical line at the end of the RT recording (line 5 of this figure).

## Measuring Coordination

One of the more interesting phenomena of recent motor learning and control research is the investigation of complex skills. One reason for this is methodologically based. Prior to the advent of computer-based technology for movement analysis, kinematic measurement of movement was an expensive, labor-intensive, and time-consuming process involving frame-by-frame analysis of slow-motion film. With the development of the computer-based movement analysis systems, there has been a dramatic increase in research involving complex skills.

A measurement issue that has developed in the study of complex skills concerns how best to assess coordination. As you will study in Concept 2.1, coordination involves the movement of limb segments in specific time- and space-based patterns. We can easily observe these patterns in angle-angle plots of the movements of limb segments, such as the ones depicted in figure 1.2–5. However, a measurement issue has arisen concerning angle-angle diagrams. Many researchers report only these qualitative kinematic descriptions and do not provide quantitative assessments of them. Some researchers question whether the qualitative pattern representation of limb segment relationships is sufficient for inferring coordination, and suggest that quantitative assessment of these descriptions is needed as well.

**FIGURE 1.2–7** Using EMG recordings to measure a movement response. The figure on the left shows the reaction-time apparatus and where each electrode was placed to record the EMG for each muscle group of interest. The figures on the right show the EMG recordings for each of the three muscle groups and the reaction-time interval for the response. (From Wynne Lee, in *Journal of Motor Behavior,* 1980, 12:187. Reprinted by permission of the author.)

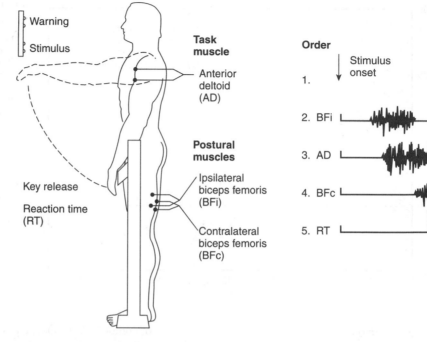

## A CLOSER LOOK

### Quantifying Coordination Patterns

Motor control researchers have suggested several techniques for quantifying the angle-angle plots that are popular for describing coordination patterns, such as the classic heart-shaped pattern of the knee-hip joints relationship during gait. While the regularity of the pattern is easy to observe, this qualitative approach does not allow for statistical between-pattern comparisons to determine reliable differences or similarities. Following are two quantitative approaches to this problem.

- The most common method is to cross-correlate time-related position changes in the angle of one joint with changes in another joint (e.g., Newell and van Emmerik 1989; Vereijken et al. 1992). The resulting correlation coefficient is interpreted as a ratio expressing the extent to which the two joints follow similar patterns of movement. A high correlation indicates strong coordination between the joints, whereas a low correlation shows little between-joint coordination.

- Sidaway, Heise, and Schoenfelder-Zohdi (1995) argue that a correlation approach is flawed because it assumes a linear relationship between the joints. In contrast, angle-angle plots of movement patterns are typically nonlinear. To accommodate both linear and nonlinear situations, they propose a normalized root-mean-squared error technique which they call NoRMS. This method involves comparing a number of cycles of a continuous task, or a series of trials for a discrete task. From this series, the mean of the angle-angle plots is calculated. Then the root-mean-squared error (RMSE) is determined for each cycle or trial of the series, totalled, and then normalized with respect to the number of cycles or trials.

A problem in resolving this issue is that there is little agreement among researchers about how to quantify coordination patterns such as the one in figure 1.2–5. Although several researchers have suggested techniques (see, e.g., Sparrow et al. 1987; Newell and van Emmerik 1989; Vereijken et al. 1992), each has inherent problems, contributing to the current lack of general acceptance of any one technique. Attempts to establish appropriate quantitative techniques continue (e.g., Sidaway, Heise, and Schoenfelder-Zohdi 1995). Until researchers can resolve this issue, qualitative presentations of limb segment relationships will remain the norm for assessing coordination.

## Summary

An essential element in understanding motor learning is the measurement of motor performance. All concepts presented in this text are based on research in which researchers observed and measured motor performance. Measuring motor performance is essential for the assessment of motor deficiencies, as well as for the evaluation of performance by students or patients as they progress through practice and therapy regimes. In this Concept, we focused on different ways to measure motor performance, along with the ways we can use these measurements in motor learning research and applied settings. We considered two categories of motor performance measures. The performance outcome measures category includes measures of time, error, and magnitude of a response. We discussed reaction time, movement time, and various error measures more extensively because of their traditional inclusion in motor learning research. The second category, performance production measures, includes kinematic, kinetic, EMG, and EEG measures, which describe characteristics of limbs, joints, muscles, and brain activity during movement. Finally, we discussed the ongoing controversy concerning the assessment of coordination characteristics of complex movement.

## Related Readings

Clarys, J. P., J. Cabri, B. DeWitte, H. Toussaint, G. de Groot, P. Huying, and P. Hollander. 1988. Electromyography applied to sport ergonomics. *Ergonomics* 31: 1605–20.

DeLuca, P. A. 1991. The use of gait analysis and dynamic EMG in the assessment of the child with cerebral palsy. *Human Movement Science* 10: 543–54.

Enoka, R. M. 1994. *Neuromechanical basis of kinesiology.* 2d ed. Champaign, IL: Human Kinetics. (Read chapters 1 and 2.)

Mah, C. D., M. Hulliger, R. G. Lee, and A. R. Marchand. 1994. Quantitative analysis of human movement synergies: Constructive pattern analysis for gait. *Journal of Motor Behavior* 26: 83–102.

Reeve, T. G., M. G. Fischman, R. W. Christina, and J. H. Cauraugh. 1994. Using one-dimensional task error measures to assess performance on two-dimensional tasks: Comment on "Attentional control, distractors, and motor performance." *Human Performance* 7: 315–19.

Spray, J. A. 1986. Absolute error revisited: An accuracy indicator in disguise. *Journal of Motor Behavior* 18: 225–38.

▪

# STUDY QUESTIONS FOR CHAPTER 1

1. Discuss how the terms *skills, actions,* and *movements* are distinct yet related when they refer to motor skills.

2. What is the benefit of developing classification systems to categorize motor skills?

3. Describe the one dimension that distinguishes the two categories in each of the following skill classification schemes, and give three examples of motor skills for each category: (a) gross vs. fine motor skills; (b) discrete vs. continuous motor skills; (c) closed vs. open motor skills.

4. (a) What are the two general skill characteristics used to classify skills in the Gentile taxonomy? (b) Describe the four classification characteristics included under each of these two general characteristics.

5. (a) What does the term *regulatory conditions* refer to in Gentile's skill classification system? (b) Why are regulatory conditions important to consider when categorizing skills?

6. Discuss how you would implement the two practical uses Gentile described for her taxonomy of motor skills.

7. (a) Describe the differences between performance outcome measures and performance production measures. (b) Give three examples for each of different measures of motor performance.

8. (a) Describe how simple RT, choice RT, and discrimination RT situations differ. (b) What does it mean to fractionate RT? (c) How does MT differ from RT?

9. What different information can be obtained about a person's performance by calculating AE, CE, and VE when performance accuracy is the movement goal?

10. How can performance error be determined for a continuous skill such as pursuit tracking?

11. Describe three kinematic measures of movement and explain what each measure tells us about the movement.

12. What is meant by the term *kinetics* as it is related to measuring human movement?

13. What information about a movement can be obtained by using EMG?

14. How can angle-angle diagrams be used to tell us something about the coordination characteristics of two limbs or two limb segments?

# UNIT

# II

# INTRODUCTION TO MOTOR CONTROL

# CHAPTER 2

# THE CONTROL OF COORDINATED MOVEMENT

### CONCEPT 2.1

Theories about how we control coordinated movement differ in terms of the roles of central
and environmental features of a control system

### CONCEPT 2.2

Proprioception and vision are important elements in motor control theories

### CONCEPT 2.3

Motor control theories provide a basis for our understanding of how we control complex motor skills

# CONCEPT 2.1

Theories about how we control coordinated movement differ in terms
of the roles of central and environmental features of a control system

## Key Terms

coordination

degrees of
freedom

degrees of
freedom
problem

open-loop
control
system

closed-loop
control
system

motor program

generalized
motor
program

invariant
features

parameters

relative timing

schema

dynamical
systems
theory

stability

attractors

collective
variables

control
parameters

self-
organization

coordinative
structures

## Application

To successfully perform the wide variety of motor
skills we use in everyday life, we must coordinate
various muscles and joints to function together.
These muscle and joint combinations differ for
many skills. Some skills, such as delivering a serve
in tennis or getting out of a chair and into a wheelchair, require us to coordinate muscles and joints of
the trunk and limbs. Other skills involve coordination of the arms, hands, and fingers; examples are
reaching to pick up a pencil, playing the guitar, and
typing on a keyboard. For still other skills, where
only one arm and hand are involved, we must coordinate only a few muscles and joints. We do this
when we manipulate a computer joystick or a car's
gearshift.

Motor skill performance has other important
general characteristics in addition to body and limb
coordination. For example, we perform some skills
with relatively slow movements; think of how we
position a bow before releasing an arrow, or pick
up a cup to take a drink from it. Other skills, such
as throwing a ball or jumping from a bench to the
floor, require fast, ballistic movements. Some
motor skills, such as writing a numeral or buttoning
a shirt, have few component parts; other skills,
such as performing a dance routine or playing the
piano, are very complex.

Also, we can produce remarkably accurate and
consistent movement patterns from one performance attempt to another. We are capable of performing well-learned skills with a remarkable degree of success in a variety of situations, even
though we have never before been in similar situations. For example, a skilled tennis player will have
to use a forehand stroke in many different situations in matches. The many different characteristics
in any situation, such as the ball's flight pattern,
speed, spin, bounce, and location on the court, as
well as the opponent's position, the wind and sun
conditions, and so on, provide little chance that any
two situations can be exactly alike. Yet a skilled
player can hit the ball successfully.

All of these performance characteristics intrigue
scholars who study how the nervous system controls
coordinated skill performance. The theories of motor
control discussed next represent some of the prominent current views addressing this complex question.

## Discussion

Before we discuss some theories of how the nervous system controls coordinated movement, we will clarify a few terms, to provide a foundation for understanding those theories.

### Coordination

Skilled motor performance involves a person's organization of the muscles of the body so that the goal of the skill being performed can be accomplished. It is this organizational feature that is at the heart of the definition of the term *coordination*. For the purposes of this textbook, we will use a definition based on one provided by Turney (1990): **coordination** is the patterning of body and limb motions relative to the patterning of environmental objects and events.

This definition contains two parts. Each is important to consider further. First, note that the definition specifies that coordination involves *patterns of body and/or limb movements*. Certain patterns of limb movement enable a person to achieve an action goal better than other patterns do. When learning a skill, the person must develop an appropriate limb movement coordination pattern. People typically begin practicing a skill by using a pattern of limb movements that they prefer. However, as they practice the skill and become more successful at performing it, a new and distinct pattern of limb movement emerges.

A common way to portray limb movement patterns is to represent graphically the relationship between the displacement patterns of each limb as it moves while performing the skill. An example of this type of representation can be seen in figure 2.1–1, where the coordination of the knee-hip joint angles during a soccer kick is shown.

The second part of the definition states that the pattern of limb and body motion is *relative to the pattern of environmental objects and events*. This is important because it establishes the need to consider motor skill coordination in relation to the context in which the skill is performed. The characteristics of the environmental context constrain the body and limbs to act in certain ways so that the goal of the action can be achieved.

For example, to walk along a pathway, people must adapt their body and limb movement patterns to the characteristics of the pathway. If, for example, a person is walking on a sidewalk and encounters a tree limb lying across it, he or she must use a new coordination pattern in order to step over the limb. The characteristics of the limb will dictate the characteristics of the movement pattern. If it is a small limb, the person may need only to take a large step, while if it is a large limb, he or she may have to climb over it.

### The Degrees of Freedom Problem

Because coordination involves body and limb movement patterns, an important question in the

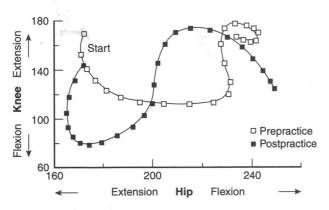

**FIGURE 2.1–1** Angle-angle diagram from an experiment by Anderson and Sidaway showing coordination changes resulting from practice for the hip and knee relationship while performing a soccer kick. (Reprinted with permission from *Research Quarterly for Exercise and Sport*, Volume 65, pp. 93–99, Copyright © 1994 American Association for Health, Physical Education, Recreation, and Dance, 1900 Association Drive, Reston, VA 20191.)

---

## A CLOSER LOOK

### Looking at the Degrees of Freedom Problem at the Level of Muscles and Joints

We know that there are 792 muscles in the human body that can act to make the one hundred joints behave in different ways. And each joint has mechanical characteristics that define its degrees of freedom for movement. Based on these features, Turvey (1990) put the coordination control problem into perspective this way: If all the joints were only hinge joints like the elbow, there would be one hundred mechanical degrees of freedom to be controlled at the joint level. But if two specific characteristics, such as position and velocity, needed to be defined for these joints to carry out a specific act, the degrees of freedom would increase to two hundred.

---

study of motor control is this: How does the nervous system control the many muscles and joints involved in producing a given pattern? To answer this question, we must consider an important problem that was first posed by Nicolai Bernstein, a Russian physiologist whose work, produced from the 1930s to the 1950s, did not become known to the Western world until 1967. Bernstein proposed that to perform a coordinated movement, the nervous system had to solve what he termed the "degrees of freedom problem."

The **degrees of freedom** of any system reflect the number of independent elements or components of the system. The **degrees of freedom problem** arises when a complex system needs to be organized to produce a specific result. The control problem is as follows: How can an effective yet efficient control system be designed so that a complex system, having many degrees of freedom, is constrained to act in a particular way?

Consider the following example of the degrees-of-freedom control problem in a mechanical system. A helicopter is designed so that it can fly up or down, to the left or the right, forward or backward, and so on, and at a variety of speeds. The helicopter designer must enable the pilot to control many different features so that the helicopter can do all these things. And the designer must help the pilot do so as simply as possible. If the pilot had to control one switch or lever for each component needed to make the helicopter fly a certain way, the pilot's job would be overwhelming. Therefore, the designer re-

duces the complexity of the task by providing control sticks and pedals that the pilot can control simultaneously with his or her hands and feet. Each stick or pedal controls several functions at once.

When the nervous system must control the human body so that it performs a complex motor skill, it faces a degrees-of-freedom control problem similar to that involving the helicopter. Our determination of the actual number of degrees of freedom that must be controlled in coordinated human movement depends on which level of control we are considering. At a very basic level, we might consider motor units as the elements that must be controlled. At another level, we could consider muscles as the element of interest. Regardless of the control level considered, it becomes evident that for any motor skill, the control problem involved in enabling a person to perform that skill is an enormous one. It is important that any theory of motor control account for how the nervous system solves this control problem.

## Open-Loop and Closed-Loop Control Systems

Most theories of how the nervous system controls coordinated movement incorporate two basic systems of control. These two systems, called **open-loop** and **closed-loop control systems,** are based on mechanical engineering models of control. Rather than provide exact descriptions of the control processes in complex human movement, these

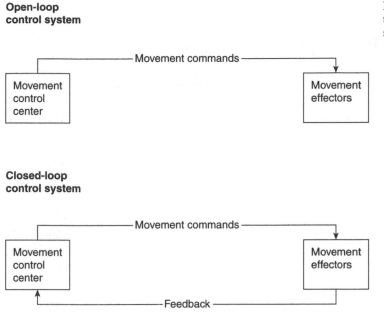

**Open-loop
control system**

**Closed-loop
control system**

**FIGURE 2.1–2**   Diagrams illustrating the open-loop and closed-loop control systems for movement control.

two models are basic descriptions of different ways the central and peripheral nervous systems initiate and control action. These models serve as useful guides that illustrate some of the basic components involved in that process.

Figure 2.1–2 presents diagrams illustrating simple open-loop and closed-loop control systems. These are the typical diagrams you would see in any general presentation of these types of control systems. Notice that each of these systems has a *control center.* The control center is sometimes referred to as an *executive.* An important part of its role is to generate and issue movement commands to the *effectors,* which, in the human, are the muscles and joints involved in producing the desired movement. Both control systems also contain *movement commands* that come from the control center and go to the effectors.

***Differences between the systems.***   These systems differ in two ways. First, a closed-loop control system involves *feedback,* while an open-loop system does not. In human movement, the feedback is *afferent* information sent by the various sensory re-

ceptors to the control center. The purpose of this feedback is to update the control center about the correctness of the movement while it is in progress.

In terms of the involvement of feedback in human movement control, figure 2.1–2 is somewhat misleading. The diagram suggests that the "effectors" that enable the body and limbs to move are the only source of feedback. But in complex human movement, feedback can come from visual and auditory receptors, as well as tactile and proprioceptive receptors.

The second important difference between open- and closed-loop control systems relates to the *movement commands* issued by the control center. In the open-loop system, because feedback is not used in the control of the ongoing movement, the commands contain all the information necessary for the effectors to carry out the planned movement. While feedback is produced and available, it is not used to control the ongoing movement. This may be so because feedback is not needed, or because there is no time to use feedback to effectively control the movement after it is initiated. In the closed-loop system, the movement commands are quite different. First, the

---

### A Closer Look

## Mechanical Examples of Open- and Closed-Loop Control Systems

**OPEN-LOOP CONTROL**

- **traffic lights**   Each light is programmed to go on at specific time intervals. Traffic conditions will not affect the intervals because the signals are impervious to that type of feedback. (Note that traffic lights can be set up to have traffic feedback override the programmed timing sequence.)
- **alarm on a clock radio**   It will turn on at the preset time regardless of whether or not you are asleep, want the radio to turn on, or are gone from the house. The only way you can stop this from occurring is by turning off the alarm.
- **videocassette recorder**   It can be programmed to tape certain programs from your television even when you are not home. The VCR will turn on and off at the time programmed into the machine.

**CLOSED-LOOP CONTROL**

- **thermostat in a house**   It controls the air-conditioning (and/or heating) system in the house. The desired room temperature is set on the thermostat. The setting becomes a reference against which actual room temperatures are compared. When the temperature is higher than the reference, a command is sent to the air-conditioning unit to turn on. If the temperature is lower than this reference, the unit stays off.
- **speed-control units**   In many stereo turntables and cruise-control systems in cars, these units control the speed of the turntable or car. Feedback continuously updates the control center about the present speed so that if there is a mismatch between the intended and the present speed, the control center can increase or decrease the speed to achieve the intended speed.

---

control center issues an initial command to the effectors that is sufficient only to initiate the movement. The actual execution and completion of the movement are dependent on feedback information that reaches the control center. In this case, then, feedback is used to help control the ongoing movement.

## Theories of Motor Control

We can clasify theories of how the nervous system controls coordinated movement in terms of the relative importance given to information provided by central components of the control system and by the environment. Theories that give prominence to the central nervous system in the control process have in common some form of memory representation, such as a motor program, that provides the basis for organizing, initiating, and carrying out intended actions. In contrast, other theories give more influence to information specified by the environment and to the dynamical interaction of this information with the body, limbs, and nervous system.

It is important to note that the theories described here address motor control from a predominantly *behavioral level of analysis*. This means that they focus on explaining observed behavior without attempting to specify neural-level features of the control process (for an example of a neural model of motor control, see Bullock and Grossberg 1991). An important goal of behaviorally based motor control theories is to propose laws and principles that govern coordinated human motor behavior. A neural-level theory would be expected to describe neural mechanisms or neural mechanism interactions that explain how the nervous system is involved in these behavioral principles.

## Motor-Program-Based Theory

At the heart of central-control-oriented theories is the **motor program,** a memory-based construct that controls coordinated movement. Various theoretical viewpoints attribute different degrees of control to the motor program. Undoubtedly, the

---

## A CLOSER LOOK

### The Evolution of the Motor Program Concept

- Early Greek philosophers such as *Plato* talked about a person's creation of an "image" of an act preceding the action itself.
- *William James* (1890) alluded to Plato when he stated that to perform an action, a person must first form a clear "image" of that action.
- *Karl Lashley* (1917) is regarded as the first person to use the actual term *motor program*. He initially viewed motor programs as "intention[s] to act," but later described them as "generalized schemata of action which determine the sequence of specific acts" (Lashley 1951, p. 122). He proposed that these schemata were organized to provide central control of movement patterns.
- *Sir Frederick Bartlett* (1932) implied that a motor program exists when he used the term *schema* to describe internal representations and organizations of movements.
- *Miller, Galanter, and Pribram* (1960) proposed the notion of a "Plan," which was "essentially the same as a program for a computer" (p. 16), and was responsible for controlling the sequence of events of an action.

- *Franklin Henry* (Henry and Rogers 1960) gave the motor program concept a needed conceptual and empirical boost. He hypothesized that the "neural pattern for a specific and well-coordinated motor act is controlled by a stored program that is used to direct the neuromotor details of its performance" (p. 449). Henry's concept of the motor program was also that of a computer program. He proposed that when initiated, the program controls the exact movement details, with essentially no modifications possible during the execution of the movement.
- *Stephen Keele* (1968) offered a view similar to Henry's by defining the motor program as "a set of muscle commands that are structured before a movement sequence begins, and that allow . . . the entire sequence to be carried out uninfluenced by peripheral feedback" (p. 387).
- *Richard Schmidt* (1975a) proposed that the motor program is not specific muscle commands, but is a memory-based representation of a class of actions, with each class defined by invariant features.

---

view that best characterizes present-day thinking about the motor program comes from the work of Richard Schmidt (1987, 1988). He proposed that a serious problem with previous views was that they limited the motor program to specific movements or sequences of movements. To overcome this limitation, Schmidt hypothesized the **generalized motor program** as a mechanism that could account for the adaptive and flexible qualities of human coordinated-movement behavior.

***Schmidt's generalized motor program.*** Schmidt proposed that a generalized motor program controls a *class of actions,* rather than a specific movement or sequence. He defined a class of actions as a set of different actions having a common but unique set of features. For Schmidt, these features, which he called **invariant features,** are the "signature" of a generalized motor program, and form the basis of what is stored in memory. In order for a person to produce a specific action to meet the demands of a performance situation, the person must retrieve the program from memory and then add movement-specific **parameters**.

Rather than use a computer metaphor, Schmidt proposed a phonograph record metaphor to describe the characteristics of the generalized motor program. The invariant features of a record specify the rhythm and the dynamics (force) of the music. The parameters include the adjustable speed and volume controls. Even if a record is played faster than normal or louder than normal, the rhythmic and dynamical structure of the music remains intact.

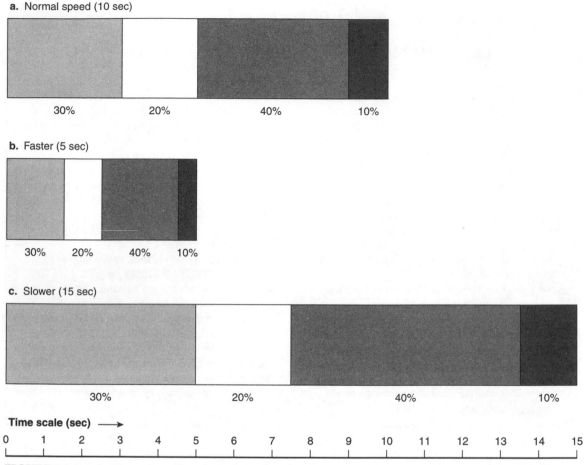

**a.** Normal speed (10 sec)

30%        20%        40%        10%

**b.** Faster (5 sec)

30%   20%   40%   10%

**c.** Slower (15 sec)

30%              20%              40%              10%

Time scale (sec) ⟶

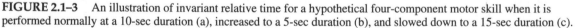

0   1   2   3   4   5   6   7   8   9   10   11   12   13   14   15

**FIGURE 2.1–3**   An illustration of invariant relative time for a hypothetical four-component motor skill when it is performed normally at a 10-sec duration (a), increased to a 5-sec duration (b), and slowed down to a 15-sec duration (c).

*Invariant features and parameters.* Although many possible characteristics could be invariant features of the generalized motor program, three are most commonly proposed. These include the **relative timing** (which is analagous to rhythm) of the components of the skill; the relative force used in performing the skill; and the order, or sequence, of the components. The term *relative* in *relative timing* and *relative force* indicates that what is invariant are the percentages, or proportions, of overall force and timing of the components of a skill.

Figure 2.1–3 presents an illustration of how to interpret the concept of relative time. Suppose

you move your arm as quickly as possible to hit four switches in sequence. Now, suppose that the four components of this task yield the following movement time proportions: component 1 takes up 30 percent of the total performance time; component 2, 20 percent; component 3, 40 percent; and component 4, 10 percent. If the performance of this skill under typical conditions has an overall duration of 10 sec (represented in part (a) of the figure), then regardless of how much you speed up or slow down this overall duration, the actual amount of time characteristic of each component changes proportionately. In figure 2.1–3,

---

**A CLOSER LOOK**

### Defining the Motor Program: A Memory Representation Versus a Plan of Action Prepared Just Prior to Moving

A problem that has arisen over the years has led to difficulties in understanding what the motor program is and how it functions. This problem is that the term *motor program* has been used to describe different functional constructs. In some discussions, the motor program refers to the memory representation of a movement or action. The generalized motor program construct in Schmidt's schema theory is a good example. The theoretical arguments about the memory-representation type of motor program focus on which characteristics of a movement or action are stored in memory as a part of the motor program. We use the term this way in the present Concept.

The other use of the term *motor program* refers to what is constructed or prepared just prior to movement initiation, but following an intention to act. This use of the term, sometimes referred to as *motor programming,* is the focus of Concept 3.1, although we do make some reference to this preparation aspect of motor-program-based control in the present Concept.

---

parts (b) and (c) represent this proportional component change for speeding up the skill (part (b)) and slowing it down (part (c)). Thus, if you typically perform this skill in 10 sec, then the amount of time you spend performing each component is 3, 2, 4, and 1 sec respectively. If you performed the skill twice as fast, in 5 sec, then each component would change proportionately to be 1.5, 1, 2, and .5 sec respectively. If you slowed down your overall performance time to 15 sec, then each component would change to 4.5, 3, 6, and 1.5 sec respectively.

While motor program theory proposes that the invariant features of a generalized motor program are rather fixed from one performance of a skill to another, it also holds that there are other features, called *parameters,* that can be varied. Examples include the *overall force,* the *overall duration,* and the *muscles* that must be used to perform the skill. Performers can easily change these from one performance situation to another, readily adapting them to the specific requirements of each situation. For example, an individual can speed up a sequence of movements and increase the overall force without altering the invariant characteristics of the motor program.

*Schmidt's schema theory.* A formalized theory of how the generalized motor program operates to control coordinated movement is Schmidt's schema theory (Schmidt 1975a, 1988). A **schema** is a rule or set of rules that serves to provide the basis for a decision. It is developed by abstracting important pieces of information from related experiences and combining them into a type of rule. For example, your concept of *dog* is the result of seeing many different types of dogs and developing a set of rules that will allow you to identify correctly as a "dog" an animal you have never seen before.

Schmidt used the schema concept to describe two control components involved in the learning and control of skills. Both are characterized as based on abstract rules. The first is the *generalized motor program*, which, as just described, is the control mechanism responsible for controlling the general characteristics of classes of actions, such as throwing, kicking, walking, and running. The second component is the *motor response schema*, which is responsible for providing the specific rules governing an action in a given situation. Thus, the motor response schema provides parameters to the generalized motor program.

The schema theory provides one explanation for a person's ability to successfully perform a skill requiring movements that have not been made in that same way before. This is possible because the person can use the rules from the motor response schema to generate appropriate parameter characteristics; the person adds these to the generalized motor program to perform the action.

Schmidt's schema theory claims to solve the degrees of freedom problem in movement coordination through an executive control operation that organizes motor programs and schemas. An important emphasis in this approach is the abstract, or general, nature of what is stored in the control center. The generalized motor program and recall schema work together to provide the specific movement characteristics needed to initiate an action in a given situation. The action initiation is an open-loop control process. However, once the action is initiated, feedback can influence its course if there is sufficient time to process the feedback and alter the action.

*Arguments promoting motor-program-based control.* Motor program advocates base one line of support for their theory on a default argument. They argue that certain motor skill performance characteristics suggest that a central command mechanism, like a motor program, must be controlling the action. Four types of research evidence illustrate the empirical basis for this argument.

One type of evidence shows that *accurate limb control can occur in the absence of sensory feedback.* For example, some experiments have shown that accurate limb positioning can occur without visual or proprioceptive feedback, and that accurate manual aiming for short distances or durations can occur without visual feedback from the arm or the target (e.g., Bizzi and Polit 1979; Elliott and Allard 1985). These kinds of results argue in favor of a central base for motor control, where motor commands can be generated by some mechanism to enable a limb to achieve its intended goal in the absence of certain sensory feedback.

Another type of evidence shows that *we prepare movements before we physically initiate them.* Research shows that RT changes as a function of a variety of movement characteristics, such as complexity and accuracy. As the movement becomes more complex or requires more accuracy, RT increases, because of the increased movement preparation demands. Evidence reported by several researchers has shown this preparation effect (e.g., Henry and Rogers 1960; Sidaway, Sekiya, and Fairweather 1995).

The third line of evidence comes from research showing that *EMG patterns are similar whether a person makes or is unexpectedly not able to make a prepared rapid limb movement.* The logic behind this research approach is this: if a central control mechanism sends commands designating when the agonist and antagonist muscles should contract in advance of movement initiation, then EMG patterns should be similar for a brief amount of time whether the limb moves or not. Research evidence showing this type of EMG effect has been reported for the biceps and the triceps for the first 100 msec after the signal to move has occurred (e.g., Young et al. 1988; Wadman et al. 1979).

Fourth, evidence shows that *there is a minimum amount of time needed to stop an intended movement.* The argument here is that if a central control mechanism prepares and initiates a rapid movement, then that movement should be initiated, once planned, even if the movement *should not* be made. Note the difference between this situation and the one described in the previous paragraph. Here, the person knows the movement should not be made rather than unexpectedly not being able to make it. For example, while typing, you see the word *there,* but for some reason you prepare, unconsciously, to type *their.* Even though you catch yourself by the time you type the *e* and begin the *i,* you probably type both the *i* and the *r.* You are not able to inhibit your typing responses in the short period of time it takes to type the last two letters. Research evidence showing this type of effect has been obtained in a variety of situations (e.g., Logan 1982; Slater-Hammel 1960), and offers support that there is a central mechanism that prepares and initiates a movement.

*Testing the invariant-relative-timing feature.* Researchers also have attempted to provide empirical

## A CLOSER LOOK

### The Difficulty We Have in Stopping a Planned Movement

In a classic experiment by A. T. Slater-Hammel (1960), participants observed the sweep hand of a clock on which one revolution took one second. Their task was to lift a finger from a response key so that this action coincided with the sweep hand's reaching a target at the *8* on a clock face (i.e., 800 msec after the hand had started). On some trials, the sweep hand unexpectedly stopped before it reached the target. Each person was told that when this happened, he or she should *do nothing* and keep his or her finger on the key. By having the hand stop unexpectedly at various points between 600 and 50 msec before it was to reach the target, Slater-Hammel could observe the length of time it took a person to inhibit a prepared movement.

The results showed that when the hand stopped approximately 140 msec before it was to reach the target, participants were able to not move from the key (as instructed) only about half of the time. When the hand stopped with less than 140 msec left before it was to reach the target, they had increasing difficulty not lifting their fingers from the key. In fact, when the hand stopped at 50 to 100 msec before the target, they almost always lifted their fingers. Only when the hand stopped 180 to 200 msec before the target could participants almost always inhibit the lifting movements.

These results demonstrate that a prepared movement will be initiated and carried out unless there is sufficient time to attend to feedback indicating that the movement should not be made, and to inhibit the movement commands issued to the musculature.

---

support for motor-program-based control by investigating Schmidt's claim that a generalized motor program controls a class of actions defined by specific invariant features. Of the proposed invariant features, relative timing has generated the most research interest. Support for the invariance of this feature has come from many experiments investigating several different skills, such as typing, gait, handwriting, prehension, and sequences of key presses, among others. (For reviews of this evidence, see Heuer 1991; Schmidt 1985, 1988.)

Researchers typically have investigated relative-timing invariance by observing changes in relative timing across a range of values of an associated parameter, such as overall duration. A good example is a study by Shapiro, Zernicke, Gregor, and Diestal (1981) in which people walked and ran at different speeds on a treadmill. The researchers were interested in what percentage of the total step-cycle time (i.e., relative time) would characterize each of the four components, or phases, of the step cycle at each treadmill speed (i.e., the overall duration parameter). If relative time is invariant for the generalized motor program involved in controlling walking and/or running gait patterns, then the percentages for a specific gait component should remain constant across the different speeds.

The results were consistent with the hypothesis of relative-timing invariance (see figure 2.1–4). They showed that as gait sped up or slowed down (at least up to 6 km/hr and beyond 8 km/hr), the percentage of time accounted for by each step-cycle component remained essentially the same for different speeds. Notice that for treadmill speeds greater than 8 km/hr a *different* motor program appears to operate: there is an obvious difference in the percentages of step-cycle time. Interestingly, at this speed, participants were no longer walking, but running. The investigators concluded that there are different generalized motor programs controlling walking and running. Within each gait pattern, the overall duration parameter could be sped up or slowed down while the relative timing among the components of the step cycle was maintained.

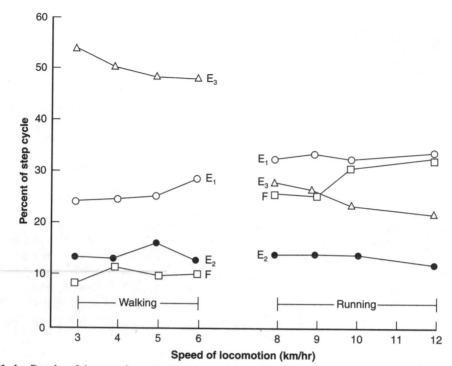

**FIGURE 2.1–4**   Results of the experiment by Shapiro et al. showing the relative timing of the four step-cycle phases (mean values), determined by comparing percentages at the different locomotion speeds. (From D. C. Shapiro, et al., "Evidence for Generalized Motor Programs Using Gait-Pattern Analysis" in *Journal of Motor Behavior,* 1966, 13:33–47. Copyright © 1966 Heldref Publications, Inc. Washington, DC. Reprinted by permission.)

*Questions about relative-timing invariance.* Schlars have advanced two major concerns about the research results demonstrating relative-timing invariance. First, they take issue with the statistical methods used to determine if relative timing is invariant. Gentner (1987) presented the most influential case, stating that conclusions from the research were based on averages of groups of people. He argued that identifying motor-program invariant characteristics requires evidence from individual data. Gentner showed that when it was reanalyzed from this perspective, the research did not provide a very strong base of support for the invariance of relative timing.

However, other researchers have offered counterarguments claiming that Gentner's approach is too restrictive. Because invariance is evaluated at the behavioral level, and motor-program invariant features are in the central nervous system, Gentner's strict analysis fails to consider the "noise" characteristics inherent in neural signals during human performance. Heuer (1991) argued that while deviations in relative timing appear when analyzed by Gentner's method, those deviations are probably still acceptable discrepancies, given that they occur at the performance end of the control process.

The second argument against relative-timing invariance as a feature of a motor program concerns the assumption that if relative timing is found to be invariant for a skill, then this characteristic is associated with a generalized motor program. The main argument here is that the relative-timing invariance observed in skilled behavior may be an outcome of the performance due to environmental features, or to the mechanical dynamics involved in body and limb movements. Rather than being specified by a central program, relative-timing invariance across behavioral variations could be an indicator of stability in the coordination pattern involved in the action.

For example, researchers typically observe relative-timing invariance when a skilled typist keystrokes a word at various overall speeds (e.g., Terzuolo and Viviani 1980). The observed timing invariance could be due to keyboard constraints rather than to motor program characteristics. That is, relative timing could occur between letter keystrokes because of the relationship among keys on the keyboard.

Those who argue against inferring a central control mechanism from evidence showing invariant relative timing state that such an inference is not necessarily valid. They point out that there are many situations in which time is a characteristic of what is observed, but there is no internal mechanism metering out time. For example, we can tell time by observing the burning characteristics of a candle, but the candle contains no time-based control mechanism.

## Dynamical Systems Theory

In sharp contrast to the motor-program-based theory of motor control is an approach commonly referred to as **dynamical systems theory.** The basis for this theoretical viewpoint is a multidisciplinary perspective involving physics, biology, chemistry, and mathematics. Proponents of this theory see human movement control as a complex system that behaves in ways similar to those of any complex biological or physical system. As a complex system, human motor control must be seen from the perspective of *nonlinear dynamics;* this means that behavioral changes over time do not follow a linear progression. For example, in the physical world, when the velocity of water through a tube is increased gradually, rather than the water flow's simply increasing steadily in speed, there is a velocity point at which the water behavior changes from smooth flow to turbulence. This behavioral change cannot be modeled mathematically with linear equations, but requires nonlinear equations.

Those who study dynamical systems theory are particularly interested in how a system changes over time from one stable state to another due to the influence of a particular variable. While this approach has been used to model many complex systems in the physical world (see Gleick 1987), only recently has it captured the attention of scientists interested in understanding how human movement is controlled.

*Nonlinear changes in movement behavior.* A series of experiments by Kelso and his colleagues provides a good example of a variable's causing a nonlinear behavioral change in human coordinated movement (e.g., Kelso 1984; Kelso and Scholz 1985). The top panel in figure 2.1–5 illustrates the type of task used in these experiments. Participants began moving their right and left index fingers at a specified rate of speed so that they were *out of phase.* This means that the muscle groups controlling the right and left fingers were operating simultaneously but in a nonhomologous fashion: when the right finger was flexed, the left finger was extended. When the experimenters compared the locations of the fingertips, they found them to be 180 degrees different from each other at any point in time. Subjects then were required to systematically increase the speed of their finger movements. The result was that the fingers eventually shifted to an *in-phase* relationship, where both were flexed or extended at the same time (i.e., a 360-degree relation of fingertips).

The *transition* between the stable out-of-phase and in-phase states was involuntary and coincided with a critical movement speed. At slower speeds, only out-of-phase movements occurred, while at faster speeds, only in-phase movements occurred. In another experiment, researchers found a similar behavioral phasing shift when subjects alternated the tapping of right and left index fingers (Kelso and Schöner 1988). In each of these situations, a linear increase in movement speed led to a nonlinear change in the fundamental type of movement.

*Stability and attractors.* At the heart of the dynamic systems view is the concept of **stability.** In dynamic terms, stability refers to the behavioral

**FIGURE 2.1–5** (a) shows the hand and finger placement for performing the finger movement task used in the experiments by Kelso. (b) and (c) show fingertip movement position as a function of time, during which movement frequency increased. (b) shows fingertip positions for both index fingers as they moved from being out of phase to in phase. (c) shows the relationship of the left index finger's peak extension to the right finger's peak extension as a different way to portray the phase transition shown in (b). (Reprinted from *Human Movement Science,* Volume 7, J.A.S. Kelso and G. Schoner, "Self-Organization of Coordinative Movement Patterns," pp. 27–46, 1988, with kind permission of Elsevier Science-NL, Sara Burgerharstraat 25, 1055 KV Amsterdam, The Netherlands.)

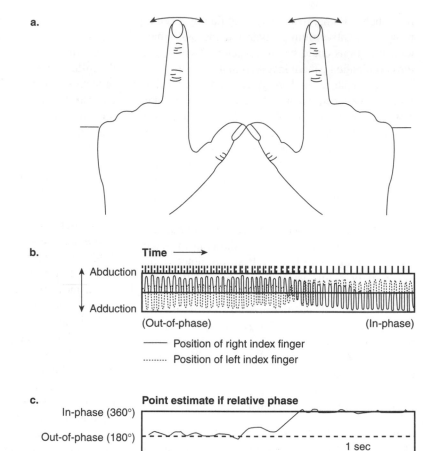

steady state of a system. This is different from the concept of invariance; stability incorporates the notion of variability by noting that when a system is slightly perturbed, it will return spontaneously to a stable state.

By observing characteristics of a stable state, scientists can gain understanding of the variables that influence a system. For example, in the rhythmic finger-moving situations in the Kelso experiment just described, the researchers observed behavioral stability when the fingers were in 180- and 360-degree phase relationships with each other. These stable states indicate coordinated movement patterns. Between these states, as finger speed increased, a *phase transition* occurred during which

instability characterized the behavioral patterns. The instability continued until finger speed reached a point at which a new stable state spontaneously occurred.

The stable behavioral steady states of systems are known as **attractors** (or *attractor states*). In terms of human coordinated movement, attractors are *preferred behavioral states,* such as the in-phase and out-of-phase states for rhythmic finger movements described in the Kelso experiment. Attractors represent stable regions of operation around which behavior typically occurs when a system is allowed to operate in its preferred manner.

For example, when a person is performing rhythmic finger tapping and attempts to produce a movement at his or her preferred rate, the person typically will produce a pattern with an in-phase relationship between fingers or arms. And if a system is slightly perturbed, it will return to the attractor state of behavior. Additionally, if a system is strongly perturbed by the continuous increase of a control parameter, the attractor state can weaken to the point at which a different attractor state influences the behavior so that a new behavioral pattern results. We saw an example of this in the rhythmic finger-movement situation, in which the continuous increase in finger speed influenced the fingers to change from an out-of-phase coordination pattern to an in-phase pattern.

Finally, attractor states are not only stable states characterized by minimal behavioral variability, but also optimally *energy-efficient states.* This means that when a person is moving at a preferred rate or using a preferred coordination pattern, that person uses less energy than he or she would if moving at a nonpreferred rate.

*Collective variables and control parameters.* Proponents of the dynamical systems view place a priority on developing formal nonlinear equations of motion that specify the stability and loss of stability of performance in addition to changes that result from learning and development (Beek and van Wieringen 1994). To develop these equations, scientists must identify the variables responsible for and associated with coordination. Primary among these variables are **collective variables,** or *order parameters,* which are functionally specific and abstract variables that define the overall behavior of a system. These collective variables enable a coordinated pattern of movement that can be reproduced and distinguished from other patterns.

Because collective variables define a movement pattern, it is essential to identify these variables. The identity of collective variables depends on the type of action. For example, at present researchers have shown that *relative phase* (illustrated in figure 2.1–3) is a collective variable for rhythmic movements, and that variables such as *equilibrium*

*points and muscle stiffness characteristics* are collective variables for discrete aiming movements.

While collective variables define a coordinated movement pattern, nonspecific **control parameters** change freely according to the specific characteristics of a situation. These include variables such as tempo (or speed) and force. In the dynamical systems approach to determining coordination principles, an experimenter will change a control parameter systematically; for example, he or she will change speed from slow to fast. As this change occurs, the researcher observes the collective variable of interest to determine any changes in its stability that are associated with specific control parameter rates. Procedures like this allow scientists to determine attractor states for patterns of limb movement.

*Self-organization.* An important element of the dynamical systems perspective is the concept of **self-organization.** This means that when certain conditions characterize a situation, a specific stable pattern of behavior emerges. Proponents of the dynamical view present many examples of self-organization within the physical world to illustrate applications of this concept to the human movement domain. For example, there is no hurricane program in the universe, but hurricanes commonly occur. However, they occur only when certain wind and water temperature conditions exist. When these variables achieve certain characteristics, a hurricane will self-organize in a distinct, identifiable fashion.

When applied to human limb coordination, the concept of self-organization means that when certain conditions characterize a situation, a specific pattern of limb movement emerges. Thus, rather than being specified by a motor program, the coordinated action self-organizes within the framework of the characteristics of environmental conditions and limb dynamics. This self-organization process follows well-established principles in the physical world. For example, the bimanual finger-movement task performed in the Kelso experiments follows principles established for a nonlinear system of coupled oscillators.

---

## A CLOSER LOOK

### Research Evidence Demonstrating Coordinative Structures

In a series of experiments investigating speech control, Kelso, Tuller, Vatikiotis-Bateson, and Fowler (1984) observed what occurred in the various components of articulators when the jaw was perturbed during an utterance. In two experiments, researchers asked each participant to say the syllable "bab." On several utterances, they then applied an unexpected force load to the participant's jaw during the upward jaw motion for the final "b" sound of the syllable. According to the coordinative structure notion, such a perturbation should result in an immediate compensation by other parts of the articulation system involved in producing this sound, because all parts work as a functional unit to achieve the common goal of the intended sound. This is, in fact, what the experimenters found. As the jaw was forced upward, there was an almost immediate compensation in the upper and lower lips so that the person still produced the sound in an understandable way. The researchers applied a similar perturbation as the participants uttered "baz." Participants made an immediate tongue compensation. Thus, the articulators can be seen to work together as functional units to achieve specified goals. When one element of the unit is disturbed, other elements compensate in a way that allows the speaker to achieve the goal. The elements involved in this compensation and the way they achieve it depend on the goal of the action.

---

*Coordinative structures.* Another important aspect of the dynamical systems view relates to the unit of behavior that is controlled. Proponents of the view assert that skilled action results when a person's nervous system constrains functionally specific *synergies of muscles and joints* to act cooperatively, so that the person can carry out an action according to the dictates of the situation. An individual may develop these functional synergies, called **coordinative structures,** through practice or experience, or they may exist naturally.

An example of a coordinative structure is the muscles and joints (the degrees of freedom to be controlled) involved in the action of reaching and grasping an object. The groups of muscles and joints that must act together to enable a person to successfully reach and grasp an object are "converted" through practice into a task-specific ensemble. The action occurs when a person has the intention to reach and grasp a cup. Then, in accordance to the characteristics of the limb and of the environmental constraints, the coordinative structure self-organizes to carry out the action.

*Perception and action coupling.* In addition to constructing mathematical models of coordinated action, proponents of the dynamical systems view also emphasize the interaction of perceptual and movement variables. Critical perceptual information includes environment invariances that specify possible behaviors. The dynamic state of the motor control system interacts with the perceptual and motor variables to produce patterns of movement appropriate for achieving the action goal of the situation.

An example of perceptual variables involved in this type of coupling process is the optical variable *tau,* which is a mathematical variable related to the time-to-contact between an object and a person's eye. (We will discuss *tau* further in Concept 2.2.) Researchers have demonstrated that *tau* guides actions such as steering a car, catching a ball, hitting a ball, jumping from a platform, and performing the long jump. As a person gains experience, the perceptual variable couples with the dynamics of movement so that a distinct coordination pattern can be reproduced as needed.

---

**A CLOSER LOOK**

## Human Gait as an Illustration of the Dynamical Systems View

The experiment described earlier in this discussion in which Shapiro and colleagues (1981) investigated walking and running at different speeds on a treadmill provides a good illustration of the various elements of the dynamical systems view of motor control. In figure 2.1–4, we saw that the relative time of each component of the step cycle remained relatively constant for speeds up to 6 km (when walking was observed), then became unstable at 7 to 9 km (during a phase transition), and then achieved a new stability at 10 km (when the subject was running).

From a dynamical systems perspective, the two relative-time patterns represent two attractor states: a walking coordination pattern and a running coordination pattern. Treadmill speed (a control parameter) influenced the relative phasing (the collective variable) of the step-cycle components to organize stably at slow speeds (walking gait), then become unstable at certain speeds, and then reorganize (self-organize) into a new behavioral pattern (running gait) at a certain faster speed.

---

***Arguments promoting a dynamical systems type of control.*** Advocates of the dynamical systems theory frequently use three lines of evidence to argue against the existence of a central control mechanism like the generalized motor program. First, because innate and learned coordinative structures exist for various coordinated acts, the human being does not need a memory representation construct such as a motor program. These structures become self-organized when the person has the intention to act in a specific situation. Modifications occur within the coordinative structure according to environmental conditions. Components of the structure adapt to compensate for each other according to constraints placed on each component.

Proponents of a dynamical systems view base their second argument on evidence showing that certain control parameter changes, such as overall speed of movement, can make dramatic changes in coordination characteristics. We saw an example of this in the rhythmic finger-movement experiments described earlier, where increasing finger-movement speed led to a spontaneous shift from an out-of-phase coordination pattern between fingers to an in-phase pattern. This type of dynamic

change is consistent with many parameter-based changes seen in the physical world. In particular, the rhythmic finger movements behave just as coupled nonlinear oscillators behave in the physical domain. Also, similar nonlinear changes occur in the rolling characteristics of fluid in cylinders when only the amount of heat applied to the cylinders is increased systematically. (See Gleick 1987 for discussion of additional physical-world examples.)

Supporters of a dynamical systems perspective offer a third argument: too many characteristics of action cannot be explained by a motor-program-based control system. Primary among these are the phase transitions that exist between stable states of behavioral patterns. For example, between the out-of-phase and the in-phase finger relationship patterns in the Kelso experiments described earlier, a transition state existed that was unstable but clearly transitory. Similarly, in the Shapiro et al. (1981) experiment involving walking and running on the treadmill, the researchers found an unstable transition state between the two stable walking and running coordination patterns. For these situations, the motor program view can accommodate only the stable conditions, not the transition stages.

***Empirical evidence supporting dynamical systems predictions.*** Relative time is a critical variable in both the motor-program-based theory and the dynamical systems theory. An impressive series of experiments by Beek and Turvey (1992) shows how relative time in cascade juggling performance follows predictions from the dynamical systems perspective, but not from the generalized motor program view. In these experiments, the relative-time measure of interest was the proportion of time a participant held a ball in his or her hand in relation to the total time the participant held the ball plus the time the ball was in flight until the next catch. According to the prediction of relative-time invariance made by the generalized motor program theory, this time proportion should remain invariant for different tempos. However, when participants juggled three balls at preferred, slower-than-preferred, and faster-than-preferred tempos, the researchers found three different relative-time proportions. Interestingly, for five-ball juggling, the relative-time proportions remained invariant across the three tempos. Beek and Turvey argue that the relative-time difference between the three- and the five-ball juggling situations fits well within the dynamical systems framework. The task constraints involved in these two juggling tasks influence the relative-time characteristics possible for each task. Because the three-ball juggling situation is less demanding in terms of avoiding ball collisions in the air, skilled jugglers can develop different stable solutions (attractors) to perform self-selected juggling tempos. But the demands of five-ball juggling do not permit such variation; these demands lead to a single stable solution for different tempos in five-ball juggling.

## The Present State of the Control Theory Issue

The motor-program-based theory and the dynamical systems theory are the predominant behavioral theories currently addressing how humans produce coordinated movement. Debate and research continue as scientists attempt to answer this important theory question more accurately. A benefit of the debate between proponents of these theories is that critical issues have become clarified and future directions more evident. We now know, for example, that a theory of control cannot focus exclusively on what movement information is specified by the central nervous system. Theorists also must take task and environmental characteristics into account. As Newell (1986) rightly stated, the optimal pattern of coordination is determined by the interaction among constraints specified by the person, the environment, and the task. At present, researchers continue to attempt to understand more clearly the unique and interactive characteristics and contributions of each of these components.

## Summary

Coordination involves a pattern of body and limb movements characterizing performance of a skill. To acquire this pattern, the nervous system must solve the degrees of freedom problem, which concerns organizing the elements of a complex system into an effective and efficient means of achieving a goal.

Most present-day theories of the control of coordinated movement incorporate features of open-loop and closed-loop control systems. Both involve a command center, commands, and effectors. However, the closed-loop system requires feedback during the action.

Theories about how the nervous system produces and controls coordinated movement attribute different roles to central and environmental factors. The motor-program-based theories hold that a central-memory-based mechanism is the primary control mechanism. This predominant current view proposes that this mechanism is a generalized motor program, which is an abstract representation of action stored in memory and retrieved when the action must be produced. Stored in the program are invariant features of the action, such as the order of events, relative time, and relative force. When a specific action must be produced, the program must be parameterized with features such as the overall duration, the overall force of the movement, and the musculature that will be used to perform the movement. Researchers investigating the invariant features of the program, as well as researchers arguing for a central representation of action, have provided evidence supporting this view of control.

An alternative view to motor-program-based control is the dynamical systems theory. This view takes issue with the idea that there is a central representation of action by proposing that factors such as environmental invariants and limb dynamics can account for much of the control ascribed to the motor program. The dynamical systems view is closely related to nonlinear dynamics; its advocates see coordinated action as following the rules and specifications found in nonlinear dynamics. The concept of stability is an essential component of this view. Stability is a preferred behavioral steady state to which behaviors are attracted. Collective variables, such as relative phase, functionally define stability. Control parameters, such as speed or frequency, influence the loss of stability of behavior. Coordinated action self-organizes as coordinative structures according to the characteristics of limb behavior and environmental constraints. Research support for this theoretical viewpoint comes from demonstrations of dynamical principles that characterize coordinated skill.

## Related Readings

Barton, S. 1994. Chaos, self-organization, and psychology. *American Psychologist* 49: 5–14.

Bruce, D. 1994. Lashley and the problem of serial order. *American Psychologist* 49: 93–103.

Kelso, J. A. S. 1994. The informational character of self-organized coordination dynamics. *Human Movement Science* 13: 393–413.

Schmidt, R. A. 1988. Motor and action perspectives on motor behavior. In O.G. Meijer and K. Roth (Eds.), *Complex motor behavior: 'The' motor-action controversy* (pp. 3–44). Amsterdam: Elsevier.

Scholz, J. P. 1991. Dynamic pattern theory—Some implications for therapeutics. *Movement Science.* Monograph. 75–91. American Physical Therapy Association.

Swinnen, S. 1994. Motor control. *Encyclopedia of human behavior.* Vol. 3. 229–43. New York: Academic Press.

Wickens, J., B. Hyland, and G. Anson. 1994. Cortical cell assemblies: A possible mechanism for motor programs. *Journal of Motor Behavior* 26: 66–82.

Worringham, C. J., A. L. Smiley-Owen, and C. L. Cross. 1997. Neural basis of motor learning in humans. In H. N. Zelaznik (Ed.), *Advances in motor learning and control* (pp. 67–86). Champaign, IL: Human Kinetics.

Zanone, P. G., and J. A. S. Kelso. 1991. Relative timing from the perspective of dynamic pattern theory: Stability and instability. In J. Fagard and P. Wolff (Eds.), *The development of timing control and temporal organization in coordinated action* (pp. 69–92). Amsterdam: Elsevier.

# CONCEPT 2.2

Proprioception and vision are important elements of motor control theories

## Key Terms

proprioception    deafferentation    prehension

## Application

When you reach for a glass of water to drink from it, both the proprioceptive and the visual sensory systems come into play as you carry out the action. Vision helps you locate the glass and grasp it with your hand and fingers. Proprioception helps you lift the glass and move it toward your mouth. Without the sensory information provided by these two key sensory systems, you would have considerably more difficulty carrying out relatively simple tasks like drinking from a glass. You accomplish other everyday skills, such as putting your door key into the keyhole, maneuvering around people as you walk in a hallway, and driving your car with ease because of the information that proprioception and vision provided to your motor control system. Similarly, sport activities also require and benefit from the roles played by the proprioceptive and visual sensory systems. For example, to catch a ball, you must see where the ball is, time its arrival to your hand, position your hand in space, and then close your fingers around the ball when it is in your hand.

Examples such as these help illustrate why proprioception and vision enable the motor control system to carry out action effectively. Without the availability of information from these sensory systems, our successful performance of a wide range of motor skills would be dramatically impaired.

## Discussion

A key feature of any theory of motor control is the role played by sensory information in controlling action. Sensory receptors located in various parts of the human body provide this information. Two of the most important types of sensory information sources influencing the control of coordinated movement are proprioception and vision.

### Proprioception and Control of Movement

**Proprioception** involves the sensory-receptor pickup of limb and body movement characteristics. Afferent neural pathways send proprioceptive information to the central nervous system about such limb and body movement characteristics as direction, location in space, velocity, and muscle activation. In closed-loop models of movement control, proprioceptive feedback plays a significant role, while in open-loop models, central commands control movement without involving proprioceptive feedback. Questions about whether human beings can control movements without proprioceptive feedback, and what role proprioceptive feedback plays in the control of coordinated movement have intrigued movement scientists for many years.

Scientists have taken a variety of experimental approaches to determine the role of proprioception in controlling coordinated action. We discuss a few of these next, to introduce you to the current thinking about this issue.

***Investigating the role of proprioception.*** Proprioception is an important source of feedback when action is under closed-loop control. One way researchers can determine the role proprioception plays in movement control is to remove this type of feedback and then observe the behavior that occurs

---

### A CLOSER LOOK

### The Sensitivity of Proprioception

A feedback-related perceptual limitation in people concerns discrimination between intensities or levels of a stimulus or signal. Such discrimination is useful when, for example, a person needs to detect different brightness levels of light before making a specific movement decision. Or, a person may need to discriminate proprioceptively between two different limb positions. From the study of *psychophysics,* which concerns the relationship between our objective world and our perception of it, we know something about how well our sensory systems can make perceptual judgments like these.

To measure the sensitivity of a perceptual system as it is used in discrimination judgments, we determine the *just noticeable difference (j.n.d.),* which is the smallest amount of change in the intensity of a stimulus that can be correctly detected by a person. Each sensory system has its own unique degree of sensitivity in detecting stimulus-intensity differences. For proprioception, the limited research evidence suggests that people have

difficulty determining whether two arm positions are different if the positions are within 1.25 cm of each other (Magill and Parks 1983).

**APPLICATION**

Suppose you are working with a person who must correct a foot positioning error while stepping, and you do not want the person to use visual feedback to position the foot. As a result, the person must use proprioceptive feedback to aid him or her in correcting the error. Now, suppose that you notice consistent errors in foot placement. After repeated efforts to correct this problem, the person states that on each attempt, it feels to him or her as though the foot is exactly where you have indicated it should be. The problem may be that the person cannot discriminate perceptually between the foot position you have indicated the foot should be in and the actual position it is in while the person is performing the skill. Your knowledge about this limitation should direct you to provide more useful information to help the person correct the problem.

---

without it. Scientists have used several techniques to remove the availability of proprioceptive feedback in such research. In general, these techniques enable researchers to compare movement without normal proprioceptive feedback with the same movement performed under normal conditions.

The most direct application of the feedback removal approach has been in animal studies. Using a procedure called **deafferentation,** researchers make proprioceptive feedback unavailable by surgically severing or removing the afferent neural pathways involved in the movement.

Taub and Berman (1963, 1968) were early users of this procedure. They observed monkeys before and after deafferentation as they performed well-developed motor skills, such as climbing, reaching, and grasping. Taub and Berman consistently found that the deafferented monkeys were still capable of

performing the skills, although the degree of precision was notably less than it had been.

Taub and Berman looked at skills that were well developed. What would happen if experimenters used the same deafferentation procedure with *newly learned skills?* Bizzi and his colleagues at Massachusetts Institute of Technology (e.g., Bizzi and Polit 1979; Polit and Bizzi 1978) took this second approach in several experiments. They placed monkeys in an apparatus like the one shown in figure 2.2–1, and trained them to point an arm at one of a series of lights when it came on. The monkeys could see the lights, but not the arm making the pointing movement. After they learned to point accurately to each light when required, the monkeys were deafferented so that no proprioceptive feedback information from the pointing arm was available during the movement. When the researchers

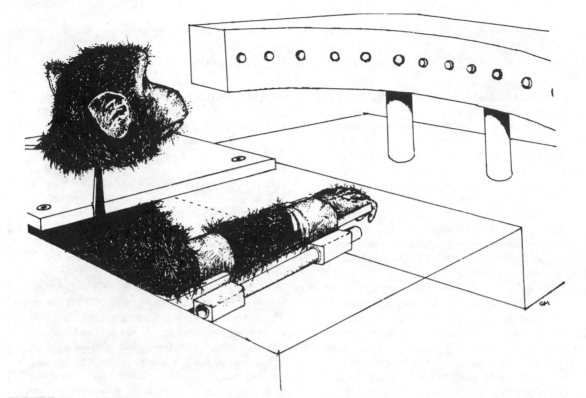

**FIGURE 2.2–1**   Monkey in the experimental apparatus used in the experiment by Polit and Bizzi. The monkey's arm is strapped to the splint that pivots at the elbow. Target lights are mounted at 5° intervals. During experimental sessions, the monkey could not see its arm and the room was darkened. (From A. Polit and E. Bizzi, in *Journal of Neurophysiology*, 1979, 42:fig. 1, p. 184. Copyright © by The American Physiological Society, Bethesda, Maryland. Reprinted by permission.)

placed them back into the positioning apparatus, the monkeys were able to position their limbs accurately in the deafferented state. In fact, they even were able to make accurate movements from starting positions that were different from the starting positions used during training.

Deafferenting human subjects for experimental purposes is not possible, for obvious reasons. However, some people are in effect deafferented because of certain trauma- or disease-related problems. For example, rheumatoid arthritis patients who have had *joint replacement* surgery have no joint receptors available. In an experiment by Kelso, Holt, and Flatt (1980), patients who had had their metacarpophalangeal joints removed and replaced with flexible silicone rubber implants per-

formed finger-positioning movements. On each trial, participants moved their fingers to a criterion finger position or a criterion distance, returned their fingers to a new starting point, and then attempted to reproduce the criterion position or distance. Results indicated that the patients had little difficulty in accurately reproducing the criterion finger *position* from a starting point that was different from the original starting point. However, they did have problems reproducing the movement *distance* from these new starting points.

Another example of deafferentation in humans involves the person who has a *sensory polyneuropathy* involving a limb. For such patients, the large myelinated fibers of the limb are lost, leading to a loss of all sensory information except pain and

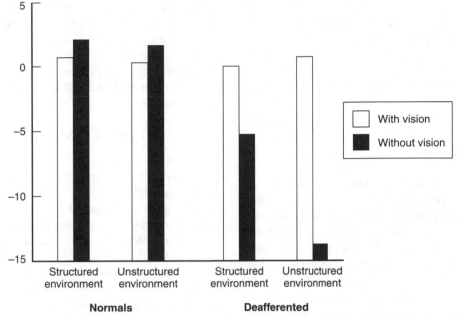

**FIGURE 2.2–2**   Results of the experiment by Blouin et al. showing the amount of error during the reproduction of an arm position for normal and deafferented subjects with vision of the environment available (structured) or not available (unstructured), and vision of the moving arm available or not. (Source: Data from J. Blouin, et al., "Reference Systems for Coding Spatial Information in Normal Subjects and a Deafferented Patient" in *Experimental Brain Research,* 93:324–331, 1993, Springer-Verlag, New York, NY.)

temperature. The efferent motor pathways are typically intact. An experiment by Blouin et al. (1993) compared a sensory polyneuropathy patient with normal participants on a pointing task involving an arm moving a pointer. On some trials, participants could see the apparatus environment, while on other trials, they performed without this visual information available. Results, shown in figure 2.2–2, were that with vision, the patient performed as accurately as the normal participants. However, without vision of either the environment or the arm while moving, the deafferented patient consistently undershot the target. Thus, without visual feedback, the deafferented patient was not able to reproduce movement accurately to a specific location in space.

Another feedback removal technique used with humans is known as the *nerve block technique.* A blood pressure cuff is placed just above the participant's elbow and then inflated until the person no longer can feel anything with the fingers. In a phe-

nomenon similar to what you experience when your arm is "asleep," the ischemic condition keeps afferent pathways from functioning. However, the efferent pathways remain unaffected. In several studies (e.g., Laszlo, 1966, 1967), people could perform motor skills in the absence of afferent sensory information from the muscles and joints of the fingers, hand, and forearm. Kelso later replicated these results using a more appropriate procedure (Kelso 1977; Kelso and Holt 1980). Here too, participants could position their fingers as accurately after the nerve block as they could prior to it.

***The role of proprioceptive feedback.***   The research evidence shows that human beings *can* carry out certain limb movements in the absence of proprioceptive feedback. However, there appear to be distinct limitations to this capability. Primary among these is the *degree of accuracy* possible. Several results from the experiments just discussed support this conclusion. In the Taub and Berman studies, the monkeys were clumsier while climbing, grasping, and reaching than they had been before deafferentation. In fact, they had difficulty grasping food with their hands in this condition. The Bizzi experiments used a relatively wide target area to indicate a correct pointing response for the monkeys. It is difficult, then, to compare the precision of the accuracy responses under normal and deafferented conditions. Researchers did note that when animal's posture was altered, pointing accuracy diminished in the deafferented condition. And in the Kelso, Holt, and Flatt experiment, the human participants maintained only positioning accuracy following joint capsule replacement. Distance movements were severely disrupted when joint capsule proprioceptive feedback was not available.

Taken together, research findings like these indicate that proprioceptive feedback provides important spatial accuracy information while a movement is in progress. Following the closed-loop control model, this means that the nervous system continuously feeds back proprioceptive information to the movement control center to provide an update on current limb position, so that the individual can make appropriate adjustments to the limb trajectory.

Proprioceptive feedback also influences the *timing of the onset of motor commands.* An experiment by Bard et al. (1992) provided evidence for this role by comparing normal participants with a patient deafferented due to a sensory polyneuropathy. Researchers asked the participants to simultaneously extend an index finger and raise the heel of the ipsilateral foot. One situation required them to do this in reaction to an auditory signal. Both the normal and the deafferented participants performed similarly by initiating the finger extension first. We would expect this if a common central command were sent to each effector. Because of the difference in distance of efferent neural pathways to the finger and heel, finger movement would occur first. Conversely, when asked to do the task at their own pace, the normal participants raised the heel first; this suggests that they based timing of the finger

movement onset on proprioceptive feedback about heel movement. In contrast, the deafferented patient performed as she had in the reactive situation, indicating that she used a central command rather than proprioceptive movements feedback as the basis for her timing of the onset of the heel and finger movements.

## Vision and Control of Movement

There are two components of visual function. Each component receives information in a different segment of the field of vision, which is said to extend to 200 degrees horizontally and 160 degrees vertically. One component is *central vision,* sometimes referred to as foveal or focal vision. Central vision can process information only in small areas, having a range of about 2 to 5 degrees. The detection information in the visual field outside these limits occurs by means of *peripheral vision.*

## Vision Predominates our Sensory-Perceptual Systems

Of all our sensory systems, human beings tend to use and trust vision the most. For example, when you first learned to type or play the piano, you undoubtedly felt that if you could not see your fingers hit each key, you could not perform accurately. Beginning dancers and stroke patients learning to walk have a similar problem. They often act as if they cannot perform accurately if they cannot watch their feet.

These anecdotal experiences illustrate our tendency to give vision a predominant role when we perform motor skills. Empirical research evidence also supports this phenomenon. The best example is a classic experiment by Lee and Aronson (1974) that is often referred to as the "moving room" experiment. Participants stood in a room in which the walls could move up or down, as well as forward or backward. However, the floor was stationary and did not move. The researchers observed the participants to record their postural responses to the movement of the walls. When the walls moved, children and adults made posture

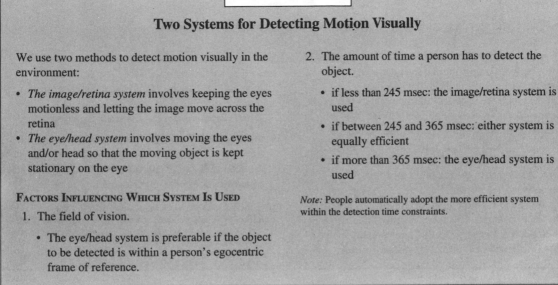

correction adjustments that were in keeping with maintaining their posture in a whole room moving in a certain direction. Because the floor did not move, their proprioceptors were not signalling that their bodies were losing stability. Only their visual systems detected any loss of balance.

The moving room experiment demonstrates nicely the special priority we assign to vision in our daily activities. In that experiment, when the proprioceptive and visual systems provided conflicting information to the central nervous system, people gave attention to vision while ignoring proprioception. The result was that they initiated unnecessary postural adjustments.

## Vision and Manual Aiming

A manual aiming task requires a person to move one or both arms over a prescribed distance to a target. In real-world settings, this action is required when a person reaches for a cup, types, or plays the piano. Manual aiming also is involved in the performance of many industrial and military jobs, as when a worker quickly picks up an item from a conveyer belt and places it in a container in which the item precisely fits. Laboratory approximations of this type of action typically involve a person's holding a stylus on a starting point and then moving it to hit a target as accurately as possible. In some experiments the participants must hit the target while moving as quickly as possible, while in others they must move at specific speeds.

***Vision's role depends on the phases of the aiming movement.***   Vision appears to be involved in different ways at different times during an aiming movement. Research evidence has shown that there are three distinct phases of performing a manual aiming movement. The role vision plays in the control of the movement is different in each phase.

The first phase is the *movement preparation phase,* which begins as soon as a person has made the decision to produce the movement to the target. Here, the person uses vision to determine important characteristics of the situation, such as the direction and distance the limb must travel and the target size. The second phase, the *initial flight*

### A CLOSER LOOK

## Time-to-Contact: The Optical Variable *Tau*

In situations in which the action involves a person's moving to an object or an object's moving toward a person, visual information that specifies *time-to-contact* with the object is an important aspect of the action control (see e.g., Lee 1974, 1980). As the person approaches the object or vice versa, the object produces a larger image on the person's retina. When this retinal image reaches a certain size, it triggers in the person a specific action response to the object.

A critical variable in these situations is not the distance from the object, but the time until the object is contacted. Lee showed that an important source of this time-to-contact information is an optical variable, which he termed *tau*.[1] This variable can be quantified mathematically as the reciprocal of the relative rate of dilation of the visual angle subtended by a moving object.

**Tau is involved in action control by influencing:**

- the triggering of the action: the action is initiated at a critical *tau* value.
- the determination of specific movement characteristics of the required action.

*Note:* Specific examples of the *tau* influence are seen in the discussions of the role of vision in the control of specific motor skills.
1. See Tresilian (1994) for a discussion of additional possible sources of time-to-contact information.

---

*phase,* includes the beginning of the actual limb movement in the general direction of the target. This phase is typically ballistic. Vision plays a minor role here, although it may provide early limb displacement and velocity information that is used later for error correction purposes. The third phase is the *termination phase,* which begins just before and ends when the target is hit. If the individual has sufficient time to use visual feedback and make movement modifications, vision plays a critical role in providing the information he or she needs to make these alterations so that the limb will hit the target.

***Factors influencing the control of manual aiming.*** We need to take several factors into account to fully understand the role of vision in human control of manual aiming skills. These factors include the movement duration, the certainty of the availability of vision, and whether the preferred limb is used to perform the action.

*Movement duration* is an important factor in manual aiming because it influences control processes involved in error correction. The error correction phase occurs *only* when the person has sufficient time to detect error and amend the move-

ment in progress. The precise amount of time that is "sufficient" to allow these correction procedures to be carried out is not well established. However, we can make a reasonable estimate from research investigating this question.

Keele and Posner (1968) performed the classic experiment addressing the error-correction-time question. They trained people to make 6-in. movements to targets of 1/4-in. diameter in times as close as possible to 150, 250, 350, and 450 msec. In half of the trials, researchers turned the lights off as soon as the participants left the starting point. In the other half of the trials, the lights remained on throughout the experiment. The logic underlying this procedure was that having the lights turned off should seriously affect accuracy if visual feedback is needed for error corrections. The results led Keele and Posner to conclude that the time required for a correction phase to occur is between 190 and 260 msec. However, later experiments (e.g., Zelaznik, Hawkins, and Kisselburgh 1983) have extended this range to between *150 and 260 msec.*

Another factor influencing the role of vision in controlling the aiming movement is the *degree of certainty about the availability of vision* during the movement. If people are uncertain about this, they prepare the movement as if vision will not be available. This means that they prepare and perform the movement in an open-loop manner. A series of experiments by Elliott and Allard (1985) produced evidence of this strategy. When participants knew before a trial began that the lights would be on, their movements, which lasted for 225 msec, benefited from their having vision available. However, when they did not know if the lights would be on or off, their error increased when the lights were on and decreased when the lights were off.

Finally, we must take one more factor into consideration to understand the role of vision in the control of an aiming movement: there is a *performance advantage for the preferred hand*. One possible reason for this advantage is that people process visual information during movement more efficiently for the preferred hand. If the hand advantage is due to more efficient processing of visual information related to that hand, it appears that this processing occurs during the preparation phase (see Roy and Elliott 1986). However, scientists need to do further research in this area to determine the extent to which the preferred-hand advantage in aiming movements is due to visual (as opposed to motor) processes.

## Vision and Prehension

**Prehension** is the act of reaching for and grasping an object, either stationary or moving. This action is very important in enabling a person to carry on daily living skills, such as reaching for and grasping a cup to drink from it, or reaching for and grasping a pen to pick it up so that he or she can write with it. Vision plays an essential role in these activities.[2]

*Influences on the role of vision in prehension.* An important influence on the role of vision in prehension control is the *phase of the action*. In the

2. See Weir, Mackenzie, Marteniuk, and Cargoe (1991) for a more complete discussion of how different variables influence the phases of prehension.

transport, or reach, phase, the arm transports the hand toward the target object. Then, in the hand-orienting phase, the person orients the hand in the correct position to grasp the object. The third step is the grasp phase, in which the person controls his or her fingers and thumb so that they grasp the object. Finally, the lift phase occurs: the person moves the grasped object, to accomplish the goal of the reach-and-grasp action.

*Task and situation variables* also influence the role of vision in prehension control. These variables include object characteristics, such as size, shape, and texture; situation characteristics, such as object location and orientation; and task requirements, such as the speed of the movement and what the person needs to do with the object. All can be influential in how prehension is controlled.

Vision is an important element in each of the reach-and-grasp phases of prehension. Before initiating a reach, a person visually picks up information about the object, such as its shape and texture, and about the distance to the object. With this advance information, he or she establishes where the arm must go, how the hand must be positioned, and how much force should be applied for the person's hand to get to the object, grasp it, and pick it up. Thus, human beings use visually detected information about the task environment to preset the motor control system to initiate and initially move the arm and hand toward the object.

If there is sufficient time, vision also provides the basis for on-line control of the hand and fingers while the arm is moving. This control, based on visual feedback, allows the hand and fingers to take the needed shape according to the object characteristics. Thus, vision provides information along the way so that the person can make whatever adjustments are needed to enable the hand to get to the object accurately, grasp it, and do something with it. If there is not sufficient time to use visual feedback, or if visual feedback is not available during the movement, the person generates movement commands specifying grasp characteristics *before* initiating the movement. He or she specifies these characteristics by visually observing the object and surrounding environment prior to initiating the movement.

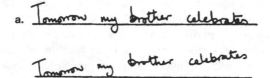

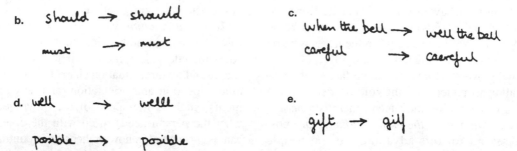

**FIGURE 2.2–3**   Handwriting examples from the experiment by Smyth and Silvers showing errors related to writing without vision available (bottom line in (a); right side of arrows in others) as compared to writing with vision available. (a) shows errors as deviating from the horizontal; (b) shows errors as adding and deleting strokes; (c) shows adding and deleting of letters; (d) shows adding or deleting of repetitions of double letters; (e) shows reversing of letters. (Reprinted from *Acta Physiologocia,* Volume 65, M.M. Smythe and G. Silvers, "Functions of Vision in the Control of Handwriting," pp. 47–64, 1987, with kind permission of Elsevier Science-NL, Sara Burgerhartstraat 25, 1055 KV Amsterdam, The Netherlands.)

Evidence supporting these two different vision-based control modes comes from research showing that it takes longer to initiate a movement when vision is not available after reach initiation than when vision is continuously available during the reach.

## Vision and Handwriting

A substantial amount of research evidence indicates that vision plays an important role in the control of handwriting actions. For example, Smyth and Silvers (1987) cited evidence showing that a person who is asked to write with his or her eyes closed adds extra strokes to some letters, omits strokes from some letters, and duplicates some letters. And if visual feedback is delayed while a person is writing, that person makes many errors, including repeating and adding letters.

Based on their own research and that of others, Smythe and Silvers proposed that vision performs two distinct functions in the control of handwriting. One function is to help the writer *control the overall spatial arrangement of words on a hori-*zontal line. We see an example of this function in figure 2.2–3, where handwriting samples taken from people writing without vision available show distinct deviations from a horizontal line. The second function for vision is to help the writer *produce accurate handwriting patterns,* such as the appropriate strokes and letters required for the written material. Again, evidence of·this is seen in figure 2.2–3. People who wrote without vision available added or omitted strokes, added extra letters, deleted letters, and reversed letters.

## Vision and Locomotion

Although scientists in a variety of fields have studied locomotion, the study of the role of vision in the control of locomotion does not have a long history. Vision plays an especially important role in locomotion when the person moving has the goal of intercepting or avoiding contact with an object. Scholars now widely agree that this action is controlled in part by the optical

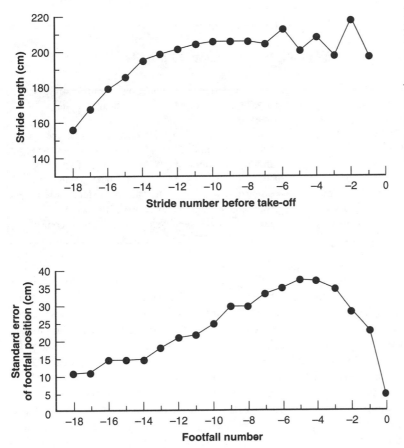

**FIGURE 2.2–4** Redrawn from results of the experiment by Lee, Lishman, and Thomson showing the stride-length characteristics (top) and the standard errors for 6 long jumps by an Olympic-class female long jumper. (From D. N. Lee, J. R. Lishman, and J. A. Thomson, "Regulation of Gait in Long Jumping." in *Journal of Experimental Psychology: Human Perception and Performance,* 1982, 8:448–459. Copyright © 1982 American Psychological Association. Reprinted by permission.)

variable *tau,* which provides information about time-to-contact with the object.

An example of research evidence demonstrating this time-to-contact influence for a locomotor skill is an experiment by Lee, Lishman, and Thomson (1982). Skilled long jumpers must run down a long trackway and accurately strike a takeoff board. In the experiment, the researchers filmed three highly skilled female long jumpers during their approaches to the takeoff board. By analyzing stride-length changes as each athlete approached and contacted the takeoff board for a series of six long jumps, the researchers observed several important gait pattern characteristics. We will examine these using the results from one of these athletes (an Olympic-level performer), presented in figure 2.2–4.

Initially, the athlete's stride length increased for the first five to six strides; it then began to become similar for the next six strides. These strides were relatively consistent across the six jumps. Then, on the final six strides, something different began to occur. The athlete made stride-length adjustments so that she could hit the board accurately. In fact, she made almost 50 percent of these adjustments on the last stride. The lower half of the figure shows why she had to make these adjustments. As the athlete ran down the track, small inconsistencies in each stride had a cumulative effect, so that when she was five strides from the board the standard error had risen to 37 cm. If she had not adjusted her stride lengths on the remaining strides, she would have missed hitting the takeoff board by a long distance.

---

## A CLOSER LOOK

### Visual Cues Can Aid Walking by Parkinson's Patients

People with Parkinson's disease commonly have the motor control problem of difficulty in controlling walking gait. The following strategy has empirical as well as clinical evidence supporting its effectiveness in helping the walking behavior of Parkinson's patients.

The therapist spaces short lines on the floor approximately 18 in. apart and perpendicular to the person. The patient is instructed to place his or her heel on each line. Research evidence (e.g., Forssberg,

Johnels, and Steg 1984) has shown that this strategy can be as effective as L-Dopa medication in its influence on walking gait.

In addition to being an effective clinical strategy, the use of spaced lines on a floor as visual cues to aid walking also demonstrates the influence of vision on locomotion. Parkinson's patients' walking gait can become almost normal when this procedure is used; this provides additional evidence of the perception-action linkage between vision and locomotor control.

---

These stride-length characteristics led the authors to describe the long jump run-up as consisting of two phases: an initial accelerative phase, where an athlete produces stereotypic stride patterns, followed by a zeroing-in phase, where the athlete modifies stride patterns to eliminate accumulated error. They concluded that a long jumper bases the correction process during the second phase on visual information obtained in advance of these strides. This means that the visual system picks up time-to-contact information from the board and directs the locomotor control system to make appropriate modfications to the stride length.

It is worth noting that the use of visual time-to-contact information to regulate gait does not depend on the expertise of the person. Although the participants in the Lee et al. long jump study were highly skilled, novice long jumpers also have demonstrated similar stride-length adjustments consistent with the influence of *tau* (Berg, Wade, and Greer 1994).

Researchers have found that other types of gait also involve adjustments during locomotion on the basis of visual time-to-contact information. Some examples are locomotor activities such as these: walking a given distance and stepping on the target with a specified foot (Laurent and Thomson 1988); running and stepping on targets, as people do when crossing a creek on rocks (Warren, Young, and Lee

1986); doing run-ups to the springboard and horse while performing the vault in women's gymnastics (Meeuwsen and Magill 1987). In all of these activities, the persons adjust stride length on the basis of time-to-contact information as they near the targets.

Visual information also guides such daily loco-motor actions as walking through doorways (Warren 1987) and stair climbing (Mark 1987). However, rather than time-to-contact, the critical variable assessed by vision in these last two activities was the ratio between the size of the door opening or the stair-step height and the shoulder width or the leg length of the individual.

## Vision and Jumping from Heights

Jumping from a platform to the floor is another skill for which experimental results have supported the view that the optical variable *tau* triggers specific preparatory actions so that a person can achieve an action goal. In an experiment by Sidaway, McNitt-Gray, and Davis (1989), people jumped from three different heights: .72 m, 1.04 m, and 1.59 m. The authors instructed the participants to land with both feet on a force plate on the floor, and to direct their visual attention toward this force plate throughout the jump.

A unique characteristic of this experiment is that the researchers measured the EMG activity of the rectus femoris so that they could assess the

---

| A CLOSER LOOK |
| :---: |

### *Tau* and Catching

The role played by the optical variable *tau* in catching an object is a much-debated issue. Wallace et al. (1992), for example, showed that *tau* acts as the sole action trigger at a specific time-to-contact only when the object approaches the person directly, on a collision course with the eye. When the object is not on this type of trajectory, as when a person catches a ball off to the side or close to the ground, that person uses *tau* along with other visual information to help him or her estimate time-to-contact. The person then must develop an appropriate movement strategy to successfully catch the object. For example, the person can use *tau* to determine the appropriate limb movement time for getting the hands into a catching position.

---

onset of activity in this prime-mover muscle in relation to the distance the person was from landing on the floor. The logic here was that according to Lee's view of the role of the optical variable *tau* as a triggering mechanism for a certain action, there should be a specific relationship between *tau* and the onset of the rectus femoris activity, regardless of the height of the jump. The results of this experiment support this prediction. Thus, the optical variable *tau* mediated the control of the onset of the muscle activity required for jumping from different heights, indicating that vision plays a critical role in the control of performing this skill.

## Vision and Catching

Three stages characterize catching an object. First, the person must move the arm and hand toward the oncoming object. Then, he or she must shape the hand to catch the object. Finally, the fingers must grasp the object. Williams and McCririe (1988) provided research evidence demonstrating the stages of catching with their study of 11-year-old boys trying to catch a ball with one hand. A movement analysis of the catching action showed no arm motion for the first 160 to 240 msec of the ball flight. Then, elbow flexion gradually began and continued slowly and uniformly for about 80 percent of the ball flight. At about the same time, the fingers began to extend. The hand began to withdraw from the oncoming ball until about one-half

of the ball flight time had elapsed. Then the upper arm accelerated about the shoulder, which resulted in the hand's being transported to the spatial position required for intercepting the ball. Boys who caught the ball began final positioning action 80 msec earlier than boys who failed to catch it. By the time 75 percent of the ball flight was complete (113 msec prior to contact), each successful boy had his hand and fingers in a ready state for catching the ball.

These results indicate that vision provides advance information enabling the motor control system to *spatially and temporally set the arms, hands, and fingers before the ball arrives*, so that the individual can catch the ball. It is especially noteworthy here that the person bases the grasping action on information obtained before the ball actually makes contact with the hand, rather than on feedback obtained after the ball has hit the hand. Tactile and proprioceptive feedback become involved after contact because the catcher needs to make adjustments to the grasp. It is apparent, then, that both central and peripheral vision operate when a person picks up information critical to catching an object.

***Time needed to see an object in order to catch it.*** We will consider here two questions concerning the role of vision in catching an object. The first is this: *How long must a person watch an object to*

**FIGURE 2.2–5** Redrawn from
results from the work of Whiting
and colleagues showing the
number of balls caught (out of 20)
under different periods of
illumination. (From H. T. A. Whiting,
"Acquiring Ball Skills," London: G. Bell &
Sons Ltd., 1969. Reprinted by permission Bell
& Hyman Ltd., London.)

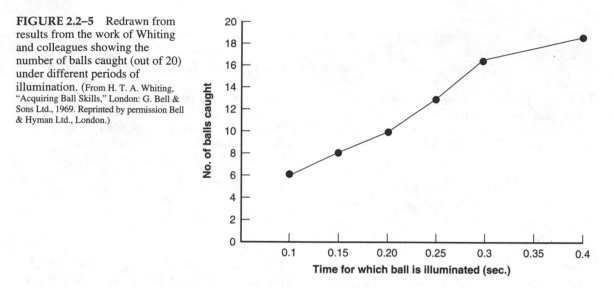

*catch it?* The classic experiment addressing this question has provided an answer.

Whiting, Gill, and Stephenson (1970) designed a special ball that could be illuminated for specific lengths of time during its flight. The participants sat in a dark room and were required to catch the ball as often as possible. The ball was illuminated for 0.1, 0.15, 0.2, 0.25, 0.3, and 0.4 sec during its flight. The longer the ball was illuminated, the more catches participants made (see figure 2.2–5 for an illlustration). However, a closer look at these results indicates that there was little difference in the number of catches they made between the 0.3- and 0.4-sec conditions. This finding suggests that after an initial period, which lasts for at least 0.3 sec (or 300 msec), visual information that people can obtain from the ball is no longer critical for their catching it. This, of course, only applies to a ball that will not unexpectedly change its course of flight after that period.

An issue related to this first question is this: *Must the object be viewed continuously?* In a series of experiments by Elliott, Zuberec, and Milgram (1994), people were required to catch a ball with one hand while having their vision intermittently occluded by special goggles that could make

the lenses either transparent or opaque. Results showed that the critical total view time was only 100 msec of the 1000-msec ball flight. Even more striking was this finding: participants were able to catch balls successfully when they intermittently saw brief snapshots (20 msec) of the ball every 80 msec during its flight. Interestingly, these results are remarkably similar to those reported for people walking on a balance beam and walking across a horizontal ladder whose vision was occluded intermittently (Assaiante, Marchand, and Amblard 1989).

Together, these experiments demonstrate that people can use visual samples of critical environmental characteristics to obtain the information they need to perform appropriate actions, if they take these samples with a very short time interval between samples (80 msec) and for a sufficient length of time (10 percent of total). We are capable of correct action when we sample visual information intermittently; this explains how people can successfully perform such diverse tasks as goal-tending in ice hockey, when they must catch a puck as it goes through several pairs of legs, and maintaining equilibrium and foot position while they walk along a narrow but crowded path.

*Vision of the hands and catching.* The second question related to catching is as follows: *Must a person be able to see his or her hands throughout the flight of a ball to successfully catch the ball?* In one of the first experiments investigating this question, Smyth and Marriott (1982) attached a screen to the participants so they could see the oncoming ball, but not their hands. When the participants were able to see their hands, they averaged 17.5 catches out of 20 balls thrown. However, when they could *not* see their hands, they were able to catch an average of 9.2 balls out of 20. More important, when they could *not* see their hands, participants typically made a hand positioning error: they could not get their hands into the correct spatial position to intercept the ball. But when they could see their hands, their typical errors involved grasping: they initiated too early the finger flexion they needed to grasp the ball.

Although additional evidence has shown that catching accuracy diminishes when a person cannot see his or her hands during the flight of a ball (e.g., Rosenberg, Pick, and von Hofsten 1988), there appears to be an important qualification to this conclusion. *Experience* is an important factor influencing a person's catching success when he or she cannot see his or her hands. We might expect this, as Davids (1988) argued, because the effective use of peripheral vision is a function of age and experience. Because we use peripheral vision to see our hands as we try to catch an oncoming object, it is logical to expect that our need to see our hands to catch a ball will depend on our age and experience.

Fischman and Schneider (1985) reported empirical evidence supporting the influence of experience. Using the same experimental procedures as those of Smyth and Marriott, they included participants who had had at least five years' experience in varsity baseball or softball. The results of this experiment (figure 2.2–6) showed that while the number of catches decreased when the people could not see their hands, the type of error did not depend on whether or not the participants could see their hands. However, for the inexperienced ball catchers, more positioning errors than grasp errors occurred when they could not see their hands.

## Vision and Striking a Moving Object

Two experiments investigating the striking of a moving object illustrate how vision is involved in this action.

*Vision and baseball batting.* The most commonly cited experiment related to the role of vision in baseball batting was performed by Hubbard and Seng (1954). Using photographic techniques, they found that their participants, including twenty-five professional baseball players, were able to track the ball only to a point, at which point they made the swing. This point did not coincide with the point where the bat made contact with the ball. Each batter tended to synchronize the start of the step forward with the release of the ball from the pitcher's hand. And, perhaps most important, the durations of the batters' swings were remarkably consistent from swing to swing, indicating that it was the initiation of the swing that batters adjusted according to the speed of the oncoming pitch. Interestingly, these findings agree precisely with expectations from a *tau*-based strategy for hitting. That is, the initiation of the batting action occurred at a critical time-to-contact.

Some of the findings of Hubbard and Seng have been either verified or extended in research reported since their study. For example, thirty years later, Bahill and LaRitz (1984) used more sophisticated technology to closely monitor eye and head movements of a major league baseball player and several college baseball players. The study was done in a laboratory situation that simulated players' responses to a high-and-outside fastball thrown by a left-handed pitcher to a right-handed batter. The major league player visually tracked the ball longer than the college players did. The college players tracked the ball to a point about 9 ft in front of the plate, at which point their visual tracking began to fall behind the ball. The major league player kept up with the ball until it reached a point about 5.5 ft in front of the plate before falling behind in his tracking. Also, regardless of the pitch speed, the major league player followed the same visual tracking pattern and was very consistent in

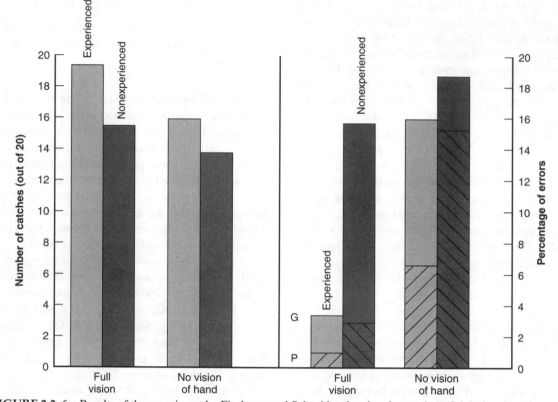

**FIGURE 2.2–6** Results of the experiment by Fischman and Schneider showing the number of right-hand catches made (out of 20 chances) for experienced softball/baseball players and nonexperienced subjects, and the percentage of errors made (based on 360 attempts) by each group that were classified as positioning (P) or grasp (G) errors when subjects either could or could not see their hands. (Source: Data from M. G. Fischman and T. Schneider, "Skill Level, Vision, and Proprioception in Simple One-Hand Catching" in *Journal of Motor Behavior,* 1985, Vol. 17, p. 219–229.)

every stance he took to prepare for the pitch. His head position changed less than one degree across all pitches. Interestingly, he made slight head movements while tracking the ball, but never moved his body.

***Vision and table tennis striking.*** In a study of five top table tennis players in the Netherlands, Bootsma and van Wieringen (1990) showed from movement analysis results that the players could not rely completely on consistent movement production. Players seemed to compensate for differences in the initiation times of their swings in order

to hit the ball as fast and as accurately as possible. For example, when time-to-contact was shorter at swing initiation, players compensated by applying more force during the stroke. And evidence suggests that some of these players were making very fine adjustments to their swings while they were moving. Thus, while visual information may trigger the initiation of the swing and provide information about its essential characteristics, vision also provides information that the player can use to make compensatory adjustments to the initiated swing, although these are very slight in terms of time and space quantities.

---

### A CLOSER LOOK

#### "Watch the Ball All the Way to Your Bat!"

A common instruction coaches give when teaching hitting in baseball is to tell players, "Watch the ball all the way to your bat." In light of this, it is interesting to note that research (e.g., Bahill and LaRitz 1984) indicates that batters probably never see the bat hit the ball. If they do, it is because they have jumped in their visual focus from some point in the ball flight to the bat contact point. They do not visually track the ball continuously all the way to bat contact because this is virtually a physical impossibility. Batters commonly track the ball to a certain point and then visually jump to a point where they predict the ball will be at bat contact.

It is worth noting that more-skilled batters watch the ball for a longer amount of time than less-skilled players. Beginners tend to have the bat swing initiation movement influence their head position and "pull" their head out of position for seeing the ball/bat contact area.

From an instruction point of view, these characteristics suggest that *it is worthwhile* to instruct a person, "Watch the ball all the way to your bat." Even though the person can't really do that, this instruction directs the person's visual attention so that the person tracks the ball for as long as physically possible, and keeps his or her head in position to see the ball/bat contact area.

---

## Summary

Proprioception and vision are two important sources of feedback involved in movement control. To investigate the role played by proprioceptive feedback in movement control, scientists have used several experimental techniques to remove proprioceptive feedback. The most direct method involves deafferentation. When animals have been deafferented after having learned a skill, they continue to perform certain skills, although with distinct performance-capability limitations. Humans who have been deafferented because of joint replacement surgery or neuropathies, or who have simulated deafferentation from a nerve block procedure, show similar characteristics. Results of these approaches have shown that proprioceptive feedback is important for controlling the degree of precision in limb movements, and in timing the onset of motor commands.

Vision tends to dominate as a source of sensory information in the control of coordinated, voluntary movement. This tendency is well illustrated by situations in which vision and proprioceptive feedback provide conflicting information, as in the moving room experiment. Research with manual aiming tasks has shown that the motor control system requires an error-correction time period of approximately 150 to 260 msec for visual feedback to alter a movement. We have examined the role vision plays in the control of movement by discussing a variety of motor skills and describing how visual information is important for performing these skills: manual aiming skills, prehension, handwriting, locomotor skills, jumping from heights, catching a ball, and hitting a baseball and a table tennis ball. One of the consistent roles for vision in these skills is to help a person preset limb and body movement in accordance with the characteristics of initial limb and body position and the characteristics of the performance environment. For skills requiring accurate limb movement, vision provides error correction information to ensure that an individual makes the movement accurately.

## Related Readings

Abernethy, B., and R. Burgess-Limerick. 1992. Visual information for the timing of skilled movements: A review. In J. J. Summers (Ed.), *Approaches to the study of motor control and learning* (pp. 343–84). Amsterdam: Elsevier.

Bootsma, R. J. 1991. Predictive information and the control of action: What you see is what you get. *International Journal of Sport Psychology* 22: 271–78.

Carnahan, H., M. A. Goodale, and R. G. Marteniuk. 1993. Grasping versus pointing and the differential use of visual feedback. *Human Movement Science* 12: 219–34.

Goodale, M. A., and P. Servos. 1997. Visual control of prehension. In H. N. Zelaznik (Ed.), *Advances in motor learning and control* (pp. 87–121). Champaign, IL: Human Kinetics.

Portier, S. J., and G. P. van Galen. 1992. Immediate vs. postponed visual feedback in practising a handwriting task. *Human Movement Science* 11: 563–92.

Savelsbergh, G. J. P., H. T. A. Whiting, and R. J. Bootsma. 1991. Grasping tau. *Journal of Experimental Psychology: Human Perception and Performance* 17: 315–22.

Tresilian, J. R. 1994. Approximate information sources and perceptual variables in interceptive timing. *Journal of Experimental Psychology: Human Perception and Performance* 20: 154–73.

Whiting, H. T. A., G. J. P. Savelsbergh, and J. R. Pijpers. 1995. Specificity of motor learning does not deny flexibility. *Applied Psychology: An International Review* 44: 315–32.

# CONCEPT 2.3

Motor control theories provide a basis for our understanding
of how we control complex motor skills

## Key Terms

speed-
  accuracy
  trade-off
Fitts' Law

index of
  difficulty
  (ID)

bimanual
  coordination

## Application

Appropriate training and rehabilitation procedures
are important to develop to help people acquire
skills effectively and efficiently. Motor control theory is an important foundation on which to base the
development of these procedures. However, an important first step is to establish how motor control
theory explains the ways we control specific motor
skills. But because the underlying mechanisms and
influences involved in the control of coordinated
skill are so complex, establishing universally accepted explanations for most skills is almost im-
possible. Even a simple limb-positioning skill, in
which a person moves a limb to a specific location
in space, involves a complex array of personal and
environmental interactions that scientists must take
into account when they explain how this action is
performed. While experts disagree in their explanations of how specific skills are controlled, all agree
on the need to look for these explanations.

## Discussion

Over the past few years an increasing number of
researchers have looked at everyday skills and
sport skills to try to establish theoretical explanations for how these skills are produced. We discuss
several of these skills here to provide a glimpse at
our present understanding of this control question.

### Manual Aiming Skills

A characteristic of most manual aiming skills is
that a person must perform the skill quickly and accurately. When both speed and accuracy are related
to successful skill performance, one of the most
fundamental principles of motor performance is
observed: *a trade-off between speed and accuracy.*
That is, when the person emphasizes speed, accuracy is reduced. And conversely, when he or she
emphasizes accuracy, speed is reduced.

*Fitts' law.*    The **speed-accuracy trade-off** is such
a common characteristic in motor skill performance that a mathematical law describes it. **Fitts'
Law,** based on the work of Paul Fitts (1954), indicates that there are two essential components of a
task in which the speed-accuracy trade-off will
occur. These are the *distance* to move and the *target size.* Fitts' Law specifies how these two components are related so that the movement time can be
derived. Fitts' Law describes this relationship as

$$MT = a + b \log_2(2D/W)$$

where

> MT is movement time
> $a$ and $b$ are constants
> $D$ is the distance moved
> $W$ is the target width, or size

That is, movement time will be equal to the $\log_2$
of two times the distance to move divided by the

<u>Same ID for different distances and target widths:</u>

**ID = 3**

Distance = 4 cm; target width = 1 cm

Distance = 8 cm; target width = 2 cm

<u>Different ID for same distance:</u>

**ID = 1**

Distance = 2 cm; target width = 2 cm

**ID = 2**

Distance = 2 cm; target width = 1 cm

**FIGURE 2.3–1** Examples of indexes of difficulty (ID) for reciprocal aiming tasks with different target size and/or distance characteristics. Task difficulty is indexed according to the ID such that the higher the ID is, the more difficult is the task. The ID is calculated according to the Fitts' Law equation: ID = $\log_2$ (2•Distance/Width). [Note that W is measured from the near edge of each target.]

width of the target. As the target size becomes smaller or as the distance becomes greater, the movement speed will decrease in order to allow for an accurate movement. In other words, there is a speed-accuracy trade-off.

Fitts indicated that because of the lawful relationship between target size and movement distance, the equation $\log_2(2D/W)$ provides an **index of difficulty (ID)** for aiming skills. The index specifies that the higher the ID is, the more difficult the

task will be, because more difficult tasks will require more movement time. Figure 2.3–1 contains several examples of IDs for different reciprocal aiming task characteristics.

Fitts based his original calculation on a reciprocal tapping task in which participants made repetitive back-and-forth movements as fast as possible between two targets for a specified period of time. For this task, they were told to place an emphasis on accuracy. Since Fitts' initial work, other researchers have found that the lawful speed-accuracy relationship for the reciprocal tapping task generalizes to a wide range of motor skill performance situations. For example, when people perform single manual aiming tasks—moving pegs from one location to insert them into a hole, throwing darts at a target, reaching or grasping containers of different sizes, moving a cursor on a screen to a target—all their actions demonstrate movement time characteristics predicted by Fitts' Law.

*Fitts' Law and motor control.*   A significant aspect of the many demonstrations of Fitts' Law is that understanding why the speed-accuracy trade-off occurs continues to interest movement scientists. Although several hypotheses have been offered, there is general agreement that the speed-accuracy trade-off is a function of open- and closed-loop processes operating during performance.

Prominent among these hypotheses is one developed by Crossman and Goodeve (1963). They proposed that when a person performs rapid aiming movements requiring accuracy, open-loop programmed control is involved in his or her initiation of the movement toward the target. Then, the person uses feedback intermittently to generate submovements that make corrections along the way until the target is contacted. MT necessarily increases because greater distances or narrower targets require more corrections. For a reciprocal tapping task, part of the MT increase occurs because the person spends more time in contact with each target before moving to the next target. This strategy allows the person to evaluate visual feedback to accurately plan the next movement.

Sometimes, people perform aiming movements so rapidly that they cannot use feedback to make corrections while moving. In these cases, the impulse-timing model proposed by Schmidt et al. (1979) appears to be relevant. According to this model, a person prepares a motor program in which commands forwarded to the musculature are translated into impulses, which are the forces produced over time. As a result, the arm is forcefully driven toward the target during the initial part of the movement. Aiming accuracy is a function of the amount of force and time involved. Because amounts of force and time are related to resulting movement variability, increasing movement velocity produces more variable movement outcomes. Therefore, if a movement at a certain velocity were inaccurate, a person would need to slow down limb movement to increase aiming accuracy.

Meyer et al. (1988) developed a model that takes into account positive elements of both the Crossman and Goodeve and the impulse-variability models; they called it the optimized initial impulse model. According to this model, a person makes an initial movement toward the target by programming and executing an initial impulse. If the movement is accurate, nothing further needs to be done. However, if the movement is inaccurate, the person prepares a submovement based on feedback that adjusts the velocity used for the first movement. This process continues until the individual produces an accurate movement. In the optimal solution, the person modifies movement time along the course of each movement so that he or she makes accurate target contact. Meyer et al. have provided mathematical support for this model, showing that the number of submovements made is related to movement time, target distance, and target width.

Scholars continue to attempt to provide evidence explaining why speed-accuracy task performance is described so well by Fitts' Law. As sophisticated movement analysis tools become available, opportunities to more appropriately assess these hypotheses should increase. At present, scientists generally agree that the appropriate hypothesis will include a combination of open- and closed-loop control processes.

## Prehension

Closely related to manual aiming skills are those requiring prehension. The earliest prehension control model, proposed by Jeannerod (1981, 1984), gave the motor program and visual feedback critical roles. In this model, different mechanisms control the transport (i.e., reach) and grasp phases of prehension. The model proposes that the grasp phase must be under feedback control to allow for

---

**A CLOSER LOOK**

## Task Constraints and Performer Objectives Influence the Speed-Accuracy Trade-off

Those who study motor control often overlook interactions between the performer and the skill. But the way people perform skills involving speed and accuracy demands emphasizes the importance of considering these interactions. An experiment by Adam (1992) nicely illustrates the interaction between a person's objective and the task's constraints.

Participants performed reciprocal tapping tasks that had different Fitts' ID characteristics. Although they were instructed to move as quickly and as accurately as possible, movement time and accuracy

performance results revealed that the participants determined their own performance objectives. These were classified as speed, accuracy, or speed-accuracy objectives. Movement analyses of their performance classified according to each of these objectives showed distinct movement kinematic characteristics for each objective. For example, when accuracy was the performer's objective, target size and distance between targets were especially influential on movement characteristics; in contrast, when speed was the performer's objective, these task constraints were not so influential.

---

specific grasping adaptations. The reach phase, including the timing of the finger-and-thumb aperture opening, is centrally represented in a motor program.

However, more recently, researchers have questioned the independence of the two prehension phases. Because certain situations were shown to influence characteristics of both the reach and the grasp phases, current speculation is that the two phases operate more in synchrony than scientists originally thought them to. For example, research evidence shows that in certain prehension situations the timing of reach and grasp events is strongly correlated (e.g., Jakobson and Goodale 1991).

It appears that the two prehension phases are under some higher-order control mechanism that monitors the entire action (see Paulignan, Jeannerod, MacKenzie, and Marteniuk 1991). This monitoring allows the coordination that occurs between the reach and the grasp phases. One example of this coordination is that hand closure occurs after approximately two-thirds of the total movement time, regardless of movement distance or object size (Chieffi and Gentilucci 1993).

A number of experiments have shown that relative-timing characteristics of prehension are typically invariant (e.g., Wallace and Weeks 1988). How-

ever, while these results are consistent with the generalized motor program view of control, Wallace and Weeks argued that these invariances can be explained without the need for a motor program. Following the arguments of the dynamical systems perspective, they proposed that the relative time observed in their experiment was not a part of any central command, but was evidence of a functional unit, or coordinative structure. Relative-time invariance emerged from the performance of this unit due to the constraints of the task being performed.

So far, both the motor program and the dynamical systems views offer explanations of the timing and prehension kinematic characteristics of prehension. We must wait for additional research to determine whether one of these views, or some other view, best explains this control.

## Handwriting

Investigation of the control mechanisms responsible for handwriting is a prominent theme in the study of motor control. Much of the research and theoretical knowledge about the control of handwriting has come from work at the University of Nijmegen in the Netherlands and at Cambridge University in England. Scholars generally agree

---

## A CLOSER LOOK

### Prehension Situations Illustrate Motor Control Adaptability

An experiment by Steenbergen, Marteniuk, and Kalbfleisch (1995) provides a good illustration of how adaptive the motor control system is. We see this adaptivity when people alter movements of a specific action to accommodate characteristics of the task situation. The authors asked the participants to reach and grasp with the right or left hand a Styrofoam cup that was either full or empty. Participants had to grasp the cup, located 30 cm in front of them, then place it on a round target 20 cm to the right or left. Movement analyses of the hand transport and grasp phases revealed interesting differences at the movement level depending on which hand a person used and whether the cup was full or empty. For example, during the transport phase, hand velocity was distinctly faster and peak velocity was earlier when the cup was empty. The grasp aperture time also varied according to the cup characteristic. Maximum grasp aperture occurred earlier in the transport phase for the full cup, a situation demanding more movement precision. In terms of coordination of the joints involved in the action, participants froze the degrees of freedom of the shoulder, elbow, and wrist joints during the prehension movements for both full and empty cups. However, when the cup was full, participants increased stabilization during the movement by making a trunk postural adjustment that moved the shoulder forward.

---

that different control mechanisms are involved in controlling what people write (letters, words, numbers, etc.) and how they write it (the writing strokes producing the letters, words, etc. on the writing surface).

When we consider the act of handwriting from an anatomical perspective, we see that there is a great deal of individual variation in terms of limb segment involvement. But when researchers obtain handwriting samples from one person, they offer strong evidence for what Bernstein (1967) referred to as *motor equivalence*. That is, a person can adapt to the specific demands of the writing context and adjust size, force, direction, and even muscle involvement to accommodate those demands. The notable outcome is that there is a great degree of similarity in characteristics such as letter forms, writing slant, relative force for stroke production, and relative timing between strokes. People have little trouble varying characteristics such as movement time and writing size, among others.[1]

1. For a more complete discussion of handwriting characteristics as they relate to motor control processes, see the special theme issue of the journal *Human Movement Science* (May 1991, Vol. 10), edited by van Galen, Thomassen, and Wing.

The complexity of handwriting control makes it difficult to develop a simple control model describing the components of this process (see van Galen 1991). A person can write his or her signature or a familiar phrase with the preferred hand, with the nonpreferred hand, with a foot, or by holding a pen in the mouth; this suggests that at least the spatial features of writing are represented in the memory system in an abstract form. Also, this motor equivalence capability suggests the involvement of coordinative structures in handwriting control.

Another interesting feature of the act of handwriting is that several control processes occur at the same time. To write a sentence, a person must use lexical and semantic as well as motor control processes. Writing requires the person to retrieve words from memory. These words must have meanings that fit what the writer intends to convey. The written sentence requires specific grammatical construction. The words require a certain spelling, which involves the person's movement of the limb to produce specific letters that are of an appropriate size and shape for what he or she is writing on. Further, the individual must hold the writing instrument with an appropriate amount of force to allow these

---

**A CLOSER LOOK**

## A HANDWRITING DEMONSTRATION OF MOTOR EQUIVALENCE

**WRITE YOUR SIGNATURE**

1. with a pen in your preferred hand.
2. with a pen in your nonpreferred hand.
3. with a pen held in your mouth by your teeth.
4. with your preferred hand on the chalkboard.

**COMPARE THE SPATIAL CHARACTERISTICS OF THE FOUR HANDWRITING SAMPLES**

1. Describe the similarities you see.
2. Describe the differences you see.

Undoubtedly, specific elements of your signature remained constant regardless of which muscle groups were involved in the writing action. Your ability to engage various muscle groups to write your signature demonstrates how the act of handwriting illustrates the concept of motor equivalence.

---

letters to be formed. The capability of human beings to carry out these various cognitive and motor elements in relatively short amounts of time demonstrates both the complexity and the elegance of the control processes underlying the act of handwriting.

## Bimanual Coordination Skills

In addition to unimanual coordination skills, human beings have many motor skills in which successful performance depends on simultaneous performance of the two arms. Sometimes the two limbs do essentially the same thing; this occurs when someone rows a boat or when a person in a wheelchair rolls the wheels of the chair in order to go straight forward or backward. But certainly more interesting from a control perspective are situations in which each limb must do something different. For example, a guitar player holds strings with one hand to determine chords, while plucking or striking strings with the other hand to produce sound. A skilled drummer can produce one rhythm with one hand while producing another with the other hand. An airplane pilot can control a lever with one hand while steering the plane with the other.

***Bimanual coordination preferences.*** An important characteristic of the performance of bimanual skills is that the two limbs prefer to do the same

thing at the same time. Try, for example, to rub your stomach with one hand while at the same time tapping the top of your head with the other hand. The reason you experience difficulty doing this relatively simple task is that your two arms want to do one of the actions, but not both. These motor skills involve **bimanual coordination.**

Kelso, Southard, and Goodman (1979) provided important empirical evidence demonstrating this limb synchrony preference. In a series of experiments, people performed simple rapid-aiming movements to targets with the right, the left, and both hands (see figure 2.3–2). In the bimanual situations, each hand moved to a target that was different from the other target in both size and distance from the hand. According to Fitts' Law, the hand moving to the target with the smaller ID should move faster. But, as we see in figure 2.3–2, this was not the case. Although the Fitts' prediction was upheld when each hand moved alone, it was not supported when the two hands moved to targets of different IDs. In these latter situations, the hands moved more in synchrony; we see this result in the similar movement times for the two hands.

Teachers and therapists who are aware of the synchrony preference of bimanual limb coordination will recognize the special attention people must devote to learn skills requiring the limbs to do

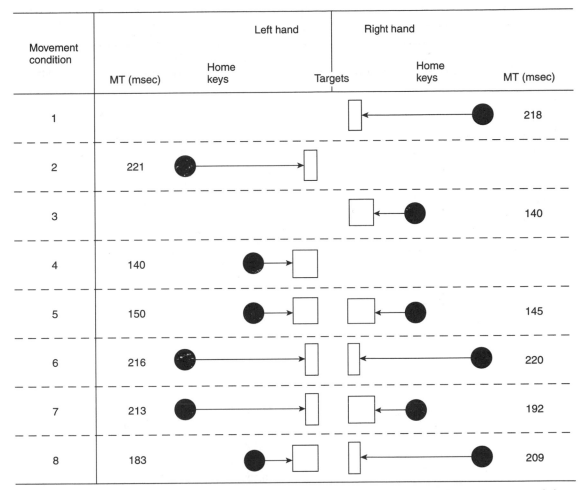

| Movement condition | MT (msec) | Home keys | Targets | Home keys | MT (msec) |
|---|---|---|---|---|---|
| | | Left hand | | Right hand | |
| 1 | | | | | 218 |
| 2 | 221 | | | | |
| 3 | | | | | 140 |
| 4 | 140 | | | | |
| 5 | 150 | | | | 145 |
| 6 | 216 | | | | 220 |
| 7 | 213 | | | | 192 |
| 8 | 183 | | | | 209 |

**FIGURE 2.3–2** Movement time scores for one- and two-hand movements to targets of different distances and sizes reported in Kelso, Southard, and Goodman's second experiment. (Source: Data from J. A. S. Kelso, et al., "On the Coordination of Two-handed Movements" in *Journal of Experimental Psychology: Human Perception and Performance,* 1979, 5:229–238.)

different things at the same time. As Swinnen and his colleagues noted (e.g., Swinnen et al. 1990; Walter and Swinnen 1992; Lee, Swinnen, and Verschueren 1995), people can modify the synchrony preference; we also know this from observing everyday skill performance. But this modification process is a difficult one that requires considerable attention to training and practice conditions. We will consider the types of practice conditions positively influencing learning synchronous bimanual skills in the discussion of Concept 6.4.

*Asymmetrical bimanual lever movements.* Asymmetrical bimanual lever movements involve the movement of a different lever by each arm, in patterns that spatially and temporally differ from each other. For example, as shown in figure 2.3–3, taken from an experiment by Swinnen et al.(1990), participants moved one lever in a simple one-direction movement while at the same time moving the other lever in a two-part flexion and extension movement. Each of these movements usually had specified goal movement times. As we would

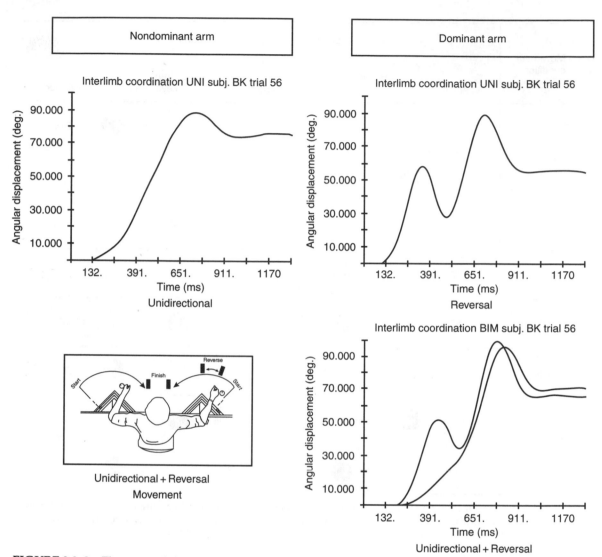

**FIGURE 2.3–3** The top panel shows the two displacement patterns for the dominant and nondominant arm lever movements in the Swinnen et al. experiment. The bottom panel contains a schematic of the experimental performance setup and also shows how the two arm movements related to each other as they were performed simultaneously. (From S. P. Swinnen, et al., "The Dissociation of Interlimb Constraints" in *Human Performance, 3,* 187–215. Copyright © 1991 Lawrence Erlbaum Associates, Mahway, NJ.)

expect given the bimanual synchrony preference of the limbs, early attempts showed the tendency of the two arms to make the same pattern. Also as usual, the more complex reversal movement took the lead. With practice, unlinking occurred and the asymmetrical lever movements could be performed.

Experiments like these provide additional evidence that the two arms are functionally linked to act together as one unit. The person must reorganize this coordinative structure if the two limbs need to perform distinct movements with different spatial patterns or time characteristics.

Scholars do not know exactly how the motor control system is involved in this process, although they continue to attempt to provide an adequate explanation. From a motor program

## A CLOSER LOOK

### Individuals Differ in Bimanual Limb Dissociation Success

An interesting individual-difference feature occurred in the many experiments by Swinnen and his colleagues in which participants had to acquire asymmetric bimanual coordination skills. A few participants in these experiments were not able to break away from the sychrony tendency, while a few others broke away from it very easily. Between these extremes were people who typified the results reported based on the group data. Unfortunately, no one has yet explored the reasons for these differences. Clearly, these results have training and rehabilitation implications. Unfortunately, the specific recommendations that take these individual differences into account await further research.

viewpoint, the two limbs act together as a unit because they are controlled by the same motor program. When each limb must acquire different movements, interference occurs between limbs until the unique specifications for each limb can be incorporated into the motor program (Schmidt 1988). Proponents of the dynamical systems approach believe that the dynamic characteristics of each limb's performance become entrained as bimanual practice progresses. The result is that a new coordinative structure develops that provides an effective means of organizing the degrees of freedom required by this skill.

One final point is worth noting about asymmetric bimanual coordination skills. It appears that the two limbs never become completely independent of each other. One limb's activity will continue to predominate over the other's even after an extensive amount of practice. However, the person can accomplish the goal of the skill, since perfect asymmetry is seldom required.

*Piano playing.*    One of the attractions for investigating the control of piano playing is that a piano can easily be interfaced with a computer to record time and force information related to the player's striking of the keys. Much of the piano-playing research has addressed the issue of timing. For example, what are the characteristics of the timing of the various events when someone plays a piano piece? Timing is critical in this task, because each hand has specified timing responsibilities. To play the piece

correctly, the player must make two hands work together to produce the notes at appropriate times.

A complex piano piece has a timing pattern for a group of notes containing a rhythmic figure. The pianist adds certain specifications to this abstract plan that allow for variations in such things as tempo and intensity from one performance to another. The skilled pianist can make these specifications differently for each hand, as well as for the two hands together.

Arguments favoring a motor program basis for the control of piano performance (e.g., Shaffer 1981) propose that a motor program contains the relative-timing characteristics evident in piano performance. According to this view, the motor program sends independent timing-based commands to the musculature to control each hand's movements. These commands are based on abstract timing requirements for the task. The performer then adds specifications related to the needs of the performance being executed.

Proponents of a dynamical systems perspective on piano performance argue that the relative-timing characteristics emerge from the interaction between the limb dynamics and the constraints imposed by the organization of the keyboard. Further control aspects of performing this skill are similar to those considered next.

*Bimanual polyrhythmic tapping.*    When a pianist or drummer must maintain different rhythms with each of the two hands, the person is performing a multifrequency task known as a polyrhythm. Although all polyrhythms are difficult to perform, those involving two rhythms where the ratio value of one of the rhythms is not 1 are especially difficult. For example, compare the difficulty of performing two rhythms having a 3:1 ratio with that of performing two rhythms with a 3:2 ratio. This suggests that the degree of difficulty is related to how much the bimanual performance must deviate from a preferred, stable state. The typical strategy a musician uses to perform these polyrhythms is to fit the slower-paced hand's rhythm within the rhythmic tapping of the faster hand.

Current views about how we control the performance of polyrhythms follow the general distinctions between the motor program and the dynamic systems views. According to a motor-program-based view (e.g., Summers et al. 1993), a common timing mechanism sends time-based muscular contraction signals to each hand. Those who ascribe to this control perspective are still debating and investigating the exact way this is accomplished. The model proposed by Summers et al. proposes that the fast hand controls the situation and that the slow-hand movements are interlaced within the fast-hand rhythmic taps. This is accomplished by an internal central "clock" that triggers fast-hand taps. The slow-hand "clock" triggers taps according to the fast-hand taps. This view of control is based on evidence showing that fast-hand timing variability seldom is influenced by the specifications of the polyrhythm, whereas timing variability for the slow hand consistently follows polyrhythm variations.

The alternative to the internal clock model of control is the dynamical systems view (see Peper, Beek, and van Wieringen 1995). The rhythmic structure observed in performance emerges from the dynamical properties of limbs performing rhythmic movements. Each limb acts as an oscillator, oscillating at the specified frequency. When each limb must perform different rhythms, practice leads to the two oscillators becoming entrained and behaving as coupled nonlinear oscillators.

Perhaps more than any other bimanual skill, polyrhythmic tapping skills provide a focus for the current debate about the control of coordinated skill. Because these skills have objective rhythmic structures, control models must take into account the need to produce specific rhythms rather than individually preferred rhythms. Further exploration is needed to establish whether these rhythms come from an organization of internal clocks or emerge from the coupling of oscillators.

*Cascade juggling.* According to those who have developed extensive research programs investigating the learning and control of juggling (e.g., Beek and Turvey 1992; Beek, Peper, and Stegeman 1995), an advantage of investigating juggling is that it lends itself to precise mathematical modeling. Currently, an impressive amount of evidence shows how well cascade juggling follows dynamical models of movement coordination. Juggling shows characteristics essential for a dynamical model, including stability, instability, and identifiable collective variables.

A good example of how well cascade juggling performance fits the dynamical systems model is a series of experiments by Beek and Turvey (1992). They filmed and analyzed limb and ball movement patterns for skilled jugglers juggling three, five, and seven balls. Their results showed that when subjects were juggling at a preferred tempo, a 3:4 ratio existed between the length of time an object was in the hand and the length of time between catches of that object. The authors found this ratio consistently, regardless of the number of balls juggled, indicating that this time proportion is a key variable describing juggling performance.

The 3:4 ratio indicates a preferred behavioral state for limbs and objects in coordination in cascade ball juggling. It is interesting to note that this time ratio provides an optimal time for objects to be in the air and held in order to minimize the chance for collision of the objects in the air. In addition, holding onto the ball for three-fourths of the time between catches yields a stable and precise throw-and-catch of the ball throughout a sequence of juggling cycles.

## Sit-to-Stand Action

The common everyday activity of moving from a sitting to a standing position is an example of a complex multijoint action. Research by Shepherd and Gentile (1994) shows how this action demonstrates that limbs and joints have functional linkages to allow intended actions to occur. Participants sat in different postures (erect trunk, trunk fully flexed, and trunk flexed between erect and fully flexed positions) on a chair and then stood up. Analysis of joint movements showed that the initial trunk position influenced the onset of extension in different ways. When a person was in the erect or partially flexed initial position, the knee started to extend before the hip joint to initiate extension. However, for an individual in the fully flexed initial position, hip joint movement preceded knee joint movement.

This initiation of joint movement at different times depending on the initial sitting position indicates that functional demands influenced the order of muscle activation. Different initial sitting positions before standing have different support, propulsion, and balance demands. By initiating leg extension from different joints for the different sitting positions, the motor control system enabled the person to carry out the intended action without losing balance.

The results of the Shepherd and Gentile study support an important component of the dynamical systems view of motor control. That is, the organization of muscle activation for an action is determined by the demands of the situation in accordance with current body position. We can consider the components of the sit-to-stand action to constitute a coordinative structure that involves a functional linkage of the joints involved in the action.

## Gait

There is little argument that at the nervous system level, we can attribute the basic control of human gait to *central pattern generators* in the spinal cord. These mechanisms provide the basis for stereotypic locomotive patterns. We can trace evi-

dence for this spinal level of control to the work of the British Nobel laureate Charles Sherrington and his colleagues at the end of the nineteenth and beginning of the twentieth centuries (e.g., Sherrington 1906).

Using a procedure known as decerebration, which involves severing the spinal cord from the brain, Sherrington observed that decerebrated cats produced locomotor rhythmic muscular activity similar to that produced by intact animals. Later, Brown (1911) went a step further by additionally severing a cat's sensory pathways to the spinal cord; still, the cat showed rhythmic leg contractions appropriate for walking. More recent research (e.g., Grillner and Zangger 1979) has confirmed and extended these earlier observations.

However, to understand how humans control the wide range of gait they are capable of, we must consider higher-level nervous system involvement, along with musculoskeletal dynamics and environmental interactions.[2] Two aspects of gait control will serve to illustrate the roles of these various factors.

A well-known feature of locomotive action is the rhythmical structure characterizing each gait variation. As you saw in figure 2.1–4, experiments observing subjects walking and running at different speeds on a treadmill demonstrate that each gait has its own unique rhythmic structure for the four components of the step cycle. Glass and Mackey (1988) emphasized that this structure is important for gait control when they described several gait pathologies attributable to abnormal rhythmic structures.

Vision provides an additional component of gait control, as we saw in Concept 2.2. Vision provides information that directs a person's walking speed, body alignment, and navigation through the environment. Warren, Young, and Lee (1986) presented a good demonstration of the navigational qualities of vision for gait. They extended the front

2. For extended discussions of the behavioral and neural levels of the control of locomotion, see Rosenbaum 1991 and Shumway-Cook and Woolacott 1995.

---

### A CLOSER LOOK

#### Applying the Dynamic Systems View of Gait Control to Therapy Environments

We can see the involvement in locomotor control of dynamical interactions between the person and the environment in the effectiveness of a therapy strategy that helps reestablish normal rhythmical gait. Based on the dynamical systems control perspective, Wagenaar and Van Emmerik (1994) recommended that therapists use various methods to help patients attain spontaneous production of the appropriate rhythmic structures for specific gait patterns by systematically altering gait speeds.

Wagenaar and Beek (1992) showed an example of the effectiveness of this procedure. They used a metronome to present rhythms to hemiplegic patients. When the authors systematically increased the rhythmical beat from 60 to 96 steps a minute, these patients improved the phase relationships of their arms and legs; this in turn positively influenced trunk rotation.

---

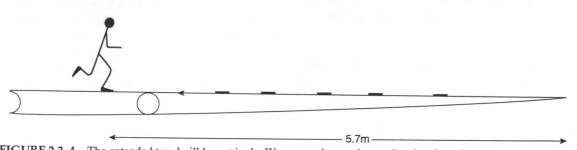

**FIGURE 2.3–4**   The extended treadmill layout in the Warren et al. experiment showing the nylon belt extension and the targets on which subjects ran. (From W. H. Warren, et al., "Visual Control of Step Length During Running Over Irregular Terrain" in *Journal of Experimental Psychology: Human Perception and Performance,* 12:259–266. Copyright © 1986 American Psychological Association. Reprinted by permission.)

---

of a treadmill trackway to provide an area in front of the participant that could be made to simulate upcoming terrain (see figure 2.3–4). While running, participants were required to step on painted markers that were placed on the trackway. The task was designed to simulate a situation such as running across a creek by stepping on stones. As you would expect from your own experience, the runners readily accomplished this navigational task. However, the important result in terms of the role played by the visual system in guiding gait was evidence that participants altered their stride characteristics in a way consistent with the influence of *tau*.

The motor-program-based theoretical explanation of gait control differs dramatically from the account proposed by a dynamical systems theory perspective. In our discussion of Concept 2.1, we described evidence from an experiment by Shapiro et al. (1981) showing that relative time was invariant for step-cycle components for walking and for running. Also, the relative-time characteristics for these two gait patterns were distinct. Those who subscribe to a motor-program-based control theory have interpreted these results thus: Walking and running are controlled by two different generalized motor programs. In contrast, the dynamical systems view holds that walking and running are stable behavioral states that self-organize according to the intention of the person and what is permitted by environmental conditions. Thus, the dynamical systems view argues that motor programs do not

---

| A CLOSER LOOK |

## Avoiding Obstacles While Walking or Running

Research by James Cutting and his colleagues at Cornell University (e.g., Cutting 1986; Vishton and Cutting 1995) has shown that if a person is walking or running and wishes to maintain footspeed while avoiding an obstacle, three time periods are critical: **The time needed to**

1. recognize that an object needs to be avoided;
2. adjust the footfall;
3. turn the foot to avoid the obstacle.

Of these three periods, the first is the most critical and takes up about 75 percent of the distance covered while the subject is approaching an object.

**IMPLICATION FOR CLINICAL REHABILITATION AND SPORT**

- Because of the importance of early visual recognition of an object to be avoided, it is important to train people to actively visually search the environment in which they locomote. To avoid collision, a person must recognize objects sufficiently early to allow appropriate movement adjustments. Therefore, the therapist or coach who focuses training on only the movement-adjustment aspect of this task ignores the most critical component of object recognition.

---

underlie the control of walking and running; instead, stable and unstable gait patterns can be explained in terms of dynamical interplay between the person and environmental conditions.

## Summary

This discussion highlighted the current controversy addressing how the nervous system controls coordinated skill by considering several different types of skills. Within each skill, discussion focused on how a motor-program-based view and a dynamical system view of control would account for specific performance characteristics. Manual aiming skills involving a speed-accuracy trade-off follow predictions of Fitts' Law, for which hypotheses following both control theories have been proposed. Other unimanual skills considered were prehension and handwriting. We also discussed bimanual skills, including bimanual aiming tasks, asymmetrical bimanual lever movements, polyrhythmic tapping tasks such as those often involved in playing the piano or drums, and juggling. For each of these skills involving both arms, theorists have proposed both motor program and dynamical systems models to account for how they are controlled. The sit-to-

stand action demonstrates functional linkages among limbs and joints to allow a person to perform an intended action. Finally, we considered gait; in general, gait follows spinal-level central pattern generator control, but an individual can adapt gait to follow higher levels of control when he or she requires specific deviations from the normal rhythmic gait.

## Related Readings

Bonnard, M., and J. Pailhous. 1993. Intentionality in human gait control: Modifying the frequency-to-amplitude relationship. *Journal of Experimental Psychology: Human Perception and Performance* 19: 429–43.

Cutting, J. E., P. M. Vishton, and P. Braren. 1995. How to avoid collisions with stationary and with moving objects. *Psychological Review* 102: 627–51.

Semjen, A., J. J. Summers, and D. Cattaert. 1995. Hand coordination in bimanual circle drawing. *Journal of Experimental Psychology: Human Perception and Performance* 21: 1139–57.

Summers, J. J. 1990. Temporal constraints on concurrent task performance. In G. E. Hammond (Ed.), *Cerebral control of speech and limb movements* (pp. 661–80). Amsterdam: North-Holland.

van Galen, G. P., and W. P. de Jong. 1995. Fitts' law as the outcome of a dynamic noise filtering model of motor control. *Human Movement Science* 14: 539–71.

# STUDY QUESTIONS FOR CHAPTER 2

1. Define the term *coordination* and describe how a limb-movement displacement graph can portray a coordinated movement pattern.

2. What is the *degrees of freedom problem* as it relates to the study of human motor control?

3. Describe the similarities and the differences between a closed-loop control system and an open-loop control system. For each system, describe a motor skill that could be characterized as having that type of control system.

4. Define a generalized motor program and describe two invariant features and two parameters proposed to characterize this program.

5. Describe the typical experimental approach taken to investigate the invariant relative-timing hypothesis of the generalized motor program. Give an example.

6. Describe the meaning of the term *nonlinear dynamics* and give an example illustrating how this term relates to human coordinated movement.

7. Define the following key terms used in dynamical systems theories of motor control: (a) stability; (b) attractors; (c) collective variables; (d) control parameters; (e) coordinative structures.

8. Describe three methods for investigating the role of proprioception in the control of movement. What do the results of the investigations using these methods tell us about the role of proprioception in controlling movement?

9. Discuss what we know about the length of time it takes to process visual feedback when performing a motor skill. How have researchers investigated this question?

10. What two roles does vision play in controlling manual aiming movements? How is the duration of the movement a variable influencing these roles?

11. Discuss the roles played by vision in controlling prehension and tell how different variables influence those roles.

12. Discuss how time-to-contact is involved in the control of locomotion when the goal is to contact a target. Include in this discussion the role vision plays in this situation.

13. Discuss how vision is involved when a person must (a) catch a thrown ball; (b) strike an oncoming ball.

14. How is Fitts' Law related to the speed-accuracy trade-off phenomenon observed in many motor skills? What are two explanations of Fitts' Law?

15. Why is an asymmetrical bimanual limb skill so difficult to perform? How does bimanual limb control provide evidence for coordinative structures?

16. Discuss how (a) a motor-program-based theory and (b) a dynamical systems theory explains how a person is able to play a piece on the piano in which both hands simultaneously perform different rhythms.

17. Discuss how relative-timing characteristics of human walking and running gaits are explained by (a) motor-program-based theory and (b) dynamical systems theory.

# CHAPTER 3

# MOTOR CONTROL PREPARATION AND ATTENTION

---

## CONCEPT 3.1

Performing voluntary, coordinated movement requires the preparation of the motor control system

## CONCEPT 3.2

Preparation for and performance of motor skills are influenced by our
limited capacity to select and attend to information

## CONCEPT 3.3

Visual selective attention plays an important role in preparing many motor skills

———————————————————— ▪ ————————————————————

# CONCEPT 3.1

Performing voluntary, coordinated movement requires
preparation of the motor control system

———

## Key Terms

movement
  preparation

Hick's Law

cost-benefit
  tradeoff

stimulus-
  response
  compatibility

foreperiod

psychological
  refractory
  period (PRP)

vigilance

## Application

Many sport and daily activities demonstrate our
need to prepare the motor control system to carry
out an intended action. For example, many sporting
events, such as running, swimming, and trap shooting, incorporate the importance of preparation into
the rules of the activity, which require an audible
signal warning the competitors to get ready.

Certain performance characteristics of activities
also provide evidence of the need to prepare for the
action. For example, when you decide to pick up a
glass of water for a drink, there is a slight delay between your decision and the intended action. In another example, if you are driving a car along a
street and another car unexpectedly pulls out in
front of you, there is a measurable time delay between the moment you see this and the moment
you begin to move your foot off the accelerator and

onto the brake pedal. In each of these very different
action scenarios, intended action is preceded by an
interval of time in which the motor control system
is prepared according to the demands and constraints of the situation.

Consider the preparation of action from a different perspective. Undoubtedly, at some time or
other you have said, following a poor performance
in an activity, "I wasn't ready!" By saying this, you
imply that if you had been "ready," you would
have performed much better than you just have. Or,
if you work with physical therapy patients, you undoubtedly have heard one tell the therapist, "Don't
rush me. If I get out of this chair before I'm ready,
I'll fall."

An important motor control question that relates to each of these situations is this: What is so
important about getting ready to perform a skill?
In other words, what makes preparation such a
critical part of successful performance? From this
question, others arise. For example, what factors
influence how long it takes to prepare an action or
how well an action is prepared? And, if a person is
prepared to move, are there limits to how long the
person can maintain this prepared state? We will
attempt to answer these questions in the following
discussion.

———————— ▪ ————————

## Discussion

In chapter 2, we focused on factors influencing the
control of an ongoing action. Although we did
mention the process of initiating the action, we
only touched on what is involved in the actual
preparation of an intended action. In the present
discussion, our interest is in what occurs between
the intention to act and the initiation of the action

itself. In the motor control literature, scholars commonly use the term **movement preparation** to designate this activity.

In this context, *preparation* means not the long-
term preparation that occurs during the days prior
to an event, but the specific preparation the motor
control system makes just prior to initiating an action. We will address two preparation issues here.

First, how do different skill, performance-context, and personal factors influence the preparation process? Second, exactly what is the motor control system preparing that makes preparation such a critical part of any performance? Before we discuss these issues, we will establish how we know that the motor control system needs to be prepared for action.

## Movement Preparation Requires Time

The principle that the motor control system needs preparation before it can initiate an action is an inferred concept. Scholars base this inference on the effects of various factors on observed differences in the amount of time between the production of a signal telling a person to begin performing a skill and the instant experimenters actually observe the beginning of movement. As you studied in Concept 1.2, we call this interval of time *reaction time (RT).* When considered in this context, *RT is an index of preparation* required to produce movement. By investigating factors that increase or decrease this time interval, we can gain some understanding of the action preparation processes our motor control system engages in to enable us to perform a skill.[1]

One of the things that the RT interval tells us is that preparing to produce voluntary movement takes time. Planned movement does not occur instantaneously. Certain movements and circumstances require more preparation than others. In the following sections, we discuss a variety of movements and circumstances that influence the amount and type of preparation needed.

## Task and Situation Characteristics Influencing Preparation

One set of factors that influence movement preparation includes characteristics of both the task itself and the situation in which it must be performed.

***The number of response choices.*** An important characteristic of task and performance situations that influences preparation time is the number of

response alternatives the performer has to choose from. *As the number of alternatives increases, the amount of time required to prepare the appropriate movement increases.* The easiest way to demonstrate this relationship is by looking at the choice-RT situation you were introduced to in Concept 1.2. RT increases according to the number of stimulus or response choices. The fastest RTs occur in simple-RT situations, which have only one stimulus and one response. RT slows down when more than one stimulus and more than one response are possible, as in the choice-RT situation. In fact, the relationship between RT increases and the number of response choices is so stable that a researcher developed a law predicting the RT when the number of choices is known.

**Hick's Law** (Hick 1952) states that RT will increase logarithmically as the number of stimulus-response choices increases. The equation that describes this law is $RT = K \log_2 (N + 1)$, where K is a constant (which is simple RT in most cases) and N equals the number of possible choices. This means that RT increases linearly as the number of stimulus-choice alternatives increases. We can predict the magnitude of this increase mathematically by applying Hick's equation.

The important component of Hick's law is the $\log_2$ function, because it designates that the RT increase is due to the information transmitted by the possible choices, rather than to the number of choice alternatives. In information theory, *$\log_2$ specifies a bit of information.* A *bit,* short for *bi*nary dig*it,* is a yes/no (i.e., 1/0) choice between two alternatives. In a 1-bit decision, there are two alternatives; there are four alternatives in a 2-bit decision; a 3-bit decision involves eight choices; and so on. The number of bits indicates the least number of "yes/no" decisions needed to solve the problem created by the number of choices involved. For example, if eight choices were possible in a situation, an individual would have to answer three yes/no questions to determine the correct choice. Thus, an eight-choice situation is a 3-bit decision situation. Accordingly, Hick's law not only correctly predicts that RT increases as the number of choice alternatives increases; it also predicts the specific size of increase to expect.

1. See Meyer, Osman, Irwin, and Yantis (1988) for an excellent overview of the history of the use of time measure for making conclusions about human information-processing activity.

A CLOSER LOOK

### Applying Hick's Law to a Sport Performance Situation

A football quarterback running an option play has three response alternatives to choose from. He can hand the ball off to a back, keep the ball and run, or run and pitch out to another back. The problem for the quarterback is that there are so many possible "stimulus" choices. All players on the defensive team, along with certain of his own offensive players, are potential sources of information to help him determine which response alternative to make.

However, given the time constraints of the situation, the quarterback must reduce the "stimulus" choices in order to reduce the decision time required. The coach can help by instructing the quarterback to look for only a very few specific characteristics in the defense. These few "keys" reduce the choice alternatives and provide the quarterback a relatively simple basis from which to decide which of the three options to select.

*The predictability of the correct response choice.* If a number of response alternatives exist in a performance situation and one alternative is more predictable than the others, response preparation time will be shorter than it would if all the alternatives were equally likely. Research evidence has consistently showed that *as the predictability of one of the possible choices increases, RT decreases.*

An experimental procedure popularized by the work of David Rosenbaum (1980, 1983) provides a good demonstration of this relationship. In this procedure, known as the *precuing technique,* researchers provide participants with differing amounts of advance information about which movement must be made in a choice situation. In Rosenbaum's experiments, participants had to move the appropriate finger as quickly as possible to hit the signaled target key. There were three response dimensions, all of which involved a two-choice situation: the *arm* to move (left or right); the *direction* to move (away from or toward the body); and the *extent* of the movement (short or long). Prior to the signal to move, the participants could receive advance information (the precue) specifying the correct upcoming response for none, one, two, or all three of the dimensions. The results showed that as the number of precued dimensions increased, the RT decreased, with the fastest RT occurring when all three dimensions were precued. The benefit of the advance information was that

participants would need to prepare only the remaining non-precued dimensions after the "go" signal.

Scientists have debated whether this predictability effect is due to response selection or to movement preparation processes. The evidence points to a response selection effect, indicating that people use the advance information in a choice situation to reduce the number of movement responses they need to select for execution (see Proctor and Reeve 1988).

*The influence of the probability of precue correctness.* An interesting twist to the precuing situation occurs when the advance information may or may not be correct. The critical factor influencing preparation time in this situation is the *probability* of the advance information's correctness. For example, in a two-choice situation, if the advance information has only a 50-50 chance of being correct, the performer will ignore it and respond as if no advance information has been given. This occurs because the probability of correctness of the advance information is no greater than the probability of correctness of the information the subject already has. However, if the advance information has an 80 percent chance of being correct, the performer will *bias* his or her preparation toward making that response.

What happens when the signal requires the nonprepared movement? In other words, what is the

---

### A CLOSER LOOK

## Biasing Actions Is Common in Many Sport Contexts

In many sport activities, athletes often bias their action preparation to produce one particular action rather than some other possible one. For example, if a basketball player knows that the player he or she is defending goes to the right to make a shot only on rare occasions, the defensive player undoubtedly will bias his or her movement preparation by "cheating" to defend moves to the left. In racquet sports, players who consistently hit to one side of the court will find their opponents "cheating" to that side. Baseball players commonly bias their hitting decisions and actions according to a pitcher's tendency to throw a certain pitch in a specific situation.

In each of these examples, the players have found that they can gain an advantage by "playing the percentages" and biasing their preparation. The clear advantage is that if they are right, they can produce the appropriate action faster than they could otherwise. But they run the risk of being wrong. If they are, the appropriate action will take longer to initiate than it would if no biasing had occurred. And this extra preparation time can lead to an unsuccessful performance.

---

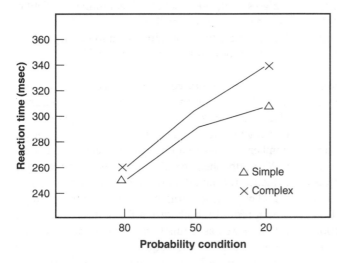

**FIGURE 3.1–1**   Results from the experiment by Larish and Stelmach showing the effects on RT of different probabilities of a cue's correctness for two different tasks. (From D. Larish and G. E. Stelmach, "Preprogramming, Programming, and Reprogramming of Aimed Hand Movements as a Function of Age," in *Journal of Motor Behavior,* 1982, 14:333. Copyright © 1982 Heldref Publications, Inc., Washington, DC. Reprinted by permission.)

price of preparing the wrong movement before preparing the correct one? We can learn the answer from the results of an experiment by Larish and Stelmach (1982). The authors provided advance information about whether the right hand or the left hand should hit the appropriate target. But this information was correct only 20 percent, 50 percent, or 80 percent of the time. The results (shown in figure 3.1–1) illustrate the **cost-benefit trade-off** associated with this situation. When there was a 50-50 chance (50 percent correct condition) of the precue's being correct, participants responded as if the task were a two-choice RT task. However, in the 80-20 condition, participants obviously biased their responses to move in the direction of the precued target. When they were correct, there was a benefit; their RTs were *faster* than if they had not biased their responses. However, when they were wrong (the 20 percent case), there was a cost: their RT was *slower* than it was in the 50-50 condition.

*Stimulus-response compatibility.*　Another task characteristic that influences the movement preparation time is the physical relationship between the stimulus and response choices. The study of what is termed **stimulus-response compatibility** has a long history that dates back to World War II (for a review of this research, see Proctor and Reeve 1990). This extensive study has shown consistently that *RT will be faster as the physical relationship between the stimulus events and their required response becomes more compatible.* Conversely, RT will be slower as this relationship becomes less compatible.

The spatial relationship between the stimulus and response devices is the most common way of considering stimulus-response compatibility. For example, suppose a person has to push one of three keys in response to the illumination of one of three lights. If the lights and keys are arranged horizontally with the key to be pushed located under the light indicating that response, then the situation is more compatible than if the lights are vertical and the buttons are horizontal. A more compatible relationship would lead to faster RTs than a less compatible situation. Also, as compatibility decreases, the number of choice errors will increase (see Fitts and Seeger 1953).

To account for the effect of stimulus-response compatibility on RT, Zelaznik and Franz (1990) argued that when stimulus-response compatibility is low, RT increases are due to response selection problems. On the other hand, when stimulus-response compatibility is high, response selection processing is minimal, so that any RT changes reflect motoric processes related to preparation of the selected response. Weeks and Proctor (1990) further developed this point by presenting evidence showing that the specific response selection problem is due to translation problems involving the mapping of the stimulus locations to the response locations. Because this translation process requires time, RT increases.

*Foreperiod length regularity.*　A part of the preparation process begins when a person detects a signal indicating that the signal to respond will occur shortly. The interval between this "warning" signal and the stimulus, or "go" signal, is known as the **foreperiod.** In simple-RT situations the regularity of the length of this interval influences RT. If the foreperiod is a constant length, i.e., the same amount of time for every trial, RT can become very short. Queseda and Schmidt (1970), for example, showed this effect for a constant 2-sec foreperiod. The average RT in this experiment was 22 msec, far below the normal 150 to 200 msec that typically characterizes simple RT.

We can attribute the fast RT associated with constant foreperiods to *anticipation* by the performer. Because it is a simple-RT situation, the person knows before the warning signal what response will be required. Then, if he or she can anticipate when the go signal will occur after the warning signal, he or she can prepare the required action in advance of the go signal, such that the actual initiation of it begins before the go signal. In terms of a fractionated RT interval, these situations undoubtedly reflect only the motor time component.

*Movement complexity.*　In Concept 2.3, we discussed evidence that the movement complexity characteristics of a task influence preparation of movement. Movement complexity is based on the number of parts to a movement. Henry and Rogers (1960) published the classic experiment providing evidence for the effect of movement complexity on RT. They demonstrated that for a ballistic task, which requires both fast RT and fast movement, RT increases as a function of the number of component parts of the required action. Numerous other experiments have confirmed these findings since that time (e.g., Anson 1982; Christina and Rose 1985; Fischman 1984; Glencross 1973). From a preparation-of-action perspective, these results indicate that the complexity of the action to be performed influences the amount of time a person requires to prepare the motor control system.

A question arising from the effect of movement complexity on RT is whether, in fact, the key factor is the number of component parts involved in the action. This question has generated research interest because the time to perform the action and the

---

| A CLOSER LOOK |

### The Classic Experiment of Henry and Rogers (1960)

Henry and Rogers (1960) hypothesized that if people prepare movements in advance, a complex movement should take longer to prepare than a simple one. In addition, the increased preparation time should be reflected in changes in reaction time (RT). To test this hypothesis, they compared three different rapid-movement situations that varied in the complexity of the movement. The least complex movement required participants to release a telegraph key as quickly as possible after a gong (movement A). The movement at the next level of complexity (movement B) required participants to release the key at the gong and move the arm forward 30 cm as rapidly as possible to grasp a tennis ball hanging from a string. The most complex movement (movement C) required participants to release the key at the gong, reach forward and strike the hanging tennis ball with the

back of the hand, reverse directions and push a button, and then finally reverse directions again and grasp another tennis ball. Participants were to perform all of these movements as quickly as possible.

The results supported the hypothesis. The average RT for movement A was 165 msec; for movement B the average RT was 199 msec; and for movement C the average RT was 212 msec.

The researchers held that the cause of the increase in RT was the increase in the amount of movement-related information that had to be prepared. They proposed that the mechanism involved in this movement preparation was a motor program, similar to a computer program, that would control the details of the sequence of events required to perform the movement.

---

number of component parts of the action are confounded when actions of different complexity are compared. That is, while the more complex action has more component parts to it, it also requires more time. Additionally, the more complex action may require the person to move a greater total distance. To investigate which of these possible factors influenced RT in the Henry and Rogers experiment, Christina and colleagues (Christina, Fischman, Vercruyssen, and Anson 1982; Christina, Fischman, Lambert and Moore 1985; Fischman 1985) carried out a series of experiments. They investigated the contributions of various characteristics of the movement responses. Their results were consistent in supporting the Henry and Rogers conclusion that the number of component parts of the action is the key variable in the RT increase.

***Movement accuracy.*** *As the accuracy demands for a movement increase, the amount of preparation time required also increases.* Researchers have nicely demonstrated this effect in comparisons of

RTs for manual aiming tasks that differed according to the target sizes. For example, Sidaway, Sekiya, and Fairweather (1995) had people perform manual aiming tasks in which they had to hit two targets in sequence as quickly as possible. Two results showed the influence on preparation of the accuracy demands of the task. First, RT increased as target size decreased. Second, when the first target was a constant size, the dispersion of the location of hits on that target was related to the size of the second target. This result indicated that preparation demands increased as movement accuracy demands increased, due to the additional preparation required for a person to constrain his or her limb to move within spatial constraints imposed by the smaller target. Interestingly, the authors observed these two effects whether or not a movement direction change was required to hit the second target.

***The repetition of a movement.*** A well-known characteristic of human performance is that when the performance situation requires a person to repeat the same response on the next attempt, that person's RT for the next trial will be shorter than it was for the previous attempt. As the number of trials increases, the influence of the repetitions on RT lessens. Again, as in other performance situations, the decrease in preparation time is due to a reduction in the response-selection process (for further discussion of this effect, see Campbell and Proctor 1993; Rabbitt and Vyas 1979).

***The time between different responses to different signals.*** There are some performance situations that require a person to respond to a signal with one action and then very quickly respond to another signal with a different action. For example, when a basketball player is confronted by a defensive player in a one-on-one situation, he or she might use a common strategy for getting around the defensive player: a head fake. The player moves his or her head in the direction opposite to the one the body will take (the first signal). The defensive player will begin to move in the direction the head indicates (the first action). However, upon seeing the offensive player's body actually going in the other direction (the second signal), the defensive player must initiate a second response in order to move in the opposite direction. In this situation, RT will be slower for the second response than for the first.

The RT delay for the second response is due to the **psychological refractory period (PRP),** which can be thought of as a delay period (the term *refractory* is synonymous with *delay*) during which a person "puts on hold" the selection of the second response while he or she selects and initiates another response. As such, the PRP reflects a distinct limitation in the action preparation process.

Figure 3.1–2 illustrates the PRP. The person is told to respond as quickly as possible to the first signal (press a button when the light goes on) and also to respond as quickly as possible to the second signal (say "bop" into the microphone when the buzzer sounds). We can see the PRP when we compare the participant's response to the buzzer alone with his or her response to the buzzer when another response has immediately preceded it. The RT for the buzzer signal will be longer when the person must respond immediately prior to it than when he or she has made no previous response. This extra time, or delay, is the PRP.

## Performer Characteristics Influencing Preparation

In addition to task and situation characteristics, certain characteristics of the performer also influence the process of action preparation. We should think

**FIGURE 3.1–2** The psychological refractory period (PRP). (a) The RTs for the $S_1$ (light)-$R_1$ (button press) and the $S_2$ (buzzer)-$R_2$ (vocal response) conditions when performed separately. (b) The effect on RT for the $S_2$-$R_2$ condition when $S_2$ arrives during the RT interval for the $S_1$-$R_1$ condition. $RT_2$ is typically lengthened by the amount of time between the onset of $S_2$ and the completion of $R_1$. This extra time is shown by the dashed line and indicates the PRP.

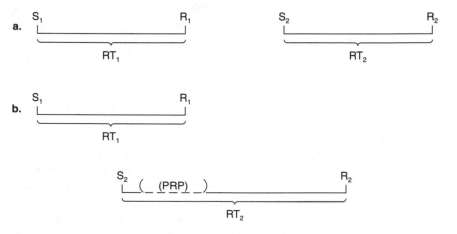

of these characteristics as situational, because they refer to the state of the person at the time a skill must be performed. It is important to note here that these performer characteristics typically influence not only the time needed to prepare a voluntary movement but also the quality of its performance.

*Alertness of the performer.*    An important principle of human performance is that the degree of alertness of the performer influences the time he or she takes to prepare a required action, as well as the quality of the action itself. In two types of performance situations, the role of alertness is especially critical. One type is the short-term RT task, where a person does not have to wait for any length of time, but must respond as quickly and as accurately as possible. The other type, involving long-term maintenance of alertness, is the task for which fast and accurate responding is important, but the signals to which the person must respond occur infrequently and irregularly.

For RT tasks, a way to increase the likelihood that a person is optimally alert to respond appropriately is to provide some type of *warning signal* that indicates he or she must respond within the next few seconds. Scientists demonstrated the benefit of this warning signal many years ago, in the early days of human performance research. For example, in a review of RT research in the first half of the 1900s, Teichner (1954) reported that there was sufficient evidence to conclude that RT is significantly faster when the signal to respond is preceded by a warning signal than when there is no warning signal.

An important point is that after the warning signal, there is an optimal length of time for the person to develop and maintain alertness while waiting for the go signal. If the go signal occurs too soon after the warning signal, or if the person must wait too long, RT will be longer than if the go signal occurs sometime between these two points in time. We can establish an optimal waiting time from RT foreperiod research, which also can be traced back to the early part of this century. For example, Woodrow (1914) reported that for simple-RT situations, maximum preparation was not reached in less than 2 sec, and was not maintained much longer than 4 sec.

These results indicate that we require a minimum amount of time to develop optimal alertness and that we can maintain that level of alertness for a limited amount of time. As you can see in figure 3.1–3, there is an optimal time range during which the go signal should occur following the warning signal. The exact amounts of time that should be used on the general time line represented in figure 3.1–3 will vary according to the skill and situation. However, as a general rule of thumb, for simple-RT situations, *the optimal foreperiod length should range between 1 and 4 sec.*

Tasks that involve long-term maintenance of alertness are known as **vigilance** tasks. In vigilance situations, an individual must take an appropriate action when he or she detects a signal to act. The problem is that *signals occur very infrequently and irregularly.* There are many vigilance situations in skill performance contexts. For example, a worker must detect and remove defective products from the assembly line. Many products move past the worker for long periods of time, but only a few are defective. Similarly, driving a car along an

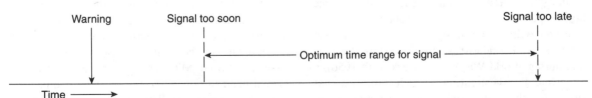

**FIGURE 3.1–3**    A time line showing a continuum of time for the occurrence of a response signal to follow a warning signal to ensure optimal readiness to respond. The actual amounts of time along this continuum should be considered as task-specific.

---

## A Closer Look

### Vigilance Problems Result from Closed Head Injury

Closed head injury involves brain damage and often results from an auto accident or a fall. Numerous cognitive and motor problems can accompany this type of injury, depending on the area of the brain that is damaged. Included in the problems associated with closed head injury is difficulty sustaining attention over a period of time in vigilance tasks.

Loken et al. (1995) provided evidence for this by comparing patients with severe closed head injuries to non-brain-injured people. All participants observed on a computer screen sets of two, four, or eight small blue circles (1.5 mm diameter). On some trials, one of the circles was solid blue (this occurred on only 60 percent of the 200 trials). When participants detected the solid blue circle, they were to hit a specified keyboard key. The set of trials lasted 20 min, with only 2 to 5 sec between trials.

The authors pointed out that the following results were most noteworthy because they added to previous knowledge of vigilance problems related to closed head injury. *In contrast to the non-brain-injured participants,* the patients showed that their

(1) **overall vigilance performance** was differentially affected by the complexity of the stimulus array on the computer screen (i.e., detection performance decreased as the set size of circles increased).

(2) **detection time latency** increased as a function of the length of time engaged in performing the task (i.e., the amount of time taken to detect a solid blue circle increased linearly across the 200 trials).

---

uncrowded freeway is a vigilance task when a person drives for an extended time. Lifeguarding at a pool or beach can be a vigilance problem, because during a long shift on duty situations requiring a response are very infrequent. Medical personnel often are required to work long hours and still be able to identify symptoms of health problems correctly and perform surgical techniques requiring precise motor skill control. A sport situation involving vigilance occurs when a baseball outfielder must maintain alertness throughout an inning in the field despite having only one ball hit his or her way, out of the many pitches thrown.

In each of these situations, RT increases as a function of the amount of time the person must maintain alertness to detect certain signals. Detection errors increase as well. Scientists first reported this phenomenon during World War II (see Mackworth 1956). In experiments investigating the detection of signals simulating those observed on a radar screen, results showed that both the RT to a signal and the accuracy of detecting signals deteriorated markedly with each half hour during a two-hour work interval.

Eason, Beardshall, and Jaffee (1965) nicely demonstrated that alertness deterioration contributes to the performance decrements associated with long-term vigilance. They provided physiological evidence consistent with decreases in vigilance performance over one-hour sessions. Skin conductance in participants decreased, indicating increased calming and drowsiness over the session. In addition, participants' neck tension steadily increased, as their nervous systems attempted to compensate by increasing muscle activity in the neck.

***Attention focused on the signal versus the movement.*** Many motor skills require a person to move as fast as possible when the signal to move occurs. In these situations, there are two important components of the total response, the RT and the movement time (MT). The person can focus on the signal itself (a *sensory set*) or on the movement required (a *motor set*). The specific component the performer is consciously focusing attention on influences RT. Franklin Henry (1961) provided the first evidence showing this influence on RT.

However, because Henry's results were based on the participants' opinions of what their sets were, Christina (1973) imposed on each participant either a sensory or a motor set. The sensory-set group was told to focus attention on the sound of the go signal, a buzzer, but to move off the response key as fast as possible. The motor-set group was told to focus on moving as quickly as possible. Results showed that the sensory-set group had an RT 20 msec faster than that of the motor-set group. Interestingly, MT was not statistically different for the two groups. Thus, subjects' focusing of attention on the signal and allowing the movement to happen naturally shortened the preparation time required and did not penalize movement speed, yielding a faster overall response time.

Jongsma, Elliott, and Lee (1987) have replicated these laboratory results in a sport performance situation. They compared sensory and motor set for a sprint start in track. To measure RT, the authors embedded a pressure-sensitive switch in the rearfoot starting block. They measured MT as the time from the release of this switch until a photoelectric light beam was broken 1.5 meters from the starting line. Results showed that for both novices and experienced sprinters, RT was fastest for the sensory-set condition.

*Practice.*    One of the most effective ways to reduce the amount of time needed to prepare a movement is by practicing the movement. Researchers have been providing evidence showing this benefit for many years. For example, Norrie (1967) found that with just 50 practice trials, people reduced by 13 percent (from 252 to 220 msec) the preparation time they needed to perform a three-part rapid arm movement involving two direction changes.

Practice also can reduce or even eliminate the effects of several factors on preparation time. For example, practice can reduce the influence of the number of stimulus choices described by Hick's Law. Mowbray (Mowbray 1960; Mowbray and Rhoades 1959) demonstrated this when he showed that after extensive practice, subjects reduced the RT for a four-choice situation to equal the RT for a two-choice situation. Also, people can reduce the

effects of stimulus-response incompatibility on RT by practicing the incompatible condition to the point at which the RT becomes comparable to that of an unpracticed compatible situation (see Duncan 1977).

What does practice do that reduces the preparation time demand? There are several possibilities. One is that practice *reduces uncertainty* in situations where much preparation time is due to people's need to translate unfamiliar stimuli or unfamiliar stimulus-response relationships. This possibility seems especially likely in the stimulus-response compatibility situation. By practicing, the person can overcome the preparation demands caused by the translation or confusion effects that were a part of the task initially. Another possibility is that practice *reduces the preparation demands* by allowing a person to better organize the movement components of an action into larger coordinative structures. Because early practice largely involves developing the appropriate coordination of muscle, joint, and limb action, early preparation time demands are greater than those later in practice, after the person has established coordination patterns.

## What Occurs During Preparation?

Based on the discussion so far, you can see that the process of preparing to produce action is complex. It includes perceptual, cognitive, and motor components. One way to demonstrate the complexity of the preparation process is to divide an EMG recording of the RT interval into components by using a technique known as *fractionating RT,* which was introduced in Concept 1.2.

*Evidence from fractionating RT.*    To fractionate RT, we divide into two distinct parts the EMG recording taken from the agonist muscle involved in a movement (see figure 3.1–4). The first part is called the *premotor time* (sometimes referred to as electromechanical delay). Notice that in the figure, the EMG signal does not change much from what it was prior to the onset of the stimulus. However, shortly after the onset of the stimulus, the EMG

**FIGURE 3.1–4** Schematization of fractionated reaction time indicating the relationship between the EMG signal activity and the premotor and motor time intervals.

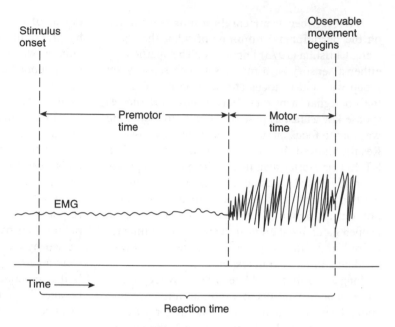

signal shows a rapid increase in electrical activity. This indicates that the motor neurons are firing and the muscle is preparing to contract, even though no observable, physical response has yet occurred. In this period of time, called the *motor time,* is the period of increased EMG activity preceding the observable response (which begins at the point marked *response*).

Premotor time and motor time represent two distinct activities that occur prior to observable movement and reflect different types of movement preparation processes. During premotor time a person is perceptually or cognitively processing the stimulus information. Motor time begins the actual motor output phase of a response. During this time, the specific muscles involved in the action are firing and preparing to begin to produce observable movement.

To gain insight into what occurs during the preparation process, researchers have looked at which of these fractionated-RT components is influenced by various factors that influence RT. For example, Christina and Rose (1985) reported that the changes in RT due to increases in *response complexity* were reflected in increases in premotor time. For a two-part arm movement, premotor time increased an average of 19 msec over that for a one-part arm movement, while motor time increased only 3 msec. Siegel (1986) found that while RT increased linearly as *response durations* increased from 150, through 300 and 600, to 1200 msec, premotor time also increased linearly. Motor time, on the other hand, remained the same until the response duration became 1200 msec; then motor time showed a slight increase. Sheridan (1984) showed that premotor time was also responsible for RT increases due to increases in *movement velocity.* However, Carlton, Carlton, and Newell (1987) found that both premotor and motor time changes resulted from altering *force-related characteristics* of the response.

***Postural preparation.*** When a person must perform arm movements while in a standing position, a part of the preparation process involves organizing supporting postural activity. EMG recordings of postural muscle activity provide evidence for this preparation. For example, Weeks and Wallace (1992) asked people to perform an elbow-flexion aiming movement in the horizontal plane while standing in an erect posture. Participants learned to make this movement in three different velocities defined by criterion movement times. The authors made EMG recordings from various muscles of both legs and the responding arm. The results (figure 3.1–5) showed that for each movement velocity, a specific sequence of supporting postural events occurred. Muscles of the contralateral and ipsilateral legs (biceps femoris and rectus femoris) activated prior to the onset of the arm agonist muscles (biceps brachii). And as the arm velocity increased, the onset of the anticipatory postural muscle activity occurred at an earlier time prior to arm agonist muscle activation. The authors found different onset orders for the various postural muscles. This finding shows that postural preparation involves organizing features of a flexibly organized synergy of postural muscles. This conclusion is important because movement scientists traditionally have assumed that postural muscle preparation is rigidly temporally organized. The advantage of the flexibly organized synergy is that anticipatory postural activity can occur according to the person's equilibrium needs of various premovement postures.

***Preparation of limb performance characteristics.***
An essential part of the movement preparation process is organizing the responding limbs to perform according to the dictates of task constraints and characteristics. Because an individual often can perform the same action using several different limbs or different segments of the same limb, he or she must specify and prepare the limb or limb segments to be involved in performing a given task.

One feature of limb movement a person must prepare is the *direction* or directions in which the limbs must move. For a very rapid movement, a person may prepare several different directions before initiating the movement. Another feature related to direction preparation is the *trajectory* the arm will follow during movement. For a task requiring a ballistic movement and spatial accuracy, an individual must prepare in advance: constraining the limb movement to meet the *accuracy* constraints of the task. In addition, as we discussed in Concept 2.2, a person catching a ball must prepare his or her hand and finger activity before an oncoming ball reaches him or her.

***Preparation of object control characteristics.***
When the skill to be performed involves manipulating an object, a part of the movement preparation process involves specifying certain features needed to control the object. Two examples illustrate what can be involved in this aspect of movement preparation.

As one feature of the preparation process for handwriting, the writer must specify pen pressure on the writing surface and grip force of the fingers on the writing instrument (Wann and Nimmo-Smith 1991). Experienced writers adjust the amount of pen pressure on the writing surface according to certain characteristics of the surface to allow energy-efficient, continuous, fluent motion. In contrast, children with handwriting problems often use excessive pen pressure and grip the pen barrel with excessive force.

Another object control feature that individuals prepare is what Rosenbaum and Jorgenson (1992) referred to as "end-state comfort." This means that when a person has several options for specifying how an object will be manipulated, as when he or she must pick up an object and place it in a specified location, the person will organize the limb movements so that a comfortable limb position will result at the completion of the action. For example, if a person must pick up an object and place it upside down on a tabletop, the person typically will pick up the object with a hand position that will yield the most comfortable position when the object is placed upside down.

***Preparation of spatial coding.***   In performance situations requiring specified responses to certain stimuli, such as choice-RT situations, people take into account the spatial relationships of the stimulus and response locations in the movement preparation process. They translate these relationships into meaningful codes that they then use to produce the required responses. Research has shown that this spatial coding accounts for many stimulus-response compatibility effects (see Weeks and Proctor 1990 for a discussion of these). The simplest spatial coding, which leads to the fastest preparation (i.e., RT), occurs when left and right

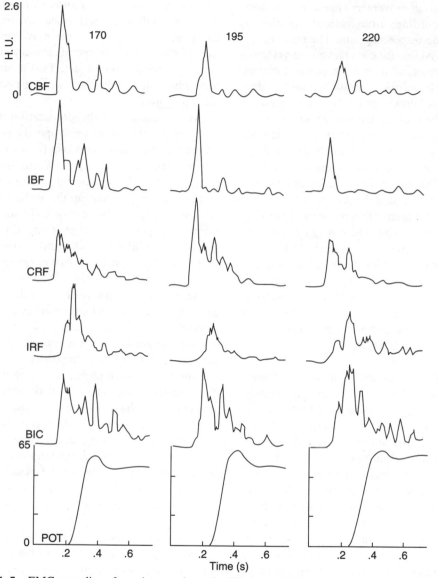

**FIGURE 3.1–5**   EMG recordings from the experiment by Weeks and Wallace. One trial of a rectified and smooth EMG record is shown for one subject performing an elbow-flexion aiming movement in the horizontal plane while standing in an erect posture. Shown are records for three different velocities (170, 195, and 220 ms) for various muscles of both legs and the responding arm (CBF = contralateral biceps femoris, IBF = ipsilateral biceps femoris, CRF = contralateral rectus femoris, IRF = ipsilateral rectus femoris, BIC = biceps brachii, POT = potentiometer). (Reprinted from *Human Movement*, Volume 11, D. L. Weeks and S. A. Wallace, 1992, with kind permission of Elsevier Science-NL, Sara Burgerhartstraat 25, 1055 KV Amsterdam, The Netherlands.)

---

## A CLOSER LOOK

### Correcting Handwriting Problems due to Grip and Pen Force

The results of the experiment by Wann and Nimmo-Smith (1991) showed that when handwriting, children with handwriting problems often do so because they use excessive pen pressure and grip the pen barrel with excessive force. They have not acquired the necessary association between the "feel" of the pen against the surface and the appropriate pen pressure to apply. The researchers speculated that adults who made the appropriate force adjustments had acquired this capability through experience, which had led to their nonconsciously learning the amount of pressure required based on sensations in the fingers holding the pen.

Teachers and therapists who work with children struggling with this type of problem can encourage an increasing sensitivity in the children to appropriate pen pressure. One way to do this is by providing handwriting experiences with a variety of writing surfaces. A teacher or therapist should monitor each child's grip force, with the goal of keeping it at the minimum amount of force needed to produce a visible trace on the writing surface.

---

stimulus locations are compatible with left and right response locations. Beyond that arrangement, it appears that up-to-right and down-to-left stimulus-to-response relationships lead to faster preparation times. The limb involved in performing the required response is not so critical as the spatial relationship of the stimulus location to the response location.

*Rhythmicity preparation.* Many skills require that the component movements follow specific rhythmic patterns. We can see this characteristic in any of the various types of gait, performance of a dance sequence, shooting of a free throw in basketball, and so on. An experiment by Southard and Miracle (1993) showed that the success skilled basketball players experienced was related to their maintaining a consistent rhythm during their free-throw-shooting ritual, regardless of the actual amount of time they took to perform this ritual. In fact, a consistent rhythm was more important than what the player actually did as part of his preparation ritual. The authors speculated that the benefit of the rhythmicity of the preparation ritual was that it prepared the rhythmicity requirements of the action to be produced by the motor system.

## Summary

To perform a motor skill, a person must prepare the motor control system. This preparation requires time, as we can see from research evidence showing that various task, situation, and personal factors influence RT. Task and situation factors include the number of response alternatives the performer has to choose from; the predictability of the correct response choice; stimulus-response compatibility; foreperiod length regularity; movement complexity; movement accuracy; the repetition of a response; and the time between different responses. Personal factors influencing preparation include the degree of the person's alertness; whether attention is focused on the signal or on the movement; and practice. We know that people prepare several action-related characteristics during the RT interval. Movement scientists have gained insight into the extent to which these are perceptual, cognitive, or motor by fractionating the RT intervals from the EMG signals of the primary agonist muscles into their premotor and motor components. Research evidence has shown that these are some of the various action features human beings prepare during the RT interval: postural organization; limb performance characteristics; object control characteristics; spatial coding; and rhythmicity.

# Related Readings

Carson, R. G., R. Chua, D. Goodman, and W. D. Byblow. 1995. The preparation of aiming movements. *Brain and Cognition* 28: 133–54.

Kasai, T., and H. Seki. 1992. Premotor reaction time (PMT) of the reversal elbow extension-flexion as a function of response complexity. *Human Movement Science* 11: 319–34.

Meulenbroek, R. G. J., D. A. Rosenbaum, A. J. W. M. Thomassen, and L. R. B. Schomaker. 1993. Limb-segment selection in drawing behaviour. *Quarterly Journal of Experimental Psychology* 46A: 273–99.

Stelmach, G. E., N. Teasdale, and J. Phillips. 1992. Response initiation delays in Parkinson's disease patients. *Human Movement Science* 11: 37–45.

Weeks, D. J., R. W. Proctor, and B. Beyak. 1995. Stimulus-response compatibility for vertically oriented stimuli and horizontally oriented responses: Evidence for spatial coding. *Quarterly Journal of Experimental Psychology* 48A: 367–83.

---

# CONCEPT 3.2

Preparation for and performance of motor skills are influenced
by our limited capacity to select and attend to information

---

## Key Terms

| | | |
|---|---|---|
| attention | multiple- | attentional |
| central- | resource | focus |
| resource | theories | automaticity |
| theories | dual-task | |
| arousal | procedure | |

## Application

When you are driving your car on an open highway that has little traffic, it is relatively easy for you to carry on a conversation with a passenger in the car or on the car phone at the same time. But what happens when the highway you are driving on becomes congested with other traffic? Isn't it difficult to carry on a conversation with your passenger or on your car phone while driving under these conditions?

This driving example raises an important human performance and learning question: Why is it easy to do more than one thing at the same time in one situation, but difficult to do these same things simultaneously in another situation? As you will discover in the discussion of this Concept, we can

consciously attend to, or think about, only so much at one time. As long as we can handle what we are doing within the capacity limits of our information processing system, we can carry out several activities effectively at the same time. But if what we are doing requires more of our attention than we can give to the things we are trying to do, we have to either stop doing some things in order to do others well, or do all of them poorly.

There are many other examples in which this concept of attention limits comes into play. For example, a skilled typist easily can carry on a conversation with someone while continuing to type—but a beginner cannot. A child learning to dribble a ball has difficulty dribbling and running at the same time, while a skilled basketball player does these two activities and more at the same time. Another type of situation in which attention limits come into play involves the instructional environment. For example, have you ever heard a physical therapy patient tell the therapist not to tell him or her to think about so many things at the same time? Or have you experienced the difficulty a beginning tennis player has determining what and how much to look for when trying to return a serve or a groundstroke?

---

## Discussion

Since the earliest days of investigating human behavior, scholars have had a keen interest in the study of attention. For example, as early as 1859, Sir William Hamilton conducted studies in Britain dealing with attention. Around the same time, William Wundt, generally acknowledged as the "father of experimental psychology," investigated the concept of attention at the University of

Leipzig in Germany. In America, William James provided one of the earliest definitions of attention in 1890, describing it as the "focalization, concentration, of consciousness."

Unfortunately, this late-nineteenth- and early-twentieth-century emphasis on attention soon waned, as those under the influence of behaviorism deemed the study of attention no longer relevant to the understanding of human behavior. A renaissance in attention research occurred, however, when the practical requirements of World War II included the need to understand human performance in a variety of military skills. Researchers were interested in several attention-related areas, such as the performance of more than one component of a skill or more than one skill at the same time; the performance of tasks where people had to make rapid decisions when there were several response choices; and the performance of tasks where people had to maintain attention over long periods of time. This renewed interest in the study of attention continues today, as scholars attempt to understand one of the most significant limitations influencing human learning and performance.

## Attention as a Human Performance Limitation

When the term is used in the context of human performance, **attention** refers to engagement in the perceptual, cognitive, and motor activities associated with performing skills. These activities may be performed consciously or nonconsciously. For example, detecting information in the environment is an attention-demanding activity. We observe and attend to the environment in which we move to detect features that help us determine what skill to perform and how to perform it.

Scholars investigating human performance have shown that attention-related activities are tied to an important human performance limitation. This limitation is well illustrated by the problem we often have doing more than one thing at a time, when we are required to divide our attention among the tasks to be performed.

Scientists have known for many years that we have attention limits that influence performance. In fact, in 1886, a French physiologist named Jacques Loeb showed that the maximum amount of pressure that a person can exert on a hand dynamometer actually decreases when the person is engaged in mental work. Unfortunately, it was not until the 1950s that researchers began to try to provide a theoretical basis for the empirical evidence.

## Attention Theories

The first theories addressing attention limitations did so from a time-based limit perspective. Most prominent here was the *filter theory* of attention, sometimes referred to as the *bottleneck theory*. This theory, which evolved into many variations, proposed that a person has difficulty doing several things at one time because the human information-processing system takes time to perform its functions, and therefore the system can perform only a limited number of functions at a time. This means that somewhere along the line, the information-processing system has a *bottleneck,* where it filters out information not selected for further processing. Variations of this theory were based on where in the system the bottleneck occurred. Some contended it existed very early, at the stage of detection of environmental information (e.g., Welford 1952, 1967; Broadbent 1958), while others argued that it occurred later, after information was perceived or after it had been processed cognitively (e.g., Norman 1968).

This type of theoretical viewpoint remained popular for many years, until it became evident that the filter theories of attention did not adequately explain all performance situations. The most acceptable alternative proposed that attention limits were the result of the *limited availability of resources* needed to carry out the information-processing functions. Just as a government has limited economic resources to pay for its activities, so too a human being has limited resources to do all the activities that he or she may be attempting at one time.

Theories emphasizing attentional resource limits propose that we can perform several tasks simultaneously, as long as the resource capacity limits of the system are not exceeded. However, if these limits are exceeded, we experience difficulty performing one or more of these tasks. Theorists following this viewpoint differ in their views of *where* the resource limit exists. Some propose that there is one central resource pool from which all attention resources are allocated, while others propose multiple sources for resources.

*Central-resource capacity theories.* According to some attention theories, there is a central reserve of resources for which all activities compete. Following the government analogy, these **central-resource theories** compare human attention capacity to a single general fund from which all activities must be funded. To further understand this view, consider the available attention resources as existing within one large circle, like the one depicted in figure 3.2–1. Next, consider as smaller circles the specific tasks that require these resources, such as driving a car (task A) and talking with a friend (task B). Each circle by itself fits inside the larger circle. But for a person to successfully perform both tasks simultaneously, both small circles must fit into the large circle. Problems arise when we try to fit into the large circle more small circles than will fit.

A good example of a central resource theory is one proposed by Kahneman (1973). In his model (see figure 3.2–2), the *capacity limits of the central pool of resources are flexible.* This means that the amount of available attention can vary depending on certain conditions related to the individual, the tasks being performed, and the situation. According to the illustration in figure 3.2–1, this flexible-central-capacity view states that the size of the large circle can change according to certain personal, task, and situation characteristics.

Kahneman views the *available* attention that a person can give to an activity or activities as a general *pool of effort,* which involves the mental re-sources necessary to carry out activities. The person can subdivide this one pool so that he or she can allocate attention to several activities at the same time. Allocation of resources is determined by characteristics of the activities and the allocation policy of the individual, which in turn is influenced by situations internal and external to the individual. Figure 3.2–2 depicts the various conditions that influence how a person will allocate the available resources.

First, notice that the central pool of available resources (available capacity) is represented as a box at the top of the model. The wavy line indicates that the amount of attention available, the capacity limit, is flexible. This limit will increase or decrease according to the *arousal level* of the person. **Arousal** is the general state of excitability of a person, reflected in the activation levels of the person's emotional, mental, and physiological systems. If the person's arousal level is too low or too high, he or she has a smaller available attention capacity than he or she would if the arousal level were in a optimal range. This means that for a person to have available the maximum attention resources, the person must be at an optimal arousal level.

Another critical factor determining whether there are sufficient attentional resources is the attention demands, or requirements, of the tasks to be performed. This factor is represented in Kahneman's model in figure 3.2–2 as the *evaluation of demands on capacity.* Because tasks differ in the

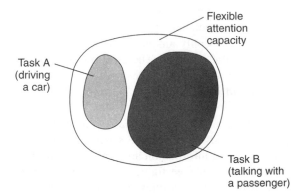

Flexible
attention
capacity

Task A
(driving
a car)

Task B
(talking with
a passenger)

**FIGURE 3.2–1** Diagram showing that two tasks (A and B) can be performed simultaneously (e.g., driving a car while talking with a passenger) if the attention demanded by the tasks does not exceed the available attention capacity. Note that the amount of available capacity and the amount of attention demanded by each task to be performed may increase or decrease, a change that would be represented in this diagram by changing the sizes of the appropriate circles.

**FIGURE 3.2–2**    Kahneman's model of attention. (From Daniel Kahneman, *Attention and Effort*, © 1973, p. 10. Reprinted by permission of Prentice-Hall, Inc., Englewood Cliffs, N. J.)

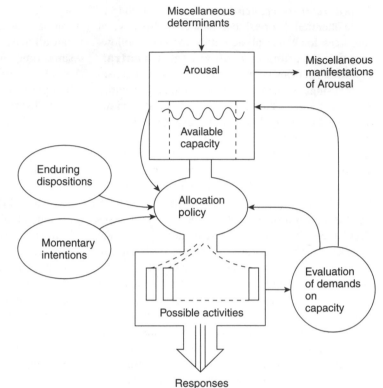

amount of attention they demand, the person must evaluate these demands to determine if he or she can do them all simultaneously, or if he or she will not be able to perform some of them.

Finally, certain rules come into play that influence how people allocate attentional resources. One is that we allocate attention to ensure that we can complete one activity. Another is that we allocate attentional resources according to our *enduring dispositions*. These are the basic rules of "involuntary" attention, or the attention we give to such things as a novel signal, a sudden noise, or the calling of our own name in a crowded room. When situations like these occur, we seem naturally to direct attention to them. The last rule concerns a person's *momentary intentions*. These are the person's own specific intentions to allocate attention in specific situations. Sometimes these are self-directed, while at other times they are based on instructions the person has received about how to direct his or her attention.

*Multiple-resource theories.*    **Multiple-resource theories** provide an alternative to theories proposing a central resource pool of attention resources. Multiple-resource theories contend that we have several attention mechanisms, each having limited resources. Each resource pool is specific to a component of performing skills. Using the government analogy, the resources are available in various government agencies and competition for the resources occurs only among those activities related to the specific agencies. The most prevalent of the multiple-resource theories were proposed by Navon and Gopher (1979), Allport (1980), and Wickens (1980, 1984).

Wickens proposed what has become the most popular of these theories. He stated that resources for processing information are available from three different sources (see figure 3.2–3). These are the *input and output modalities* (e.g., vision, limbs, and speech system), the *stages of information process-*

## An Attention-Capacity Explanation of the Arousal-Performance Relationship

A widely held view of the relationship between arousal and performance is that it takes the form of an inverted U. This means that when we graph this relationship, placing on the vertical axis performance level ranging from poor to high, and placing on the horizontal axis arousal level ranging from very low to very high, the plot of the relationship resembles an inverted U. This type of relationship indicates that arousal levels that are either too low or too high will result in poor performance. However, between these extremes is a range of arousal levels that should yield high performance levels.

If, as Kahneman's model indicates, arousal levels influence available attention capacity in a similar way, then it would follow that we can attribute the arousal level–performance relationship to available attention capacity. This means that arousal levels that are too low or too high lead to poor performance, because the person does not have the attentional resources needed to perform the activity. When the arousal level is optimal, sufficient attention resources are available and the person can achieve a high level of performance.

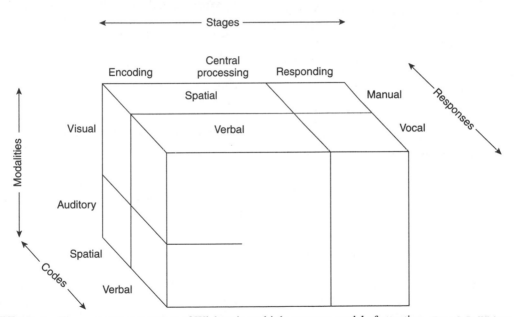

**FIGURE 3.2–3**　The component structure of Wickens's multiple-resource model of attention. (From C. D. Wickens, "Processing Resources in Attention" in R. Parasuraman and R. Davies (eds.), *Varieties of Attention*, 1984. Copyright © 1984 Academic Press, Orlando, FL. Reprinted by permission.)

ing (e.g., perception, memory encoding, response output), and the *codes of processing information* (e.g., verbal codes, spatial codes). Our success in performing two or more tasks simultaneously depends on whether those tasks demand our attention from a common resource or from different resources. When two tasks must be performed simultaneously and share a common resource, they will be performed less well than when the two tasks compete for different resources.

For example, the multiple-resource view would explain variations in the situation involving driving a car while talking with a passenger in the following way. When there is little traffic, driving does not demand many resources from any of the three different sources. But when traffic gets heavy, resource demand increases from these two sources: input-output modalities and stages of information processing. These are the same two sources involved in providing attention resources for carrying on a conversation with a friend. As a result, to maintain safe driving, the person must reduce the resource demand of the conversation activity.

If the multiple-resource view is accurate, we would predict that performance of a tracking task and a verbal memory task together should be more successful than performance of a tracking task and a verbal task requiring spatial decisions. We expect this result because the tracking task and the spatial task should compete for the same resource, since they each involve spatial coding of information. When we take task difficulty into account, we predict that two difficult tasks can be performed simultaneously if they require different resources, but cannot if they compete for the same resources (see Wickens, Sandry, and Vidulich 1983 for examples of experiments supporting the predictions of this model).

An advantage of multiple-resource theories is their focus on the types of demands placed on various information-processing and response outcome structures, rather than on a nonspecific resource capacity. The resource-specific attention view provides a practical guide to help us determine when task demands may be too great to be performed simultaneously. For example, if one task requires a hand response and one requires a vocal response, a person should have little difficulty performing them simultaneously, because they do not demand attention from the same resource structure. Conversely, people have difficulty performing two different hand responses simultaneously, because they both demand resources from the same structure.

## Procedures for Assessing Attention Demands

The most common experimental procedure used to investigate attention-limit issues has been the **dual-task procedure.** The general purpose of experiments using this technique is to determine the attention demands and characteristics of two different tasks that are performed simultaneously. Experimenters' general approach has been to determine the attention demands of one of the two tasks by noting the degree of interference caused on that task while it is performed simultaneously with another task, called the *secondary task.*

The *primary task* in the dual-task procedure is typically the task of interest, whose performance experimenters are observing in order to assess its attention demands. Depending on the purpose of the experiment, the performer may or may not need to maintain consistent primary-task performance, whether performing that task alone or simultaneously with the secondary task.

If instructions in the experiment require the participant to pay attention to the primary task so that it is performed as well alone as with the secondary task, then secondary-task performance is the basis researchers use to make inferences about the attention demands of the primary task. On the other hand, if the experiment does not direct the person to attend primarily to either task, performance on both tasks is compared to performance when each task is performed alone.

*Continuous-secondary-task technique.* One approach to the use of the dual-task procedure requires people to maintain performance on a primary task while continuously performing a secondary task. For example, in a commonly cited experiment by Kantowitz and Knight (1976), participants had to maintain a metronome-paced rate of speed on the primary task. In this task, known as a reciprocal tapping task, they moved a stylus back and forth between two targets. The secondary task was the continuous performance of a mental task, such as adding columns of digits. Participants were told to perform both tasks at

| A CLOSER LOOK |
| --- |

## Comparison of Attention Demands of Balance Control for People With and Without Lower-Limb Amputations

Geurts and Mulder (1994) studied people in the Netherlands with and without unilateral lower-limb amputations to determine the degree of attention those with amputations needed to control their balance. The participants with amputations had been fit with prostheses for the first time when this study began. All participants performed a static balance task of standing on a force platform on the floor for 30 sec. They were instructed to stand as still and symmetrically as possible with their hands folded behind their backs. After establishing baseline fore-aft and lateral sway characteristics while doing this task, participants simultaneously performed an arithmetic task. They had to listen to a relatively simple addition problem and state verbally if the sum was correct or incorrect. The participants without amputations showed, as expected, no postural difficulties in the dual-task situation. In contrast, those with amputations showed an increase in both body sway and the number of arithmetic errors. Interestingly, eight weeks later, after weekly rehabilitation therapy, participants with amputations did not show these same dual-task deficits and performed more as the no-amputation participants had.

These results demonstrate that

- people who are initially acquiring the capability to use a lower-limb prosthesis following amputation require attention capacity to perform a simple static postural control task. A sufficient amount of attention to perform a mental task simultaneously is not available.
- the attention participants need to balance using a prosthesis decreases after a period of therapy to a point at which they can allocate attention to a mental task, so that they can perform both tasks successfully.

the same time but to maintain the proper tapping speed at all times. The authors reasoned that if sufficient attention capacity were available for a person to perform the tapping task and the adding task together, the person should be able to perform the secondary task while doing the primary task as well as he or she could when performing the secondary task alone. In other words, a type of "time-sharing" can go on in the processing system to enable both tasks to be done simultaneously.

The results showed that two tasks could be done together with little difficulty when the secondary task was an easy one. However, as the secondary task became more difficult, performance on the secondary task worsened. These results demonstrate the limited-resource-capacity concept by showing how various task demands require different amounts of attention, which in turn influence a person's capability to perform the tasks simultaneously.

*Secondary-task probe technique.* An alternative dual-task procedure is called the *probe technique.* Researchers use a discrete secondary task to "probe" attention demands of performing various parts of the primary task by requiring the subject to perform the secondary task at various times while performing the primary task. This approach is especially popular when a researcher is interested in the attention demands of the individual components of a task. In this situation, a person usually is told to concentrate on the primary task. He or she is also instructed to perform the secondary task as well as possible. The rationale behind this procedure is that if a phase of the primary task demands attention capacity, it will reduce the attentional resources available for performing the secondary task. Thus, secondary task performance should suffer when the secondary task is performed with the primary task, compared to when it is carried out alone.

**FIGURE 3.2–4** Results of the experiment by Posner and Keele showing differences in secondary-task performance (RT) as a function of where the response was made during the 135° rapid primary task. RT effects are shown for primary-task movements to large and small targets. (Source: Data from M. I. Posner and S. W. Keele. "Attention Demands of Movements," in *Proceedings of the 16th Congress of Applied Psychology,* 1969.)

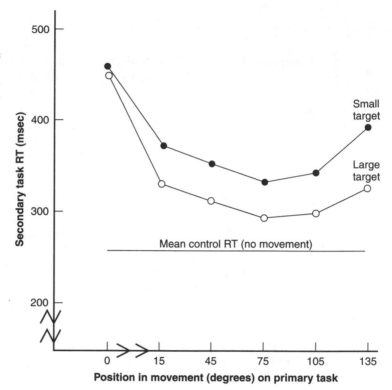

For example, the probe technique would be a useful procedure if you were interested in knowing when attention is required in the course of a walk through a cluttered environment. You could require the person to perform a reaction-time task (secondary task) by depressing a hand-held response button when a signal sounds while the person is walking (primary task). You could set the signal to sound at various phases of the walking task, such as at its initiation, or when an obstacle is encountered, or when the person is walking without any obstacles nearby.

Experiments using the probe technique to assess attention demands of performing motor skills have shown that all phases of performing a skill do not require the same degree of attention. An example from the performance of a simple skill will illustrate this point. Attention demands appear to be high as a person initiates a manual aiming movement. But the continuing movement toward the target demands very little attention. Finally, completing the movement may or may not demand a lot of attention, depending on the characteristics of the target and on how the movement must be completed. For example, in a classic experiment by Posner and Keele (1969), the participants moved to a target and made a correction of the movement if they overshot the target. As you can see in figure 3.2–4, when the target was small, attention demand to complete the movement was high. But when the target was large, a participant needed to devote much less attention to stopping the movement.

## Focusing Attention

In addition to having to divide attention among several activities, people also direct attention to specific features of the environment and to action preparation activities. This attention-directing process is known as **attentional focus.** As opposed

---

| A CLOSER LOOK |

## An Attention-Related Strategy for Preparing to Perform a Closed Skill

Based on a review of research related to attention and performance, Singer and colleagues (Singer et al. 1991) presented a three-component strategy that should be employed by people as they prepare to perform a closed skill. People can use this strategy when performing a variety of sport skills (e.g., shooting a free throw in basketball, serving in tennis or badminton, shooting in archery and gun sports, hitting a golf ball) and everyday skills (e.g., getting out of bed, getting out of a chair, walking along a designated pathway, buttoning a jacket).

Those who use this strategy engage in three activities just prior to performing a skill:

1. **Relaxation** involves using breathing control and muscle relaxation to reduce tensions, to enhance attention focus and develop an optimal arousal level
2. **Visualization** involves mentally seeing and feeling the desired performance before actually performing it
3. **Focus** involves concentrating on a positive aspect of task performance that is vital to performing effectively

---

to attentional demands, which concern the distribution of attentional resources to various tasks that need to be performed simultaneously, attentional focus concerns the marshalling of available resources in order to direct them to specific information sources.

We can consider attentional focus in terms of both width and direction of focus. *Width* indicates that our attention can have a *broad or narrow* focus on environmental information and mental activities. *Direction* indicates that our attention focus can be *external or internal:* attention may be focused on cues in the environment or on internal thoughts, plans, or problem-solving activities. Nideffer (1993) has shown that the broad and narrow focus widths and the external and internal focus directions interact to establish four types of attention-focus situations that relate to performance.

Individuals in performance situations require specific types of attention focus to achieve successful performance. For example, a person needs a broad/external focus to walk successfully through a crowded hallway, but a narrow/external focus to catch a ball. Sometimes, situations require us to shift the type of attention focus and the object of that attention. We do this by engaging in what is referred to as *attention switching*. It is an advantage

to switch attention focus rapidly among environmental and situational pieces of information when we must use a variety of sources of information for rapid decision making. For example, a football quarterback may look to see if the primary receiver is open; if not, he must find an alternate receiver. In the meantime, the quarterback must be making certain that he is not about to be tackled or kept from delivering a pass. Each of these activities requires attention and must be carried out in the course of a few seconds. To do this, the player must rapidly switch attention between external and internal sources of information.

However, certain kinds of attention switching can be a disadvantage in the performance of some activities. For example, a person performing a skill that requires a rapid, accurate series of movements, such as typing, piano playing, or dancing, will be more successful if he or she focuses attention on a primary source of information for extended periods of time. Problems can arise if the person's attention is switched too frequently between appropriate and inappropriate sources of information. For example, if a pianist is constantly switching visual attention from the written music to the hands and keys, he or she will have difficulty maintaining the precise timing structure required by the piece being played.

## Attention and Consciousness

The term *attention* is often inappropriately used to imply only conscious awareness. The result has been that terms like "high attention demands" and "low attention demands" are equated with how much a person has to think consciously about or concentrate on something. However, the concept of attention should not be limited to conscious activities.

Clearly, conscious involvement in attention activities characterizes many skill performance situations. For example, when a child is learning to bounce a ball with one hand and run at the same time, we can almost observe the child thinking about what he or she needs to do. The same thing occurs when a rehabilitation patient is working on handwriting. Therapists often observe such patients verbally directing the action as it occurs.

However, some attention-demanding activities appear not to involve conscious awareness. We saw an example in the study of the long jumpers by Lee, Lishman, and Thomson (1984) considered in Concept 2.2. Their results indicated that while visual attention was important for the precise hitting of the takeoff board, skilled long jumpers and coaches were not consciously aware of the corrections the athletes made as they were completing the approach run.

In the following two sections, we discuss two important issues relating attention to conscious awareness. The first concerns the notion of *automaticity,* a term that is commonly used in reference to skilled performance. The second concerns conscious awareness and the learning of a skill.

*Automaticity.*    A common assumption about skilled performance is that the skill is performed "automatically." **Automaticity** implies that skills can be performed without demands on attention capacity. Logan (1985) provided some important insights into the concept of automaticity and its relationship to motor skill performance. He pointed out that the concept of skilled performance and the concept of automaticity are closely related. Automaticity is an important component of skilled performance, in that it consists of knowledge and procedures that can be called upon and carried out automatically.

Both automaticity and skill can be acquired through practice. It is best to think of automaticity as a continuum of varying degrees. It is possible, for example, that some processing activity required in the performance of a skill may be only partially automatic. If this is so, then we need to restructure the dichotomous yes/no question that researchers have asked regarding attention demands when dual-task procedures are employed. One approach to addressing this need would be to assess dual-task performance at various stages of practice.

An important skill-learning question that comes out of this view of automaticity is this: *How automated do complex skills become?* Some skills such as performing a dance or gymnastics routine or playing a piano piece, are highly complex. Do these become automated all the way through the piece so that little, if any, attention is needed? The reasonable response to this question seems to be that the performer develops automated "chunks" of the entire piece. These chunks are parts of the pieces that have been put together into groups and performed with little attention directed toward what is in the chunks. Attention is demanded, however, at the beginning or initiation of each chunk.

Anecdotal evidence for this view comes from discussions with skilled individuals. During performances, individuals indicate that they perform many parts of a routine without thinking about these parts. However, these performers indicate that there are also places in the routine to which they must direct conscious attention. Those places seem to be identified by distinct characteristics. The dancer may attend to the place where the tempo changes or a partner must be contacted or lifted; the pianist may attend to tempo changes. The gymnast may direct attention to parts of the routine that would be dangerous if missed. All of these individuals indicate that they give attention to parts of the routine with which they have had difficulty.

There is, unfortunately, almost no research evidence supporting this view of attention and the performance of complex skills. One reason is that it is difficult to test. However, some studies concerned with simple movements have shown that attention demand changes as a result of practice. These studies (e.g., Reeve 1976; Wrisberg and Shea 1978) have shown that while a performer may reduce attention for some aspects of the movement, the movement does not reach what might be considered a completely automated state. For some parts of the skill, attention remains critical, regardless of the amount of practice. What remains to be determined are the characteristics of the parts of a complex skill that will always demand the performer's conscious attention, regardless of the stage of learning.

*One feature of skills that does not achieve automaticity is timing.* According to Peters (1977), when two different motor activities must be performed at the same time, only one set of time commands will be issued at one time. Thus, we would expect that there are certain skills in which different timing activities must be performed simultaneously, and in which some degree of interference will always exist. Peters (1985) reported evidence of this when he compared novice and skilled pianists as they performed rubato, which involves one hand's temporary departure from the common time base and playing of another while the other hand continues playing the common time base. Novices were essentially unable to do this. While the skilled pianists were better than the novices, their performances also showed evidence of interference.

**Is conscious attention to environmental cues needed for learning?** The second issue concerning consciousness and attention relates to the common instructional technique of telling people what in the environment to look for that will help them perform a skill. Sometimes we ask people to tell us what they were looking for or looking at when they performed a skill, so that we can help them correct their visual attention focus. However, research investigating the need for conscious awareness of environmental cues when learning skills reveals that these types of techniques do not have to be in-

cluded in the student-teacher or patient-therapist interaction. This research shows that we learn to select relevant cues from the environment without being consciously aware of what those cues are.

A good example of research demonstrating that skill learning occurs in the absence of conscious awareness of critical environmental cues is an experiment reported by Richard Pew (1974). Participants watched a target cursor move in a complex waveform pattern on an oscilloscope for 60 sec. The participants' task involved pursuit tracking of the target cursor: they were to manipulate a joystick to make their own cursor stay as close as possible to the target cursor. The unique feature of the target-cursor movement was that it moved randomly for the first and third 20-sec segments on every trial, but it made the same movements on every trial during the middle 20-sec segment. The participants practiced this pursuit-tracking task for approximately 24 trials on each of 16 days. The results showed that as they practiced, they performed better on the middle segment than on the other two segments. But what is more important is that when interviewed, none of the participants indicated that they knew that the target cursor made the same pattern during the middle segment. Thus, the participants picked up and used the regularity of the cursor movement during the middle segment, even though they were unaware of that characteristic.

The results Pew found have been replicated in experiments in which the repeated segment was the middle of the three segments (Magill and Hall 1989), and the first of the three segments (Magill, Schoenfelder-Zohdi, and Hall 1990). The results of this latter experiment, shown in figure 3.2–5, illustrate the degree of superior performance by subjects on the repeated segment of the tracking pattern as compared to the random-pattern segments. Again, no participants in either of these experiments reported that they were aware that one segment in the patterns they tracked was repeated on every practice trial.

These experiments reveal an important characteristic of the visual selection process. That is, visual cue selection can occur without people's

**FIGURE 3.2–5** The results of the experiment by Magill, Schoenfelder-Zohdi, and Hall (1990) showing the superior performance on the repeated segment A compared to the random segments B and C for a complex tracking task. (Source: R. A. Magill, et al., "Further Evidence for Implicit Learning in a Complex Tracking Task" paper presented at the annual meeting of the Psychonomics Society, November, 1990. New Orleans, LA.)

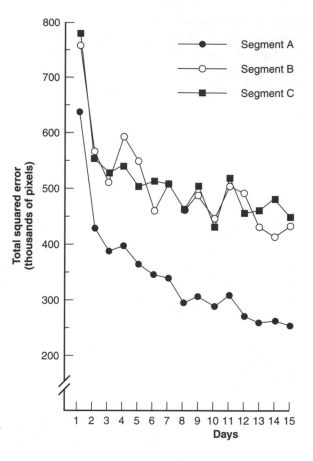

conscious awareness of the cues they are selecting. People do not have to be told which cues to look for, nor do they need to be able to report verbally which cues they are looking for or using. However, it is essential that they see the relevant cues in a large variety of environmental contexts in which the relevant cues occur each time, and that the persons are attending to the context and trying to improve performance on each trial.

## Summary

We have considered attention as our capacity to engage in the perceptual, cognitive, and motor activities associated with performing skills. Human beings have a limited capacity to engage in these activities. As a result, we often have difficulty per-

forming more than one task at a time. The most popular theories of attention limits propose that we have a limited capacity to process information. Some theories consider this limitation to be a central pool of attentional resources. For example, Kahneman's flexible limited-capacity model proposes that attentional resources are allocated from a single pool. Allocation is influenced by several factors related to the individual and to the activities to be performed. Multiple-resource theories arise from an alternative view that proposes several resources from which attention can be allocated. The typical experimental procedures used to support a limited-capacity view are called dual-task procedures.

An important aspect of attention and motor skill performance is *attentional focus:* where and how a

| A CLOSER LOOK |
| --- |

## Awareness of Relevant Cues Can Be Detrimental to Skill Learning

It is a common assumption that making people aware of relevant environmental cues will facilitate skill acquisition. However, an experiment by Green and Flowers (1991) showed that this is not the case when those cues do not occur on every trial. Participants played a computer game in which they manipulated a joystick to move a paddle horizontally across the bottom of the monitor to try to catch a "ball," which was a dot of light, that moved for 2.5 sec from the top to the bottom of the screen. The ball moved according to one of eight pathways, four of which involved a single curve and four of which involved an S-curve. On some trials (75 percent), the ball made one of two types of deviations from the normal pathway. When these occurred, they related to a specific final position of the ball. Thus, participants'

detection of these characteristics could help them increase their catching accuracy. One group of participants received explicit instruction about this characteristic and its probability of occurring; the other group did not. Participants practiced for five days for a total of 800 trials. The results showed that both groups improved. However, the explicitly instructed group made more errors than the group that had had no instruction and obviously implicitly acquired the capability to use the predictive information. The authors concluded that the instructed participants directed so much of their attentional resources to trying to remember the rule and looking for its occurrence that their performance was disrupted, because they did not have sufficient resources to devote to the catching task itself.

person directs his or her attention in a performance situation. Attention can be focused either broadly or narrowly, and either externally, on some aspect of the environmental situation, or internally, on some aspect of the skill preparation or performance. People can switch focus quickly among these widths and directions.

Finally, attention is not limited to conscious awareness. People carry out many attention-demanding activities without being consciously aware of them. One example is the visual attention people give to environmental cues directing performance. These cues demand attentional focus; however, people are not always consciously aware of the characteristics of the cues.

## Related Readings

Abernethy, B. 1988. Dual-task methodology and motor skills research: Some applications and methodological constraints. *Journal of Human Movement Studies* 14: 101–32.

Allport, A. 1987. Selection for action: Some behavioral and neurophysiological considerations of attention and action. In H. Heuer and A. F. Sanders (Eds.), *Perspectives on perception and action* (pp. 395–419). Hillsdale, NJ: Erlbaum.

Franz, E. A., H. N. Zelaznik, and A. Smith. 1992. Evidence of common timing in the control of manual, orafacial, and speech movements. *Journal of Motor Behavior* 24: 281–87.

Peters, M. 1994. When can attention not be divided? *Journal of Motor Behavior* 26: 196–99.

# CONCEPT 3.3

Visual selective attention plays an important role in preparing many motor skills

## Key Terms

visual search

## Application

To carry out many of the motor skills you use in your daily activities, you need to visually attend to specific features of the environmental context before actually carrying out the actions. For example, when you reach for a cup to drink the coffee in it, you visually note where the cup is and how full it is before you reach to pick it up. When you put your door key into the keyhole, you first look to see exactly where it is. When you need to maneuver around people and objects as you walk along a corridor, you look to see where they are, what direction they are moving in, and how fast they are going. To drive your car, you also must visually select information from the environment so that you can get safely to your destination.

In sport activities, visual attention to environmental context information is also essential. For many skills, unless athletes attend to critical cues first, their performance success is seriously impaired. For example, visually attending to ball-and server-based cues allows the player to prepare to hit a return shot in tennis or racquetball. Skills such as determining where to direct a pass in soccer or hockey, or deciding which type of move to put on a defender in basketball or football, are all dependent on a player's successful attention to the visual cues prior to initiating action.

In each of these daily living and sport activities, vision plays a critical role in preparing a person to perform a skill. Visually searching the environment helps the individual obtain information he or she needs to make decisions about what actions to produce, how to carry out the actions, and when to initiate the actions.

## Discussion

**Visual search** is the process of directing visual attention to locate appropriate environmental cues. During the preparation process for performing many skills, people carry out visual search to select from the environment those cues that are relevant for the performance demands of specific situations. In the following sections, we discuss the actual process of selecting appropriate information from the environment, and give examples from various sport and everyday skills to illustrate how visual search is an important component of the performance preparation process.

## Procedures for Investigating Visual Search in Motor Skills

Before considering the visual search process itself, we will examine how researchers have investigated visual selective attention as it relates to performing motor skills. Three experimental procedures have become popular for determining the visual search strategies used in skill performance situations. Two involve video simulation of a skill performance situation. The third involves monitoring of the person's eye movements as he or she performs a skill.

*Video simulation techniques.* In one popular technique for investigating visual search, researchers videotape real skill performance situations and then use the video to simulate the real situation. In the testing situation, the participant observes the video (or sometimes a film or a series of slides), and then is asked to perform specific actions as if he or she were actually in that situation. For example, a tennis player may be asked to act as if he or she is actually receiving the serve of the tennis player in the video. For the action component, the participant may be required to designate as quickly as possible the ball's landing position on the court of the serve.

Scientists have used two different procedures in the video simulation technique. Each determines one of two characteristics of the visual search process. One procedure assesses the amount of time the person takes to select the information he or she needs in order to respond. The other determines which characteristics of the observed performance the person uses to make a correct response.

The procedure for addressing the time issue is the *temporal occlusion procedure.* The film or video stops at various time points during the action and the observer is required to make a response. An example of the use of this procedure is an experiment by Abernethy and Russell (1987), in which badminton players watched film sequences of a player making different shots. When the film stopped, participants marked their predictions of the landing positions of the shuttle. To determine when in the course of the observed action the participants made their decisions, the film stopped at different times prior to, during, and after ball contact. By noting the relationship between the accuracy of a participant's predicted shuttle landing location and the moment he or she made the decision, the researchers could determine when in the time course of the observed action the participant had picked up by visual search the information needed to make a decision.

To determine what information a person uses to make the required response, researchers use the *event occlusion procedure.* Parts of each frame of film or video are masked so that the observer cannot see selected parts of the action. Figure 3.3–1 presents an example of this procedure, taken from the second part of the Abernethy and Russell (1987) study. The logic of this approach is that if the person performs worse without being able to see a specific cue, then that cue is important for successful performance.

*Eye movement recording technique.* Another experimental procedure researchers use to investigate visual attention issues in motor skills is the *eye movement recording.* This procedure requires the use of specialized equipment that tracks the movement of the eyes and records where the eyes are "looking" at a particular time. A researcher can record the displacement of central vision for a specific time interval, as well as the place and the length of time the person fixates his or her gaze while tracking. One way scientists use this approach is to have the participant observe a film simulation of a performance situation and then make a response. They then plot the movement of the eye as a function of the film scene, so that they can determine the spatial location of the participant's eye movements (displacement), along with his or her gaze fixation characteristics related to observing the serving action. A more difficult way to use this procedure is to record eye movements while a person is actually performing a skill in the performance setting.

*Eye movements and visual attention.* Although eye movement recordings track the displacement characteristics of focal vision while people observe a scene, an important question arises concerning how well this procedure assesses visual attention. The logic underlying the use of the procedure is that what a person is looking at should give researchers insight into what information in the environment the person is attending to. But there is an important research question here: Is this a valid assumption? Can we validly relate eye movements to visual attention?

**FIGURE 3.3–1** Examples of what subjects saw in the Abernethy and Russell experiment when they watched a film of a badminton serve where various parts of the serving action were masked and could not be seen. (*Source:* Abernethy, B., and D. G. Russell, 1987. Expert-novice differences in an applied selective attention task. *Journal of Sport Psychology* 9: 326–345.)

Research evidence (e.g., Shepherd, Findlay, and Hockley 1986) has shown consistently that it is possible to give attention to a feature in the environment without moving the eyes to focus on that feature. However, it is not possible to make an eye movement without a corresponding shift in attention. This means that eye movement recordings may underestimate what a person is visually attending to. With this caution in mind, these recordings provide good estimates of what the person is attending to.

## How We Select Visual Cues

One of the more popular answers to questions about how certain cues in the environment are selected comes from the *feature integration theory* of visual attention proposed by Anne Treisman (Treisman and Gelade 1980; Treisman 1988). This view indicates that during visual search, we initially group stimuli together according to their unique features, such as color, shape, or movement. This grouping occurs automatically. These groups of features form "maps" related to the various

## A CLOSER LOOK

### Visual Search and Attention Allocation Rules

If the key to successful selection of environmental information when performing motor skills is the distinctiveness of the relevant features, an important question is this:

**WHAT MAKES CERTAIN FEATURES MORE DISTINCTIVE THAN OTHERS?**

Insight into answering this question comes from the attention allocation rules in Kahneman's theory of attention (1973):

• **Unexpected features attract our attention.** You can see this in your own daily experience. While concentrating on your professor during a lecture, haven't you been distracted when a classmate has dropped some books on the floor? Undoubtedly, you switched your visual attention from the

professor to the source of the noise. When the environment includes features that typically are not there, the distinctiveness of those features increases. The result is that people have a tendency to direct visual attention to them.

• **We allocate attention to the most meaningful features.** In performance environment, the most meaningful cues "pop out" and become very evident to the performer. Meaningfulness is a product of experience and instruction. As a person experiences performing in certain environments, critical cues for successful performance are invariant and increase in their meaningfulness, often without the person's conscious awareness. Instruction also plays a part in the way certain features of cues become more meaningful than others.

values of various features. For example, a color map would identify the various colors in the observed scene, while a shape map would indicate which shapes are observed. These maps become the basis for further search processes when the task demands that the person identify specific cues. For further processing, we must use attention, and must direct it to selecting specific features of interest.

The selection of features of interest occurs when a person focuses the *attentional spotlight* on the master map of all features. People can direct attention over a wide or a narrow area, and it appears that the spotlight can be split to cover different map areas. If the person's task is to search for a target having a certain distinct feature, then the target will "pop out" as a result of this search process, because the feature is distinct among the groupings of features. Thus, the more distinctive the feature is that identifies the target of the visual search, the more quickly the person can identify and locate the target. If the distinctive feature is a part of several cues, the search slows as the person

assesses each cue in terms of how its characteristics match those of the target.

## Visual Search and Action Preparation

Visual search picks up critical cues that influence three parts of the action control process: *action selection, constraining of the selected action,* and *timing of action initiation.* By influencing these processes, the visual system enables a person to prepare and initiate an action that conforms to the specific requirements of the performance situation.

Research investigating visual search in performance situations has produced evidence about what is involved in these important preparation processes. Sport performance situations have been the most popular context in which scientists have investigated the role of visual search in action preparation. The following research examples, investigating different sport situations, provide a sense of what we currently know about the characteristics of visual search processes related to the performing of motor skills.

---

**A CLOSER LOOK**

## Two Examples of Severe Time Constraints on Visual Search

There are some situations in sport in which researchers can determine the actual amount of time a person has to engage in visual search and to prepare an action. Two of these are returning a serve in tennis and hitting a baseball. In each of these situations, it is clearly to the player's advantage to detect the information needed as early as possible, in order to prepare and initiate the appropriate action.

**PREPARING TO RETURN A TENNIS SERVE**

A serve traveling at 40 to 45 m/sec allows the receiver only 500 to 600 msec to hit the ball. This means that the person must search as soon as possible for the cues that will provide information about the

direction, speed, landing point, and bounce characteristics of the ball, so that he or she can select, organize, and execute an appropriate return stroke.

**PREPARING TO HIT A BASEBALL**

When a pitcher throws a ball at a speed of 90 mph, it will arrive at home plate in approximately .45 sec. Suppose that it takes .1 sec for the batter to get his or her bat to the desired point of ball contact. This means that the batter has less than .35 sec after the ball leaves the pitcher's hand to make a decision and to initiate the swing. If the pitcher releases the ball 10 to 15 feet in front of the rubber, the batter has less than .3 sec of decision and swing initiation time.

---

*Visual search in badminton.* The experiments by Abernethy and Russell (1987) described earlier in this Concept provide a good example of visual search by expert badminton players. They found that the time between the initiation of the badminton server's backswing and the shuttle's hitting the floor in the receiver's court is approximately 400 msec. Within that time period, there appears to be a critical time window for picking up critical cues predicting where the shuttle will land. This window, which lasts from about 83 msec before until 83 msec after racquet shuttle contact, provides information about racquet movement and shuttle flight that seems to resolve uncertainty about where the served shuttle will land. Experts use the 83-msec period prior to racquet-shuttle contact more effectively than novices. As a result, experts have more time to prepare their returns. The racquet and the arm are the primary sources to visually search for the anticipatory cues needed to prepare the return.

*Visual search in baseball batting.* An example of research describing characteristics of the visual search processes involved in baseball batting is a study by Shank and Haywood (1987). They

recorded eye movements for college and novice players as they watched a videotape of a right-handed pitcher as if they were right-handed batters. Twenty randomly presented fastballs and curves from both the wind-up and stretch positions were observed. For each pitch, the players' task was to indicate verbally if the pitch was a fastball or a curve. The expert players correctly identified almost every pitch, whereas the novices were correct only about 60 percent of the time. Members of both groups did not begin to track the ball until about 150 msec after the ball had left the pitcher's hand. During the wind-up, experts fixated on the release point, whereas novices tended to shift fixations from the release point to the pitcher's head. These results show that the expert batter, knowing where the most relevant cues are prior to the release of a pitch, visually attends to the release point and ignores other possible sources of information prior to the release.

*Visual search in returning a tennis serve.* Results from two experiments by Goulet, Bard, and Fleury (1989) demonstrate how critical visual search strategies are to preparing to return tennis

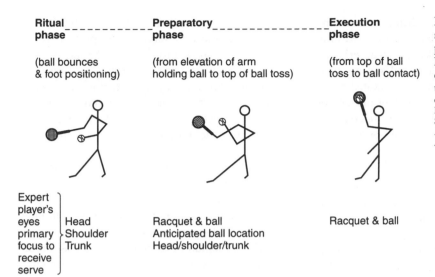

| Ritual phase | Preparatory phase | Execution phase |
|---|---|---|
| (ball bounces & foot positioning) | (from elevation of arm holding ball to top of ball toss) | (from top of ball toss to ball contact) |

Expert player's eyes primary focus to receive serve

| Head Shoulder Trunk | Racquet & ball Anticipated ball location Head/shoulder/trunk | Racquet & ball |

**FIGURE 3.3–2** Illustration showing where expert tennis players in the Goulet, Bard, and Fleury experiment were looking during the three phases of a tennis serve. (Source: Based on discussion in C. Goulet, et al., "Expertise Differences in Preparing to Return a Tennis Serve: A Visual Information Processing Approach" in *Journal of Sport and Exercise Psychology,* 11:382–398, 1989.)

serves. Expert and novice tennis players watched a film showing a person serving and were asked to identify the type of serve as quickly as possible. The authors recorded the participants' eye movements as they watched the film. Three phases of the serve were of particular interest: the "ritual phase" (the 3.5 sec preceding the initiation of the serve); the "preparatory phase" (the time between the elevation of the arm for the ball toss and the ball's reaching the top of the toss); and the "execution phase" (from the ball toss to racquet-ball contact).

As illustrated in figure 3.3–2, during the ritual phase, the expert players focused mainly on the head and the shoulder/trunk complex, where general body position cues could be found. During the preparatory phase, they directed visual search primarily around the racquet and ball, where it remained until ball contact. An interesting note was that the experts also looked at the server's feet and knees during the preparatory phase. The important difference between experts and novices was that the visual search patterns of the expert players allowed them to correctly identify the serve sooner than novices could.

*Visual search in soccer actions.* To determine whether to shoot, pass, or dribble in soccer, the player must use visual search that is different from that involved in the situations described above. The soccer situation involves many players in the visual scene that must be searched for relevant cues. An experiment by Helsen and Pauwels (1990) provides a good demonstration of visual search patterns used by experienced and inexperienced players to determine these actions. Participants acted as ball handlers as they viewed slides of typical attacking situations. For each, the person indicated as quickly as possible whether he would shoot at the goal, dribble around the goalkeeper or opponent, or pass to a teammate. As expected, the experts took less time to make the decision. More important, eye-tracking results showed that the experts gained this time advantage because they knew what to look for in a scene. Although the visual search patterns of the experts and the novices were similar, the experts fixated on fewer features of the scene and spent less time at each fixation.

Another visual search situation in soccer involves anticipating where a pass will go. Williams et al. (1994) showed that experienced players and inexperienced players look at different environmental features to make this determination. Results based on subjects' eye-tracking characteristics while watching action from an actual soccer game showed that the experienced players fixated more on the positions and movements of other players, in addition to the ball and the ball handler. In contrast, inexperienced players typically fixated only on the ball and the ball handler.

***Visual search while driving a car.*** Driving a car is a non-sport performance situation in which vision provides information to select and constrain action. In a study of novice and experienced drivers, Mourant and Rockwell (1972) had subjects drive a 2.1-mi neighborhood route and a 4.3-mi freeway route. The novices were students in a driver education class. The authors recorded students' eye movements while they drove. The results showed that novice drivers concentrated their eye fixations in a smaller area as they gained early driving experience. In comparison to the experienced drivers, the novices looked more immediately in front of the car and more to their right (note that this study was done in England). This indicates that novices have a smaller scanning range while driving than do experts, thus increasing the likelihood that they will not detect important cues in the environment. On the freeway, the novices made pursuit eye movements, whereas the experienced drivers made specific eye fixations. That is, the experts knew what cues were important and specifically searched for those cues. The experienced drivers looked into the rear- and side-view mirrors more frequently than the novices, while the novices looked at the speedometer more than the experienced drivers did.

***Visual search during prehension while walking.*** When a person must walk to a table to pick up an object, such as a pen or book, visual search plays an important role in setting into motion the appropriate action coordination. An experiment by Cockrell, Carnahan, and McFayden (1995) demonstrated this role for visual search. Participants were required to walk 3.75 m to a table and pick up an aluminum can or a pencil as they walked by. Results showed that before they began any prehensive action, their eyes moved to fixate on the target. Head movement also preceded the initiation of reaching movements. Thus, the eyes' searching of the environment to determine the location and characteristics of the object started a chain of events to allow the participants to grasp the object successfully.

***Visual search while moving through a cluttered environment.*** Movement through a cluttered environment can occur in everyday situations—we walk around furniture in the house or walk through a crowded mall—and in sport situations: a player runs with a football or dribbles a basketball during a game. People's ability to maneuver through environments like these indicates that they have detected relevant cues and used them in advance to avoid collisions. Visual search is an important part of this process.

According to research by Cutting, Vishton, and Braren (1995), the most important cues involved in avoiding collision in these situations come from the relative location or motion of objects around the object the person needs to avoid. When visually fixating on the object he or she needs to avoid, the person uses relative-displacement and/or velocity information about both the object to be avoided and other objects in front of or behind the object. It is important to note that this decision making is done automatically by the visual system and provides the basis for appropriate action by the motor control system. The key practical point here is that the person needs to visually fixate on the object or objects that he or she wishes to avoid.

## Teaching Visual Search Strategies

If a person is instructed to look for and attend to certain things and continues to practice doing that, then those things become the environmental cues that "pop out" when the person is in that situation. Movement scientists have demonstrated the effectiveness of this type of visual search training many times in research settings (see Czerwinski, Lightfoot, and Shiffrin 1992). With training, people

---

## A CLOSER LOOK

### Acquiring Effective Visual Search Strategies

Certain conditions are important to facilitate a person's acquiring the capability of automatic effective visual search:

- The person needs an extensive amount of practice in situations that include common relevant cues.
- The environmental context in which these cues occur needs to be varied during practice. The

situational characteristics should vary as much as possible, but the person needs to search for the same cues each time.

- The person must actively engage in the search process, although it is not necessary that he or she be instructed to look for specific cues or to indicate verbally which cues he or she is searching for.

---

develop the capability to detect relevant information from the environment automatically.

An interesting instruction question arises here: Must the person be told specifically which cue or cues to look for and attend to? Research discussed in Concept 3.2 concerning the implicit learning of invariant environmental cues directing action suggests that explicit instruction about which cue(s) to look for is not essential. What is more important is that the person is directing visual attention to the area in which the critical cues occur, and that the critical cues regularly occur in situations in which the skill is performed. The visual system seems to detect these invariances automatically. As a result, experiencing these invariant cues will increase the likelihood that the cues will "pop out" in similar situations.

The key requirement here is that the critical cues occur regularly. Recall from the discussion in Concept 3.2 that when critical cues occur infrequently or irregularly, the person's explicit search for them can hinder performance. It is the regular occurrence of cues that establishes their invariance and enables the visual system to automatically detect and make use of them.

## Summary

Visual attention to critical cues in the environment is an important part of preparing to perform a skill. An individual selects these cues by visually search-

ing the environment for advance information that will enable the person to anticipate the action required in a situation. Effective visual search influences action selection, constraining of the selected action, and timing of action initiation. We have discussed examples of visual search in motor skill situations involving badminton, baseball batting, tennis, soccer, and driving a car. Research evidence shows that training can facilitate the use of effective visual search strategies.

## Related Readings

Abernethy, B., and R. Burgess-Limerick. 1992. Visual information for the timing of skilled movements: A review. In J. J. Summers (Ed.), *Approaches to the study of motor control and learning* (pp. 343–84). Amsterdam: Elsevier.

Bootsma, R. J. 1991. Predictive information and the control of action: What you see is what you get. *International Journal of Sport Psychology* 22: 271–78.

Carnahan, H., M. A. Goodale, and R. G. Marteniuk. 1993. Grasping versus pointing and the differential use of visual feedback. *Human Movement Science* 12: 219–34.

Tresilian, J. R. 1994. Approximate information sources and perceptual variables in interceptive timing. *Journal of Experimental Psychology: Human Perception and Performance* 20: 154–73.

Whiting, H. T. A., G. J. P. Savelsbergh, and J. R. Pijpers. 1995. Specificity of motor learning does not deny flexibility. *Applied Psychology: An International Review* 44: 315–32.

# STUDY QUESTIONS FOR CHAPTER 3

1. Discuss how we can use reaction time (RT) as an index of the preparation required to perform a motor skill.

2. Discuss how Hick's Law is relevant to helping us understand the characteristics of factors that influence motor control preparation.

3. What is the cost-benefit trade-off involved in biasing the preparation of an action in the expectation of making one of several possible responses? Give a motor skill performance example illustrating this tradeoff.

4. Discuss what is meant by the term "movement complexity." Tell how it influences motor control preparation to perform a rapid movement.

5. Describe two performer characteristics that can influence movement preparation. Discuss how these characteristics can influence preparation.

6. Select a motor skill and describe two motor control features of that skill that a person prepares prior to the initiation of performance of the skill.

7. Discuss how central-resource theories and multiple-resource theories of attention differ in how they characterize limitations in the ability to perform several skills simultaneously.

8. Describe a motor skill performance situation in which a dual-task procedure could be used to assess attention demands of that situation. Indicate why this assessment would provide useful information to a practitioner.

9. Discuss how the concept of automaticity in motor control illustrates the appropriate way to view the relationship between attention and consciousness.

10. If people can acquire and use knowledge about environmental-cue regularities without being able to describe verbally what those cues are like, then how can people acquire and use this information?

11. What is meant by the term *visual search* when it is used in reference to performing motor skills? Give an example.

12. Describe how video simulation techniques and eye movement recordings can provide evidence about visual search processes related to performing motor skills.

13. What three aspects of the motor control process does visual search influence? Select a motor skill in which visual search is important and describe how visual search influences these three control processes.

© Jean-Claude Lejuene

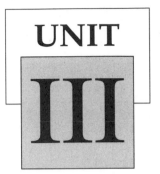

# UNIT
# III

# THE LEARNING
# ENVIRONMENT

# CHAPTER 4

# INTRODUCTION TO MOTOR SKILL LEARNING

## CONCEPT 4.1

People who assess learning must make inferences from observing performance during practice and tests

## CONCEPT 4.2

Distinct performance and performer characteristics change during skill learning

## CONCEPT 4.3

Transfer of learning from one performance situation to another is an integral part of skill learning and performance

# CONCEPT 4.1

People who assess learning must make inferences from
observing performance during practice and tests

## Key Terms

performance          performance          transfer tests
learning                 curve              performance
stability             retention tests        plateau

## Application

Any professional involved in motor skills instruction typically has to provide some type of assessment to determine whether or not the student or
patient has learned what the professional has
taught. The following two situations, common in
physical education and rehabilitation settings, provide examples of the importance of assessing
learning.

Suppose you are a physical educator teaching
a tennis unit. If you are teaching your students
to serve, how do you determine if they are actually learning what you are teaching them? What
will you look for to assess their progress in
learning to serve? How can you be certain that

what you are observing is the result of learning
and not just luck?

Or suppose you are a physical therapist helping
a stroke patient to learn to walk without support.
What evidence will tell you that this patient is
learning to do what you have taught him or her to
do? What characteristics of the patient's performance will make you confident that the patient is
learning this skill and will be able to walk without
assistance at home as well as in the clinic?

The answers to these questions are important for
effective professional practice in any setting in
which people need to learn motor skills. As you
think about possible answers to these questions, consider two important characteristics of learning that
you need to take into account whenever you assess
skill learning. First, we do not directly observe
learning; we directly observe behavior. Second, because of this, we must make inferences about learning from the behavior we observe. Any learning assessment procedure must incorporate these two
critical characteristics of learning.

## Discussion

In this discussion about the assessment of learning,
we need to keep two important terms distinct: *performance* and *learning*. This distinction helps us establish an appropriate definition for the term *learning;* it also helps us consider appropriate conditions
under which we should observe performance, so
that we can make valid inferences about learning.

### Performance Distinguished from Learning

Simply put, **performance** is *observable behavior.*
If you observe a person walk down a corridor, you

are observing a performance of the skill of walking. Similarly, if you observe a person hitting a
baseball, you are observing a performance of the
skill of hitting a ball. When used in this way, the
term *performance* refers to the execution of a skill
at a specific time and in a specific situation. *Learning,* on the other hand, cannot be observed directly,
but can only be inferred from characteristics of a
person's performance.

Before considering a more formal definition
for learning, think about how often we make inferences about people's internal states based on
what we observe them doing. For example, when

someone smiles (an observable behavior), we infer that he or she is happy. When someone cries, we infer that he or she is sad, or perhaps very happy. When a person's face gets red, we believe that person is embarrassed. In each of these situations, certain characteristics about the individual's behavior are the basis for our making a particular inference about some internal state we cannot observe directly. However, because we must base our inference on observed behavior, it is possible for us to make an incorrect inference. If a student sitting beside you in class yawns during the lecture, you might infer from that behavior that the person is bored. However, it may be that he or she is very interested and the yawning is due to extreme tiredness because of lack of sleep the night before.

*Learning defined.*  We will use the following general definition for the term **learning:** *a change in the capability of a person to perform a skill that must be inferred from a relatively permanent improvement in performance as a result of practice or experience.* It is important to note from this definition that the person has increased his or her capability, or potential, to perform that skill. Whether or not the person actually performs the skill in a way that is consistent with this potential will depend on the presence of what are known as *performance variables.* These include such factors as the alertness of the person, the anxiety created by the situation, the uniqueness of the setting, fatigue, and so on. As a result, it is critical that methods used to assess learning take factors such as these into account to allow accurate inferences about learning.

## General Performance Characteristics of Skill Learning

We can observe four general performance characteristics as skill learning takes place.

*Improvement.*  First, *performance of the skill shows improvement over a period of time.* This means that the person performs at a higher level of skill at some later time than at some previous time. It is important to note here that learning is not nec-essarily limited to improvement in performance. There are cases in which practice results in bad habits, which in turn result in the observed performance's failure to show improvement. In fact, performance actually may become worse as practice continues. But because this text is concerned with skill acquisition, we will focus on learning as it involves improvement in performance.

*Consistency.*  Second, as learning progresses, *performance becomes increasingly more consistent.* This means that from one attempt to another, a person's performance levels should become more similar. Early in learning, performance levels are typically quite variable from one attempt to another. Eventually, however, the performance becomes more consistent.

A related term here is **stability**. As performance consistency of a skill increases, certain behavioral characteristics of performance become more stable. This means that the acquired new behavior is not easily disrupted by minor changes in personal or environmental characteristics.

*Persistence.*  The third general performance characteristic we observe during learning is this: *the improved performance capability is marked by an increasing amount of persistence.* This means that as the person progresses in learning the skill, the improved performance capability lasts over increasing periods of time. An important characteristic of skill learning is that a person who has learned a skill should be able to demonstrate the improved level of performance today, tomorrow, next week, and so on. The persistence characteristic relates to the emphasis in our definition of learning on a relatively permanent improvement in performance.

*Adaptability.*  Finally, an important general characteristic of performance associated with skill learning is that *the improved performance is adaptable to a variety of performance context characteristics.* We never really perform a skill for which everything in the performance context is exactly the same each time. Something is different every time we perform a skill. The difference may be our own emotional state, the characteristics of the skill itself, an environmental difference such as a change in weather conditions, the place where we perform the skill, and so on. Thus, successful skill performance requires adaptability to changes in personal, task, and/or environmental characteristics. The degree of adaptability required depends on the skill and the performance situation. As a person progresses in learning a skill, his or her capability to perform the skill successfully in these changed circumstances also increases.

## Assessing Learning by Observing Practice Performance

One way we can assess learning is to record levels of a performance measure during the period of time a person practices a skill. A common way to do this is to illustrate performance graphically in the form of a **performance curve.** This is a plot of the level achieved on the performance measure for each time period, which may be time in seconds or minutes, a trial, a series of trials, a day, etc. For any performance curve, the levels of the performance measure are always on the Y-axis (vertical axis), and the time over which the performance is measured is on the X-axis (horizontal axis).

*Performance curves for outcome measures.* We can graphically describe performance by developing a performance curve for an outcome measure of performance. An example is shown in figure 4.1–1, which depicts one person's practice of a complex pursuit tracking task. The task required the person to track, or follow the movement of, a cursor on a computer monitor by moving the mouse on a tabletop. The goal was to track the cursor as closely as possible in both time and space. Each trial lasted about 15 sec. The outcome measure of performance was root-mean-squared error (RMSE).

Notice that in this graph we can readily observe two of the four behavioral characteristics associated with learning. First, *improvement* is evident by

the general direction of the curve. From the first to the last trial, the curve follows a general downward trend (indicating decreasing error). Second, we can also see *increased performance consistency* in this graph. The indicator of this performance characteristic is performance on adjacent trials. According to figure 4.1–1, this person showed a high degree of inconsistency early in practice but became slightly more consistent from one trial to the next toward the end of practice.

When a person is acquiring a new skill, the performance curve for an outcome measure typically will follow one of four general trends from the beginning to the end of practice. These are represented by the four different shapes of curves in figure 4.1–2. Curve (a) is a *linear curve,* or a straight line. This indicates proportional performance increases over time; that is, each unit of increase on the horizontal axis (e.g., one trial) results in a proportional increase on the vertical axis (e.g., one second). Curve (b) is a *negatively accelerated curve,* which indicates that a large amount of improvement occurred early in practice, with smaller amounts of improvement later. This curve represents the classic power function curve of skill learning, which we will discuss in some detail in Concept 4.3 as a characteristic of the power law of practice. Curve (c) is the inverse of curve (b) and is called a *positively accelerated curve.* This curve indicates slight performance gain early in practice, but a substantial increase later in practice. Curve (d) is a combination of all three curves, and is called an *ogive* or *S-shaped curve.*

It is important to note that each curve in figure 4.1–2 shows better performance as the curve slopes upward. There are, however, instances in which the slope of the curve in a downward direction indicates performance improvement. This occurs when the performance measure is one for which a decrease in the performance level means better performance. Measures involving error or time (such as absolute error and reaction time) follow this characteristic, as performance is improving when the amount of error or time decreases. In such

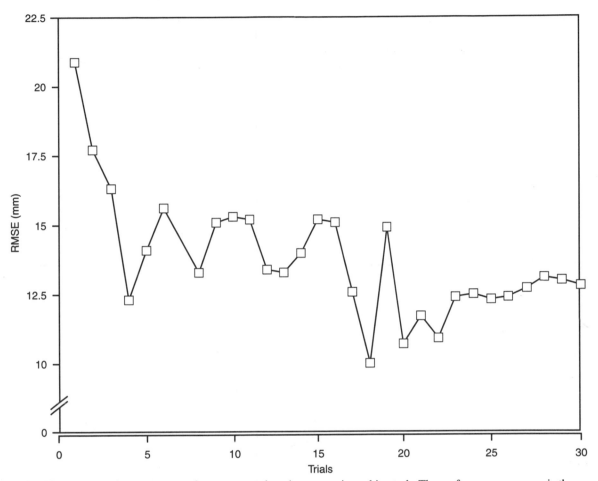

**FIGURE 4.1–1**   Performance curve for one person learning a pursuit tracking task. The performance measure is the root mean-squared error (RMSE) for each trial.

cases, the directions of the performance curves would be opposite to those just described, although the shapes of the curves would be the same.

We must make one further point concerning performance curves. The four curves presented in figure 4.1–2 are hypothetically smoothed to illustrate general trends of performance curves. Typically, performance curves developed for individuals are not smooth but erratic, like the one in figure 4.1–1.

***Performance curves for kinematic measures.*** We can record and graphically display not only outcome measures, but also performance production measures, such as kinematics. When scientists or clinicians use these types of measures to assess performance, they cannot always develop performance curves like the one in figure 4.1–1. This is so because a kinematic measure typically does not lend itself to being represented by one number value for each trial. A kinematic measure involves

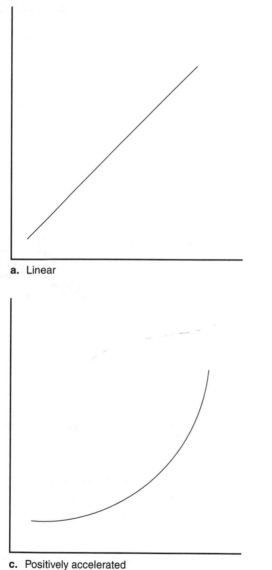

**a.** Linear

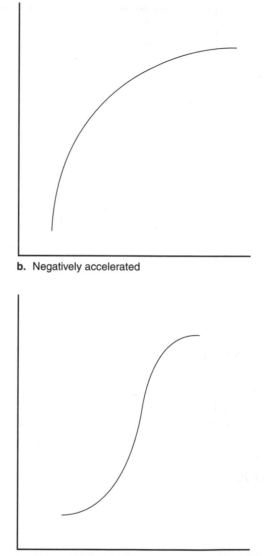

**b.** Negatively accelerated

**c.** Positively accelerated

**d.** Ogive or S-shaped

**FIGURE 4.1–2**    Four general types of performance curves.

performance over time within a trial. It is important to include this time component when we graphically represent a kinematic measure.

To assess improvement and consistency in performance for a series of practice trials, researchers commonly show one performance curve graph for each trial. To show improvement and consistency

changes, they depict a representative sample of trials from different stages of practice.

We can see an example of this approach to kinematic measures in figure 4.1–3. In an experiment by Marteniuk and Romanow (1983), participants performed a task in which they moved a lever on a tabletop to produce the criterion movement pattern

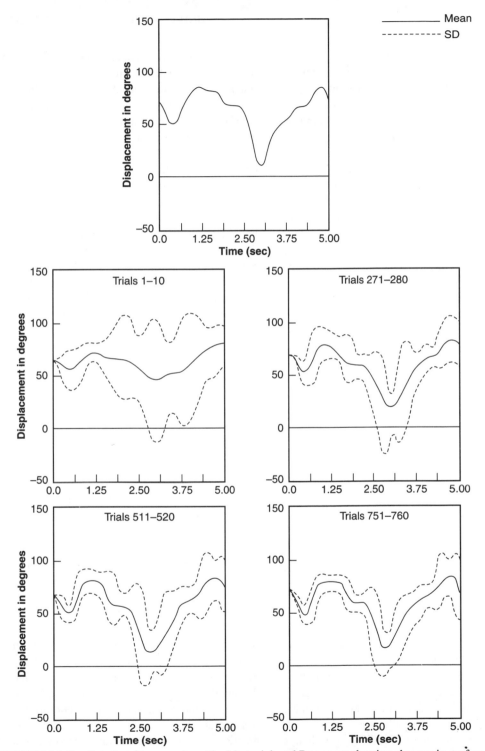

**FIGURE 4.1–3** Results of an experiment by Marteniuk and Romanow showing changes in performance accuracy (displacement) on a tracking task at different practice trial blocks for one participant. The graph at the top shows the criterion pathway for the tracking task. (From R.G. Marteniuk and S.K.E. Romanow," "Human Movement Organization and Learning as Revealed by Variability of Movement, Use of Kinematic Information, and Fourier Analysis," in R.A. Magill (Ed.), *Memory and Control of Action.* Copyright © 1983 Elsevier/North-Holland, Amsterdam, The Netherlands. Reprinted by permission.)

also shown in this figure. Each participant observed the criterion movement on a computer monitor. The graphs in figure 4.1–3 represent the performance of one person for 800 trials. To obtain a more representative picture of performance, the researchers analyzed practice trials in blocks of 10 trials each. To represent performance changes during practice, figure 4.1–3 shows four blocks of trials, each representing a different segment of the 800-trial session. Each graph shows two performance characteristics. One is the person's average pattern drawn for the block of trials; this is indicated by the solid line (mean). The second is the variability of the patterns drawn for that same block of trials; this is indicated by the dashed lines (SD, or standard deviation).

To determine *improvement in performance,* compare the early to the later practice trials by examining how the shape of the person's produced pattern corresponds to the shape of the criterion pattern. As the person practiced more, the produced pattern became more like the criterion pattern. In fact, in trials 751 through 760, the participant was making a pattern almost identical to the criterion pattern.

To assess *changes in consistency,* compare how far the standard deviation lines are from the mean pattern for each block of trials. For trials 1 through 10, notice how far the standard deviation lines are from the mean. This shows a large amount of trial-to-trial variability. However, for trials 751 through 760, these lines are much closer to the mean, indicating that the person more consistently produced the same pattern on each trial of that block of trials.

## Assessing Learning by Retention Tests

Another means of inferring learning from performance examines *the persistence characteristic of improved performance* due to practicing a skill. The most common means of assessing this characteristic is to administer a retention test. You have been experiencing this approach to assessing learning since you began school. Teachers are always giving tests that cover units of instruction. They use these **retention tests** to determine how much

you know, or have retained from your study. Note that a teacher makes an inference concerning how much you have learned about a particular unit of study on the basis of your test performance.

The typical way to administer a retention test in a motor skill situation is to have people perform the skill they have been practicing after a period of time during which they have not actually practiced the skill. The purpose of a retention test is to determine the degree of permanence or persistence of the performance level achieved during practice; having a period of time with no practice allows this type of assessment. The actual length of time between the end of practice and the test is arbitrary. But the amount of time should be sufficiently long to allow any factors to dissipate that may have influenced practice performance artificially. The critical assessment is the difference between the person's performance level on the first practice day and that on the test. If there is a significant improvement between these two periods of time, then you can be confident that learning has occurred.

## Assessing Learning by Transfer Tests

The third means of inferring learning examines the *adaptability aspect of performance changes* related to learning. This assessment method involves using **transfer tests,** which are tests involving some novel situation, so that people must adapt the skill they have been practicing to the characteristics of this new situation. Two types of novel situations are especially interesting. One is a new context in which the people must perform the skill; the other is a novel variation of the skill itself.

*Novel context characteristics.*   Test administrators can use various kinds of context changes in transfer tests. One characteristic they can change is the *availability of augmented feedback,* which is the performance information a person receives from some external source. For example, in many practice situations, the person receives augmented feedback in the form of verbal information about what he or she is doing correctly or incorrectly. If you were assessing learning to discover how well the person can rely on his or her own resources to perform the skill, then your requirement that the person perform without augmented feedback available would be a useful context change for the transfer test.

Another context characteristic a test administrator can change is the *physical environment* in which a person performs. This is especially effective for a learning situation in which the goal is to enable a person to perform in locations other than those in which he or she has practiced. For example, if you are working in a clinic with a patient with a gait problem, you want that patient to be able to adapt to the environmental demands of his or her everyday world. While performing well in the clinic is important, it is less important than performing well in the world in which the patient must function on a daily basis. Because of this need, the transfer test in which the physical environment resembles one in the everyday world is a valuable assessment instrument.

The third aspect of context that can be changed for a transfer test is the *personal characteristics* of the test taker as they relate to skill performance. Here, the focus is on how well a person can perform the skill while adapting to characteristics of himself or herself that were not present during practice. For example, suppose you know that the person will have to perform the skill while he or she is physically fatigued. A test requiring the person to perform the skill while fatigued would provide a useful assessment of his or her capability to adapt to this situation.

*Novel skill variations.* Another aspect of adaptability related to skill learning is a person's capability to successfully perform a novel variation of a skill he or she has learned. This capability is common in our everyday experience. For example, no one has walked at all speeds at which it is possible to walk. Yet, we can speed up or slow down our walking gait with little difficulty. Similarly, we have not grasped and drunk from every type of cup or glass that exists in the world. Yet when we are

confronted with some new cup, we adapt our movements quite well to the cup characteristics and successfully drink from it. These examples illustrate the importance to people of producing novel variations of skills. One of the ways to assess how well a person can do this is to use a transfer test that incorporates this movement adaptation characteristic.

Note that one of the ways we get people to produce a novel skill variation is to alter the performance context in some way so that they must adapt their movements to it. In this way, the transfer test designed to assess capability to produce novel skill variations resembles a transfer test designed to assess capability to adapt to novel performance context features. The difference is the learning assessment focus.

## Assessing Learning from Coordination Dynamics

In another method of assessing learning, a researcher or clinician observes the stabilities and transitions of the dynamics of movement coordination while a person practices a skill. Proponents of this approach, which is gaining in popularity in learning research, assume that when a person begins to learn a new skill, he or she is not really learning something new, but is evolving a new spatial and temporal coordination pattern from an old one. These theorists view learning as the transition between the initial pattern, represented by a preferred coordination mode the person uses when first attempting the new skill, to the establishment of the new coordination mode. *Stability* of the coordination pattern is an important criterion for determining which of these three states (initial, transition, or new) characterizes the person's performance.

For example, a person who is learning handwriting experiences an initial state represented by the coordination characteristics of the limb movements at the beginning of practice. These characteristics make up the preferred spatial and temporal structure the person and the task itself impose on the limb, so that the limb can produce movement approximating what is required. This initial stable state must be changed to a new stable state at which the person can produce fluent handwriting. Learning is the transition between these two states.

An example of this approach to assessing skill learning is an experiment by Lee, Swinnen, and Verschueren (1995). The task (see figure 4.1–4) required participants to move two levers toward and away from the body at the same rate (15 times in 15 sec.) to produce ellipses on the computer monitor. But to accomplish this, the participants had to coordinate the movement of their arms so that the right arm on each cycle was always 90° out of phase with the left arm. The initially preferred movement coordination for the two arms for one subject is shown in figure 4.1–4 as the arm-to-arm displacement relationship demonstrated on the pretest on the first day of practice. The series of diagonal lines resulted when the person moved the arms in phase, in a motion resembling that of windshield wipers. The stability of this coordination pattern is indicated by the consistency of the 15 diagonal lines produced during the pretest trial, and by the person's tendency to produce that same pattern on the pretest trial on day two, after having performed 60 practice trials of the ellipse pattern on day one.

By the end of day three, this person had learned successfully to produce the ellipse pattern. Evidence for this is the consistent production of 15 ellipses in both the pretest and the posttest trials on day three. However, notice the instability of the performance in the many trials between the old and the new stable patterns (exhibited on the day one pretest and the day three posttest). This instability occurs during the transition between two stable states and characterizes the process of learning a new skill.

## Practice Performance May Misrepresent Learning

It may be misleading to base an inference about learning solely on observed performance during practice. There are several reasons for this. One is that the practice environment may involve a vari-

able that artificially inflates performance. Another possibility is that the practice environment may involve a variable that artificially depresses learning. Third, practice performance may be misleading if it involves performance plateaus.

***Practice performance may overestimate or underestimate learning.***   In this textbook, you will see examples of variables whose presence during practice influences performance in such a way that performance overestimates or underestimates learning. One way you can overcome these problems is to use retention tests or transfer tests to assess learning. If a person's practice performance does represent learning, then that person's performance on a retention test should demonstrate the persistence characteristic and not deviate too much from his or her performance at the end of practice. Similarly, transfer test performance should demonstrate the person's increased capability to adapt to novel conditions.

***Performance plateaus.***   Over the course of learning a skill, it is not uncommon for a person to experience a period of time during which improvement seems to have stopped. But for some reason, at some later time, improvement starts to occur again. This period of steady state during which there appears to be no further improvement is known as a **performance plateau.**

Figure 4.1–5 provides a good illustration of a performance plateau, taken from an experiment by Franks and Wilberg (1982). This graph shows one individual's performance on a complex tracking task for ten days, with 105 trials each day. Notice that this person showed consistent improvement for the first four days. Then, on days five through seven, performance improvement stopped. However, this was a temporary characteristic; performance began to improve again on day eight and the improvement continued for the next two days. The steady-state performance on days five through seven is a good example of a performance plateau.

Those studying motor learning have debated the idea that plateaus exist as a normal phase of the learning experience since the end of the last

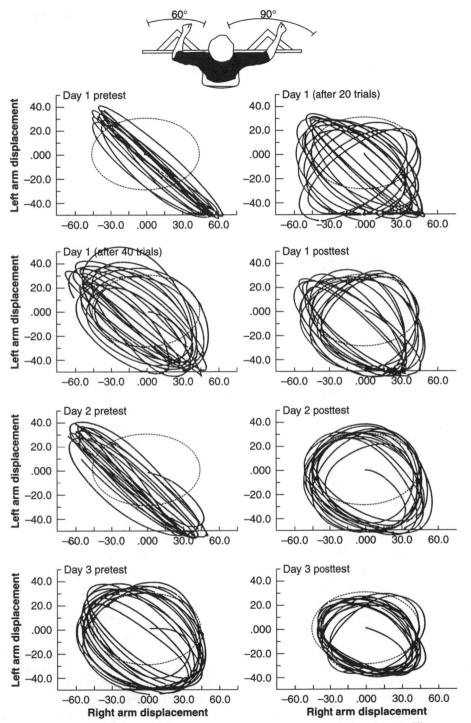

**FIGURE 4.1–4**   The task and results from the experiment by Lee, Swinnen, and Verschueren. The top panel shows the task, in which participants moved two levers to draw ellipses on the computer monitor (the dotted lines on each graph represent the goal ellipse pattern). The series of graphs shows the results as the left-arm × right-arm displacements of one person for the pretest and posttest (and some intermediate) trials for each of three practice days.

(From T.D. Lee, et al., "Relative Phase Alterations During Bimanual Skill Acquisition" in *Journal of Motor Behavior,* 27:263–274, 1995. Reprinted with permission of the Helen Dwight Reid Educational Foundation Published by Heldref Publications, 1319 Eighteenth Street NW, Washington, DC 20036–1802. Copyright © 1995.)

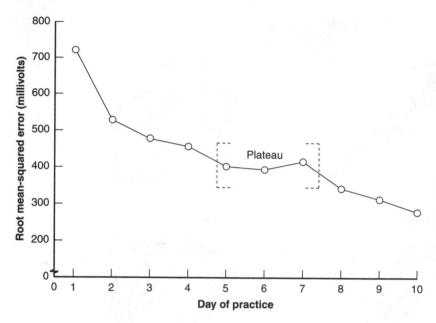

**FIGURE 4.1–5**   Results from the experiment by Franks and Wilberg showing the results from one participant performing the complex tracking task for 10 days, with 105 trials per day. Notice the performance plateau for 3 days (days 5, 6, and 7) where performance leveled off before the subject showed improvement again. (From I.M. Franks and R.B. Wilberg. "The Generation of Movement Patterns During the Acquisition of a Pursuit Tracking Task" in *Human Movement Science*, 1982, 1:251–272. Copyright © 1982 Elsevier/North-Holland, Amsterdam, The Netherlands. Reprinted by permission.)

century, when Bryan and Harter (1897) observed telegraphers learning Morse code. The authors noted steady improvement in the telegraphers' letters-per-minute speed for the first twenty weeks. But then a performance plateau occurred that lasted six weeks; this was followed by further performance improvement for the final twelve weeks. Since this early demonstration, researchers have been debating about whether a plateau is a real learning phenomenon or merely a temporary performance artifact (see Adams 1987 for an excellent review of plateau research). At present, most agree that plateaus are *performance rather than learning characteristics.* This means that plateaus may appear during the course of practice, but it appears that learning is still going on during these times; performance has plateaued, but learning continues.

There are several *reasons performance plateaus occur.* One is that the plateau represents a period of transition between two phases of acquiring certain aspects of a skill. Other possible explanations for a given performance plateau may be a period of poor motivation, a time of fatigue, or a lack of attention directed to an important aspect of a skill. Finally, the plateau may be due not to these performance

characteristics but to limitations imposed by the performance measure. This is the case when the performance measure involves what are known as *ceiling* or *floor effects.* These effects occur when the performance measure will not permit the score to go above or below a certain point.

## Summary

We have discussed four methods for assessing learning. One method is to look for improvement and consistency characteristics of performance as the person practices. We can see these when we plot performance curves of outcome or kinematic performance measures during practice. The second method is to use retention tests. In this method, a tester assesses the persistence characteristic of a learned skill by requiring a person to perform a practiced skill after a period of time during which he or she has not practiced. Transfer tests are a third method of assessing the amount a person has learned, as well as his or her acquired capability to adapt to new performance conditions. A transfer test requires a learner to perform either the practiced skill in a new situation or a new variation of the

## An Example of Artificially Depressed Practice Performance

Fatigue is a good example of a practice variable that can artificially depress practice performance. A research example that illustrates this effect is an experiment by Godwin and Schmidt (1971). The authors required participants to learn an arm movement task known as the sigma task (because the movement pattern produced resembles σ, the lowercase Greek letter sigma). They had to move a handle with one hand as rapidly as possible in a complete circle in one direction, then reverse direction to make another circle, then let go of the handle, and finally knock down a small barrier a few inches from the handle. The researchers required that one group of participants (the fatigued group) engage in arm-cranking activity for 20 sec between trials; the other group (the nonfatigued group) rested during these 20-sec periods. The performance of these two groups is shown in figure 4.1–6.

Notice that at the end of the practice trials the nonfatigued group performed better than the fatigued group did. But on the transfer test, where both groups performed the task with a 20-sec rest between trials, the two groups performed similarly. The important thing about these results is that if the authors had observed practice performance only, they would have drawn an incorrect conclusion about learning. This was evident in the results of the transfer test. The authors concluded that the between-trials exercise influenced practice performance, but *not* learning.

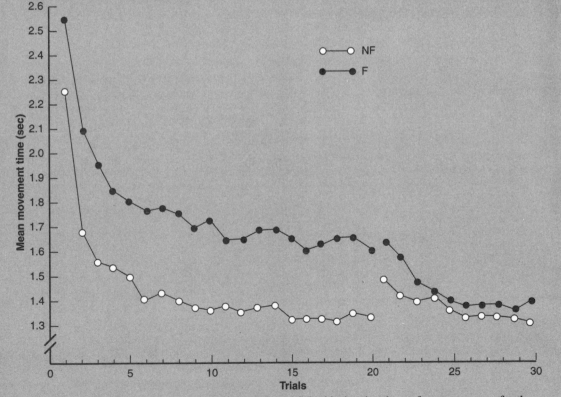

**FIGURE 4.1–6**   Results of the experiment by Godwin and Schmidt showing the performance curves for the fatigued group (closed circles) and the nonfatigued group (open circles) for the sigma task. Note that trials 21–30 are the transfer test, during which both groups performed nonfatigued. (From M.A. Godwin and R.A. Schmidt, "Muscular Fatigue and Discrete Motor Learning" in *Research Quarterly for Exercise and Sport*, 1971, Vol. 42, pp. 374–383. Copyright © 1971 American Alliance for Health, Physical Education, Recreation, and Dance. Reprinted by permission.)

practiced skill. In the fourth learning assessment method, the tester observes consistency and stability characteristics of coordination patterns during practice and on tests. This method gives the tester an opportunity to observe transitions between previously learned and newly acquired coordination patterns.

The assessment of learning only on the basis of practice performance can sometimes lead to invalid inferences. Certain performance variables can artificially inflate or depress performance, so that the test over- or underestimates the amount a person has learned. Additionally, a performance artifact known as a performance plateau can occur, giving the appearance that learning has stopped when it has not. To avoid being misled about learning by these performance artifacts, testers can use retention and transfer tests, as well as further observation of learners' performance of the skills being learned.

## Related Readings

Carron, A. V., and R. G. Marteniuk. 1970. An examination of the selection of criterion scores for the study of motor learning and retention. *Journal of Motor Behavior* 2: 239–44.

Higgins, J. R., and R. K. Spaeth. 1972. Relationship between consistency of movement and environmental condition. *Quest,* Monograph 17: 61–69.

Lee, T. D., and S. P. Swinnen. 1993.Three legacies of Bryan and Harter: Automaticity, variability, and change in skilled performance. In J. L. Starkes and F. Allard (Eds.), *Cognitive issues in motor expertise* (pp. 295–315). Amsterdam: Elsevier.

Zanone, P., and J. A. S. Kelso. 1994. The coordination dynamics of learning: Theoretical structure and experimental agenda. In S. P. Swinnen, H. Heuer, J. Masson, and P. Caesar (Eds.), *Interlimb coordination: Neural, dynamical, and cognitive constraints* (pp. 461–90). San Diego: Academic Press.

---

# CONCEPT 4.2

Distinct performance and performer characteristics change during skill learning

---

## Key Terms

cognitive stage

associative stage

autonomous stage

"getting the idea of the movement"

regulatory conditions

nonregulatory conditions

fixation/ diversification

power law of practice

freezing the degrees of freedom

## Application

Have you ever noticed that people who are skilled at performing an activity often have difficulty teaching that activity to a beginner? This difficulty is due in part to the expert's failure to understand how the beginner approaches performing the skill each time he or she tries it. To facilitate successful skill acquisition, the instructor or therapist must consider the point of view of the student or patient and ensure that instructions, feedback, and practice conditions are in harmony with the person's needs.

Think for a moment about a skill you are proficient in. Remember how you approached performing that skill when you first tried it as a beginner. For example, suppose you were learning the tennis serve. Undoubtedly you thought about a lot of things, such as how you held the racquet, how high you were tossing the ball, whether you were transferring your weight properly at contact, and so on. During each attempt and between attempts, your thoughts focused on fundamental elements of the serve. Now, recall what you thought about after you had had lots of practice and had become reasonably proficient at serving. You probably did not continue to think about all the specific elements each time you served. If you continued practicing

for many years so that you became very skilled, your thoughts while serving undoubtedly changed even further. Rather than thinking about the specific elements involved in serving, you could concentrate on other aspects of the skill. Although you still concentrated on looking at the ball while tossing it and during contact, you also thought about things like where you were going to place this serve in your opponent's service court, or what you were going to do after you served.

Although this performance example involves a sport skill, the underlying concept helps to explain the difficulty experienced by skilled people teaching beginners in all skill instruction contexts. In the rehabilitation clinic, for example, the same problem exists. Imagine that you are a physical therapist working with a stroke patient and helping him or her to regain locomotion function. Like the tennis pro, you are a skilled performer (here, of locomotion skills); the patient is like a beginner. While there may be some differences between the sport and the rehab situations because the patient was skilled prior to the stroke, in both cases you must approach skill acquisition from the perspective of the beginner.

In the examples just described, we have seen that different characteristics distinguish beginners from skilled people. At the instruction level, this indicates that the skilled person teaching the beginner must approach performing the skill the way he or she did as a beginner. The extent to which the skilled person can do this will influence the degree of success he or she has teaching beginners. In addition, those who teach or coach skilled people likewise must understand characteristics of the skilled performer. In both cases, those who provide motor skill instruction benefit from being aware of those characteristics people demonstrate at these different skill levels.

---

## Discussion

An important characteristic of learning motor skills is that all people seem to go through distinct stages as they acquire skills. Several theorists have proposed models identifying and describing these stages. We discuss three of them here.

## The Fitts and Posner Three-Stage Model

Paul Fitts and Michael Posner presented the acknowledged classic learning stages model in 1967. They proposed that learning a motor skill involves three stages. During the *first stage,* called the **cognitive stage** of learning, the beginner focuses on cognitively oriented problems. For example, beginners typically try to answer questions such as these: What is my objective? How far should I move this arm? What is the best way to hold this implement? Where should this arm be when my right leg is here? Additionally, the learner must engage in cognitive activity as he or she listens to instructions and receives feedback from the instructor.

Performance during this first stage is marked by a large number of errors, and the errors tend to be large ones. Performance during this stage also is highly variable, showing a lack of consistency from one attempt to the next. And although beginners may be aware that they are doing something wrong, they generally do not know what they need to do to improve.

The *second stage* of learning in the Fitts and Posner model is called the **associative stage** of learning. The cognitive activity that characterized the cognitive stage changes at this stage, because the person has learned to associate certain environmental cues with the movements required to achieve the goal of the skill. The person makes fewer and less gross errors since he or she has ac-

quired the basic fundamentals or mechanics of the skill, although they need to be improved. Because this type of improvement still is required, Fitts and Posner referred to this stage as a *refining* stage, in which the person focuses on performing the skill successfully and being more consistent from one attempt to the next. During this refining process, performance variability begins to decrease. Also during this associative stage, people acquire the capability to detect and identify some of their own performance errors.

After much practice and experience, which can take many years, some people move into the **autonomous stage** of learning, which is the *final stage* of learning. Here the skill has become almost *automatic,* or habitual. People in this stage do not consciously think about what they are doing while performing the skill, because they can perform it without conscious thought. They often can do another task at the same time; for example, they can carry on a conversation while typing. Performance variability during this stage is very small: skilled people perform the skill consistently well from one attempt to the next. Additionally, these skilled performers can detect their own errors, and make the proper adjustments to correct them. Fitts and Posner pointed out the likelihood that not every person learning a skill will reach this autonomous stage. The quality of instruction and practice as well as the amount of practice are important factors determining achievement of this final stage.

It is important to think of the three stages of the Fitts and Posner model as parts of a continuum of practice time, as figure 4.2–1 depicts. Learners do not make abrupt shifts from one stage to the next. There is a gradual transition or change of the learner's characteristics from stage to stage. Because of this, it is often difficult to detect which stage an individual is in at a particular moment.

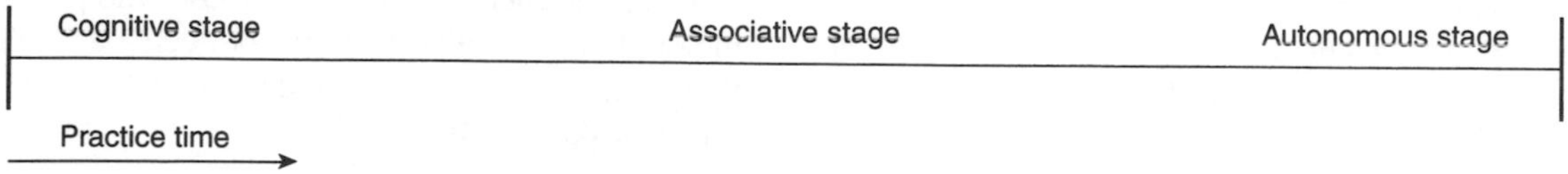

| Cognitive stage | Associative stage | Autonomous stage |

Practice time →

**FIGURE 4.2–1**    The stages of learning from the Fitts and Posner model placed on a time continuum.

However, as we will consider in more detail later in this discussion, the beginner and the skilled performer have distinct characteristics that we can observe and need to understand.

## Gentile's Two-Stage Model

A model that is gaining acceptance in the motor learning literature after many years of being ignored was proposed by Gentile (1972, 1987). She viewed motor skill learning as progressing through two stages. In contrast to Fitts and Posner, Gentile presented these stages from the perspective of the goal of the learner in each stage.

In the *first stage* the goal of the learner is **"getting the idea of the movement."** We can understand the "idea of the movement" in general terms as what the person must do to achieve the goal of the skill. In movement terms, the "idea" involves the *appropriate movement pattern* required for achieving the action goal of the skill. For example, if a person is rehabilitating his or her capability to reach for and grasp a cup, the person's focus in the first stage of learning is on acquiring the appropriate arm and hand coordination that will lead to his or her successfully reaching for and grasping a cup.

In addition to establishing the basic movement pattern, the person also must learn to *discriminate between environmental features* that specify how the movements must be produced and features that do not influence movement production. Gentile referred to these features as regulatory and nonregulatory environmental conditions. You may recall from the discussion in Concept 1.1 of Gentile's taxonomy of motor skills that **regulatory conditions** are characteristics of the performance environment that influence, i.e., regulate, the characteristics of the movements used to perform the skill. In the example of learning to reach for and grasp a cup, the regulatory conditions include information such as the size of the cup, the shape of the cup, the distance the cup is from the person, and so on. On the other hand, there are characteristics of the performance environment that do not influence the movement characteristics of the skill. These are called **nonregulatory conditions.** For example, the color of the cup or the shape of the table the cup is on are nonrelevant pieces of information for reaching for and grasping the cup.

In the *second stage* the learner's goal is described as **fixation/diversification.** During this stage the learner must acquire several characteristics to continue skill improvement. First, the person must develop the capability of *adapting* the movement pattern he or she has acquired in the first stage to the specific demands of any performance situation requiring that skill. Second, the person must increase his or her *consistency* in achieving the goal of the skill. Third, the person must learn to perform the skill with an *economy of effort.*

The terms *fixation* and *diversification* specify that closed and open skills have distinct requirements associated with the accomplishment of these second-stage goals. *Closed skills require fixation.* The person must refine the movement pattern acquired during the first stage so that he or she can correctly and consistently produce this pattern at will. Practice of closed skills during the second stage must give the learner the opportunity to refine the basic movement pattern he or she has acquired in the first stage. Performing *open skills,* on the other hand, *require diversification.* Because learners must adapt to the changing environment in order to perform open skills successfully, during practice in this stage they must focus on developing the capability to modify movement characteristics.

Higgins and Spaeth (1972) nicely illustrated the relationship of closed and open skills to the stages of learning when they analyzed movement patterns a person developed for throwing a dart at stationary and moving targets. Figure 4.2–2 shows schematic representations of the patterns, derived from displacement data for the head, shoulder, elbow, and wrist during throws across 200 practice trials. For throwing at both the stationary and the moving targets, the person developed one basic movement pattern during early practice. However, with further practice, the essential character of each pattern became distinct according to which type of target was involved. For the stationary target, representing a closed skill, the person refined

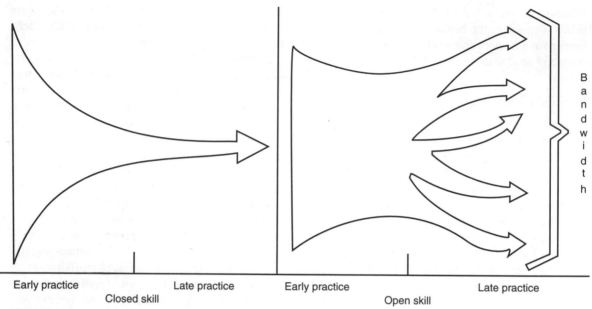

Early practice                    Late practice          Early practice                    Late practice
          Closed skill                                              Open skill

**FIGURE 4.2–2**    Schematic representations by Higgins and Spaeth of the characteristics of displacement patterns developed during practice of closed and open motor skills. For both, the subject develops a basic displacement pattern during early practice. Late practice yields results related to the type of skill. For a closed skill, the subject refines the basic pattern and produces it more consistently in late practice. For an open skill, the basic pattern develops into a well-defined distribution of displacement pattern variations. (From J.R. Higgins and R.A. Spaeth, "Relationship Between Consistency of Movement and Environmental Conditions" in *Quest,* 17:61–69, 1979. Reprinted by permission of the National Association for Physical Education and Higher Education.)

the basic throwing pattern and produced it more consistently. This process is represented by the narrow bandwidth of movement patterns characterizing late practice. In contrast, the movement pattern the person had developed during early practice for throwing at the moving target started to diversify as a function of the target speed. In late practice, a "well-defined distribution of displacement patterns" (p. 66) emerged. These are represented in figure 4.2–2 by the branching arrows in late practice.

## The Coordination and Control Stages Model

Newell (1985) developed a model of skill learning stages that had been suggested earlier by Kugler, Kelso, and Turvey (1980). It has some features similar to those of the Gentile model. The unique-

ness of Newell's model is its focus on the development of coordinated movement. According to this model, skill learning progresses through two stages. Each is labeled according to the primary emphasis of the learner during that stage.

The *first stage* is the *coordination stage.* Here the emphasis is on acquiring the basic coordinated movement pattern needed to accomplish the goal of the action. In this sense, this model is similar to the Gentile model. The *second stage* is the *control stage.* After acquiring the appropriate limb coordination pattern, the person must learn to add to this pattern situation-specific characteristics that will allow him or her to accomplish the action goal in a specific situation. Adding these characteristics is known as *parameterizing the movement pattern.* In movement terms, parameterizing involves adding to the basic movement pattern a specific set of kinematic and kinetic values in accordance to the

---

| A CLOSER LOOK |
|:---:|

## Implications of Gentile's Learning Stages Model for Instruction and Rehabilitation Environments

**DURING THE FIRST STAGE**

- Have the learner focus in practice on developing the basic movement coordination pattern of the skill for both open and closed skills.
- Establish practice situations that provide opportunities to discriminate regulatory from nonregulatory characteristics.

**DURING THE SECOND STAGE**

- **Closed skills**   In practice situations, include characteristics as similar as possible to those the learner will experience in his or her everyday world, or in the environment in which he or she will perform the skill.

  *Examples:*

  walking on similar surfaces in similar environments

  writing with the same type of implement on the same type of surface

shooting basketball free throws as they would occur in a game

shooting arrows under match conditions

- **Open skills**   In practice, systematically vary the controllable regulatory conditions of actual performance situations, while allowing naturally varying characteristics to occur as they normally would.

  *Examples:*

  walking from one end of a hallway to the other while various numbers of people are walking in different directions and at various speeds (systematically vary the hallway size and numbers of people; allow the people to walk at any speed or in any direction they wish)

  returning volleyball serves under game-like conditions (systematically vary the location of the serve, the offensive alignment of players, etc.; the speed and action of the ball will vary at the server's discretion)

---

demands of the performance situation. The person's goal during this second stage, then, is to acquire the capability to parameterize the movement pattern effectively so that he or she can adapt to the unique demands of any performance situation. Additionally, the efficiency with which the person accomplishes the action should increase in this stage, so that he or she performs the skill with a minimum of energy.

While this model of skill learning is similar to the Gentile model, there are two reasons for discussing it. First, it focuses directly on the development of coordination. Second, it has become more popular than the Gentile model among researchers promoting the dynamical systems view of motor control and learning discussed in chapter 2.

## Performer and Performance Changes Across the Stages of Learning

Stages-of-learning models indicate that in each learning stage, both the person and the skill performance show distinct characteristics. In this section, we will look at a few of these characteristics. This overview has two benefits: it provides a closer look at the skill-learning process, and it helps explain why instruction or training strategies need to be developed for people in different learning stages.

*Changes in rate of improvement.*   As a person progresses along the skill-learning continuum from the beginner stage to the highly skilled stage, the *rate* changes at which the person improves.

---

## A CLOSER LOOK

### Calculating the Power Function of the Power Law of Practice

Skill improvement from initial to later practice trials typically follows a mathematical power function, as Snoddy first demonstrated in 1926. A power function is a linear relationship between the logarithm of time and the logarithm of the output. In skill learning, time is the amount of practice and output is the performance measure.

Snoddy proposed this equation:

$$\log C = \log B + n \log x$$

where $C$ is the performance measure, $x$ is the number of trials, and $B$ and $n$ are constants.

This equation means that if the log of the performance measure is plotted against the log of the number of trials, the plot will be a straight line.

---

Although, as figure 4.1–2 shows, there are four different types of performance curves representing different rates of improvement during skill learning, the negatively accelerated pattern is more typical of skill learning than the others. This means that early in practice, a learner usually experiences a large amount of improvement relatively quickly. But as practice continues, the amount of improvement decreases.

Snoddy mathematically formalized this change in the rate of improvement during skill learning in 1926, in a law known as the **power law of practice.** According to this law, early practice is characterized by large amounts of improvement. However, after this seemingly rapid improvement, further practice yields improvement rates that are much smaller. Exactly how long the change in rates takes to occur depends on the skill.

Crossman (1959) performed a classic experiment concerning cigar makers in England to demonstrate the power law of practice. He examined how long it took a worker to produce a cigar as a function of how many cigars the worker had made in her career. Some workers had made 10,000 cigars, while others had made over 10 million. The skill itself was a relatively simple one that could be done very quickly. The first notable thing Crossman found was that workers still showed performance improvement after seven years of experience, during which time they had made over 10 million cigars (see figure 4.2–3). In

addition to this remarkable result, he found evidence of the power law of practice for these workers. As you can see in figure 4.2–3, the majority of all the improvement occurred during the first two years. After that, performance improvement increments were notably smaller.

The difference in rate of improvement between early and later practice is due partly to the amount of improvement possible at a given time. Initially, there is room for a large amount of improvement. The errors people make during early practice trials are large and lead to many unsuccessful attempts at performing the skill. Because many of these errors are easy to correct, the learner can experience a large amount of improvement quickly. However, as practice continues, the amount of improvement possible decreases. The errors people make later in practice are much smaller. As a result, their correction of these errors yields less improvement than they experienced earlier in practice. And certainly from the learner's perspective, attaining notable improvement seems to take longer than it did before.

***Changes in limb-segment coordination.***   When the skill being learned requires the learner to coordinate various segments of a limb, the typical learner will use the common initial strategy of trying to control the many degrees of freedom of the limb segments by holding some joints rigid. Referring to Bernstein's (1967) original thinking about

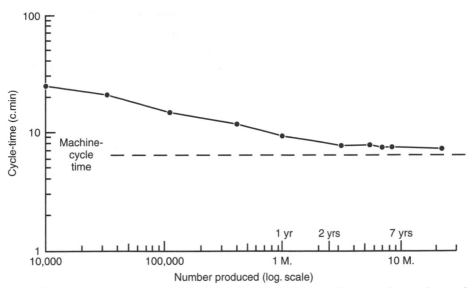

**FIGURE 4.2–3**   The results from the study by Crossman showing the amount of time workers took to make a cigar as a function of the number of cigars made across seven years of experience. Note that both axes are log scales. (From E.R.F.W. Crossman, "A Theory of the Acquisition of Speed Skill" in *Ergonomics,* 1959, 2:153–166. Copyright © 1959 Taylor and Francis, London.)

the development of coordination, some movement scientists have called this strategy **freezing the degrees of freedom** of the limb. For example, the person may move his or her arm like a stick because the elbow joint is locked during the movement, making the two arm segments act as one. But as the person practices the skill, a *freeing of the degrees of freedom* emerges, as the "frozen" limb segments seem to unlock and begin to operate as a coordinated multisegment unit. The segments of this new unit will demonstrate a functional synergy that enables the person to perform the action in a more effective and efficient way.

Researchers have provided evidence for this type of coordination development for a variety of skills. For example, Southard and Higgins (1987) showed that when beginners first tried to perform a racquetball forehand shot, they locked the elbow and wrist joints of the arm. But with practice, these joints began to work together in functionally appropriate ways that led to improved performance. One notable benefit of this acquired synergistic linkage was a dramatic increase in racquet velocity at ball impact.

Anderson and Sidaway (1994) showed a similar performance benefit for coordination development in novice soccer players' kicking. When they first were learning to kick the ball properly, the players constrained the movements of their hip and knee joints. The problem with this strategy is that it limits the velocity that can be generated by the hip joint, because the player cannot use the knee joint effectively. With practice, however, players' kicking velocity increased, as their hip and knee joints acquired greater freedom of movement and increased functional synergy.

The skill of handwriting also has shown these types of segmental relationship changes (Newell and van Emmerik 1989). As figure 4.2–4 shows, when a person began practicing writing his or her name with the nondominant hand (in the equivalent of performance by a beginner), the pen and wrist segments operated as one segment. Note the contrast with segmental operations when the subject was writing with the dominant hand. Subject performance with the highly practiced dominant hand showed an elbow-wrist-pen synergy that permitted effective and efficient writing.

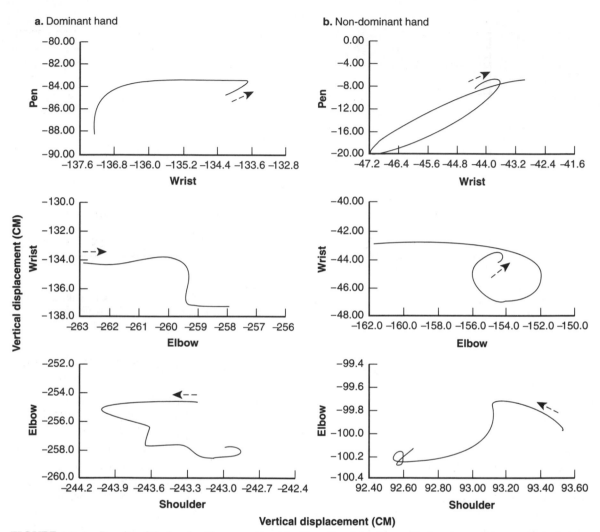

**FIGURE 4.2–4** Results of the handwriting experiment by Newell and van Emmerik showing position-position plots of pairs of pen and joint movements for the same signature written with (a) the dominant and (b) the nondominant hands.
(Reprinted from *Human Movement Science,* Volume 8, K.M. Newell and R.E.A. van Emmerik, "The Acquisition of Coordination: Preliminary Analysis of Learning to Write," pp. 17–32. 1989 with kind permission of Elsevier Science–NL, Sara Burgerharstraat 25, 1055 KV Amsterdam, The Netherlands.)

In a final example, note that these coordination changes are not limited to people acquiring new skills. Stroke patients going through therapy to help them move from sitting to standing and then to sitting again show coordination development characteristics similar to those of people acquiring a new skill (Ada, O'Dwyer, and Neilson 1993). In this experiment, recovering stroke patients progressed from being able to sit-stand-sit without assistance one time to being able to perform this

sequence three times in a row in 10 sec. It is noteworthy that the coordination between the hip and the knee joints showed marked improvement changes as the patients progressed, demonstrating the development of the basic synergy required for these joints to allow unaided standing.

***Changes in altering a preferred coordination pattern.*** Because we have learned to perform a variety of motor skills throughout our lives, we

---

**A CLOSER LOOK**

### Controlling Degrees of Freedom as a Training Strategy in Occupational Therapy

A case study of a 34-year-old hemiplegic woman who had suffered a stroke demonstrates how a therapist can use an understanding of the degrees of freedom problem to develop an occupational therapy regime (Flinn 1995). To increase impaired left-arm strength and function during the first two months of outpatient therapy, the therapist engaged the patient in using the impaired arm to perform several functional tasks for which the degrees of freedom were restricted. To achieve this, the therapist decreased the number of joints involved in the task by stabilizing or eliminating some joints and decreasing the amount of movement of the limb against gravity. For example, the patient used the impaired arm to lock her wheelchair brakes, dust tables, and provide stability while she stood and brushed her teeth using her sound arm. During the next two months, as the patient's left-arm use improved, the therapist increased the degrees of freedom by requiring the control of more joints. For example, initially the patient simply had pushed silverware from the counter into the drawer; now the patient grasped the objects from the counter, lifted them, and placed them in the drawer. Finally, the therapist again increased the degrees of freedom demands a couple of months later. Now the treatment focused specifically on the everyday multiple degrees of freedom tasks the patient would have to perform at her regular workplace.

---

have developed preferred ways of moving. In fact, each of us has developed a rather large repertoire of movement patterns that we prefer to use. When confronted with learning a new skill, we often determine that it resembles a skill we already know how to perform. As a result, we typically begin practicing the new skill using movement characteristics similar to those of the skill we already know. For example, it is common for an experienced baseball player to use a swing resembling baseball batting when he or she first practices hitting a golf ball.

When a person is learning a new skill that requires altering an established coordination pattern, an interesting transition from old to new pattern occurs. The experiment by Lee, Swinnen, and Verschueren (1995) that we discussed in Concept 4.1 provides a good example of this change. Recall that participants had to learn to bimanually move two levers simultaneously in a 90° out-of-phase arm movement relationship in order to draw ellipses on the computer monitor. Figure 4.1–4 showed that when they first were confronted with this task, the participants' preferred way of coordinating their arms was to move both arms at the same time, producing diagonal patterns. The influence of this stable preferred pattern remained for more than 60 practice trials. Participants did not produce the new coordination pattern consistently until they had performed 180 practice trials. Instability characterized the coordination patterns they produced on trials between these two demonstrations of stable patterns.

The Lee et al. experiment demonstrates several things. First, it shows that people approach skill-learning situations with distinct movement pattern biases that they may need to overcome to achieve the goal of the skill to be learned. Second, it is possible for people to overcome these biases, but often this takes a lot of practice (the actual amount varies among people). Finally, an observable pattern of stability-instability-stability characterizes the transition between production of the preferred movement pattern and production of the goal pattern. The initially preferred and the newly acquired goal movement patterns are distinguished by unique but stable kinematic characteristics over repeated performances. However, during the transition period between these stable patterns, the limb kinematics are very irregular or unstable.

## A CLOSER LOOK

### Muscle Activation Changes During Dart-Throwing Practice

An experiment by Jaegers et al. (1989) illustrates how the sequence and timing of muscle activation reorganizes as a function of practice so that a person can make consistent and accurate dart throws. Individuals who were inexperienced in dart throwing made 45 throws at a target on each of three successive days. Several arm and shoulder muscles were monitored by EMG.

The three muscles primarily involved in stabilizing the arm and upper body were the anterior deltoid, latissimus dorsi, and, clavicular pectoralis. On the first day, these muscles erratically activated both before and after the dart release. But at the end of the last day, these muscles followed a specific sequence of

activation initiation. The clavicular pectoralis and anterior deltoid muscles became active approximately 40 to 80 msec prior to the dart release and turned off at release. The latissimus dorsi became active just before the release and remained active for 40 msec after release. Then, the anterior deltoid became active again.

The primary muscle involved in producing the forearm-extension-based throwing action was the lateral triceps. During the initial practice trials, this muscle initiated activation erratically, before and after dart release. But by the end of the third day, it consistently initiated activation approximately 60 msec prior to dart release and remained active until just after release.

---

People who provide skill instruction should note that this transition period can be a difficult and frustrating time for the learner. The instructor or therapist who is aware of this can be influential in helping the person work through this transition stage. One helpful strategy is providing extra motivational encouragements to keep the person effectively engaged in practice.

***Changes in muscles used to perform the skill.*** If practicing a skill results in coordination pattern changes, we should expect a related change in the muscles a person uses while performing the skill. EMG patterns produced while people practiced skills have shown that early in practice a person uses his or her muscles inappropriately. Two characteristics are particularly noteworthy. First, more muscles than are needed commonly are involved. Second, the timing of the firing of the involved muscle groups is incorrect. As a person continues to practice, the amount of muscle involvement decreases, so that eventually a minimal number of muscles needed to produce the action arc activated, and the timing of firing patterns becomes appropriate.

Researchers have provided evidence showing these types of change during practice for a variety

of physical activities. For example, muscle activation changes occur as people learn sport skills such as the single-knee circle mount on the horizontal bar in gymnastics (Kamon and Gormley 1968), ball throwing to a target (Vorro, Wilson, and Dainis 1978), and dart throwing (Jaegers et al. 1989). Also, researchers have shown muscle activation differences resulting from practice in laboratory tasks, such as complex, rapid arm-movement and manual aiming tasks (Schneider et al. 1989), as well as simple, rapid arm-extension tasks (Moore and Marteniuk 1986).

The change in muscle use that occurs while a person learns a skill reflects a reorganization of the motor control system as that skill is acquired. As Bernstein (1967) first proposed, this reorganization results from the need for the motor control system to solve the degrees of freedom problem it confronts when the person first attempts the skill. By structuring muscle activation appropriately, the motor control system can take advantage of physical properties of the environment, such as gravity or other basic physical laws. By doing this, the motor control system reduces the amount of work it has to do and establishes a base for successful skill performance.

*Changes in movement efficiency.* Since the performer and performance changes we have described in the preceding sections occur as a result of practicing a skill, then we can reasonably expect that the amount of energy a person uses while performing the skill should change with practice as well. While there has been little empirical study of this effect, evidence supports this expectation. Economy of movement refers to minimizing the energy cost of performing a skill. Beginners expend a large amount of energy (have a high energy cost), whereas skilled performers perform more efficiently, with a minimum expenditure of energy.[1]

Several energy sources have been associated with performing skills. One is the physiological energy involved in skilled performance; researchers identify this by measuring the amount of oxygen a person uses while performing a skill. They also determine physiological energy use by measuring the caloric cost of performing the skill. People also expended mechanical energy while performing; scientists determine this by dividing the work rate by the metabolic rate of the individual. As we learn a skill, changes in the amount of energy we use occur for each of these sources. The result is that we perform with greater efficiency; in other words, our energy cost decreases as our movements become more economical.

Scientists have been accumulating research evidence only recently to support the widely held assumption that movement efficiency increases as a result of practicing a skill. For example, *oxygen use* decreased for people learning to perform on a complex slalom ski simulator in 20-min practice sessions over a period of five days (Durand et al. 1994). Sparrow and Irrizary-Lopez (1987) offered evidence that *caloric costs* decrease with practice of a motor skill for persons learning to walk on their hands and feet (crawling) on a treadmill moving at a constant speed. And Heise (1995) showed *mechanical efficiency* to increase as a function of practice for people learning to perform a ball-throwing task.

1. Note that many prefer the term *economy* to *efficiency;* see Cavanagh and Kram (1985).

*Changes in achieving the kinematic goals of the skill.* Kinematic characteristics define the spatial and temporal features of performing a skill. Skilled performance has certain displacement, velocity, and acceleration limb-movement-pattern goals. As a person practices a skill, he or she not only becomes more successful in achieving these goals, but also acquires these kinematic goals at different times during practice, although in the same sequence. Displacement is the first kinematic goal persons achieve, indicating that spatial characteristics of a skill are the first ones people successfully acquire. The next goal people achieve is velocity; this is followed by acceleration.

Marteniuk and Romanow (1983) demonstrated this systematic progression of kinematic goal acquisition in an experiment that we briefly introduced in Concept 4.1. Participants practiced moving a horizontal lever back and forth to produce a complex displacement pattern (shown in figure 4.1–3). During 800 trials of practice, they became increasingly more accurate and consistent at producing the criterion pattern. An evaluation of the kinematic performance measures showed that the participants subjects first achieved accuracy and consistency with the displacement characteristics. Then they acquired the velocity and finally the acceleration characteristics as practice progressed.

*Changes in visual attention.* Because vision plays a key role in the learning and control of skills, it is interesting to note how the use of vision changes as a function of practicing a skill. Because we discussed most of these changes at length in Concept 2.2, we will mention them only briefly here. Beginners typically look at too many things; this tendency leads them frequently to direct their visual attention at inappropriate environmental cues. As a person practices a skill, he or she directs visual attention toward sources of information that are more appropriate for guiding his or her performance. In other words, the person gains an increased capability to direct his or her vision to the regulatory features in the environment that will provide the most useful information for performing

---

A CLOSER LOOK

## Changes in Conscious Attention Demands Resulting from Practice

An experiment by Leavitt (1979) for skating and stickhandling skills in ice hockey is an excellent example of how conscious attention demands change as a result of long-term practice. Subjects were players from hockey programs in six different age groups, ranging from pre-novice through university varsity. Each player had to skate and/or stickhandle under four conditions: skating only, skating while identifying geometric figures shown on a screen, skating while stickhandling a puck, and skating while both stickhandling a puck and identifying geometric figures.

Skating speed was the primary skill. Results showed that for players with less than one year of experience, skating speed slowed dramatically when they were simultaneously either stickhandling or identifying figures. In fact, it took eight years of experience before players could skate, stickhandle, and identify figures at the same time without slowing their skating speed. During the intervening years, the players showed systematic improvements in skating speed while doing the other skills, although their doing one or both of the other skills still affected their skating speed.

---

the skill. Also, people get better at appropriately directing their visual attention earlier during the time course of performing a skill. This timing aspect of directing visual attention is important because it increases the time available in which the person can select and produce an action required by the situation.

***Changes in conscious attention when performing a skill.*** According to the Fitts and Posner learning stages model, early in practice the learner consciously thinks about almost every part of performing the skill. But as the person practices the skill and becomes more proficient, the amount of conscious attention he or she directs to performing the skill itself diminishes to the point at which he or she performs it almost automatically.

We see an everyday example of this change in the process of learning to shift gears in a standard-shift car. If you have learned to drive a standard-shift car, you undoubtedly remember how you approached shifting gears when you first learned to do so. Each part of the maneuver required your conscious attention. You thought about each part of the entire sequence of movements: when to lift off the accelerator, when to push in the clutch, how to coordinate your leg movements to carry out these clutch and accelerator actions, when and where to move the gear shift, when to let out the clutch, and

finally, when to depress the accelerator again. But what happened as you became a more experienced driver? Eventually, you performed all these movements without conscious attention. In fact, you undoubtedly found that you were able to do something else at the same time, such as carry on a conversation or sing along with the radio. You would have had great difficulty doing any of these things while shifting when you were first learning to drive.

***Changes in error detection and correction capability.*** Another performance characteristic that improves during practice is the capability to identify and correct one's own movement errors. An individual can use this capability either during or after the performance of the skill, depending on the time constraints involved. If the movements are slow enough, a person can correct or modify an ongoing movement while the action is occurring. For example, if a person grasps a cup and brings it to the mouth to drink from it, he or she can make some adjustments along the way that will allow him or her to accomplish each phase of this action successfully. However, for rapid movements, such as initiating and carrying out a swing at a baseball, a person often cannot make the correction in time during the execution of the swing, because the ball

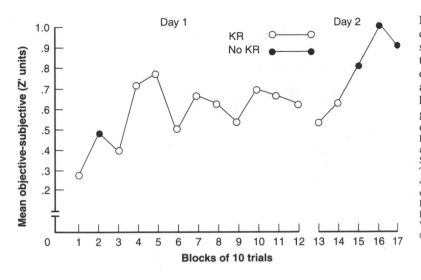

**FIGURE 4.2–5** Results from the experiment by Schmidt and White showing the correlation between the participants' estimates of their error (subjective error) and their actual error (objective error) when knowledge of results (KR) was given or withheld during 170 trials of practice over two days. (From R.A. Schmidt and J. L. White, "Evidence for an Error Correction Mechanism in Motor Skills: A Test of Adam's Closed-Loop Theory," in *Journal of Motor Behavior,* 4:143–152. 1972. Reprinted with permission of the Helen Dwight Reid Educational Foundation. Published by Heldref Publications, 1319 Eighteenth Street, NW, Washington, DC 20036–1802. Copyright © 1972.)

has moved past a hittable location by the time the person makes the correction. For both types of skills, performers can use errors they detect during their performance to guide future attempts.

An experiment by Schmidt and White (1972) demonstrates the development of this error detection and correction capability. The authors required participants to learn to move a lever 9 inches in 150 msec. Notice from figure 4.2–5 that early in practice there was a low correlation (.30) between the participants' actual performance error and their own estimates of that error. However, after 140 practice trials, this correlation had risen to above .90. But the authors found even more convincing evidence of how well these people had acquired the capability to detect and correct their own error: they continued to demonstrate accurate error estimation capability even after the researchers no longer told them their actual error after each trial.

## Expertise

If a person practices a skill long enough and has the right kind of instruction, he or she eventually may become skilled enough to be an *expert*. On the learning stages continuum we presented earlier in this discussion (see figure 4.2–1), the expert is a person who is located at the extreme right end. This person is in an elite group of people who are

exceptional and outstanding performers. Although motor skill expertise is a relatively new area of study in motor learning and control research, we know that experts have distinct characteristics. Most of our knowledge about experts in the motor skills domain relates to athletes, dancers, and musicians. Although they are in seemingly diverse fields, experts in these skill performance areas have some similar characteristics. Some of these will be examined next.

***Amount and type of practice leading to expertise.*** In an extensive study of experts from a diverse number of fields, Ericsson, Krampe, and Tesch-Romer (1993) reported that expertise in all fields is the result of *intense practice for a minimum of ten years.* Critical to achieving expertise is not only the length of time in which the person practices intensely, but also the type of practice. According to Ericsson and his colleagues, the specific type of intense practice a person needs to achieve expertise in any field is *deliberate practice.* During this type of practice, the person receives optimal instruction, as well as engaging in intense, worklike practice for hours each day. As the person develops toward expertise, he or she begins to need personalized training, or supervision of the practice regime.

## A CLOSER LOOK

### Four Phases of Achieving Expertise

Ericsson, Krampe, and Tesch-Romer (1993) noted these phases in the achievement of expertise.

1. Introduction to the activity; formal instruction and practice begin.
2. Continuation of instruction and practice; phase ends with a commitment to do the activity full-time.

3. Commitment to improve performance while engaged full-time in the activity.
4. Achievement of knowledge and capabilities beyond the teacher's; person becomes an eminent performer.

A characteristic of expertise that emerges from the length and intensity of practice required to achieve expertise in a field is this: *expertise is domain specific* (see Ericsson and Smith 1991). This means that characteristics of experts are specific to the field in which they have attained this level of success. There is little transfer of the capabilities in the field of expertise to another field in which the person has no experience.

*Experts' knowledge structure.* A notable characteristic common to expert skill performers is that they know more about an activity than nonexperts do. More important, this expert knowledge is structured quite differently, as well. Research investigating experts in a number of diverse skills, such as chess, computer programming, bridge, and basketball, has shown that the expert has developed his or her knowledge about the activity into more organized concepts and is better able to interrelate the concepts. The expert's knowledge structure also is characterized by more decision rules, which he or she uses in deciding how to perform in specific situations. Additionally, because of the way the knowledge is structured, the expert can remember more information from one observation or presentation. The benefit of these knowledge structure characteristics is that they enable the expert to solve problems and make decisions faster and more accurately than a nonexpert can, and to adapt to novel environments more easily. For example, an expert basketball player bringing the ball down the floor can look

at one or two players on the other team and know which type of defense the team is using; he or she then can make decisions about whether to pass, dribble, or shoot. The beginner would need to take much more time to make these same decisions because he or she would need to look at more players to obtain the same information.

*Experts' use of vision.* When experts perform an activity, they use vision in more advantageous ways than nonexperts do. We discussed many of these characteristics in Concept 2.2. For example, experts search their environment faster, give more attention to this search, and select more meaningful information in less time. Also, experts do not need as much environmental information for decision making, primarily because they "see" more when they look somewhere. Undoubtedly due in part to their superior visual search and decision-making capabilities, experts can use visual information better than nonexperts to anticipate the actions of others. And experts recognize patterns in the environment sooner than nonexperts do. Experts achieve these vision characteristics after many years of experience performing a skill; studies have shown the characteristics to be a function more of experience than of better visual acuity or eyesight.

## Summary

Learning is a process that involves time and practice. As an individual moves from being a beginner in an activity to being a highly skilled performer, he or she progresses through several distinct, although continuous, stages. Three different models attempt to describe these stages. Fitts and Posner proposed that the learner progresses through three stages: the cognitive, the associative, and the autonomous stages. Gentile proposed two stages, which she identified in terms of the goal of the learner. The learner's goal in the first stage is "getting the idea of the movement." In the second stage, the learner's goal is fixation or diversification for closed and open skills, respectively. The third model, proposed by Newell, is closely related to Gentile's, but focuses on the development of coordination. According to this model, the first stage is the coordination stage, in which the basic pattern of coordination is established. The second stage is the control stage. During this stage, the performer learns to apply to the coordination pattern the movement parameter values he or she requires to achieve optimal performance of the skill in various situations.

As people progress through the learning stages, distinct performer and performance changes are notable. We have discussed several here: changes in the rate of improvement, coordination characteristics, the muscles involved in performing the skill, movement efficiency, the achievement of the kinematic goals of the skill, visual attention, conscious attention, and the learner's capability of detecting and correcting errors.

Finally, we discussed the expert end of the learning continuum. Experts are characterized by exceptional performance. They take a minimum of ten years of deliberate practice to achieve expertise. These highly skilled people have common performance characteristics in their use of vision and in their knowledge structures, which provide the basis for their exceptional performance capability.

## Related Readings

Abernethy, B., K. T. Thomas, and J. T. Thomas. 1993. Strategies for improving understanding of motor expertise [or mistakes we have made and things we have learned!!]. In J. L. Starkes and F. Allard (Eds.), *Cognitive issues in motor expertise* (pp. 317–56). Amsterdam: Elsevier.

Allard, F., and J. L. Starkes. 1991. Motor-skill experts in sports, dance, and other domains. In K. A. Ericsson and J. Smith (Eds.), *Toward a general theory of expertise: Prospects and limits* (pp. 126–52). Cambridge, England: Cambridge University Press.

Beek, P. J., and A. A. M. van Santvoord. 1992. Learning the cascade juggle: A dynamical systems analysis. *Journal of Motor Behavior* 24: 85–94.

Sanders, R. H., and J. B. Allen. 1993. Changes in net joint torques during accommodation to change in surface compliance in a drop jumping task. *Human Movement Science* 12: 299–326.

Schöner, G., P. Zanone, and J. A. S. Kelso. 1992. Learning as change of coordination dynamics: Theory and experiment. *Journal of Motor Behavior* 24: 29–48.

Summers, J. J., S. K. Ford, and J. A. Todd. 1993. Practice effects on the coordination of the two hands in a bimanual tapping task. *Human Movement Science* 12: 111–33.

Vereijken, B., R. E. A. van Emmerik, H. T. A. Whiting, and K. M. Newell. 1992. Free(z)ing degrees of freedom in skill acquisition. *Journal of Motor Behavior* 24: 133–42.

# CONCEPT 4.3

Transfer of learning from one performance situation to another
is an integral part of skill learning and performance

## Key Terms

transfer of
   learning
positive
   transfer
negative
   transfer
intertask
   transfer
percentage of
   transfer

savings score
intratask
   transfer
identical
   elements
   theory
transfer-
   appropriate
   processing

bilateral
   transfer
asymmetric
   transfer
symmetric
   transfer

## Application

Why do we practice a skill? One reason is to increase our capability of performing the skill in a situation requiring it. We want to be able to accomplish specific action goals when we need to when we perform everyday skills like walking or drinking from a cup, as well as sport skills. For example, if your goal is to get up from the chair you are sitting in and walk to the television to turn it off, you will want to perform the required actions without problems. Similarly, if your goal is to pitch well for your baseball team, you will need to perform well the skills involved in pitching a baseball. To achieve goals like these, we practice the skills we need to perform the appropriate actions involved in accomplishing these goals.

These skill performance examples involve an important motor learning concept known as *transfer of learning*. This concept lies at the very heart of understanding the processes underlying skill learning. An important focus of this concept is the capability we acquire through experience to perform a skill in some novel situation. We want to be able to do what we have done before in any new situation we may experience. This suggests, then, that one of the goals of practicing a skill is developing the capability to transfer performance of the skill from the practice environment to some other environment in which the individual must perform the skill, so that he or she can achieve the same action goal.

Consider this point in light of the examples we have just described. If you were working with a stroke patient, you would want the hours of rehabilitation to help that person be able to successfully walk from a chair in his or her living room to the television set to turn it off. In terms of transfer of learning, this example illustrates that an important goal of the rehabilitation experience is to help the patient develop the capability to transfer the skill acquired in the clinic to his or her everyday world. Similarly, if you were working with a baseball pitcher, you would want that person to be able to pitch effectively in a game, and not just in a practice environment.

## Discussion

*Transfer of learning* is one of the most universally applied principles of learning in education and rehabilitation. In educational systems, this principle is the foundation for curriculum and instruction

development, because it provides the basis for arranging the sequence in which the students will learn skills. In the rehabilitation clinic, this principle forms the basis for the systematic approaches to protocols that therapists develop and implement. Because of the widespread importance of transfer of learning, you must have an understanding of this learning phenomenon as part of your conceptual foundation for studying motor learning.

In Concept 4.1, we used the concept of transfer of learning when we discussed transfer tests as a method of assessing learning. Those tests are in fact based on the transfer of learning principle. That discussion provided you with a good basis for the present discussion, which will provide you with an understanding of the transfer of learning principle itself.

## What Is Transfer of Learning?

Learning researchers generally define **transfer of learning** as the influence of previous experience on performing a skill in a new context or on learning a new skill. This influence may be positive, negative, or neutral (zero). **Positive transfer** occurs when experience with a skill aids or facilitates performance of the skill in a new context or learning of a new skill. Each of the examples we used at the beginning of this Concept involved positive transfer. **Negative transfer** occurs when experience with a skill hinders or interferes with performance of the skill in a new context or learning of a new skill. For example, a person who has learned the forehand in tennis before learning the forehand in badminton often experiences some initial negative transfer for learning the mechanics of the stroke. The badminton forehand is a wrist snap, whereas the tennis forehand requires a relatively firm wrist. The third type of transfer of learning effect is *zero transfer,* which occurs when experience with a skill has no influence on performance of the skill in a new context or learning of a new skill. Obviously, there is no transfer from learning to swim to learning to drive a car. Nor can we assume that experience with some motor skills will always have an influence on learning new motor skills.

## Why Is Transfer of Learning Important?

We pointed out earlier that the principle of transfer of learning forms the basis for educational curriculum development and instructional methodology, as well as for the development and implementation of systematic approaches to rehabilitation protocols. Thus, from a practical point of view, the transfer principle is very significant. But the transfer principle also has theoretical significance, since it helps us to understand processes underlying the learning and control of motor skills.

*Sequencing skills to be learned.* The sequencing of mathematics skills provides a very useful practical example of the transfer principle. The school curriculum from grades 1 through 12 is based on a simple-to-complex arrangement. Teachers must present numeral identification, numeral writing, numeral value identification, addition, subtraction, multiplication, and division in this specific sequence, because each concept is based on the preceding one. A person presented with a division problem before having learned addition, subtraction, or multiplication would have to learn those skills before completing the problem. We do not teach algebra before basic arithmetic. We do not reach trigonometry before geometry.

We can make the same point about skills taught in a physical education program, a sports program, or a rehabilitation clinic. Those who develop a curriculum or a protocol should take advantage of the transfer of learning principle when they sequence skills. Learners should acquire basic or foundational skills *before* more complex skills that require mastery of these basic skills. In other words, there should be a logical progression of skill experiences. An instructor should decide when to introduce a skill by determining how the learning of that skill will benefit the learning of other skills. If the instructor does not use this approach, time is wasted while people "go back" to learn prerequisite basic skills.

Gentile's taxonomy of motor skills (discussed in Concept 1.1) provides a good example of how the transfer principle can be implemented in a training regime. That taxonomy presents sixteen categories of skills, systematically sequenced from less to more complex according to specific skill characteristics (see table 1.1–1). One use for this taxonomy is as a guide to help the therapist select functionally appropriate activities for a rehabilitation patient after making a clinical evaluation of the patient's motor function problems. Gentile based this taxonomy on the principle of positive transfer. She organized the sequence of activities by listing first the activities that a person must perform before performing more complex or difficult ones. The therapist can select appropriate functional activities for a rehabilitation regime by starting with activities related to the taxonomy category in which the therapist identified the skill performance deficit. Then, the therapist can increase activity complexity by moving up the taxonomy from that point.

***Instructional methods.***   The second important practical application of the transfer of learning principle to motor skill instruction is in the area of instructional methods. For example, an instructor might use dry land drills when teaching students the basic swimming strokes, before letting them try the strokes in the water. Such an instructor assumes that there will be positive transfer from the dry land drills to the performance of the strokes in water.

There are numerous other examples of incorporating the transfer principle in instructional settings. It is common, for example, to practice a part of a skill before practicing the entire skill (we will discuss this practice method in Concept 6.4). Sometimes an instructor simplifies an activity for a person before requiring the person to perform the skill in its actual context; for example, the coach has a person hit a baseball from a batting tee before hitting a moving ball. If the skill being acquired involves an element of danger, the instructor often allows the person to perform the skill with some type of aid so that the danger is removed. For example, a therapist provides physical assistance to a patient who is learning to get out of bed and into a wheelchair, so that the patient will not fall when first practicing this skill.

***Assessing the effectiveness of practice conditions.***   When an instructor or therapist designs a practice regime, he or she also must assess the effectiveness of that regime. A transfer test can

provide such an assessment effectively. In fact, when an instructor or therapist is comparing the effectiveness of several practice conditions, he or she should identify the one that leads to the best transfer test performance as the preferred practice condition, and implement that one in a training or rehabilitation protocol. Thus, the principle of transfer of learning comes into play once again, as it provides the basis for assessing the effectiveness of the practice conditions an instructor selects to facilitate skill learning.

Bransford, Franks, Morris, and Stein (1979) underscored the importance of the transfer basis for assessing the effectiveness of practice conditions several years ago, when they were addressing a related issue. They asserted that *the effectiveness of any practice condition should be determined only on the basis of how the practiced skill is performed in a "test" context.* This means that if we are deciding whether one procedure is superior to another to facilitate skill learning, we should not reach a conclusion until we have observed the skill in a test performance situation.

We can think of the "test" referred to here in several ways. It may be a specific skills test, where a person performs the practiced skill in a test constructed for that skill. In another type of test, the person performs the practiced skill in an everyday functional environment. Or, the test may require the person to use the skill in an organized competition or game. The point is that regardless of the exact nature of the test, the person's performance in the test itself should be the only measure of the effectiveness of any practice condition.

## Assessing How Much Transfer Has Occurred

Before considering the theoretical implications of the transfer of learning principle, we should become acquainted with the ways to assess transfer. In Concept 4.1, we presented examples of ways to use transfer tests to make appropriate inferences about the learning that has resulted from practice. The goal of such tests is to help the therapist or instructor make a general inference about performance

---

### A CLOSER LOOK

#### Benefits of Dry Land Training for Scuba Skills

An experiment by John Brady (1979) provides an interesting illustration of the way a skill training context can take advantage of the positive transfer phenomenon. Certified scuba divers were required to assemble as fast as possible underwater a complex mechanical device known as the UCLA Pipe Puzzle, developed for the U.S. Navy. This assembly task involved eight subtasks and required the use of a box-end wrench. Two groups of divers watched and participated in a demonstration of the assembly task. One group then practiced assembling the device one time on dry land before attempting to perform the task underwater. Another group received additional dry land practice by performing eight assembly trials before doing the task underwater. The results indicated that the group with extra dry land practice performed the task underwater significantly faster than the other group. Thus, the dry land practice facilitated (i.e., positively transferred to) the divers' underwater performance of assembling the complex mechanical device. From an instructional perspective, the results of this experiment show that the generally safer and less expensive dry land practice facilitates task performance underwater, while decreasing underwater training time.

---

adaptability resulting from learning. While the approach described in that discussion provides an appropriate means of achieving the learning inference goal, such an assessment does not provide information about how much transfer has occurred. The type of assessment procedure to use depends on the type of transfer situation involved.

*Assessing intertask transfer.*   Researchers use the **intertask transfer** experimental design to assess the influence of experience with one skill on the performance of a new skill, with the new skill either a different skill or a variation of the first one. This type of design is particularly well suited for assessing how well a practice condition prepares a person to adapt what he or she has learned to perform a novel variation of the practiced skill.

The simplest and most frequently used experimental design to assess intertask transfer is as follows:

| | | |
|---|---|---|
| *Experimental group* | Practice task A | Perform task B |
| *Control group* | No practice | Perform task B |

Performance on task B by both groups is the result of interest in this experimental design. If ex-perience with task A facilitated the learning or performing of task B, then the experimental group would show more rapid improvement on task B than the control group. On the other hand, if experience with task A interfered with the learning or performing of task B, then the experimental group would take longer to learn task B or show hindered performance of task B when compared to the control group.

*To quantify the amount of intertask transfer,* researchers have proposed various methods. Two of the more frequently used have been percentage of transfer and savings score. The **percentage of transfer** is the percentage of improvement on the new task (task B) that is attributable to having performed the first task (task A). A high percentage of transfer would indicate a strong influence of task A on task B, while a low percentage would suggest a much smaller, though positive, influence. The **savings score** is the amount of *practice time saved* learning the novel task (task B) because of prior experience with another task (task A). Researchers can use this score to show that the task A experience saved a quantity of practice trials on task B. For example, if the experimental group reached a criterion of 100 points on task B in 20 trials while the control group took 30 trials to do so, the savings score would be 10 trials.

---

**A CLOSER LOOK**

### Calculating the Percentage of Transfer

**INTERTASK TRANSFER**

Note that the scores used in this calculation should be the initial performance on task B.

$$\text{Percentage of Transfer} = \frac{\text{Experimental Group} - \text{Control Group}}{\text{Experimental Group} + \text{Control Group}} \times 100$$

**INTRATASK TRANSFER**

Use the same principle expressed in the formula to calculate intertask transfer. However, use the initial performance scores from condition C. Two separate calculations are required: one to determine the percentage of transfer from practicing under condition A, and one to determine it from practicing under condition B.

$$\text{Percentage of Transfer due to Practicing A} = \frac{C_A - C_B}{C_A + C_B} \times 100$$

$$\text{Percentage of Transfer due to Practicing B} = \frac{C_B - C_A}{C_A + C_B} \times 100$$

---

For practical applications, the savings score has particular merit. This is especially true when an instructor wants to know whether or not a training procedure effectively aids the learning of a skill or performance of that skill in a real context. The savings score would indicate how much time spent practicing the skill itself the procedure could save. If no practice time were saved, the instructor would have some concern about its continued use.

*Assessing intratask transfer.* The **intratask transfer** experimental design is best suited to compare how different types of practice conditions enable a person to adapt a practiced skill in order to perform this same skill in a novel context. The basic research paradigm to assess intratask transfer is this:

| Group A | Practice condition A | Perform in condition C |
| Group B | Practice condition B | Perform in condition C |

Three questions are important to answer when we analyze the intratask transfer experimental design. First, how did performance under practice conditions A and B compare? Second, how did the two groups compare when performing under condition C? Third, did each group improve, get worse, or show no change in performance from the last practice trial to the first transfer trial? Researchers often overlook this last question. Its importance becomes evident when groups show different performance levels on the transfer trials than they did during the practice trials.

To quantify the amount of transfer involved in intratask transfer, we can calculate both the percentage of transfer and the savings score measures. The savings score calculation is the same as that used to find intertask transfer.

## Why Does Positive Transfer of Learning Occur?

The theoretical significance of the concept of transfer of learning becomes evident as we attempt to determine why transfer occurs. For example, if we know why transfer occurs, we have a better understanding of what a person learns about a skill that enables the person to adapt to the performance requirements of a new situation. This kind of knowledge helps learning theorists understand such things as what people learn and what accounts for the adaptability that typically characterizes learned skills.

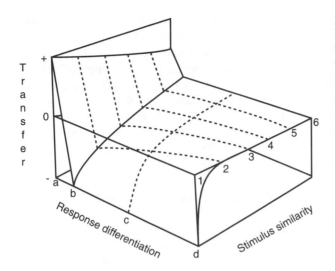

**FIGURE 4.3–1** The transfer surface proposed by Holding showing the expected transfer between two tasks in terms of the similarity or difference of characteristics of stimulus and response aspects of the skills. Holding predicts maximum positive transfer when the stimulus and response characteristics are identical, and negative transfer when the stimuli for the two tasks are identical but the two responses are completely different from each other. (From D. Holding, "An Approximate Transfer Surface" in *Journal of Motor Behavior,* 8:1–9, 1976. Reprinted with permission of the Helen Dwight Reid Educational Foundation. Published by Heldref Publications, 1319 Eighteenth Street, NW, Washington, DC 20036–1802. Copyright © 1976.)

Although researchers have proposed several reasons over the years to explain why transfer of learning occurs, we will discuss only two of the more popular hypotheses here. Both consider the similarities between the two situations to be critical for explaining transfer. However, the two hypotheses differ in their explanations of what similarities account for transfer. One hypothesis proposes that transfer of learning occurs because the components of the skills and/or the context in which skills are performed are similar. The other proposes that transfer occurs primarily because of similarities between the amounts and types of learning processes required.

*Similarity of skill and context components.* The more traditional view of why positive transfer occurs contends that transfer is due to the similarity between the components of two skills or of two performance situations. In this view, the more similar the component parts of two skills or two performance situations are, the greater will be the amount of positive transfer between them. Therefore, we would expect the amount of transfer between the tennis serve and the volleyball serve to be greater than that between the tennis serve and the racquetball serve. We likewise would expect a high degree of transfer to occur when practice conditions emphasized performance characteristics similar to those required in a "test" situation. In a clinical situation, for example, this means that therapy protocols that involved functional rehabilitation procedures would lead to a high degree of transfer to the performance of a skill in its everyday context.

This view has its roots in some of the earliest motor learning research, which Thorndike did at Columbia University in the early part of the 1900s. To account for transfer effects, Thorndike (1914) proposed the **identical elements theory.** In this theory, "elements" are general characteristics of a skill or performance context—such as the purpose of the skill or the attitude of the person performing the skill—or specific characteristics of the skill, such as components of the skill being performed. Additionally, Thorndike considered identical elements to include mental processes that shared the same brain cell activity as the physical action.

Work by Holding (1976, 1987) best represents the present-day versions of Thorndike's view as they relate to motor skills. Holding proposed that the amount and direction of transfer is related to the *similarity of the stimulus and the response aspects* of two skills. This means that the more similar both the stimuli and the responses are, the more transfer will occur between the skills. To formalize this relationship, Holding (1976) developed a "transfer surface" (see figure 4.3–1) to predict the type and amount of transfer to expect given the stimulus and response characteristics of two skills. Holden's model predicts maximum positive transfer when the stimulus (S) and the response (R) for one task are the same as for the second task. As the stimuli decrease in similarity, transfer progresses toward 0.

To apply the Holding transfer surface to specific motor skills, it is helpful to adapt the terms *stimulus* and *response* to more appropriate skill performance characteristics. We can think of elements along the stimulus dimension as the *perceptual input requirements of actions*. Some examples are visual sources of environmental information, such as object shape or speed; these are particularly important in defining regulatory conditions that guide action. Other examples are context characteristics of the performance environment, such as the regularity or randomness of objects, which provide perceptual cues that influence skill performance. Elements along the response dimension involve those movement characteristics that define the *basic movement pattern* required to produce an action. In particular, kinematic features of skills are included along this dimension. The more similar two skill are in the characteristics of either or both of these two skill dimensions, the more positive transfer we would expect between the skills.

***Similarity of processing requirements.*** The second hypothesis explaining why positive transfer occurs proposes that it results from the *similarity of learning or performance process characteristics* required by the two skills or two performance situations. This hypothesis finds its clearest expression in the view that explains transfer effects in terms of transfer-appropriate processing (see Lee 1988). This view maintains that although similarity in skill and context components explains some transfer effects, it cannot explain all transfer effects. A key point of the **transfer-appropriate-processing** view is the similarity between the learning or performance processes required by the two performance situations. In this view, two components of positive transfer are critical: what a person must do to be successful in performing the transfer task, and the similarity between that activity and the activity required during the training experience.

An example of transfer-appropriate processing occurs when the transfer task requires a person to engage in problem-solving activity. For positive transfer to occur between the training and transfer tasks, the training task also must involve problem-solving activity. Damos and Wickens (1980) provided a demonstration of transfer resulting from similar processing activities in the training and the test situations. They showed that even when training and transfer task characteristics were not similar, positive transfer resulted when they trained people to do two tasks simultaneously. The interesting feature of this situation was that the transfer task was a two-hand tracking task, while the training tasks were dual-task cognitive tasks. According to the view requiring similarity between task components, no transfer should have occurred. However, the similarity between the processing demands of the training tasks and those of the transfer tasks led to positive transfer between them.

***Merit in both hypotheses.*** Although much remains unknown about the cause of transfer of learning, evidence points to the value of both hypotheses in accounting for transfer effect. Clearly, we can expect the amount of positive transfer to increase as a function of increasing similarity between skills and performance contexts. It appears that the similarity-of-processing view is actually an extension of the components view that comes into play only when skill components and context similarities are minimal, while processing activities are highly similar. However, as Schmidt and Young (1987) concluded in their extensive review of transfer in motor skills, we do not know very much about what accounts for the transfer phenomenon. Unfortunately, research investigating this question has been minimal during recent years, despite the fact that much more research is needed if we are to answer the question of *why* transfer occurs.

## Negative Transfer

Although negative transfer effects appear to be rare in motor skill learning (e.g., see Annett and Sparrow 1985; Schmidt 1987), people involved in

---

### A CLOSER LOOK

## An Experimental Demonstration of the Transfer-Appropriate-Processing Account of Positive Transfer

The transfer task in the experiment by Damos and Wickens (1980) was a compensatory tracking task. To perform this task, participants had to keep a moving circle on a video screen centered on a horizontal bar that was also on the screen. They could do this by making left-to-right movements with a control stick. On the screen at the same time was a moving vertical bar that they had to move up and down on the screen to keep it in contact with a constant horizontal line. Participants controlled this task by a different control stick; they held one control stick in each hand.

Damos and Wickens used two cognitive dual tasks for training. In one, participants had to specify whether two simultaneously presented digits were alike in size, in name, or in both. The other was a

short-term memory task in which participants observed between one and four digits in a sequence and then had to recall the second-last digit in the sequence. In the experiment, one group of participant received training on both tasks, another group received training on only one task, and a third group received no training on either cognitive dual task. Notice that in terms of task or context components, there is minimal similarity or no similarity between the training and test tasks. The commonality is that both tasks require attention-capacity timesharing, which can be considered a cognitive process. Results showed that the group that practiced both cognitive dual tasks performed the tracking task better than the other two training groups.

---

motor skill instruction and rehabilitation need to be aware of what may contribute to negative transfer. Because negative transfer effects can occur, it is important to know how to avoid such effects and to deal with them when they occur.

***Negative transfer situations.*** Simply stated, negative transfer effects occur *when an old stimulus requires a new but similar response.* This means that the perceptual input characteristics of two performance situations are similar, but the movement characteristics are different. Two situations that are especially susceptible to negative transfer effects involve *change in the spatial locations of a movement* in response to the same stimulus and *change in the timing characteristics of the movement* in response to the same stimulus.

An example of the *spatial location change* occurs when you must drive a car different from your own. If both cars are five-speed stick shifts, what happens when reverse is in a different location

from the one you are accustomed to in your own car? Typically, you find yourself trying to shift to the location of reverse for your own car. This happens especially when you are not paying close attention to shifting. This example demonstrates that when we learn a specific spatially oriented movement to accomplish an action goal, we take time to learn a movement that is similar but to a new location, because of the negative transfer effect of the previous learning experience.

An experiment by Summers (1975) provides an illustration of the negative transfer effects of *changing the timing characteristics of a movement.* Participants practiced a specific sequence of nine key presses for which each interval from key press to key press required a specified criterion time; they successfully learned these after many practice trials. Then they were told to produce the same sequential response, but to ignore the just-learned timing structure, and just do the sequence as quickly as possible. The interesting result was that

---

## A CLOSER LOOK

### Teaching and Rehabilitation Implications of Factors Influencing Positive Transfer of Learning

**SIMILARITY OF ENVIRONMENTAL AND MOVEMENT COMPONENTS**

Compare what the person must do during the training procedure with what he or she must do to perform the skill in its normal context.

**Rehab environment example:** If the normal context requires the person to walk through randomly cluttered environments, such as crowded rooms or hallways, the training environment should be similarly cluttered.

**Sport skill training environment example:** In a basketball game, players can do freethrows in situations involving one, two, three, or one-and-one shot(s). Practice should include all of these situations, when players are both not fatigued and very fatigued.

**SIMILARITY OF INFORMATION-PROCESSING DEMANDS**

Compare the information-processing demands of the training procedure with those of performance of the skill in its normal context.

**Rehab environment example:** If the person will use handwriting skills to take notes of what another person is saying, during training he or she should practice this dual task.

**Sport skill training environment example:** Because a swimmer must adjust stroke characteristics in competition primarily on the basis of his or her own intrinsic feedback, practice must provide the swimmer ample opportunity to make adjustments on his or her own.

**FUNCTIONAL EQUIVALENCE**

Certain nonfunctional procedures are useful for enhancing specific components of a skill, e.g., strength, balance, flexibility. The training regime also should include procedures that emphasize practicing functional aspects of the skill.

---

while the participants were able to perform the entire sequence more rapidly as instructed, they maintained the learned timing structure.

***Why do negative transfer effects occur?*** One possible reason making a new movement to a familiar stimulus produces negative transfer effects is this. As a result of much practice performing a skill in one specific way, a specific perception-action coupling has developed between the perceptual characteristics of the task and the motor system. When a person sees a familiar perceptual array, the motor system has a preferred way of organizing itself to respond to those characteristics. While this perception-action coupling allows for fast and accurate performing, it is problematic when the familiar stimulus requires a different movement response. Change from the preferred state to a new state is difficult and takes practice.

Another possibility is that the negative transfer results from *cognitive confusion*. In the car shift example, the requirements for shifting into reverse in the new car undoubtedly lead to some confusion in the driver about what to do. Undoubtedly you have had a similar experience when you have had to type on typewriters or keyboards that differ in the locations of certain keys, such as the backspace key. When you first begin typing on the new keyboard, you have difficulty striking the keys that are in different locations. What is notable here is that the problem is not with your limb control; you know how to strike keys in a sequence. Rather, the problem is related to the confusion created by the novel position of the keys.

Fortunately, negative transfer effects can be overcome with practice. You probably have experienced this for either gear shifting or the typing, or for both. Just how much practice is required depends on the person and the task itself.

## Bilateral Transfer

When the transfer of learning relates to learning of the same task but with different limbs, it is known as **bilateral transfer.** This well-documented phenomenon demonstrates our ability to learn a particular skill more easily with one hand or foot after we already have learned the skill with the opposite hand or foot.

*Experimental evidence of bilateral transfer.* Experiments designed to determine whether bilateral transfer does indeed occur have followed similar experimental designs. The most typical design has been the following:

|  | Pretest | Practice Trials | Posttest |
|---|---|---|---|
| Preferred limb | X | X | X |
| Nonpreferred limb | X | | X |

This design allows the experimenter to determine if bilateral transfer to the nonpracticed limb occurred because of practice with the other limb. In the sample experimental design, note that the practice limb is the preferred limb. However, this does not need to be the case; the preferred limb/nonpreferred limb arrangement could be reversed. In either case, the researcher compares pretest-to-posttest improvements for each limb. While the practiced limb should show the greatest improvement, a significant amount of improvement should occur for the nonpracticed limb, indicating that bilateral transfer has occurred.

Investigation of the bilateral transfer phenomenon was popular from the 1930s through the 1950s. In fact, the bulk of the evidence demonstrating bilateral transfer in motor skills can be found in the psychology journals of that period. One of the more prominent investigators of the bilateral transfer phenomenon during the early part of that era

was T. W. Cook. Between 1933 and 1936, Cook published a series of five articles relating to the various concerns of bilateral transfer, or cross education, as he called it. Cook terminated this work by asserting that the evidence was sufficiently conclusive to support the notion that bilateral transfer does indeed occur for motor skills.

Given such a foundation of evidence, few experiments published since those by Cook have investigated only the question of the occurrence of the bilateral transfer phenomenon. The research literature since the 1930s has addressed several issues related to bilateral transfer. These include topics such as reminiscence, practice distribution, the overload principle, fatigue, and the direction of the greatest transfer, as well as the reason bilateral transfer occurs and its significance in terms of underlying processes involved in the learning and control of skills.

*Symmetry versus asymmetry of bilateral transfer.* One of the more intriguing questions about bilateral transfer effect concerns the direction of the transfer. The question is this: Does a greater amount of bilateral transfer occur when a person learns a skill using one specific limb before learning it using the other limb (**asymmetric transfer**), or is the amount of transfer similar no matter which limb the person practices with first (**symmetric transfer**)?

Reasons for investigating this question are theoretical as well as practical. From a theoretical perspective, knowing whether bilateral transfer is symmetric or asymmetric would provide insight, for example, into the role of the two cerebral hemispheres in controlling movement. That is, do the two hemispheres play similar or different roles in movement control? A more practical reason for investigating this question is that its answer can help professionals design practice to facilitate optimal skill performance with either limb. If asymmetric transfer predominated, the therapist or instructor would decide to have a person always train with one limb before training with the other; however, if symmetric transfer predominated, it would not make any difference which limb the person trained with first.

The generally accepted conclusion about the direction of bilateral transfer is that it is *asymmetric.* But there is some controversy about whether this asymmetry favors transfer from preferred to non-preferred limb, or vice versa. The traditional view, based on an influential review of the research literature by Ammons (1958), was that we could expect greater transfer when a person practiced initially with the preferred limb. However, some more recent evidence favors the opposite direction for greater transfer. This direction appears to be specific for skills involving complex finger sequencing (e.g., Taylor and Heilman 1980; Elliott 1985).

Although movement scientists have not yet resolved the question of which limb a person should practice with initially, it is evident that for most skill training and rehabilitation situations, the greatest amount of transfer occurs from the preferred to the nonpreferred limb. This approach not only is consistent with the bulk of the research literature concerned with bilateral transfer, but also is supported by other factors that need to be taken into account, such as motivation. Initial preferred-limb practice has a greater likelihood of yielding the types of success that will encourage the person to continue pursuing the goal of becoming proficient at performing the skill.

*A cognitive explanation of bilateral transfer.* Some theorists think that bilateral transfer is cognitively based. They postulate that what is transferred is important cognitive information related to what to do to achieve the goal of the skill. This view of common cognitive elements has much in common with the "identical elements" theory Thorndike suggested, which we discussed earlier in this Concept.

The cognitive explanation gives strong consideration to those elements of a skill related to the performer's knowing "what to do." For example, we can consider the performance of a skill with one limb and then the other to be essentially two distinct skills. Throwing a ball at a target using the right arm is a different task from throwing a ball with the left arm. However, elements of these skills are common to both, regardless of the hand the thrower is using. Examples would be the arm-leg opposition principle, the need to keep the eyes focused on the target, and the need to follow through. Each of these elements represents what to do to successfully throw the ball at a target and does not specifically relate to either arm.

Proponents of this view argue that if a person achieves proficiency at a skill using the right arm, the person does not need to relearn the common cognitive "what to do" elements when he or she begins practicing with the left arm. The person should begin with the left arm at a higher level of proficiency than he or she would have had if he or she had never practiced with the right arm.

An experiment by Kohl and Roenker (1980) provides an example of empirical support for the cognitive explanation of bilateral transfer. A physical practice group practiced a pursuit rotor task (60 rpm for 30 sec) with their right hands. Those in a mental imagery group held the stylus with their right hands and, with eyes closed, imaged themselves tracking the target for the same number of trials (they had observed the experimenter perform one trial prior to these imagery trials). The third group, the control group, had neither type of right-hand practice and did not see the apparatus until the transfer trials. Figure 4.3–2 shows what happened on these trials when all three groups performed with their left hands. As you can see, the physical practice and mental imagery practice groups performed similarly, but both did better than the control group.

*A motor control explanation of bilateral transfer.* Other movement scientists propose a motor control explanation for bilateral transfer that incorporates the generalized motor program and the transfer of motor output characteristics through the nervous system. There are two ways of establishing this explanation. In the first, theorists look at the control construct described in Concept 2.1 as the generalized motor program. Recall that the muscles required to produce an action are *not* an invariant characteristic of the generalized motor

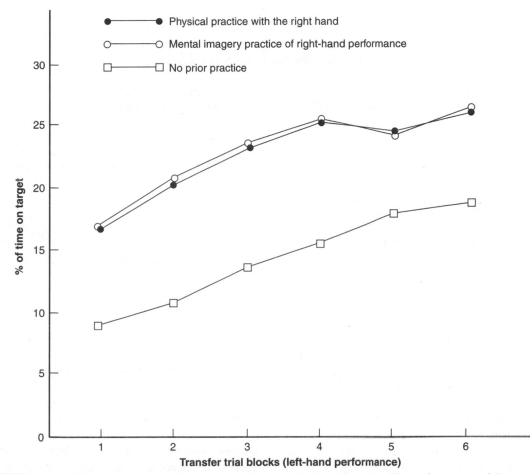

FIGURE 4.3–2  Transfer trial results from the experiments by Kohl and Roenker. The performances of three groups experiencing different practice conditions during the preceding 18 trials are shown here. (Source: Data from R.M. Kohl and D.L. Roenker, "Bilateral Transfer as a Function of Mental Imagery" in *Journal of Motor Behavior*, 1980, 12:197–206.)

program. Rather, muscles are a *parameter* that a person must add to achieve the goal of the action.

This view of the motor program provides one explanation for a person's ability to write his or her name with a pen held in the preferred hand, by some other limb, or even between the teeth. In fact, Raibert (1977) demonstrated movement pattern similarities for this type of handwriting regardless of the muscle group required to produce the movement. Thus, bilateral transfer as a motor control phenomenon is consistent with the view that the generalized motor program operates as a control mechanism by specifying time and space features of movement. And a person can adapt this program to produce a goal-directed action for a muscle group that has not been involved previously in performing the skill.

Because the generalized motor program develops from practice, we would expect that following sufficient practice with one limb, a person would develop an appropriate memory representation of the action so that he or she could perform at a better-than-beginning level with a nonpracticed limb. However, due to other factors, such as problems

---

## A CLOSER LOOK

### Implementing Bilateral Transfer Training

For the person involved in motor skill instruction or rehabilitation, an important question concerns how to take advantage of the bilateral transfer phenomenon and implement it into the instructional or rehabilitation setting.

#### RECOMMENDED GUIDELINES

• Initiate practice with the preferred limb.
• In early practice sessions, concentrate on developing a reasonable degree of proficiency with one limb *before* beginning practice with the other limb.

• After initiating practice with the second limb, alternate practice for both limbs, based on set blocks of trials or amounts of time for practice with each limb.
• Use verbal encouragement to motivate the person to continue to practice with the nonpreferred limb.

---

with perception, biomechanics, and specificity of training, we would not expect initial performance with the nonpracticed limb to be as good as performance with the practiced limb. But we would expect this initial performance to be better than it would if there were no practice at all with the other limb.

The second argument proponents of a motor control explanation offer is based on evidence showing that at least some bilateral transfer of skill is mediated in the brain by interhemispheric transfer of the motor components of the task (Hicks, Gualtieri, and Schroeder 1983). Researchers have demonstrated this mediation by measuring the EMG activity in all four limbs when one limb performs a movement. When EMG activity occurs, it tells researchers that the central nervous system has forwarded commands to those muscles. Results from earlier research by Davis (1942) indicated that the greatest amount of EMG activity occurs for the contralateral limbs (i.e., the two arms), a lesser amount occurs for the ipsilateral limbs (i.e., arm and leg on the same side), and the least amount occurs for the diagonal limbs.

Additionally, Hicks, Frank, and Kinsbourne (1982) showed that when people practiced a typing task with one hand, bilateral transfer occurred only when the other hand was free. When the nontyping hand grasped the table leg during typing, the authors observed no bilateral transfer effects. They interpreted these results to indicate that when the control centers for the muscles that will be involved in the test trials are otherwise engaged, as they were when the fingers were flexed to grasp the table leg, those centers are unavailable for the "central overflow of programming" that goes on during an action.

*A cognitive-motor explanation of bilateral transfer.* Research evidence provides support for the view that both cognitive and motor factors are involved in bilateral transfer. There is no doubt that cognitive components related to "what to do" account for much of the transfer that results from practicing a skill with one limb. This is quite consistent with what we have discussed thus far in this book. For example, the various models of the stages of skill learning described in Concept 4.2 propose that determining "what to do" is a critical part of what a learner acquires in the first stage of learning. There is likewise no doubt that bilateral transfer involves motor components of a skill. This is consistent with our discussion in Concept 2.3 of the control of coordinated action. It is also consistent with empirical evidence that there is some motor outflow to other limbs when one limb performs a skill.

# Summary

Transfer of learning concerns the influence of previous experiences on the learning or performance of a new skill or on its performance in a new context. The influence of the previous experience may facilitate, hinder, or have no effect on the learning of the new skill. The transfer of learning concept is integral to curriculum development in educational environments, as well as to training protocol development in rehabilitation programs. The concept also forms the basis for many methods instructors, coaches, and rehabilitation therapists use to enhance skill acquisition. In addition, the transfer of learning concept is an essential part of understanding motor learning, because it is basic to the process of making inferences about the influence of practice conditions on learning skills. Researchers can quantify the amount of transfer between skills or situations for both intertask and intratask transfer.

We have discussed two hypotheses that attempt to account for positive transfer. The first states that positive transfer increases as a function of the similarities of the components of motor skills and of the contexts in which the skills are performed. The second hypothesis states that the amount of positive transfer is related to the similarity of the processing demands of the two situations.

Negative transfer effects occur primarily when a new movement response is required for a familiar perceptual context. Movement scientists attribute negative transfer to the difficulty inherent in altering the preferred perception-action coupling state that a person has developed for responding in a specific context. Negative transfer also may result from initial cognitive confusion that results when a person does not know what to do in a new performance situation. People usually overcome negative transfer effects with practice.

Bilateral transfer is a phenomenon in which a person experiences improvement in the performance of a nonpracticed limb as a result of practice with the opposite limb. Typically, bilateral transfer is asymmetric, although researchers debate about whether the preferred-to-nonpreferred direction yields greater transfer or vice versa. A cognitive factor involved in explaining bilateral transfer is that people acquire knowledge about what to do with initial practice. And advocates of a motor control explanation point out that factors related to generalized motor program characteristics and the motor outflow of motor commands to the opposite limb are involved in bilateral transfer.

## Related Readings

Annett, J., and J. Sparrow. 1985. Transfer of training: A review of research and practical implications. *Programmed Learning and Educational Technology* 22: 116–24.

Lee, T. D. 1988. Testing for motor learning: A focus on transfer-appropriate-processing. In O. G. Meijer and K. Roth (Eds.), *Complex motor behaviour: 'The' motor-action controversy* (pp. 210–15). Amsterdam: Elsevier.

Schmidt, R. A., and D. E. Young. 1987. Transfer of movement control in motor skill learning. In S. M. Cormier and J. D. Hagman (Eds.), *Transfer of learning,* (pp. 47–79). Orlando, FL: Academic Press.

Winstein, C. J. 1991. Designing practice for motor learning: Clinical implications. In M. J. Lister (Ed.), *Contemporary management of motor control problems* (pp. 65–76). Fredericksburg, VA: Bookcrafters.

# STUDY QUESTIONS FOR CHAPTER 4

1. Explain how the terms *performance* and *learning* differ, and why we must *infer* learning from performance situations.

2. What four performance characteristics are generally present if learning of a skill has occurred?

3. What is an advantage of using transfer tests in making a valid assessment of learning? Give an example of a real-world situation that illustrates this advantage.

4. What is a performance plateau? What seems to be the most likely reason a performance plateau occurs in motor skill learning?

5. Describe some characteristics of learners as they progress through the three stages of learning proposed by Fitts and Posner.

6. How does Gentile's learning stages model differ from the Fitts and Posner model? How does her model relate specifically to differences in learning open and closed skills?

7. How do the coordination and control stages differ in Newell's learning stages model?

8. Describe four performer or performance changes that research has shown to occur as a person progresses through the stages of learning a motor skill.

9. Describe what an expert is and how a person can become an expert motor skill performer. What are some characteristics that distinguish an expert from a nonexpert?

10. Give two reasons understanding the concept of transfer of learning is important. What are two ways that the amount of transfer can be quantified?

11. What are two reasons proposed to explain why transfer occurs? For each of these, give a motor skill example.

12. What type of situation characteristics predict negative transfer? Give two motor skill performance examples of these characteristics and indicate why negative transfer would occur.

13. What is bilateral transfer? What is the issue underlying the question of whether bilateral transfer is symmetric or asymmetric?

14. Discuss two hypotheses that attempt to explain why bilateral transfer occurs.

15. Describe how you would organize practice for a skill in which the capability to use either arm or either leg would be beneficial.

# INSTRUCTION AND
# AUGMENTED FEEDBACK

### CONCEPT 5.1

The most effective method of providing instructions for helping a person
to learn a motor skill depends on the skill and the instructional goal

### CONCEPT 5.2

Augmented feedback can improve, hinder, or have no effect on skill learning

### CONCEPT 5.3

The motor skills professional can provide augmented feedback in a variety of ways

### CONCEPT 5.4

Several timing characteristics of augmented feedback can influence skill learning

# CONCEPT 5.1

The most effective method of providing instructions for helping a person to learn a motor skill depends on the skill and the instructional goal

## Key Terms

modeling

observational learning

point-light technique

cognitive mediation theory

dynamic view of modeling

verbal cues

serial position effect

## Application

If you wanted to teach someone how to do a skill, how would you do it? Probably, you would verbally describe what to do, demonstrate the skill, or use some combination of both approaches. But do we know enough about the effectiveness of these different means of communication to know which one we should prefer or when we should use each one or both?

Demonstrating skills is undoubtedly the most common means of communicating how to perform them. We find demonstrations in a wide range of skill acquisition situations. For example, a physical education teacher may demonstrate to a large class how to putt in golf. An aerobics teacher may demonstrate to a class how to perform a particular sequence of skills. A baseball coach may show a player correct form for bunting a ball. In a rehabilitation context, an occupational therapist may demonstrate to a patient how to button a shirt, or a physical therapist may demonstrate to a wheelchair patient how to get from the floor into the chair.

The instructor demonstrates a skill because he or she believes that in this way, the learner receives more information in less time than he or she could through a verbal explanation of performing the skill. Whether you are teaching a large class, working with a small group, or providing individual instruction, and whether you are teaching a complex skill or a simple skill, you probably hold this generally accepted view that demonstration is the preferred instruction strategy. But we should not assume the wisdom of this view of demonstration without addressing numerous issues. Above all, we must establish when demonstration is effective, and when it may be less effective than some other means of communicating how to perform a skill.

## Discussion

As we have mentioned, the two most popular ways to communicate how to perform a skill are to demonstrate the skill and to give verbal instructions about how to do so. One of the problems encountered by any person providing skill instruction is determining which of these communication forms is better for a particular skill or skill instruction situation.

### Demonstration

It is ironic that although demonstration is a very common method of providing information about how to perform a skill, there is very little research related to it. In fact, most of what we know about the use of demonstration comes from research and theory related to modeling and social learning (e.g., Bandura 1984). However, in recent years movement scientists have shown an increase in interest about the role of demonstration in motor skill learning. (Note that the terms **modeling** and **observational learning** often are used interchangeably with the term *demonstration*. Because *demonstration* is more specific to the context of instruction about how to perform a skill, we will use this term in this text.)

There seem to be at least two reasons for the increased interest in demonstration and skill learning. One reason is the phenomenal growth of interest in the role of vision in skill learning. Because demonstrating how to do a skill involves visual observation on the part of the learner, researchers have been able to use the study of demonstration and skill learning to assess how the visual system is involved in skill acquisition and performance. Another reason for current interest is that we know so little about how to effectively implement this very common instructional strategy. As a result, researchers have been making an increased effort to improve our understanding of the role of demonstration in skill instruction and learning.

In a comprehensive review of research investigating the role of demonstration in motor skill acquisition, McCullagh, Weiss, and Ross (1989) concluded that demonstration is more effective under certain circumstances than under others. This conclusion suggests that an instructor should use demonstration only after determining that the instructional situation indeed warrants the use of demonstration, rather than some other form of providing information about skill performance. In the following sections, we consider some of the concerns that professionals need to take into account before making this instructional decision.

***What the observer perceives from a demonstration.***   Before considering conditions influencing the effectiveness of demonstration, we should examine what a person actually "sees" when a skill is demonstrated. Note the use of the word "sees" rather than "looks at." As we pointed out in Concept 2.2, what we see and what we look at can be very different. What we "see" is what we *perceive* from what we look at. This distinction is particularly relevant to the discussion of demonstration, because what a person perceives from a skill demonstration is not necessarily something that he or she specifically looks at or looks for. In fact, if people are asked later to describe verbally what information they used from a demonstration to help them perform a skill, they do not always give a very accurate accounting of that information. Thus, perception of information from a demonstration appears to be another example of attention without awareness in a skill learning situation.

Research evidence has shown consistently that the observer perceives from the demonstration information about the coordination pattern of the skill (e.g., Scully and Newell 1985; Schoenfelder-Zohdi 1992; Whiting 1988). More specifically, the observer perceives and uses *invariant features of the coordinated movement pattern* to develop his or her own movement pattern to perform the skill. Two types of research evidence support this view. One results from researchers' investigation into visual perception of motion; the other, from their investigation into the influence of demonstration on learning a complex skill.

Research on the perception of human motion investigates questions about how people recognize movement patterns they see in their world. An important principle developed from this research is that people rarely use specific characteristics of the individual components of a pattern to make judgments about the pattern. Rather, they use relative information about the relationships among the various components.

Using a procedure known as the **point-light technique,** several researchers have identified the relative information involved in the perception of human movement. This procedure involves placing lights or bright spots on the joints of a model who is then filmed or videotaped performing an action. Then the researcher plays the film or video so that the person participating in the experiment sees only bright dots, not the whole model. Evidence from the first reported use of this procedure (Johansson 1973) showed that people could accurately label different gait patterns, such as walking and running, by observing the moving dot patterns. Others (e.g., Cutting and Kozlowski 1977) showed that from observing moving dot patterns, people actually could identify their friends. Using a computer simulation, Hoenkamp (1978) showed that the movement characteristic people use to identify different gait patterns is the ratio of the time duration between the forward and return swings of the lower leg.

## A CLOSER LOOK

### Perceiving a Throwing Action from Observing a Point-Light Display

An experiment by Williams (1988) provides an example of use of the point-light technique. Eighty adults (ages 18 to 25 yrs) and eighty children (ages 14 to 15 yrs) observed a video point-light display of a side view of the arm of a seated person throwing a small plastic ball at a target (see figure 5.1–1). The video showed only dots of light at the shoulder, elbow, and wrist joints of the person throwing the ball. The author showed participants the video three times and then asked them what they had seen. Results showed that 66 percent of the children and 65 percent of the adults responded that they had seen a throwing motion. An additional 25 percent of the adults and 23 percent of the children made this response after seeing the video one additional time.

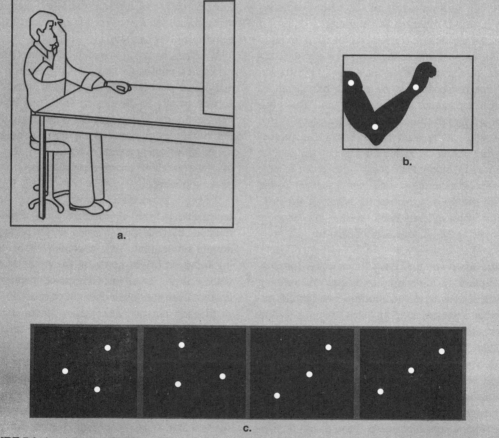

a.

b.

c.

**FIGURE 5.1–1**   An example of use of the point-light technique in motor learning research. (a) shows the model demonstrating the throwing of a small ball at a target. (b) shows a static image of the point-light display of the model's arm with lights at the shoulder, elbow, and wrist joints. (c) shows four still frames of the video shown to subjects. From left to right, these depict the arm at the start of the throw, at maximal flexion, at release of the small ball, and at completion of the throw. (Reproduced with permission of author and publisher from: Williams, J. G. "Visual demonstration and movement production: effects of timing variations in a model's action." *Perceptual and Motor Skills*, 1989, 68, 891–896. © Perceptual and Motor Skills 1989.)

**FIGURE 5.1–2** A person performing on the slalom ski simulator. Note that the person has attached light-reflecting markers for videotape-based movement analysis.

This groundbreaking research on the perception of human movement has shown two things that help our understanding of observational learning. First, people can recognize different gait patterns accurately and quickly without seeing the entire body or all the limbs move. Second, the most critical information people perceive in order to distinguish one type of gait pattern from another is not any one characteristic of the gait, such as velocity of the limbs. Instead, people use the invariant relative-time relationship between two components of gait. From these conclusions we can hypothesize that these invariant relationships in coordinated movement constitute the critical information involved in observational learning.

The second type of research providing evidence about what an observer uses from a skill demonstration also·provides a test of the hypothesis that people perceive invariant relationships. An example is an experiment by Schoenfelder-Zohdi (1992) in which subjects practiced the slalom ski simulator

task shown in figure 5.1–2. This simulator consisted of two rigid, convex, parallel tracks on which a movable platform stood. A participant stood on the platform with both feet and was required to move the platform to the right and then the left as far as possible (55 cm to either side) with rhythmic slalom-ski-like movements. The person needed coordination and effort to perform this skill, because the platform had rigid springs on either side that ensured that the platform always returned to the center (normal) position. Thus, the participant had to learn to control the movement of the platform from side to side as far as possible using smooth ski-like movements, just as he or she would if actually skiing. Participants practiced this skill for several days after they had either observed a skilled model perform the task or received verbal information about the goal of the task. A movement analysis of limb movements showed that participants who had observed the skilled demonstration developed coordinated movement patterns

**FIGURE 5.1–3**  Angle-angle diagrams of the left knee and left hip for two people practicing on the slalom ski simulator. Both graphs show the relationship of these joints after one day of practice. The top graph is from the person who watched a skilled model demonstrate; the lower graph is from the person who did not watch a demonstration. (From B.G. Schoenfelder-Zohdi, 1992, *Investigating the Informational Nature of a Modeled Visual Demonstration,* Ph.D. Dissertation, Louisiana State University. Reprinted by permission.)

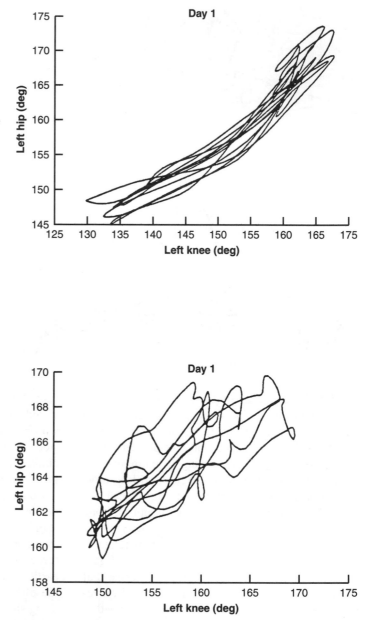

earlier in practice than did those who had not observed the demonstration. Figure 5.1–3 shows one example of these results.

Taken together, these two types of research indicate that the visual system automatically detects in a movement pattern invariant information that is relevant for determining how to produce the observed action. In some manner, which scientists do not fully understand and continue to debate, the person translates the perceived information into movement commands to produce the action. The perceived information may be not specific components of the actual movement, but rather some kind of information about how different components of the skill act in relation to each other.

***The influence of skill characteristics.*** Research investigating the influence on learning of demonstration has produced equivocal findings about the effectiveness of skill demonstration. Some researchers have found that demonstration leads to better skill learning than other forms of instruction; others have found that it does not. But as Magill and Schoenfelder-Zohdi (1996) pointed out, a closer inspection of that research should lead to the conclusion that the influence of demonstration on skill acquisition depends on characteristics of the skill being learned. The most important characteristic leading to the beneficial effect of demonstration is that the skill being learned requires the *acquisition of a new pattern of coordination.*

We see this clearly when we organize into two categories results of research investigating the effect of demonstration on skill learning. In one category are those experiments in which participants learned more quickly after demonstration than after other forms of instruction. It is interesting that in experiments in this category, typically participants learned skills requiring them to acquire new patterns of limb coordination. In the other category are experiments in which participants usually learned skills no better after observing demonstrations than after receiving other forms of instruction. In these experiments, the participants practiced skills that required them to acquire new parameter characteristics for well-learned patterns of limb coordination.

***Observing correctly performed demonstrations.*** A common guiding principle for demonstrating a skill is that the demonstrator should perform the skill correctly. Research support for this direction comes from experiments like one by Landers and Landers (1973), in which the authors compared the influence of skilled and unskilled models on acquiring a ladder-climbing task. The results showed that use of a skilled model led to better student performance than use of an unskilled model.

Why would more accurate demonstration lead to better learning? Two reasons are evident from the research literature. The first reason follows our discussion of perception of information in the preceding section. If the observer perceives and uses information on invariant movement patterns, it seems logical to expect the quality of performance resulting from observing a demonstration to be related to the quality of the demonstration. Another reason is that in addition to picking up coordination information, an observer also perceives information about the strategy used by the model to solve the movement problem. Typically, the observer then tries to imitate that strategy on his or her initial attempts at performing the skill.

An experiment by Martens, Burwitz, and Zuckerman (1976, experiment 3) offers research evidence that strategy imitation is involved in observational learning. Participants had to learn the commercially available "shoot-the-moon" task, which involved moving a ball up an incline formed by two metal rods held by a participant and moved back and forth to make the ball go up the incline. The score is based on where the ball falls through the rods to the base below. Participants first observed models performing the task using one of two strategies. One strategy, called the "creep strategy," involved moving the ball slowly up the incline. The other strategy, the "explosive strategy," involved moving the rods in a way that rapidly propelled the ball up the incline. The results showed that the participants typically adopted the same strategy they had seen a model use.

***Observing unskilled demonstrators.*** Although the theoretical predictions and the empirical evidence point to the preferability of observing skilled demonstrators, evidence indicates that beginners can derive learning benefits even from observing unskilled demonstrators. Note that this kind of demonstration is effective only if both the observers and the models are beginners learning the skill. What this means is that models are "demonstrators" only in that the observers are watching them practice.

## A CLOSER LOOK

### Beginners Learn by Observing Other Beginners: Learning the Tennis Volley

An experiment by Hebert and Landin (1994) nicely illustrates how instructors can facilitate skill acquisition for beginners by having them observe other beginners. Female university students who had no previous formal training or regular participation in tennis practiced the tennis forehand volley with the nondominant hand. All of these students first saw a brief instructional videotape emphasizing the basic elements of the volley. Then, one group practiced the volley for 50 trials while receiving verbal feedback from the instructor after each trial. Each of these students had a fellow participant observe and listen to a videotape of their practice trials. Then these observers were divided into two groups and began their own 50 trials of practice. One of these latter groups received verbal feedback from the instructor during practice, while the other group did not. A fourth control group practiced without either observing other participants or receiving verbal feedback. The results showed that those who had observed other beginners practice before beginning practice performed better on a posttest than those who had not, regardless of the feedback condition during practice.

One proposed benefit of this use of demonstration is that it discourages imitation of a skilled model's performance of the skill, and encourages the observer to engage in more active problem solving. We can trace evidence for the benefit of this approach to the 1930s (e.g., Twitmeyer 1931), although widespread interest in this approach did not develop until Adams (1986) published some experiments. Since then, others have pursued the investigation of the use and benefit of observing an unskilled model (e.g., McCullagh and Caird 1990; Pollock and Lee 1992; Weir and Leavitt 1990).

One situation in which observing an unskilled model is beneficial occurs when the observer not only can watch the model but also can hear the augmented feedback the instructor or experimenter gives. Under these conditions, the observer actively engages in problem-solving activity that is beneficial for learning. The learner observes what the unskilled model does, what the "expert" tells him or her is wrong with the attempt, what the model does to correct errors, and how successful he or she is on the succeeding attempts.

***The frequency of demonstrating a skill.*** One of the reasons for demonstrating a skill is to communicate how to perform the skill. For the beginner,

demonstration provides an effective means of communicating the "idea" of the movement. As we discussed in Concept 4.2, Gentile considered this to be the goal of the first stage of learning. When applied to the use of demonstration, Gentile's view suggests two things. The first is that it is beneficial to demonstrate a skill before the person begins practicing it. The second, and perhaps more important, is that the instructor should continue demonstrating during practice as frequently as necessary. At least two research studies support this latter point. One, by Carroll and Bandura (1990), involves the learning of complex movement patterns of a computer joystick; the other, by Hand and Sidaway (1993), involves the learning of a golf skill. Both experiments provided evidence that more frequent observations of the model yielded better skill learning.

***Auditory modeling.*** Our discussion so far has focused on visual demonstration. However, there are skills for which visual demonstration is less effective for learning than other forms of demonstration. An example is a skill for which the goal is to move in a certain criterion movement time. For this type of skill an auditory form of demonstration seems to work best.

A good research example illustrating the use and effectiveness of auditory modeling is an experiment by Doody, Bird, and Ross (1985). The task required people to use one hand to knock down seven small wooden barriers in a specified sequence in 2,100 msec. Visual and auditory demonstration groups observed a videotape of a skilled model before each practice trial. The visual demonstration group saw only the video portion of the tape and heard no sound. The auditory demonstration group heard only the audio portion of the modeled performance and did not see the task performed by the model. A control group only was told the goal movement time. Results indicated that the group that heard the audio portion of the performance did better than both the visual-demonstration-only group and the control group. It is interesting that the visual-only group did no better than the control group.

Additionally, there are skills for which auditory modeling can be as effective for learning as visual modeling. A good example of this is learning the rhythmic sequence of a series of dance steps. For example, in an experiment by Wuyts and Buekers (1995), people who had no prior dance or music experience learned a sequence of thirty-two choreographed steps. For acquiring the rhythmical timing of this sequence, members of a group that only heard the structure learned the timing structure as well as members of groups who both saw and heard the sequence performed by a model.

***How the observing of demonstrations influences learning.*** At the learning theory level, an important question is this: How does observing demonstrations influence learning in a beneficial way? Two different views address this question.

The predominant current view of the way observing a demonstration benefits skill learning is based on the work of Bandura (1984) concerning modeling and social learning. This view, called the **cognitive mediation theory,** proposes that when a person observes a model, he or she translates the observed movement information into a symbolic memory code that forms the basis of a stored representation in memory. The reason the person transforms movement information into a cognitive memory representation is so that the brain can then rehearse and organize the information. The memory representation then serves as a guide for performing the skill and as a standard for error detection and correction. To perform the skill, the person first must access the memory representation and then must translate it back into the appropriate motor control code to produce the body and limb movements. Thus, cognitive processing serves as a mediator between the perception of the movement information and the performance of the skill by establishing a cognitive memory representation between the perception and the action.

According to Bandura, four subprocesses govern observational learning. The first is the *attention process,* which determines what the person observes and what information he or she extracts from the model's actions. The second is the *retention process,* in which the person transforms and restructures what he or she observes into symbolic codes that the person stores in memory as internal models for action. Certain cognitive activities, such as rehearsal, labeling, and organization, benefit the development of this representation. The *behavior reproduction process* is the third subprocess; during it, the person translates the memory representation of the modeled action and turns it into physical action. Successful accomplishment of this process requires that the individual possess the physical capability to perform the modeled action. Finally, the *motivation process* involves the incentive or motivation to perform the modeled action. This process, then, focuses on all those factors that influence a person's motivation to perform. Unless this process is completed, the person will not perform the action.

The second view of how observing a demonstration benefits skill learning is based on the direct perception view of vision proposed by Gibson (1966, 1979) and extended by Turvey (1977) to the performance of motor skills. Scully and Newell (1985) proposed this view, which has been called the **dynamic view of modeling,** as an alternative to Bandura's theory. The dynamic view questions the need for a symbolic coding (the

## A CLOSER LOOK

### Implementing Demonstration in Skill Instruction Settings

- Keep in mind that demonstrating a skill will have its greatest benefit when the skill being learned requires the acquisition of a new pattern of coordination. Examples include learning to serve in tennis, learning a new dance step, and learning to get into a wheelchair from the floor.
- Be aware also that if the skill being learned involves learning a new control parameter characteristic for a previously learned pattern of coordination, demonstration will be no more beneficial than verbal instructions. Examples include learning to throw a ball at different speeds, learning to kick a ball from different distances, and learning to grasp and lift different sizes of cups.
- Demonstrate frequently and provide no verbal commentary while demonstrating, to reduce a potential attention-capacity problem.

- Be certain the observer can see the critical aspects of the skill you are demonstrating. It may be helpful to direct the observer's attention to these aspects verbally just before the demonstration.
- If you cannot demonstrate a skill very well, use some other way to provide a skilled demonstration, such as a film or videotape, or another person who can demonstrate the skill.
- In some situations, allow beginners to observe other beginners practice a skill. This can be an effective use of demonstration, and works well when there is limited space and/or equipment for every person in a group to perform the skill at the same time.
- Use auditory demonstrations of timing goals. This is an effective way to communicate how to achieve these types of action goals.

memory representation step) between the observation of the modeled action and the physical performance of that action. Instead, it maintains, the visual system is capable of automatically processing visual information in such a way that it constrains the motor response system to act according to what the vision detects. The visual system "picks up" from the model salient information that effectively constrains the body and limbs to act in specific ways. The person does not need to transform the information received via the visual system into a cognitive code and store it in memory. This is the case because the visual information can directly provide the basis for coordination and control of the various body parts required to produce the action. Thus, the critical need for the observer in the early stage of learning is to observe demonstrations that enable him or her to perceive the important invariant coordination relationships between body parts. Additional modeling will benefit the learner if it enables the person to parameterize the coordinated action.

Unfortunately, there is no conclusive evidence in the research literature that shows one of these two views of the modeling effect to be the more valid one. At present, both views appear to be viable theoretical explanations of why modeling benefits skill acquisition. The cognitive mediation theory has been the more prominent of the two, receiving more attention in motor skills research (e.g., Carroll and Bandura 1987, 1990). However, the dynamic view is growing in popularity; this should lead to research that will test its viability as an alternative explanation of the modeling effect (see Whiting 1988).

## Verbal Instructions and Cues

Verbal instructions rank with demonstration as undoubtedly the most commonly used means of communicating to people how to perform motor skills. Evidence supports the value of verbal instructions for facilitating skill acquisition. Several factors are particularly important for developing effective verbal instruction.

*Verbal instructions and attention capacity.*    An important performer characteristic that an instructor needs to keep in mind when presenting verbal instructions is that the person has a limited capacity to attend to incoming information. This means that the instructor must take into account the quantity of instructions. It is easy to overwhelm the person with instructions about what to do to perform a skill. Based on our knowledge of attention-capacity limits, we can reasonably expect that a beginner will have difficulty paying attention to more than one or two instructions about what to do. Because the beginner will need to divide attention between remembering the instructions and actually performing the skill, a minimal amount of verbal information can exceed the person's attention-capacity limits (e.g., Wiese-Bjornstal and Weiss 1992).

*Verbal instructions influence goal achievement strategies.*    Another factor that we need to consider is that verbal instructions direct the person's attention to certain performance aspects of the skill. A good example of this is the way verbal instructions can bias a person in terms of the strategy he or she uses to learn skills that must be performed both quickly and accurately. An experiment by Blais (1991) illustrates the way verbal instructions can invoke strategy bias for learning these skills. The task was a serial pursuit tracking task in which participants controlled a device like a steering wheel to align a pointer in one of four positions on a screen in front of them. When a target position was illuminated, a participant had to move the pointer to that small area as quickly and as accurately as possible. When the person had achieved that goal, another target area was illuminated. This process was repeated many times. Three groups of participants received verbal instructions that emphasized being accurate, being fast, or being both accurate and fast.

The instruction emphasis was especially evident during the first of the five days of practice. On this day, the "speed instruction" group recorded the fastest movement times, while the "accuracy group" produced the most accurate performance. An interesting result was that the group told to em-phasize both speed and accuracy adopted a strategy that led to fast movement times—but at the expense of performance accuracy. And while the "accuracy instruction" group performed the most accurately, its members did so in a manner that eventually gave them the fastest average overall response time, which included reaction time, movement time, and movement-correction time for errors. Thus, for this task, where both speed and accuracy were equally important for overall performance, instructions emphasizing accuracy led to the best achievement of the two-component goal.

*Verbal cues.*    One of the problems associated with verbal instructions is that they can contain too little or too much information and not provide the learner with what he or she needs to know to achieve the goal of the skill. To overcome this problem, Landin (1994) has suggested that instructors use verbal cues to direct people to know what to do to perform skills. **Verbal cues** are short, concise phrases that serve to (1) direct people's attention to regulatory information relevant for performing skills, or (2) prompt key movement-pattern elements of performing skills. For example, the cue "Look at the ball" directs visual attention, while the cue "Bend your knee" prompts an essential movement component. Research has shown these short, simple statements to be very effective as verbal instructions to facilitate learning new skills, as well as performing well-learned skills.

Teachers, coaches, or therapists can implement verbal cues in several different ways in skill learning settings. One way is to *give verbal cues along with a demonstration* to supplement the visual information (e.g., Carroll and Bandura 1990; McCullagh, Stiehl, and Weiss 1990). When used this way, verbal cues aid in directing attention, and can guide rehearsal of the skill a person is learning. One caution about this use of verbal cues is that they may interrupt attention to the relative-timing patterns of skills and actually hinder skill learning (see Wiese-Bjornstal and Weiss 1992).

Another way to use verbal cues is to *give cues to help learners focus on critical parts of skills.* For example, in an experiment by Masser (1993),

---

### A CLOSER LOOK

## Guidelines for Using Verbal Cues for Skill Instruction and Rehabilitation

- Cues should be short statements of one or two words.
- Cues should relate logically to the aspects of the skill to be prompted by the cues.
- Cues can prompt a sequence of several movements.
- Cues should be limited in number. Cue only the most critical elements of performing the skill.

- Cues can be especially helpful for directing shifts of attention.
- Cues are effective for prompting a distinct rhythmic structure for a sequence of movements.
- Cues must be carefully timed so that they serve as prompts and do not interfere with performance.

---

first-grade classes were taught to do headstands. In one class, before students made each attempt to swing their legs up into the headstands, the instructor said, "Shoulders over your knuckles," to emphasize the body position critical to performing this skill. The cued students maintained their acquired skill three months after practice, whereas the students who had not received this verbal cue performed the headstand poorly three months later. A similar result occurred in an experiment using verbal cues to emphasize critical parts of the forward roll.

Performers also can *use verbal cues while performing* to cue themselves to attend to or perform key aspects of skills. Sport psychologists have referred to this approach as *self-talk.* They have used it to help skilled athletes keep their attention focused while performing skills. Cutton and Landin (1994) provided a research example demonstrating the effectiveness of this technique for nonskilled individuals. Instructors taught university students in a beginning tennis class five verbal cues to say out loud each time they were required to hit a ball. These were as follows: "ready," to prompt preparation for the oncoming ball; "ball," to focus attention on the ball itself; "turn," to prompt proper body position to hit the ball, which included turning the hips and shoulders to be perpendicular with the net and pointing the racquet toward the back fence; "hit," to focus attention on contacting the ball; and "head down," to prompt the stationary position of the head after ball contact. The students

who used verbal cues learned tennis groundstrokes better than those that did not, including a group that received verbal feedback during practice.

Verbal cues have been used to improve the performance of skilled tennis players. For example, Landin and Hebert (1995) had university female varsity tennis players use self-cueing to help them improve their volleying skills. Players learned to say the word "split," to cue them to hop to a balanced two-foot stop that would allow them to move in any direction. Then, they said, "turn," to cue them to turn their shoulders and hips to the ball. Finally, they said, "hit," to direct their attention to tracking the ball to the point of contact on the racquet and to cue themselves to keep the head still and hit the ball solidly. After practicing this cueing strategy for five weeks, the players showed marked improvements in both performance and technique.

It is interesting to note that people develop verbal cues for two different purposes. Sometimes the cue *directs attention* to a specific environmental event or to specific sources of regulatory information (in our example, "ready," "ball," and "hit" are such cues). In other cases, the cue *prompts action,* for either a specific movement ("head down") or a sequence of movements ("turn"). The key to the effectiveness of verbal cues is that as the person practices and continues to use the cues, an association develops between the cue and the act it prompts. The benefit to the learner is that he or she does not need to give attention to a large number of verbal instructions and can allocate attention to the perceptual and movement components of the skill.

## The Influence of Serial Position

Many motor skills require people to learn a specific sequence of actions or movements. Dance, piano playing, gymnastics, figure skating, and synchronized swimming are some of the many activities that require people to learn sequences. In a rehabilitation environment, occupational therapy patients may need to learn to assemble parts of a piece of equipment by combining the components in a precise order so that the desired finished product will result. For these types of skills, a factor that we need to take into account when providing instructions is where in the sequence a specific component comes.

To establish appropriate instructions for skills involving sequence learning, we can apply a memory phenomenon known as the **serial position effect.** Because of this effect (also known as the *primacy-recency effect*), the items in a sequence that were presented first and those that were presented last usually are recalled best, while those that were in the middle are recalled worst. This means that how well a person recalls a series of events is a function of each event's position in the sequence. And the longer the sequence is, the more pronounced the effect tends to be. Experimental evidence has demonstrated this effect for both verbal items and movements (e.g., Magill and Dowell 1977). One important fact is that the serial position effect is especially evident in initial practice trials and typically is eliminated as the person becomes more skilled.

The implication of the serial position effect for instruction is that when someone teaches a sequential skill, learners will have the most difficulty remembering what to do in the middle portions of the sequence. People will learn this segment best when the instructor emphasizes it by demonstrating it more often than the first and last segments, or by verbally directing attention to this middle portion of the sequence. Another strategy relates to how

learners practice the sequence. As we will discuss in Concept 6.4, the instructor can encourage people initially to practice segments of the sequence, rather than the entire sequence. A sufficient amount of practice can eliminate the serial position effect, so that a learner can perform the entire sequence correctly.

## Summary

A demonstration conveys information about how a learner should perform a skill. The benefit of observing a skilled demonstration is that it presents to the observer the invariant characteristics of the coordination pattern necessary for performing the skill. Because of this, more learning benefits will result from observing skills requiring new patterns of coordination than from observing skills for which people must learn new parameters for already-established patterns of movement. Observing another beginner learning a skill also can lead to skill learning benefits. Increased frequency of demonstration appears to influence skill learning positively. When people must learn timing characteristics of skills, auditory modeling is an effective technique for communicating these characteristics.

Two prominent theoretical viewpoints attempt to explain how modeling influences skill learning. One view, called the cognitive mediation theory, argues that a person develops a memory representation from observing a model, and that the person must access this representation prior to performing the skill. The alternative view, called the dynamic view, holds that people do not need cognitive mediation, because the visual system can automatically constrain the motor system to act in accordance with what has been observed.

When an instructor uses verbal instructions to provide information about how to perform a motor skill, the information must direct the learner's attention to important aspects of the skill. Verbal cues provide a means of communicating verbally which aspects of a skill are critical for successful performance and how to perform the skill.

An additional concern for people presenting demonstrations or giving verbal instructions relates to skills in which they must teach sequences of movements. Because of the serial position effect, during early practice, learners remember parts of a sequence presented first or last better than those in the middle. Middle components of a sequential skill may require additional instruction and practice emphasis.

## Related Readings

Gray, J. T., U. Neisser, B. A. Shapiro, and S. Kouns. 1991. Observational learning of ballet sequences: The role of kinematic information. *Ecological Psychology* 3: 121–34.

McCullagh, P. 1993. Modeling: Learning, developmental, and social psychological considerations. In R. N. Singer, M. Murphey, and L. K. Tennant (Eds.), *Handbook of research on sport psychology* (pp. 106–26). New York: Macmillan.

McCullagh, P., and J. K. Caird. 1990. Correct and learning models and the use of model knowledge of results in the acquisition and retention of a motor skill. *Journal of Human Movement Studies,* 18: 107–16.

Rink, J. E. 1994. Task presentation in pedagogy. *Quest* 46: 270–80.

---

■

---

# CONCEPT 5.2

Augmented feedback can improve, hinder, or have no effect on skill learning

——

## Key Terms

task-intrinsic
  feedback

augmented
  feedback

concurrent
  augmented
  feedback

terminal
  augmented
  feedback

knowledge of
  results (KR)

knowledge of
  performance
  (KP)

## Application

Think about a time when you were beginning to learn a new physical activity. How much success did you experience on your first few attempts? Most likely, you were not very successful. As you tried to improve, you probably had many questions that you needed someone to answer to help you better understand what you were doing wrong and

what you needed to do to improve. How were these questions answered for you? If you were in a class or taking lessons from a private instructor, you probably sought the answers from the instructor. Although you may have been able to answer many of your questions on your own as you continued to try different things while you practiced, you found that getting an answer from the instructor saved you time and energy.

This situation is an example of what commonly occurs in the early stage of learning a skill. It is equally typical for a person learning a new sport skill and a person relearning a skill following an injury or illness. The significance of this example is that it points out an important role played by the teacher, coach, therapist, or trainer. This role involves providing information to the learner to facilitate the skill acquisition process. The information is known as augmented feedback.

---

■

---

## Discussion

While movement scientists generally agree that augmented feedback can be an important part of skill instruction, they do not agree on how instructors should implement it to influence skill learning most effectively. As a first step in the process of addressing this issue, we will discuss what augmented feedback is. This step is important because of the long history of terminology problems that have characterized discussions about this important instructional variable. Our goal here is to establish a common ground of terms and definitions so that we can see more clearly that augmented feedback can have various effects on skill learning, depending on the type of information given and the skill being learned.

## The Feedback Family

When a person performs a motor skill, there are several sources of information (i.e., feedback) about the outcome of an action or about what caused the outcome. One of these sources is the person's own sensory feedback system (which we discussed in chapter 2). This information source involves all the various components of the sensory-perceptual system and comes into play during and after the person's performance of a skill. For example, the visual system provides information about performance success or errors as a person walks through a cluttered environment. Another source of information is outside the person's own sensory feedback system. For example, when a teacher tells a student what he or she did correctly or incorrectly and what the student should do to make corrections, feedback is coming from a source that is external to the performer. This type of feedback is always in addition to the feedback provided by the person's own sensory-perceptual system, and as such is called *augmented feedback.* Thus, it is helpful to think of *two sources of feedback* related to performing a skill, one internal and one external to the performer.

With regard to the terminology issue, it is important to note that we use the term *feedback* throughout this book as a generic term describing information a person receives about the performance of a skill *during or after* its performance. Because feedback can come from various sources, it is helpful to distinguish different types of feedback on the basis of *where the feedback originates.* To make these distinctions, we can consider the various types of feedback as related members of the same family. Figure 5.2–1 graphically demonstrates this *feedback family,* in which there are two principal forms of feedback. **Task-intrinsic feedback** is the sensory feedback available during or after a person performs a skill that is a naturally occurring part of the skill performance situation itself. **Augmented feedback,** on the other hand, always refers to feedback that comes from sources external to the person and adds to or enhances task-intrinsic feedback.

## Types of Augmented Feedback

Augmented feedback augments task-intrinsic feedback in two distinct ways. In some situations, augmented feedback *enhances* the task-intrinsic feedback the person's sensory system can readily detect on its own. For example, a teacher or coach might tell a golfer where his or her hands were positioned at the top of the swing, even though the person could feel for himself or herself where they were. In a clinical environment, a therapist might show an amputee patient EMG traces on a computer monitor to enhance the patient's own proprioceptive feedback as it helps the patient know when the appropriate muscles are functioning.

In other situations, augmented feedback *adds* information that the person cannot detect using his or her sensory system. For example, the golf teacher or coach might tell the golfer where the ball went because the golfer did not see it after it was hit. Likewise, a therapist might tell a clinical patient how much his or her body swayed because vestibular problems prevent the patient from being able to detect this information. In each of these situations, augmented feedback provides performance information that otherwise would not be available to the person.

In Figure 5.2–1, it is important to note that there are *two categories of types of augmented feedback:* knowledge of results and knowledge of

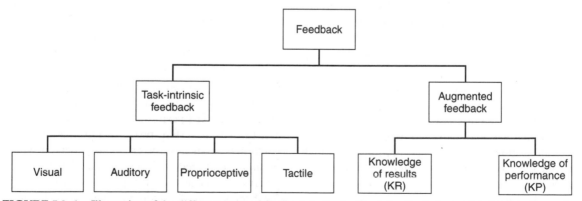

**FIGURE 5.2–1**   Illustration of the different types of feedback in the feedback family that are related to learning and performing motor skills.

performance. Each category can involve a variety of ways of presenting augmented feedback; this will be the topic of discussion in Concept 5.3.

Also, it is important to point out here that augmented feedback can be provided at different times. Learning researchers use different terms to designate the time periods when it is given. If augmented feedback is given *while the movement is in progress,* we call it **concurrent augmented feedback.** If it is given *after the skill has been performed,* we call it **terminal augmented feedback.**

*Knowledge of results (KR).* The category of augmented feedback known as **knowledge of results** (commonly referred to as **KR**) consists of *externally presented information about the outcome of performing a skill or about achieving the goal of the performance.* In some situations, KR describes something about the performance outcome. For example, if a teacher tells a student in an archery class, "The shot was in the blue at 9 o'clock," the teacher is providing performance outcome information. Similarly, if a therapist shows a patient a computer-generated graph indicating that this leg extension was three degrees more than the last one, the therapist is giving KR to the patient about the outcome of his or her leg extension movement.

Sometimes, KR does not describe the performance outcome, but simply tells the performer whether he or she has achieved the goal of the performance. This is the case when some external device gives a "yes" or "no" signal indicating whether or not the performance goal was achieved. For example, to augment proprioceptive and visual feedback for a patient working on achieving a goal leg extension, the therapist could set a buzzer to be activated when the patient achieved the goal number of degrees of movement. Although the buzzer would provide no information about how close to the goal or how far from it the movement was if it had not been achieved, the patient would know that he or she had not achieved the goal unless the buzzer sounded.

*Knowledge of performance (KP).* The second category of augmented feedback is **knowledge of performance** (known as **KP**). This is information about the *movement characteristics that led to the performance outcome.* The important point here is that KP differs from KR in terms of which aspect of performance the information refers to. For example, in the archery situation described above, the teacher would provide KP by telling the student that he or she had pulled the bow to the left at the release of the arrow. Here, the teacher would be verbally augmenting the task-intrinsic feedback by telling the student what he or she had done that caused the arrow to hit the target where it did.

In addition to giving KP verbally, there are various nonverbal means of providing KP. For example, videotape is a popular method of showing a person what he or she did while performing a skill. Videotape allows the person to see what he or she actually did while performing that led to the outcome of that performance. Another means of providing KP that is increasing in popularity as computer software becomes more accessible is showing the person computer-generated kinematic characteristics of the just-completed performance. In clinical environments, therapists also use biofeedback devices to give KP. For example, a therapist can attach a buzzer to an EMG recording device so that the person hears the buzzer sound when he or she activates the appropriate muscle while performing a movement. In each of these situations, sensory feedback is augmented in a way that informs the person about what he or she did while performing the skill that yielded the outcome of that performance.

## The Roles of Augmented Feedback in Skill Acquisition

Augmented feedback plays two roles in the skill learning process. One is to *facilitate achievement of the goal of the skill.* Because augmented feedback provides information about the success of the skill in progress or just completed, the learner can determine whether what he or she is doing is appropriate for performing the skill correctly. Thus, the augmented feedback can help the person achieve the skill goal more quickly or more easily than he or she could without this external information.

---

| A CLOSER LOOK |

### Augmented Feedback as Motivation

An instructor can use augmented feedback to influence a person's perception of his or her own ability in a skill. This is an effective way to influence the person's motivation to continue pursuing a task goal or performing a skill. The verbal statement "You're doing a lot better" can indicate to a person that he or she is being successful at an activity. Evidence supporting the motivational effectiveness of this type of verbal feedback comes from research relating to self-efficacy and performance of skills.

For example, Solmon and Boone (1993) showed that in a physical education class environment, students with high ability perceptions demonstrated longer persistence at performing a skill and had higher performance expectations than those with low ability perceptions. In her review of the self-efficacy literature as it relates to skill performance, Feltz (1992) concluded that the success or failure of past performance is a key mediator of a person's self-perceptions regarding ability. The logical implication of these findings is that an instructor or therapist can present augmented feedback in a way that influences a person's feelings of success or failure. Because of this, augmented feedback can influence a person to persist at performing a skill.

---

The second role played by augmented feedback is to *motivate the learner to continue striving toward a goal*. In this role, the person uses augmented feedback to compare his or her own performance to a performance goal. The person then must decide to continue trying to achieve that goal, to change goals, or to stop performing the activity. This motivational role of augmented feedback is not the focus of our discussion in the present Concept. Others, however, have discussed it in the motor learning literature (e.g., Adams 1978, 1987; Little and McCullagh 1989; Locke, Cartledge, and Koeppel 1968). In addition, scholars interested in the pedagogical aspects of physical education teaching (e.g, Solmon and Lee 1996) increasingly are studying the effects of augmented feedback on people's motivation to engage in, or continue to engage in, physical activities.

## How Essential Is Augmented Feedback for Skill Acquisition?

When a researcher or practitioner considers the use of augmented feedback to facilitate skill acquisition, an important theoretical and practical question arises: Is augmented feedback *necessary* for a person to learn motor skills? The answer to this question has theoretical implications for the understanding of the nature of skill learning itself. The need, or lack of need, for augmented feedback to acquire motor skills tells us much about what characterizes the human learning system and how it functions to acquire new skills. From a practical perspective, determining the necessity for augmented feedback for skill learning can serve to guide the development and implementation of effective instructional strategies. As you will see, the answer to this question is not a simple yes or no. Instead, there are *four different answers*. Which one is appropriate depends on certain characteristics of the skill being learned and of the person learning the skill.

***Augmented feedback can be essential for skill acquisition.*** In some skill performance situations, performers cannot use critical sensory feedback to determine what they need to do to improve performance. For performers to learn skills in such situations, augmented feedback is essential. There are at least three types of situations in which a person may not be able to use important task-intrinsic feedback effectively.

First, some skill situations do not make critical sensory feedback available to the person. For example, when a performer cannot see a target that he or she must hit, the performer does not have important visual feedback available. In this case, augmented feedback can add critical information that is not available from the task performance environment itself.

Second, in some situations the person, because of injury, disease, etc., does not have available the sensory pathways needed to detect critical task-intrinsic feedback for the skill he or she is learning. For these people, augmented feedback can serve as a substitute for this missing information.

Finally, in some situations the appropriate task-intrinsic feedback provides the necessary information and the person's sensory system is capable of detecting it, but the person cannot use the feedback. For example, a person learning to move a limb a certain distance or to throw a ball at a certain rate of speed may not be able to determine the distance moved or the rate of speed of the throw, due to lack of experience. In these situations, augmented feedback helps to make the available task-intrinsic feedback more meaningful to the performer.

Research evidence supports the need for augmented feedback in these learning situations. For example, many of the earliest experiments on this topic showed the need for augmented feedback in situations in which the performance environment did not provide the learner with critical sensory feedback. In many of these experiments, participants were blindfolded and thus could not see their movements or the performance environments. These experiments consistently showed augmented feedback, typically in the form of KR, to be essential for learning when, for example, the blindfolded persons had to learn to draw a line of a certain length (Trowbridge and Cason 1932) or move a lever to a criterion position (e.g., Bilodeau, Bilodeau, and Schumsky 1959). When the authors did not give KR in these situations, participants did not learn the skills.

An experiment by Newell (1974) illustrates the situation in which the task-intrinsic feedback needed to perform the skill is available, but the person is not capable of using it. Participants had to learn to make a 24-cm lever movement in 150 msec. Although they could see their arms, the lever, and the target, the results showed that their success at learning the movement depended on how many times (out of 75 trials) they had received KR about the accuracy of their responses (see figure 5.2–2). These results indicated that in the initial learning stage, those participating did not have a good internal referent for determining what a 150-ms movement was. They needed augmented feedback for at least 52 trials to establish such a referent, which they then could use to perform the movement without the need for augmented feedback.

***Augmented feedback may not be needed for skill acquisition.*** Some motor skills inherently provide sufficient task-intrinsic feedback, so that augmented feedback is redundant. For these types of skills, learners can use their own sensory feedback systems to determine the appropriateness of their movements and to make adjustments on future attempts. An experiment by Magill, Chamberlin, and Hall (1991) provides a laboratory example of this type of situation. Participants learned a coincidence-anticipation skill in which they simulated striking a moving object by sequentially lighting a series of LEDs along a 281-cm-long trackway (see figure 5.2–3). As they faced the trackway, they had to knock down with a hand-held bat a small wooden barrier directly under a target LED coincident with the lighting of the target. KR was given as the time they took to knock the barrier down (number of msec before or after the target lighted). Four experiments showed that participants learned this task regardless of the number of trials on which they received KR during practice. In fact, receiving KR during practice did not lead to better learning than practice without KR.

A motor skill that does not require a person to have augmented feedback to learn it has an important characteristic: a detectable external referent in the environment that the person can use to determine the appropriateness of an action. For the

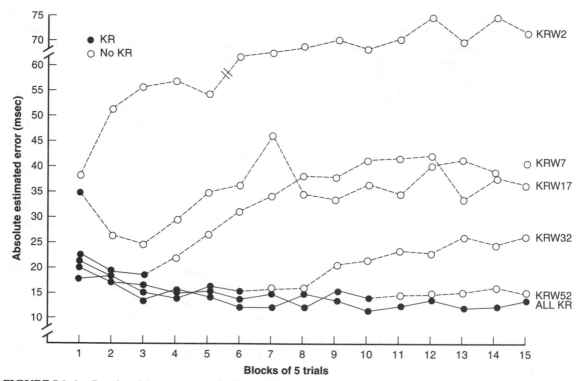

**FIGURE 5.2–2** Results of the experiment by Newell showing the performance curves for learning to make a linear movement in 150 msec of groups who had KR withdrawn at various points during the 75 trials. The open circles indicate blocks of trials during which no KR was given; the closed circles show blocks of trials with KR. The number following each KRW indicates the trial on which KR was withdrawn. (From K.M. Newell, "Knowledge of Results and Motor Learning" in *Journal of Motor Behavior,* 1974, 6:235–244. Copyright © 1974 Heldref Publications, Inc., Washington, DC. Reprinted by permission.)

**FIGURE 5.2–3** A subject in the experiment by Magill, Chamberlin, and Hall performing the coincidence-anticipation task. On the wall at eye level was a series of LEDs that sequentially lit up to simulate a moving object. The subject used a small wooden bat to knock down the small wooden barrier directly under a target LED coincident with the lighting of the target. (Author photo)

anticipation timing task in the Magill et al. experiment, the target and other LEDs were the external referents. The learner could see when the bat made contact with the barrier in comparison to when the target lighted; this enabled him or her to see the relationship between his or her own movements and the goal of those movements. It is important to note here that the learner may *not* be consciously aware of this relationship. The sensory system and the motor control system operate in these situations in a way that does not demand the person's awareness of the environmental characteristics. Thus, the enhancement of these characteristics by providing augmented feedback does not increase or speed up learning of the skill.

In addition to skill characteristics, practice condition characteristics also influence the need for augmented feedback. One of these characteristics is the existence of an observational learning situation. Experimental results have shown that two different types of observational learning conditions can be influential. In one, the learner observes a skilled model perform the skill. For example, in an experiment by Magill and Schoenfelder-Zohdi (1996), people who observed a skilled demonstration learned a rhythmic gymnastics rope skill as well as did those who received verbal KP after each trial. In addition, Hebert and Landin (1994) showed that beginning tennis players who watched other beginners practice learned the tennis forehand volley as well as or better than beginning players who received verbal KP. In both of these situations, the observational learning situation provided beginners an opportunity to acquire knowledge about how to do the skill correctly; they then were able to practice and improve on their own without needing augmented feedback.

There is an interesting parallel between skill learning situations in which learners do not need augmented feedback and results of studies investigating the use of teacher feedback in physical education class settings. These studies consistently have shown low correlations for the relationship between teacher feedback and student achievement (e.g., Eghan 1988; Pieron 1982; Silverman, Tyson, and Krampitz 1991). This finding suggests that

the amount and quality of teacher feedback is influential for improving the skills of beginners in sport skills class settings, but we should not see it as the *most* important variable. Other variables, such as observational learning, appear to be capable of precluding the need for augmented feedback. Our understanding of the extent of this influence awaits further research.

*Augmented feedback can enhance skill acquisition.* Many motor skills can be learned without augmented feedback. However, people will learn many of these more quickly or perform them at a higher level if they receive augmented feedback during practice. For these skills, augmented feedback is neither essential nor redundant. The effect of augmented feedback on the learning of these skills is to *enhance* it.

Skills in this category include those for which improvement does occur through task-intrinsic feedback alone, but because of certain skill or learner characteristics, performance improvement reaches only a certain level. The research literature has shown two types of skill characteristics to fit this description.

The first type involves relatively simple skills for which achievement of the performance goal is initially easy to assess. An example is a movement goal of moving as quickly as possible. Initially, a person can assess if a particular attempt was faster than a previous one. However, usually due to the learner's lack of experience, which results in his or her decreased capability to discriminate small movement-speed differences, improvement seems to stop at a certain level of performance. To improve beyond this level of performance, the person requires augmented feedback (e.g., Stelmach 1970; Newell, Quinn, Sparrow, and Walter 1983). Research evidence shows that there is a point during practice at which people who receive KR about movement time for this type of skill continue to improve performance, while those who do not receive it level off in their performance.

The second type of skill for which augmented feedback enhances learning is any complex skill

---

**A CLOSER LOOK**

### The "Typical" Physical Education Teacher and Augmented Feedback

Research evidence consistently has shown that physical education teachers provide various types of augmented feedback and present that feedback with varying degrees of frequency to students in their classes. An example of this evidence is in one of the earliest and most comprehensive studies of this issue, by Fishman and Tobey (1978).

**SUBJECTS**

    teachers in 81 elementary and secondary physical education classes

**AUGMENTED FEEDBACK PRESENTATION CHARACTERISTICS**

    KP = 94%; KR = 6%

**INTENTION OF AUGMENTED FEEDBACK**

    appraisal of performance = 53%

    instruction about how to improve performance = 41%

    praise or criticism of performance = 5%

**FREQUENCY OF GIVING AUGMENTED FEEDBACK**

    average = just over one instance per min/ 35-min class

    range across the classes = 1 to 297 instances (median = 47)

---

that requires a person to acquire an appropriate multi-limb pattern of coordination. For such skills, learners can attain a certain degree of success simply by making repeated attempts to achieve the performance goal. But this goal achievement process can be speeded up with the addition of KP. More specifically, the KP that works best is information about critical components of the coordination pattern.

A good illustration of the effect of this type of KP for this type of skill is an experiment by Wallace and Hagler (1979). The complex skill subjects learned was a one-hand basketball set shot with the nondominant hand. The shot they practiced was 3.03 m from the basket and 45° to the left side of the basket. After each shot, one group of subjects received verbal KP about errors in their stance and limb movements during the shot. Another group received only verbal encouragement after each shot. Both groups could see the outcome of each shot. Figure 5.2–4 depicts the results. Note that KP provided an initial boost in performance for the first 15 trials. Then, the verbal encouragement group caught up. However, similarity in performance between the two groups lasted only about 10 trials;

after this point, the verbal encouragement group showed no further improvement, while the group receiving KP continued to improve.

***Augmented feedback can hinder skill learning.*** An effect of augmented feedback on skill learning that many might not expect is that it can hinder the learning process, and, in some cases, actually make learning worse than it would have been otherwise. This effect is especially evident when a beginning learner becomes dependent on augmented feedback that will not be available in a test situation. Typically, the performance improvement the learner experienced during practice deteriorates in the test situation. In fact, in some situations, not only does performance deteriorate when augmented feedback is withdrawn, but the test performance is no better than if augmented feedback had not been given at all.

There are *three different skill learning situations* in which research has shown this hindering effect to exist. One occurs when the instructor or therapist presents augmented feedback *concurrently* with the person's performance of the skill. This effect is well documented in the research literature. An

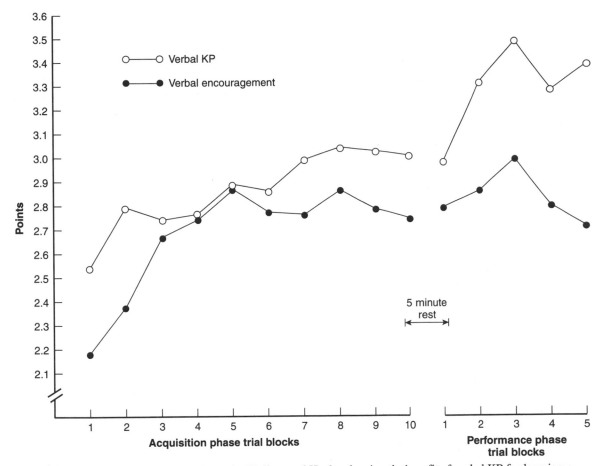

**FIGURE 5.2–4** Results of the experiment by Wallace and Hagler showing the benefit of verbal KP for learning a basketball shooting skill. (Reprinted with permission from *Research Quarterly for Exercise and Sport,* Volume 50, pp. 265–271, Copyright © 1979 by the American Alliance for Health, Physical Education, Recreation and Dance, 1900 Association Drive, Reston, VA 20191.)

experiment Annett (1959) performed many years ago in England provides an example. Participants had to learn a very simple skill, which involved producing a specified amount of force by either depressing a movable plunger or pressing against a fixed metal bar. The author provided augmented feedback either concurrently or terminally. He provided concurrent augmented feedback by graphically showing on an oscilloscope whether the force produced was within a certain range of the criterion force. To provide terminally presented augmented feedback, the author either verbally told the partici-

pant the amount of force exerted or allowed the subject to see the oscilloscope reading. The results showed that although participants receiving the concurrent feedback performed well during training, their test performance without augmented feedback showed an immediate deterioration, as the amount of error became very large.

The characteristic of the force production task that led to a dependency on augmented feedback was that the task-intrinsic feedback was minimal or difficult to interpret. No naturally occurring environmental information indicated the amount of force a person's movement produced. Participants had to rely on their own proprioceptive feedback to perform the task. In this type of situation, people typically substitute concurrently provided augmented feedback for task-intrinsic feedback, because it gives them an easy-to-use guide for performing correctly. There is a problem with this approach, however: rather than learning the sensory feedback characteristics associated with performing the skill, people become dependent on the augmented feedback to perform the skill (see Lintern, Roscoe, and Sivier 1990).

It is important to note before we continue that the use of concurrent augmented feedback does not always hinder learning. We will discuss conditions favoring the effective use of concurrent augmented feedback in Concepts 5.3 and 5.4.

A second situation in which augmented feedback during practice can lead to performance deterioration during transfer occurs when the instructor or therapist presents terminal augmented feedback *after every practice trial.* A research example illustrating this situation is an experiment by Winstein and Schmidt (1990). Participants performed almost 200 practice trials of the skill, which was moving a lever back and forth on a tabletop to produce a complex wave-form pattern on a computer monitor. Researchers gave KP by showing participants on the computer monitor the pattern they had produced, overlaying the criterion pattern. The results showed that people who received KP after every practice trial performed well during practice—but on the test trials without KP, they performed at essentially the same level they had been on during the first 24 practice trials. On the other hand, subjects who had seen the KP on only two-thirds of the practice trials showed little performance deterioration on the test trials. These results nicely demonstrate that KP can be available too frequently, causing people to become so dependent on it that they need to have it available to perform the skill.

Proteau and his colleagues (Proteau et al. 1987; Proteau and Cournoyer 1990) proposed an interesting hypothesis about why dependency on augmented feedback occurs in this type of situation. They suggested that the augmented feedback becomes a part of the memory representation that develops during practice, and thus becomes a part of what the person has learned. Thus, when the person must perform the skill in a situation without augmented feedback, task-intrinsic feedback alone is not sufficient for them to perform the skill successfully.

A third situation in which augmented feedback can hinder skill learning occurs when the instructor or therapist presents augmented feedback *erroneously* for a skill that the person could learn without augmented feedback. In this situation, task-intrinsic and augmented feedback are in conflict with each other. Especially in the early stage of skill learning, people resolve this conflict by performing according to the augmented feedback. When this information is erroneous, they learn the skill incorrectly.

An experiment by Buekers, Magill, and Hall (1992) illustrates this type of feedback conflict resolution. Participants practiced an anticipation timing task similar to the one described earlier in this Concept in the experiments by Magill, Chamberlin, and Hall (1991). Recall that people did not need augmented feedback to learn this skill. In the Buekers, Magill, and Hall experiment, participants practiced for 75 trials. After every trial, one group received correct KR: the direction and amount of timing error for that trial. A second group received erroneous KR after every trial. The researchers gave these people error information indicating that they had struck the barrier 100 msec later than they actually did. A third group received correct KR for the first 50 trials and then received the incorrect KR for the last 25 trials. A fourth group received no KR. Following the practice trials, all subjects performed the same task without KR, first one day later and then one week later. The results (see figure 5.2–5) showed that while participants did not need KR to learn the skill, the erroneous KR information led the people who received it to perform according to the KR rather than according to the feedback intrinsic to the task itself. This effect occurred even when participants had received correct KR for the first 50 trials, and only then began to receive the erroneous information. Even more

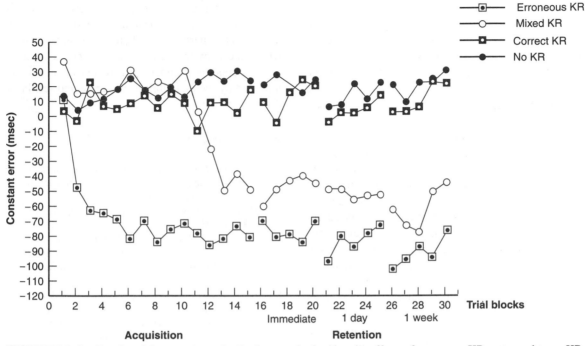

**FIGURE 5.2–5**   Results of the experiment by Buekers et al., showing the effects of erroneous KR compared to no KR and correct KR for learning an anticipation timing skill. Note that members of the mixed-KR group received correct KR for their first 50 trials and then received erroneous KR for their last 25 practice trials. (From M.J. Buekers, R.A. Magill, and K.G. Hall, "The Effect of Erroneous Knowledge of Results on Skill Acquisition When Augmented Information is Redundant" in *Quarterly Journal of Experimental Psychology,* 1992, 44(A):105–117. Reprinted by permission of The Experimental Psychology Society.)

striking was the persistence of the effect of the erroneous information one week later, when participants performed the skill without KR.

The results of this experiment have important implications for skill acquisition environments. The primary reason people resolved the conflict between sensory and augmented feedback in favor of the erroneous information is that they were not certain how to use or interpret the task-intrinsic feedback. As a result, they chose the augmented feedback as their information source for making movement adjustments on future trials. Beginners are the most likely learners to be influenced in this way. These results should tell instructors and therapists that the information they provide as augmented feedback must be appropriate and should establish a means by which the learners can inter-

pret sensory feedback. People will ignore their own sensory feedback, even though it is correct, and base their movement correction on what the instructor tells them.

## Summary

Augmented feedback is information provided by an external source that either adds to or enhances feedback directly available from performing a skill (called task-intrinsic feedback). We distinguish the two types of augmented feedback based on the part of a skill performance to which the information refers. Knowledge of results (KR) refers to the outcome of the skill performance, whereas knowledge of performance (KP) refers to performance characteristics that led to the outcome. An instructor can provide augmented feedback concurrently, while the learner is performing the skill, or terminally, after the performance is completed. Augmented feedback can serve to inform the learner about the success of the skill performance or the performance errors made; it also can serve to motivate the learner to continue striving toward a goal.

Augmented feedback can have four different effects on skill learning. Research evidence has shown that augmented feedback can be essential, not essential, an enhancement, or even detrimental for learning skills. The effect varies according to certain skill and learner characteristics. What remain to be determined from future research are the specific skill and learner characteristics and/or skill learning conditions that underlie each of these four effects. Some hypotheses do exist concerning these characteristics and conditions. It appears that when the performance of a skill provides the performer with task-intrinsic feedback that the performer can interpret effectively so that he or she can evaluate the performance, augmented feedback is not necessary. When the person cannot interpret task-intrinsic feedback from the environment or from the movements involved in the skill itself, he or she needs some form of augmented feedback. The

exact type the person needs and how or when it should be provided appear to depend on the skill the person is performing. Three situations exist in which the learner can become dependent on augmented feedback and therefore learning will be hindered by the availability of augmented feedback during practice.

## Related Readings

Adams, J. A. 1987. Historical review and appraisal of research on the learning, retention, and transfer of human motor skills. *Psychological Bulletin* 101: 41–74. (Read the sections on KR: pp. 43–44, 48–49, 61–62.)

Lee, A. M., N. C. Keh, and R. A. Magill. 1993. Instructional effects of teacher feedback in physical education. *Journal of Teaching in Physical Education* 12: 228–43.

Magill, R. A. 1993. Augmented feedback and skill acquisition. In R. N. Singer, M. Murphey, and L. K. Tennant (Eds.), *Handbook on research in sport psychology* (pp. 193–212). New York: Macmillan.

Salmoni, A. W., R. A. Schmidt, and C. B. Walter. 1984. Knowledge of results and motor learning: A review and critical reappraisal. *Psychological Bulletin* 95: 355–86.

# CONCEPT 5.3

The motor skills professional can provide augmented feedback
in a variety of ways

## Key Terms

quantitative
  augmented
  feedback

qualitative
  augmented
  feedback

performance
  bandwidth

descriptive KP

prescriptive
  KP

biofeedback

## Application

When you are helping a person learn or relearn a skill, do you ever think about the effectiveness of the augmented feedback you provide? For example, when you give a person verbal feedback, how do you decide what to tell the person? If the person is making a lot of mistakes while performing the skill, how many mistakes do you tell him or her about and which do you choose? Do you think about the possibility that there may be more effective ways to provide augmented feedback? What are the advantages, disadvantages, or limitations of these various means?

Consider the following situations. Suppose that you are teaching a golf swing to a class, or working in a clinic with a patient learning to locomote with an artificial limb. In each of these situations, the people practicing these skills can make lots of mistakes and can benefit from receiving augmented feedback. When they make mistakes, which they probably do in abundance, how do you know what to tell them to try to correct on subsequent attempts? If you had a video camera available, would you videotape them and then let them watch their own performances? Or would it be even more beneficial to take the videotapes and have them analyzed so that you could show them what their movements looked like kinematically? There are many alternative methods you can use to provide augmented feedback. But before you as the instructor or therapist use any one of these, you should know how to implement that method most effectively and when to use it to facilitate learning.

All of these questions relate to a fundamental issue confronting every person involved in motor skill instruction, regardless of setting or type of skill. The issue is how to provide adequate information for the learner's optimal benefit. In the following discussion we address these questions, to increase your understanding of motor skill learning processes and to provide useful practical information.

## Discussion

In this discussion, we will focus on important issues concerning the content of augmented feedback, and then examine several types of augmented feedback that professionals can use in instructional settings. Before we look at these, we will consider a characteristic of augmented feedback that has direct bearing on the choice of type and content of augmented feedback an instructor makes in any situation.

## Augmented Feedback Directs Attention

When deciding the type and content of augmented feedback to give, an instructor must consider this: the feedback will influence how the learner directs his or her attention while performing a skill. Recall from our discussion of Kahneman's model of attention (Concept 3.2) that an influential factor in determining how attention capacity is allocated is what Kahneman called "momentary intentions."

---

### A CLOSER LOOK

### A Research Example Showing How Augmented Feedback About Certain Aspects of a Skill Helps Correct Other Aspects

Participants in an experiment by den Brinker, Stabler, Whiting, and van Wieringen (1986) learned to perform on the slalom ski simulator. Their three-part goal was to move the platform from left to right as far as possible at a specific high frequency, and with a motion that was as fluid as possible. Based on these performance goals, each of three groups received a different type of information as KP after each trial. Researchers told participants in one group the distance they had moved the platform; they told another group's participants how close they were to performing at the criterion platform movement frequency; and they told participants in the third group how fluid their movements were. All three groups practiced for four days, performing six 1.5-min trials each day, with a test trial before and after the block of practice trials. Early in practice, the type of KP an individual received influenced the performance measure specifically related to that feature of performing the skill. However, on the last two days of practice, KP about distance caused people to improve in all the performance goal characteristics. Thus, the directing of learners' attention to improvement in one performance feature led to their developing not only that one, but also the two other performance features.

---

Augmented feedback can serve as a type of momentary intention, because it can direct the individual's attention to a particular feature of performing the skill.

Because of the attention-directing influence of augmented feedback, it is important to make sure that the feedback you give directs the person's attention to the particular aspect of the skill that, if improved, will improve significantly the performance of the entire skill or of the part of the skill the person is trying to improve. For example, suppose you are teaching a child to throw a ball at a target. Also suppose this child is making many errors, as is typical of beginners. The child may be looking at his or her hand, stepping with the wrong foot, releasing the ball awkwardly, or not rotating the trunk. Probably the most fundamental error is not looking at the target. This, then, is the error about which you should provide feedback, because it is the part of the skill to which you want the child to direct his or her attention. It is the part of the skill that, if corrected, will have an immediate, significant, positive influence on performance. By correcting this error, the child undoubtedly will also correct many of the other errors that characterize his or her performance.

## Augmented Feedback Content Issues

We will consider here three issues related to the content of augmented feedback. Each of these concerns the kind of information augmented feedback should contain.

***Information about errors versus correct aspects of performance.*** A continuing controversy about augmented feedback content is whether the information the instructor conveys to the learner should concern the mistakes he or she has made or those aspects of the performance that are correct. The answer to this question is difficult to determine, primarily because of the different roles augmented feedback can play in the skill acquisition process. When the instructor is giving error information, augmented feedback is functioning in its informational role related to facilitating skill improvement. On the other hand, when the instructor is telling a person what he or she did correctly, augmented feedback has a more motivational role.

Research evidence consistently has shown that error information is more effective for encouraging skill improvement. This evidence supports a hypothesis by Lintern and Roscoe (1980), which is an expanded version of one originally proposed by Annett (1959). The hypothesis is that focusing on what is done correctly while learning a skill, especially in the early stage of learning, is not sufficient by itself to produce optimal learning. Rather, the experience the person has in correcting errors by operating on error-based augmented feedback is especially important for skill acquisition.

Another way of looking at this issue is to consider the different roles augmented feedback plays. Error information directs a person to change certain performance characteristics; this in turn facilitates skill acquisition. On the other hand, information indicating that the person performed certain characteristics correctly tells the person that he or she is on track in learning the skill and encourages the person to keep trying. When we consider augmented feedback from this perspective, we see that whether this feedback should be about errors or about correct aspects of performance depends on the goal of the information. Error-related information works better to facilitate skill acquisition, whereas information about correct performance serves better to motivate the person to continue.

It makes good sense to provide both error-based and correct performance information during practice. The real question of importance, then, concerns the optimal proportion of each type. Unfortunately, no research results exist on which we can base an answer to this question. However, Siedentop (1983) has provided a guideline. He proposed that instructors give both types of augmented feedback according to a ratio of four error-based statements to one statement based on correct performance. A conclusion on whether this is the optimal combination to facilitate skill learning awaits experimental study. However, it seems that some such combination is an excellent way to involve both roles of augmented feedback in a skill-learning setting.

*Qualitative versus quantitative information.* Augmented feedback can be qualitative, quantitative, or both. If the augmented feedback involves a numerical value related to the magnitude of some performance characteristic, it is called **quantitative**

**augmented feedback.** In contrast, **qualitative augmented feedback** is information referring to the quality of the performance characteristic without regard for the numerical values associated with it.

For verbal augmented feedback, it is easy to distinguish these types of information in performance situations. For example, a therapist helping a patient to increase gait speed could give that patient qualitative information about the latest attempt in statements such as these: "That was faster than the last time"; "That was much better"; or "You need to bend your knee more." A physical education teacher or coach teaching a student a tennis serve could tell the student that a particular serve was "good," or "long," or could say something like this: "You made contact with the ball too far in front of you." On the other hand, the therapist could give the patient quantitative verbal augmented feedback using these words: "That time you walked 3 sec faster than the last time," or "You need to bend your knee 5 more degrees." The coach could give quantitative feedback to the tennis student like this: "The serve was 6 cm too long," or "You made contact with the ball 10 cm too far in front of you."

Therapists and instructors also can give quantitative and qualitative information in nonverbal forms of augmented feedback. For example, the therapist could give qualitative information to the patient we have described by letting him or her hear a tone when the walking speed exceeded that of the previous attempt, or when the knee flexion achieved a target amount. The teacher or coach could give the tennis student qualitative information in the form of a computer display that used a moving stick-figure to show the kinematic characteristics of his or her serving motion. Those teaching motor skills often give nonverbally presented quantitative information in combination with qualitative forms. For example, the therapist could show a patient a computer-based graphic representation of his or her leg movement while walking along, displaying numerical values of the walking speeds associated with each attempt, or the degree of knee flexion observed on each attempt. We could describe similar examples for the tennis student.

How do these two types of augmented feedback information influence skill learning? Motor learning researchers traditionally have investigated this question in experiments designed to address the *precision* of verbally presented KR. In doing so, they have assumed that quantitative KR is more precise than qualitative KR. The traditional view is that quantitative is superior to qualitative information for skill learning. However, researchers have been questioning this conclusion following a reassessment by Salmoni, Schmidt, and Walter (1984) of the research on which the conclusion is based. They showed that most of the experiments investigating the precision issue did not include retention or transfer tests.

Consider the following experiment as an example of a more appropriate conclusion about the precision effect. Each participant in an experiment by Magill and Wood (1986) learned to move his or her arm through a series of wooden barriers to produce a specific six-segment movement pattern. Each segment had its own criterion movement time, which participants had to learn. Following each of 120 practice trials, participants received either qualitative KR for each segment (i.e., "too fast," "too slow," or "correct") or quantitative KR for each segment (i.e., the number of msec too fast or too slow). As you can see from figure 5.3–1, the first 60 trials showed no difference in performance of participants based on the type of information

**FIGURE 5.3–1** Absolute constant error scores during practice with KR (blocks 1–10) and without KR (blocks 11–12) on a six-segment timing pattern in the experiment by Magill and Wood. (From R.A. Magill and C. Wood, "Knowledge of Results Precision as a Learning Variable in Motor Skill Acquisition" in *Research Quarterly for Exercise and Sport,* 1986, Vol. 57, pp. 170–173. Copyright © 1986 American Alliance for Health, Physical Education, Recreation, and Dance. Reprinted by permission.)

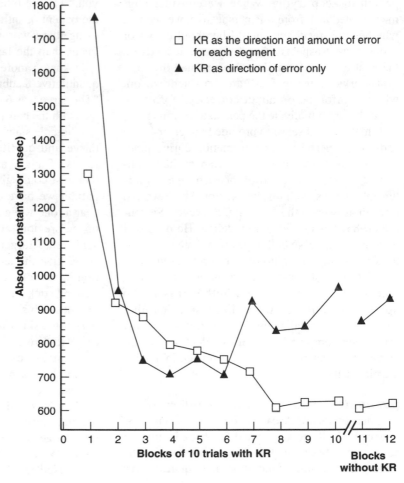

□  KR as the direction and amount of error for each segment

▲  KR as direction of error only

received. However, during the final 60 trials and on the 20 no-KR retention trials, the quantitative-KR condition yielded better performance.

From these results we can conclude that the answer to the question about whether qualitative or quantitative information is better for skill learning cannot be an either/or response. Determining which type of information is better depends on the individual learner's stage of learning. People in the early stage of learning give attention primarily to the qualitative information, even if they have quantitative information available. The advantage of this attention focus is that the qualitative information provides an easier way to make a first approximation of the required movement. Put another way, this information allows learners to control more easily the many degrees of freedom and produce an action that is "in the ballpark" of what they need to do. After they achieve this "ballpark" action, quantitative information is more valuable to them, because it enables them to refine the action to make it more effective for achieving the action goal. In terms of Gentile's learning stages model, qualitative information can allow a person to "get the idea of the movement," but the learner needs quantitative information in the next stage to achieve its fixation or diversification goals.

***Augmented feedback based on performance bandwidths.*** Closely related to the issues we have addressed in the preceding two sections is the question of how large an error a performer should make before the instructor or therapist gives augmented feedback. This question has distinct practical appeal because it undoubtedly reflects what occurs in actual instruction situations. To many teachers and therapists, it seems reasonable to provide feedback only when errors are large enough to warrant attention. This practice suggests that in many skill-learning situations, teachers or therapists develop **performance bandwidths** that establish error tolerance limits specifying when they will or will not give augmented feedback. When a person performs within the tolerance limits of the bandwidth, the teacher or therapist does not give augmented feedback. But if the person makes an error that is out-

side that performance bandwidth, the person instructing does give feedback.

There is some laboratory-based research support for the effectiveness of the performance bandwidth approach. For example, in the first reported experiment investigating this procedure, Sherwood (1988) had subjects practice a rapid elbow-flexion task with a movement-time goal of 200 msec. Members of one group received KR about their movement-time error after every trial, regardless of the amount of error (i.e., had a 0 percent bandwidth). Members of two other groups received KR only when their error exceeded bandwidths of 5 percent and 10 percent of the goal movement time. The results of a no-KR retention test showed that the 10 percent bandwidth condition resulted in the least amount of movement time variability (i.e., variable error), while the 0 percent condition resulted in the most variable error. Other researchers have replicated these results (see, e.g., Lee, White, and Carnahan 1990; Cauraugh, Chen, and Radlo 1993).

## Examples of Different Types of Knowledge of Performance

Most of the research on which we base our knowledge of augmented feedback and skill learning comes from laboratory experiments in which researchers gave knowledge of results (KR) to participants. Although most of the conclusions from that research also apply to knowledge of performance (KP), it is useful to look at some of the research that has investigated different types of KP. Based on evidence from teacher performance research, it seems that most people engaging in motor skill instruction give KP more than they give KR. And as movement analysis technology becomes more sophisticated and available, nonverbal forms of KP are becoming more prominent in skill acquisition settings.

***Verbal knowledge of performance.*** One of the reasons providers of skill instruction give verbal KP more than verbal KR is that KP gives people more information to help them improve the movement aspects of skill performance. Because KR is

## A CLOSER LOOK

### Quantitative versus Qualitative Augmented Feedback and the Performance Bandwidth Technique

Cauraugh, Chen, and Radlo (1993) had subjects practice a timing task in which they had to press a sequence of three keys in 500 msec. Participants in one group received quantitative KR about their movement times (MT) when MT was *outside* a 10 percent performance bandwidth. A second group, in the reverse of that condition, received quantitative KR only when MT was *inside* the 10 percent performance bandwidth. Two additional groups had participants "yoked" to individual participants in the outside and inside bandwidth conditions. Members of these two groups received KR on the same trials their "yoked" counterparts did. This procedure provided a way to have two conditions with the same frequency of augmented feedback, while allowing a comparison between bandwidth and no-bandwidth conditions.

In terms of KR frequency, those in the outside bandwidth condition received quantitative KR on 25 percent of the 60 practice trials, while those in the inside condition received KR on 65 percent of the trials. The interesting feature of this difference is that the remaining trials for both groups were implicitly qualitative KR trials, because when they received no KR, the participants knew that their performance was "good" or "not good." The retention test performance results showed that the two bandwidth conditions did not differ, but both yielded better learning than the non-bandwidth conditions. These results show that establishing performance bandwidths as the basis for providing quantitative KR yields an interplay between quantitative and qualitative KR that facilitates skill learning.

based on performance outcome, it seems to have little effect on skill acquisition, except in situations where KR has been shown to be essential for skill learning (as described in Concept 5.2). One of the problems that arise with the use of verbal KP is determining the appropriate content of what to tell the person practicing the skill. This problem occurs because skills are typically complex and KP usually relates to a specific feature of skill performance. The challenge for the instructor or therapist, then, is selecting the appropriate features of the performance on which to base KP.

To solve this problem, the first thing a teacher or therapist must do is perform a *skill analysis* of the skill being practiced. This means identifying the various component parts of the skill. Then, the professional must organize the parts by prioritizing how critical they are for performing the skill correctly. He or she should list the most critical part first, then the second most critical, and so on. To determine which part is most critical, he or she decides which part of the skill absolutely must be done properly for the entire skill to be performed

correctly. For example, in the relatively simple task of reaching for and grasping a pencil, the most critical component is looking at the pencil. This part of the skill is the most critical because even if the beginning learner did all other parts of the skill correctly (which would be unlikely), there is a very low chance that he or she would perform the skill correctly without looking at the pencil. In this case, then, looking at the pencil would be first on the skill analysis priority list, and would be the first part of the skill the professional assessed in determining what to give KP about.

*Verbal KP statements are of two types.* In **descriptive KP,** the KP statement simply describes the error the performer has made. The other type, **prescriptive KP,** not only identifies the error, but also tells the person what to do to correct it. For example, if you tell a person, "You moved your right foot too soon," you only describe the problem. However, if you say, "You need to move your right foot at the same time you move your right arm," you also give prescriptive information about what the person needs to do to correct the problem.

---

| A CLOSER LOOK |
| --- |

### An Example of Basing KP on a Skill Analysis

In an experiment by Magill and Schoenfelder-Zohdi (1996), people practiced a rhythmic gymnastics rope skill. The skill involved first holding the rope with both knots at the ends of the rope in one hand and then circling the rope two times forward in the sagittal plane. At the end of the second circle, the person let go of one knot so that the rope went to full extension and hit the floor. At the same time, the person did a half turn to face the direction opposite to the starting position. As the rope came back, the person caught the knot at the end of the rope.

The authors did a skill analysis. From this, they developed the following priority list of thirty-six KP statements. (The statement for a given trial was chosen based on what the experimenter saw as the most critical error to be corrected on the next trial.)

1. Hold both knots in one hand
2. Circle the rope two times
3. Circle the rope forward
4. Move your arm away from your body
5. Circle the rope in the sagittal plane
6. Circle the rope slower
7. Circle the rope faster
8. Make a half turn
9. Do not turn your body to the left
10. Turn your feet
11. Turn earlier
12. Turn later
13. Do not turn too much
14. Do not twist your body
15. Do not turn abruptly
16. Let the knot go earlier
17. Let the knot go later
18. Do not let go of the other knot
19. Move your arm down when letting the knot go
20. The rope should hit the floor
21. Do not hit the rope so hard on the floor
22. Do not interrupt the motion of the rope
23. Move your arm to your right
24. Move your arm to the side of your body
25. Move your arm to shoulder height
26. Let the rope slide far enough
27. Keep your arm straight
28. Pull the rope downward
29. Pull the rope back earlier
30. Pull the rope back later
31. Pull the rope back more strongly
32. Pull the rope back more weakly
33. Do not grab the middle of the rope
34. Guide the rope better
35. Try to catch the knot
36. That was correct

---

Which type of KP better facilitates learning? Although there is no empirical evidence, common sense dictates that the answer varies with the stage of learning of the person practicing the skill. The statement, "You moved your right foot too soon," would be helpful to a beginner only if he or she knew that the right foot was supposed to move at the same time as the right arm. Thus, descriptive KP statements are useful to help people improve performance only once they have learned what they need to do to make a correction. This suggests that prescriptive KP statements are more helpful for beginners. For the more advanced person, a descriptive KP statement often will suffice.

*Videotape as augmented feedback.* The increasing use of videotape as augmented feedback argues for the need for instructors and therapists to know more about how to use it effectively. Unfortunately, very little research has been done on which to base guidelines for using videotape as augmented feedback. In fact, Rothestein and Arnold (1976) published the only extensive review of the research literature, reviewing over fifty studies that involved eighteen different sport activities. In most of these studies, the students were beginners, although a few studies included intermediate- and advanced-level performers. Although results about the effectiveness of videotape were generally mixed, two points were clear. First, while the type of activity was not a critical factor, the skill level of the student was critical. When beginners watched a videotape replay, they needed someone to point out the important information to them. Advanced or intermediate performers did not appear to need this type of assistance. Second, videotape replays were most effective when used for sustained periods of time. Studies included in the review for which videotape was an effective learning aid included videotape as part of the practice regime for at least five weeks.

An experiment by Kernodle and Carlton (1992) provides one example of research evidence supporting the benefit of having beginners watch videotape replays. Participants practiced throwing a soft, spongy ball as far as possible with their nondominant arm. People in one group received specific focus cues about what to look for on videotape replays of each trial. People in another group received this cue plus a prescriptive KP statement related to a critical error they had made on the trial. Members of both of these groups eventually threw the ball farther and developed better throwing forms than members of a group that only watched the videotape replay and members of a group that only received KR about the distance of their throws.

When considering the use of videotape as augmented feedback, teachers and therapists should acknowledge the important point that videotape does not transmit to the beginner every type of performance information that may be critical to improving performance. Videotape replays clearly transmit certain types of performance information to the learner better than they transmit other types. Selder and Del Rolan (1979) gave an excellent example of this. In their study, twelve- and thirteen-year-old girls were learning to perform a balance beam routine. A control group received only verbal feedback about their performance on each trial. Another group observed videotape replays of their performances. One result supported the need for sustained use of videotape to benefit learning. Although there were no performance differences between the two groups at the end of

four weeks of practice, the videotape group scored significantly higher than the verbal feedback group at the end of six weeks (see figure 5.3–2). But what was particularly notable in these results was that the gymnasts in the videotape group scored significantly higher on only four of the eight factors making up the total score. These factors were precision, execution, amplitude, and orientation and direction. Their observation of videotape replays provided them with no advantage over those who received verbal feedback for rhythm, elegance, coordination, and lightness of jumping and tumbling.

***Graphically presented kinematics as augmented feedback.*** The capability to do sophisticated kinematic analysis of movement has become increasingly more common in rehabilitation clinics, as well as in sports instruction clubs. Therapists and teachers use this type of analysis to portray kinematic characteristics of skill performances graphically as augmented feedback. Just as it should for videotape, research should determine the effectiveness of kinematic analysis in providing augmented feedback, and establish guidelines for implementing its use.

The idea of using kinematic characteristics as augmented feedback for enhancing skill learning did not begin with the advent of computers. One of the earliest studies investigating this feedback method involved the training of machine operators in industry (Lindahl 1945). The workers had to cut thin discs of tungsten precisely and quickly with a machine that required fast, accurate, and rhythmic coordination of the hands and feet. The typical training method for this job was trial and error. However, Lindahl developed an alternative training method that involved providing augmented feedback in the form of a paper tracing of the foot pattern a worker produced while cutting the tungsten discs. An example of a tracing for the correct foot action is at the top of figure 5.3–3. Trainers presented the trainees with charts illustrating this correct foot action

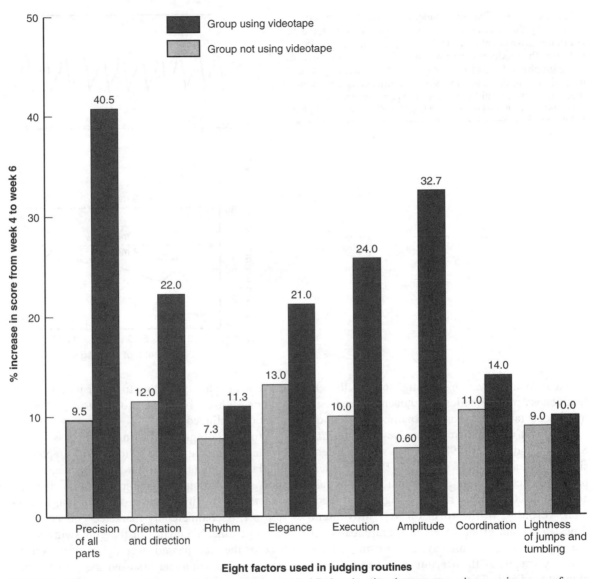

**FIGURE 5.3–2** Results of the experiment by Selder and Del Rolan showing the percentage increase in scores of a gymnastics group using videotape and a group not using videotape. (Source: Data from D.J. Selder and N. Del Rolan, "Knowledge of Performance, Skill Level and Performance on the Balance Beam" in *Canadian Journal of Applied Sport Sciences,* 1979, 4:226–229.)

and then periodically showed them the results of their own foot movements. The benefit of this procedure is shown in the bottom portion of figure 5.3–3. It is notable in this figure that the trainees who received the augmented feedback achieved in eleven weeks production performance levels that had taken other trainees five months to achieve. Additionally, the trainees reduced their percentages of broken cutting wheels to almost zero in twelve weeks, a level not achieved by those trained with the traditional method in less than nine months.

**FIGURE 5.3–3**    The upper panel illustrates the foot action required by the machine operator to produce an acceptable disc cut in the experiment by Lindahl. The graph at the bottom indicates the production performance achieved by the trainees using graphic information during 12 weeks of training. The dashed lines indicate the levels of performance achieved by other workers after 2, 5, and 9 months of experience. (Source: L.G. Lindahl, "Movement Analysis as an Industrial Training Method" in *Journal of Applied Psychology,* 1945, Vol. 29:420–436, 1945 American Psychological Association.)

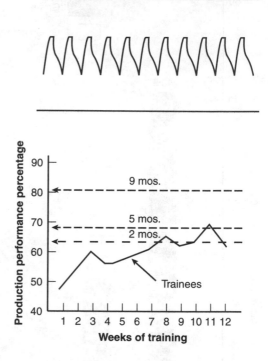

Most of the research investigations of the effectiveness of kinematics as augmented feedback have been laboratory-based experiments. A good example is an experiment by Newell, Quinn, Sparrow, and Walter (1983), which was an extension of an earlier study by Hatze (1976). Participants practiced moving a lever to a target as fast as possible. One group received augmented feedback verbally, in the form of their movement times; a second group received it graphically, in the form of computer displays of their movement-velocity traces. A third group received no augmented feedback. The group receiving the graphic kinematic display showed the best performance during two days of practice. It is interesting to note here that all three groups practiced initially with no augmented feedback for 25 trials and showed steady improvement before reaching a steady state around trial 20. Both augmented feedback groups showed immediate improvement when they began receiving their forms of augmented feedback, with the graphic presentation of

movement velocity leading to better initial performance, which became more pronounced as practice continued.

Wood, Gallagher, Martino, and Ross (1992) provided a good example of the use of graphically displayed movement kinematics for learning a sport skill. Participants practiced a full-swing golf shot with a five iron from a platform into a backstop net. A commercially marketed golf computer monitored the kinematics of the golf swing as the head of the club passed over light sensors on the platform. The computer assessed the velocity, displacement, and trajectory path of each swing and displayed this information on a monitor for learners in two groups. One group saw a template of an optimum pattern along with the kinematics; the other group did not see this template. A third group received kinematic information verbally in the form of numbers referring to kinematic outcomes of the swing. A fourth group received no augmented feedback. On a retention test given one week later without augmented feedback, the group that had observed the graphic presentation of the swing kinematics along with the optimum pattern template performed best.

Finally, it is important to point out that when teachers, coaches, and therapists use graphic displays of movement kinematics as augmented feedback, they should take the stage of learning into account. Beginners benefit from kinematic information only when they can interpret and use it to improve their own performance. Thus, it is useful to show a template of the kinematic goal to beginners. More skilled people can take advantage of more complex kinematic information.

*Biofeedback as augmented feedback.* **Biofeedback** involves the use of instrumentation to provide information about physiological processes involved in performing a skill. The most commonly used form of biofeedback in motor skill learning research has been *EMG biofeedback.* Most of what we know about the effect of EMG biofeedback on skill learning comes from research done in rehabilitation settings. Results of this work have shown beneficial effects on skill learning. The rationale underlying the effectiveness of EMG biofeedback is that movement disorder patients are often unaware of their movements, and that biofeedback provides a means of enhancing their awareness.

A study by Mulder and Hulstijn (1985) is a good example of evidence supporting the effectiveness of EMG biofeedback. Participants practiced selective muscle control by learning to abduct the big toe while keeping the other toes of the foot from moving. The authors used this task because it required participants to control a specific muscle group to perform the action; this is a common characteristic of rehabilitation situations. Each member of one group received normal proprioceptive feedback, but could not see his or her foot and received no verbal feedback about his or her performance. Another group received both proprioceptive and visual feedback, but no verbal feedback. The third group had both proprioceptive and visual feedback plus tactile feedback, which came from a force meter, but received no verbal feedback. After this stage, two groups received biofeedback by seeing either an EMG signal or a force meter display in addition to normal proprioceptive and visual feedback. Results showed that the two augmented biofeedback groups performed better than the nonaugmented groups on each of the two days of training.

It is worth noting that the results from the laboratory-based situation in the Mulder and Hulstijn (1985) experiment have been supported in a real-world context. In an experiment by Montes, Bedmar, and Martin (1993), researchers trained piano students to control their thumb attack while playing. This action involved their striking with maximum force and then immediately relaxing the thumb. By means of a monitor, students received EMG biofeedback from the abductor pollicis brevis muscle, which is the agonist for this thumb movement. They observed a graph of the amplitude and relaxation rates of thumb abduction during the movement. Researchers compared these students to a group that did not receive this biofeedback, and found the biofeedback condition to be more effective for facilitating acquisition of this action.

Researchers also have found *other types of biofeedback* to aid skill acquisition. For example, experimenters provided heartbeat information auditorily to subjects while they were engaged in rifle shooting training, in an experiment reported by Daniels and Landers (1981). Previous work had shown that elite shooters squeeze the rifle trigger between heartbeats. To help beginners acquire this characteristic, the authors provided heartbeat biofeedback to the students during their shooting performance. Results indicated that the use of this form of biofeedback facilitated acquisition of this important performance characteristic and led to improved shooting scores.

Chollet, Micallef, and Rabischong (1988) used another type of biofeedback with skilled swimmers to help them improve and maintain their high level of performance. The authors developed swimming paddles that would provide information to enable highly skilled swimmers to maintain their optimal velocity and number of arm cycles in a training

---

**A CLOSER LOOK**

### Guidelines for Giving Augmented Feedback

- **The person must be capable of using the information.** More specific or sophisticated augmented feedback is not necessarily better. Beginners need information to help them make a "ballpark" approximation of the required movements; they need more specific information as skill learning progresses.
- **A combination of error-based augmented feedback and information based on what was done correctly is most helpful,** to take advantage of the roles of augmented feedback for facilitating skill improvement and for motivating a person to continue practicing the skill.
- **Verbal KP should be based on the most critical error** made during a practice attempt; the professional should identify this based on a skill analysis and a prioritized list of components of the skill.

- **Prescriptive KP is better for novices,** while descriptive KP is more appropriate for more skilled people.
- **Videotape replays can be effective with beginners** if instructors or therapists provide direction to help them detect and correct errors as they watch the tape.
- **Computer-generated displays of the kinematics of a skill performance will be more effective for more advanced performers** than for novices to help facilitate skill improvement.
- **Biofeedback needs to give people information they can use to alter movements.** In addition, it must be presented in such a way that people do not become dependent on it.

---

session. The swimming paddles contained force sensors and sound generators that transmitted an audible signal to transmitters in a swimmer's cap. The sensors were set at a desired water-propulsion-force threshold; when the swimmer reached this threshold, the paddles produced a sound audible to the swimmer. The authors found this device to help swimmers maintain their stroke count and swimming speed when they otherwise would have found it decreasing through the course of a long distance practice session.

## Summary

Because augmented feedback is such an important part of skill learning, it is important to understand what information the therapist or instructor should provide to facilitate learning and how often he or she should give that information. The professional

should keep three important points in mind when deciding what augmented feedback information to give. First, he or she should determine the precision of the information. Augmented feedback can be either too precise or too general to aid learning. Second, he or she should determine the content of the augmented feedback. In doing so, the therapist or teacher must understand that augmented feedback serves to direct attention to certain parts of the skill; therefore, augmented feedback should direct attention to the part of the skill that it is most important to improve on the next trial. Third, the professional should establish the form of presenting the augmented feedback. While verbal augmented feedback is the most common type, alternative methods such as videotape replay, graphic representations of movement kinematics, and augmenting sensory feedback also can be effective.

# Related Readings

Beckham, J. C., F. J. Keefe, D. S. Caldwell, and C. J. Brown. 1991. Biofeedback as a means to alter electromyographic activity in a total knee replacement patient. *Biofeedback and Self-Regulation* 16: 23–35.

Lee, A. M., N. C. Keh, and R. A. Magill. 1993. Instructional effects of teacher feedback in physical education. *Journal of Teaching in Physical Education* 12: 228–43.

Newell, K. M., and P. M. McGinnis. 1985. Kinematic information feedback for skilled performance. *Human Learning* 4: 39–56.

Schmidt, R. A., and D. E. Young. 1991. Methodology for motor learning: A paradigm for kinematic feedback. *Journal of Motor Behavior* 23: 13–24.

Swinnen, S. P., C. B. Walter, J. M. Pauwels, P. F. Meugens, and M. B. Beirincks. 1990. The dissociation of interlimb constraints. *Human Performance* 3: 187–215.

Winstein, C. J. 1991. Knowledge of results and motor learning. Implications for physical therapy. *Physical Therapy* 71: 140–49.

Wrisberg, C.A., G. A. Dale, Z. Liu, and A. Reed. 1995. The effects of augmented information on motor learning: A multidimensional assessment. *Research Quarterly for Exercise and Sport* 66: 9–16.

# CONCEPT 5.4

Several timing characteristics of augmented feedback can influence skill learning

## Key Terms

KR-delay
  interval

post-KR
  interval

subjective
  error
  estimation

trials-delay
  procedure

fading
  technique

guidance
  hypothesis

summary
  augmented
  feedback

## Application

Three important questions arise about the timing of giving augmented feedback. First, should the motor skills instructor present it during or after the performance of a skill? Second, how do the length of and activity during time intervals preceding and following the presentation of augmented feedback affect skill learning? Third, how often should a person give augmented feedback during practice? The following example illustrates how each of these questions is a part of skill instruction.

Suppose that you are teaching a person to play golf. Each of our three questions comes into play in a practice session. The first question is relevant here because you could give augmented feedback while the person swings, after he or she has hit the ball, or at both times. If you give feedback after the person hits the ball, the second question comes into play, because two time intervals are now important. The first is the time interval from the person's hitting of the ball until you give augmented feedback. The second is the time that elapses from your giving of that information until the person hits another ball. Finally, the third question is involved in this situation because you could give augmented feedback every time the learner hits the ball, or only a few times during practice.

The three timing questions are related to some important practical concerns. For example, does it matter whether the feedback is given during or after a movement is completed? Does it matter how long a person must wait to get augmented feedback after completing a movement? How important is the amount of time between the completion of one movement and the beginning of the next movement? Does it matter how frequently during practice the learner receives augmented feedback? Does the notion that "more is better than less" apply here? We address these questions in the following discussion section.

## Discussion

The first of the three augmented feedback timing issues we will consider here is whether it is better to give augmented feedback while a person is performing a skill, in what is known as *concurrent augmented feedback,* or to give it at the end of a practice attempt, in what we call *terminal augmented feedback.* In addressing the second issue, we consider two specific intervals of time that are created when a learner receives terminal augmented feedback. One interval (the **KR-delay interval**) is between the end of one practice attempt and the augmented feedback. It is important to consider this interval because as we do so, we examine the question of when after a skill is performed a teacher or therapist should give augmented feedback. The other interval (the **post-KR interval**) is between the augmented feedback and the beginning of the next practice attempt. The third timing issue concerns how often the professional should give augmented feedback during practice to facilitate skill learning. This issue has generated a great deal of research in recent years under the label of the *frequency* of augmented feedback.[1]

## Concurrent versus Terminal Augmented Feedback

An important training question is whether concurrent or terminal presentation of augmented feedback is better for facilitating skill acquisition. Unfortunately, a search through the motor learning research literature suggests that there is no unequivocal answer to this question. However, a guideline emerges from that literature that can help us answer the question. Terminal augmented feedback can be effective in almost any skill learning situation, although the teacher or therapist must consider the nature of its effect in light of our discussion in Concept 5.2 of the four different effects augmented feedback can have on skill learning. Concurrent augmented feedback, on the other hand, seems to be most effective when task-intrinsic feedback is very low and the person cannot determine from the task-intrinsic feedback how to perform the skill or improve performance. It is in these situations that concurrent augmented feedback seems to work best.

## Implementing Concurrent Augmented Feedback

When augmented feedback is concurrent with a learner's performing of a skill, the feedback typically is presented by some mechanical or electronic device that enhances either or both of two performance context characteristics. In some situations, concurrent augmented feedback *enhances certain regulatory features* of the environmental context; this occurs, for example, when the pathway is illuminated while a person is on target in a tracking task. Concurrent augmented feedback also can *enhance certain movement features* of the skill; this occurs when electromyographic (EMG) biofeedback is used as augmented feedback.

Two types of learning outcomes are possible when people give concurrent augmented feedback in skill acquisition situations. The more positive outcome is that the feedback enhances certain characteristics of the learner's performance of the skill; this can be an effective training technique. The second type of learning outcome is a negative one. In certain situations, concurrent feedback leads to very good initial practice performance, but then performance shows no further improvement for the remainder of practice. On transfer trials, for which the augmented feedback is removed, performance actually may decline.

Two experiments illustrate these two different effects of concurrent feedback on skill learning. An experiment by Vander Linden, Cauraugh, and Greene (1993) comparing concurrent and terminal augmented feedback demonstrated the *negative effect* of the former. Participants learned a 5-sec isometric elbow-extension force production task. One group received concurrent kinetic augmented feedback during every trial. The force of a person's response was shown on an oscilloscope matched against a visible template of the correct response (see figure 5.4–1 for an example). The group that received this information concurrently while performing each trial did better during practice than two groups that received terminal augmented feedback. Members of one of these latter groups saw the oscilloscope results after every trial (100 percent frequency), while members of the other group saw their results only after every other trial (50 percent frequency). However, forty-eight hours later, on a retention test during which participants received no augmented feedback, the concurrent group showed the worst performance of the three.

An experiment by Hadden, Magill, and Sidaway (1995) illustrates the *beneficial effects* of using concurrent augmented feedback. Participants practiced a task that required them to coordinate the movement of two levers, one for each arm, to draw

1. Note that the terminology used to describe these two intervals follows the traditional labels used in the majority of the research literature, even though we have been using the term KR in a more specific way than these interval labels imply. It is important to see these intervals as relevant to all forms of augmented feedback.

**FIGURE 5.4–1** An example from the Vander Linder et al. experiment of what a participant saw during and/or after a trial on which they attempted to produce a 5-sec elbow-extension force trace that replicated as closely as possible the template trace. (Reprinted from *Physical Therapy.* D.W. Vander Linden, et al., "The Effect of Frequency of Kinetic Feedback on Learning an Isometric Force Production Task in Nondisabled Subjects," 1993, 73:79–87 with permission of the American Physical Therapy Association.)

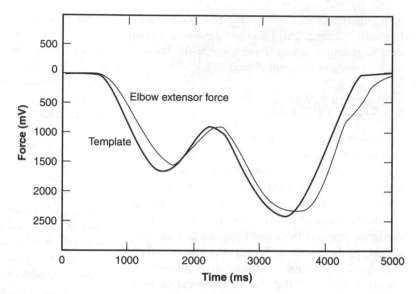

a circle on a computer monitor. Those in the concurrent feedback condition saw what they were drawing as they drew it by observing the movement of a line on the screen as they moved the levers. Those in the terminal feedback condition saw what they drew only after they completed the trial. The results showed that the concurrent condition led not only to better practice trial performance, but also to better retention test performance one day later, with no augmented feedback given.

*Predicting learning outcomes of concurrent augmented feedback.* How we can know which of the two learning outcomes of concurrent augmented feedback we should expect for a skill learning situation? According to Lintern, Roscoe, and Sivier (1990), the important factor is the extent to which the augmented feedback directs the person's attention to how to control his or her own perceptual and motor control characteristics to perform the skill. When the augmented feedback influences people to direct their attention away from critical task-intrinsic feedback and toward the augmented feedback instead, the augmented feedback becomes a crutch that they will need for future performance (see, e.g., Karlin and Mortimer 1963; Lintern and Roscoe 1980). The more the augmented feedback

directs attention to important perceptual and motor control features involved in performing the skill, the more effective the augmented feedback will be for training.

To help clarify the Lintern et al. hypothesis, consider how it applies to the two experiments we described in the previous section. For the isometric force production task in the Vander Linden et al. experiment, task-intrinsic feedback is minimal and difficult to interpret. When people try to learn this task, their tendency is to direct attention toward the augmented feedback on the oscilloscope and away from the task-intrinsic feedback. As a result, concurrent augmented feedback leads to rapid improvement, but also to a dependence that causes a deterioration in performance when the learners cannot observe the oscilloscope while performing. Now, consider the bimanual coordination task in the Hadden, Magill, and Sidaway (1995) experiment, in which participants had to coordinate the movement of the two arms to draw a circle on the computer screen. When people first attempt this task, task-intrinsic feedback is initially low, because there is nothing inherent in the task itself that tells the person what to do. The concurrent augmented feedback provides this essential information. But once performers acquire this

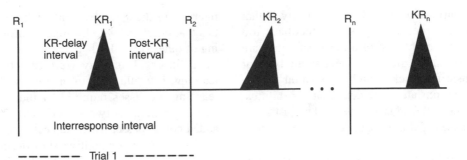

**FIGURE 5.4–2**  Intervals of time related to KR during the acquisition of a skill.

knowledge, task-intrinsic feedback is adequate. Augmented feedback is no longer so important and does not appear to distract performers' attention from this essential task-intrinsic feedback.

Thus, the need for concurrent augmented feedback is highest when task-intrinsic feedback does not provide information on what people must do to achieve the action goal. In Gentile's terms, concurrent augmented feedback aids learning when the skill itself does not provide sufficient information to allow the person to get the idea of the movement, and when terminally presented augmented feedback will not provide this information either.

## The KR-Delay and Post-KR Intervals

The second timing issue related to augmented feedback concerns when the feedback is given terminally. Two intervals of time are created between two trials: the KR-delay interval and the post-KR interval. These intervals are depicted graphically in figure 5.4–2. To understand the relationship between these intervals and skill learning, we must understand the influence of two variables: *time,* or the length of the interval, and *activity,* the cognitive and/or motor activity during the interval.

***The length of the KR-delay interval.***  It is not uncommon to see statements in textbooks indicating that a learner should receive augmented feedback as soon as possible after performing a skill, because delaying it beyond a certain amount of time would lead to poorer learning. A significant prob-

lem with this viewpoint is that it has little research evidence to support it. Such a view comes from research based predominantly on animal learning (see Adams 1987). Research has established that human learners see augmented feedback as more than a reward: augmented feedback has informational value that humans use to solve problems associated with learning a skill. Whereas animal learning studies have shown that delaying reward leads to decreased learning (e.g., Roberts 1930), human skill learning studies have shown that delaying augmented feedback does not have this negative effect (e.g., Bilodeau and Bilodeau 1958b).

While delaying the presentation of augmented feedback does not appear to affect skill learning, there does seem to be a *minimum* amount of time that must pass before it is given. Two experiments by Swinnen, Schmidt, Nicholson, and Shapiro (1990) demonstrated this. In these experiments, participants learned to move a lever through a two-reversal movement to achieve a specific movement-time goal (experiment 1), or to move a lever coincident in time with the appearance of a target light (experiment 2). They received KR after three different intervals: immediately upon completing the required movement (i.e., "instantaneously"), 8 sec after completing it (experiment 1) or 3.2 sec after completing it (experiment 2). The results of both experiments showed that giving KR instantaneously upon completing a movement had a negative effect on learning.

Why would receiving augmented feedback immediately after completing a movement not be good for learning a skill? One possibility is that when learners receive augmented feedback too soon after the completion of a movement, they are not able to engage in the subjective analysis of task-intrinsic feedback, which is essential for developing appropriate error-detection capabilities. When augmented feedback is delayed by just a few seconds, these capabilities can develop effectively.

*Activity during the KR-delay interval.* Researchers investigating the effects of activity during the KR-delay interval have found three types of outcomes. In some circumstances, activity has no effect on skill learning. In others, activity hinders learning. At still other times, activity benefits learning. These different types of results have provided insight into the learning processes involved in the KR-delay interval, as well as providing distinct implications for developing effective instructional strategies.

The most common effect of activity during the KR-delay interval on skill learning is that it has *no influence on learning.* Experiments have demonstrated this result for many years (e.g., Bilodeau 1969; Boulter 1964; Marteniuk 1986). For example, in the Marteniuk experiment, subjects practiced moving a lever to produce a specific sine-wave-like pattern on a computer screen. One group received KR within a few seconds after completing the movement and engaged in no activity during the KR-delay interval; another group had a 40-sec KR-delay interval, but did not engage in any activity during the interval; and a third group also had a 40-sec KR-delay interval, but engaged in a lever-movement task in which the subjects attempted to reproduce a movement pattern that the experimenter had just performed. The results showed no differences among the groups on a no-KR retention test.

There is some evidence, although it is sparse, that activity during the KR-delay interval *hinders learning.* The most important result of this research has been to enable researchers to identify situations in which this outcome occurs. Two types of activities have shown this negative effect and suggest which types of learning processes occur during this

interval. In the study by Marteniuk (1986), activities that interfered with learning involved the learning of other skills. He hypothesized that if the KR-delay interval activity were to interfere with learning, it would have to interfere with the exact learning processes required by the primary task being learned. In two experiments, Marteniuk added conditions in which subjects had to learn either a motor or a cognitive skill during the KR-delay interval. Results of both experiments indicated that these types of learning activities interfered with learning of the primary skill.

The other type of KR-delay interval activity that research has shown to hinder skill learning involved estimating the movement-time error of another person's lever movement, which the second person performed during the interval. In an experiment by Swinnen (1990), people learned to move a lever a specified distance, involving two reversals of direction, in a criterion movement time. Subjects who had to engage in the error estimation activity during the KR-delay interval showed worse performance on a retention test than those who did nothing or who performed a nonlearning task during the interval.

Finally, results of some experiments indicate that certain activities during the KR-delay interval actually can *benefit learning.* In the type of activity showing this effect, the person estimates his or her own error, in what is called **subjective error estimation,** before receiving augmented feedback. Hogan and Yanowitz (1978) first reported evidence of this beneficial activity effect. Participants practiced a task for which the goal was to move a handle along a trackway a specified distance of 47 cm in 200 msec. One group did not engage in any activity before receiving KR. A second group was required to give a subjective error estimation in the form of a verbal estimate of their own error for each trial before receiving KR for that trial. The results showed that although there were no differences between groups at the end of the 50 trials of practice, the group that had engaged in the error estimation activity during the KR-delay interval performed significantly better on no-KR retention trials.

In the experiment described previously, Swinnen (1990) found the same error estimation benefits. What is important about the Swinnen experiments is that they involved a comparison of subjective error estimation with participants' estimation of the error in a movement made by the experimenter. A comparison of these two conditions (see figure 5.4–3) showed that a person's estimate of his or her own error benefitted learning, whereas the person's estimate of error in a different person's movement hindered learning.

We find an interesting parallel to the subjective error estimation situation in what researchers call the **trials-delay procedure.** Here, experiment participants receive KR not when they complete a trial, but after they complete performance on a later trial. Anderson, Magill, and Sekiya (1994) used this technique for subjects learning to make a blindfolded aiming movement. One group received KR about distance error after every trial (delay–0). A second group received KR two trials later (delay–2), which meant that they were told their error for trial 1 after completing trial 3. Results (figure 5.4–4) were that while the delay condition hindered performance during practice, it led to better performance on a 24-hr retention test. When we

compare the beneficial results from this delay procedure to those reported for the subjective error estimation procedure, we must acknowledge the importance of people's directing their attention to task-intrinsic feedback to facilitate error detection processes.

What do these different effects of activity reveal about learning processes that occur during the KR-delay interval? Our conclusion is that during this time interval the learner is actively engaged in learning processes involving activities such as developing an understanding of the task-instrinsic feedback and establishing essential error detection capabilities (see Swinnen 1990; Swinnen et al. 1990). When activity requiring similar processing occurs at the same time, interference with essential learning processes occurs, because the learner's attention capacity is too limited to allow both to occur simultaneously. On the other hand, when other activity during this interval enhances these processes, learning is facilitated.

***The length of the post-KR interval.*** Researchers traditionally have viewed the post-KR interval as a very important interval for skill acquisition. They reason that it is during this period of time that the

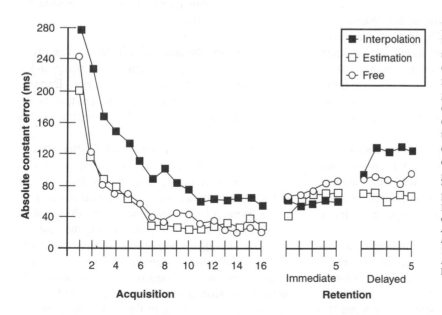

**FIGURE 5.4–3** Results from the experiment by Swinnen showing the influence of estimating the experimenter's movement error (interpolation group) and the influence of estimating the subject's own error (estimation group) during the KR-delay interval, compared with no activity during the interval (free group). (From S.P. Swinnen, "Interpolated Activities During the Knowledge-of-Results Delay and Post-Knowledge-of-Results Interval: Effects on Performance and Learning." in *Journal of Experimental Psychology: Learning, Memory, and Cognition,* 1990, 16:692–705. Copyright © 1990 American Psychological Association. Reprinted by permission.)

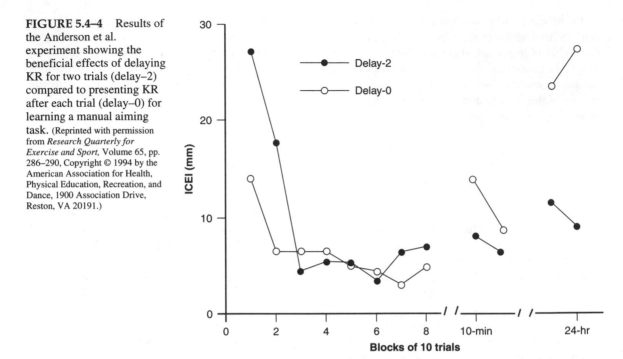

**FIGURE 5.4–4**  Results of the Anderson et al. experiment showing the beneficial effects of delaying KR for two trials (delay–2) compared to presenting KR after each trial (delay–0) for learning a manual aiming task. (Reprinted with permission from *Research Quarterly for Exercise and Sport,* Volume 65, pp. 286–290, Copyright © 1994 by the American Association for Health, Physical Education, Recreation, and Dance, 1900 Association Drive, Reston, VA 20191.)

learner develops a plan of action for the next trial. This planning occurs at this point because the learner now has available both task-intrinsic feedback and augmented feedback.

If the learner processes critical skill-learning information during the post-KR interval, we would expect there to be a minimum length for this interval. In fact, empirical evidence has shown that indeed, this interval can be too short. For example, for learning a limb-positioning movement, researchers found a 1-sec post-KR interval to lead to poorer learning than 5-, 10-, or 20-sec intervals (Weinberg, Guy, and Tupper 1964; see also Rogers 1974; Gallagher and Thomas 1980). In this way the post-KR interval resembles the KR-delay interval; for optimal learning to be achieved, a learner needs a minimum amount of time to engage in the learning processes required.

However, there is no evidence indicating an optimal length for the post-KR interval. Research consistently has shown no apparent upper limit for the length of this interval. Magill (1977) provided an example of the type of research addressing this

question. For this comparison of post-KR interval lengths of 10 sec and 60 sec for subjects learning three limb positions on a curvilinear positioning device, results showed no differences between the two interval lengths.

*Activity during the post-KR interval.*  The effect of engaging in activity is similar for the post-KR interval to that for the KR-delay interval. Depending on the type of activity, activity can have no effect on learning, interfere with learning, or benefit learning.

The most common finding has been that activity during the post-KR interval *has no effect on skill learning.* For example, in an experiment by Lee and Magill (1983a) people practiced making an arm movement through a series of three small wooden barriers in 1050 msec. During the post-KR interval, one group engaged in a motor activity (learning the same movement in 1350 msec), one group engaged in a cognitive activity involving number guessing, and a third group did not do any activity. As you can see in figure 5.4–5, at the end

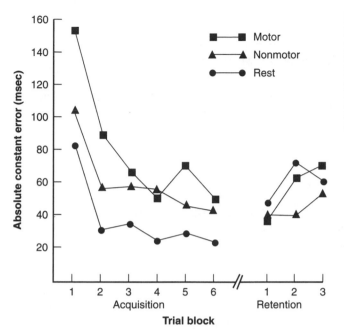

**FIGURE 5.4–5** Results of the experiment by Lee and Magill showing acquisition and retention performance for absolute constant error as a function of activity during the post-KR interval. Retention performance is without KR. (From T.D. Lee and R.A. Magill, "Activity During the Post-KR Interval: Effects Upon Performance or Learning" in *Research Quarterly for Exercise and Sport*, 1983, Vol. 54, pp. 340–345. Copyright © 1983 American Alliance for Health, Physical Education, Recreation, and Dance. Reprinted by permission.)

of the practice trials the two activity groups showed poorer performance than the non-activity group. However, this was a temporary performance effect rather than a learning effect: on a no-KR retention test, the three groups did not differ.

Several researchers have reported results indicating that activity during the post-KR interval *hinders learning*. Of these, only those by Benedetti and McCullagh (1987) and by Swinnen (1990, experiment 3) included appropriate tests for learning. In both of these experiments, the interfering activity was a cognitive activity. Participants in the experiment by Benedetti and McCullagh engaged in a mathematics problem-solving task, whereas those in the experiment by Swinnen guessed the movement-time error of a lever movement the experimenter made during the post-KR interval.

Only one experiment (Magill 1988) has demonstrated that *beneficial learning effects* can result from activity in the post-KR interval. Participants learned a two-component arm movement in which each component had its own criterion movement time. During the post-KR interval, one group had to learn two additional two-component movements,

one group had to learn a mirror-tracing task, and a third group did not engage in activity. Results showed that while there were no group differences on a no-KR retention test, the two groups engaged in activity during the post-KR interval performed better than the no-activity group on a transfer test in which participants learned a new two-component movement.

What do these different effects of activity tell us about learning processes that occur during the post-KR interval? They support the view we discussed earlier that learners engage in important planning activities during this time period. They use this planning time to take into account the discrepancy between the task-intrinsic and the augmented feedback, to determine how to execute the next attempt at performing the skill. Much of this planning seems to require cognitive activity; we see this in the experiments showing that engaging in cognitive problem-solving activity during this interval hinders learning. Why would beneficial transfer effects result when people must learn another motor skill in this interval? One hypothesis follows the transfer-appropriate-processing view we discussed

---

## A CLOSER LOOK

### Practical Implications of the Effects of KR-Delay and Post-KR Intervals

- A brief time interval should occur between a person's completion of a movement and the teacher's or therapist's giving of augmented feedback.
- Although an instructor's delaying of augmented feedback for a considerable length of time does not negatively affect learning of the skill, it undoubtedly influences the motivation of the person to continue to try to achieve the activity goal.
- A useful technique to facilitate skill learning is to have the person overtly focus attention on what he

or she did wrong on a practice attempt, by having the person respond, before being told what he or she did wrong, to this question: "What do you think you did wrong that time?"

- There is little need to be concerned about the length of the activity engaged in during the post-KR interval in terms of its influence on the degree of skill learning. However, the teacher or therapist should take motivational considerations into account on an individual basis.

---

in Concept 4.3. This type of activity is beneficial because it increases the person's motor skill problem-solving experience; this in turn enables the person to transfer more successfully to a situation that requires similar problem-solving activity.

## Frequency of Presenting Augmented Feedback

Three issues are important as we consider the frequency question. First, is type of frequency—absolute or relative—important. Second, what frequency is optimal for learning? And third, can augmented feedback be given less often, but in a summary format that includes performance information about a certain number of practice attempts?

*Absolute versus relative frequency.* In one of the approaches to the augmented feedback frequency question, researchers have tried to determine whether there is a specific number of times that motor skills instructors should give augmented feedback in practice (i.e., *absolute frequency*), or there is a specific optimal percentage of practice attempts for which they should give augmented feedback (i.e., *relative frequency*). Traditionally, motor learning researchers have concluded that greater augmented feedback frequency leads to better learning (e.g., Bilodeau and Bilodeau 1958a). However,

the important research literature review by Salmoni, Schmidt, and Walter (1984), as well as experimental results since that review, lead us to the more appropriate conclusion that relative frequency, rather than absolute frequency, of augmented feedback is critical for skill learning. This means that the research literature does not support the view that "more is better" with regard to the frequency of augmented feedback. In fact, in many cases "less" is actually better than "more" for learning skills. What is important, then, is how often the learner receives augmented feedback with respect to the number of practice attempts he or she makes.

*Determining the optimal relative frequency.* Sufficient research evidence has now accumulated for us to say confidently that the optimal relative frequency for giving augmented feedback is *not* 100 percent. A good example of this type of evidence is an experiment by Winstein and Schmidt (1990). They had participants practice producing the complex movement pattern shown in the top panel of figure 5.4–6 by moving a lever on a tabletop to manipulate a cursor on a computer monitor. During the two days of practice, participants received KR after either 100 percent or 50 percent of the trials. For the 50 percent condition, experimenters used a **fading technique** in which they systematically reduced the KR frequency; they

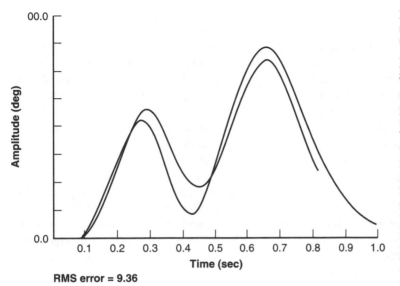

RMS error = 9.36

**FIGURE 5.4–6**  The top panel shows the goal movement pattern in the Winstein and Schmidt experiment. A sample of one subject's attempt to produce this pattern is superimposed. The RMS error score is shown as the subject saw it. Note that the goal pattern lasted for .80 sec while the subject produced a 1.0-sec pattern. The bottom panel shows the results of this experiment for the 100% KR frequency and 50% KR frequency groups, where the 50% group had KR frequency "faded" from 100% to 0%. (From C.J. Winstein, and R. A. Schmidt, "Reduced Frequency of Knowledge of Results Enhances Motor Skill Learning" in *Journal of Experimental Psychology: Learning, Memory and Cognition*, 1990, 16:677–691. Copyright © 1990 American Psychological Association. Reprinted by permission.)

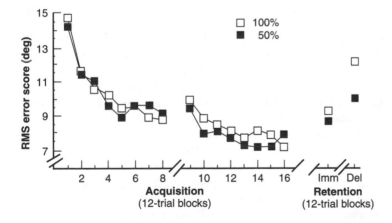

provided KR after each of the first 22 trials of each day, then had participants perform 8 trials with no KR, then provided KR for 8, 7, 4, 3, 2, and 2 trials for each of the remaining 8-trial blocks each day. The results of this procedure are presented in the bottom panel of figure 5.4-6. In a no-KR retention test given one day later, the faded 50 percent frequency condition led to better retention perfor-

mance than the 100 percent condition produced. In fact, people who had received KR after every practice trial showed retention test performance at a level resembling that of their first day of practice.

These results demonstrate that for skills for which augmented feedback benefits learning, optimal learning does not depend on a person's receiving augmented feedback after every practice trial.

Research has been consistent in demonstrating that when people receive augmented feedback on fewer than 100 percent of the practice trials, their learning is as good as or better than their learning with augmented feedback provided on every practice trial. In fact, there is sufficient evidence that we can conclude that receiving augmented feedback after every trial of practice increases the likelihood that a person will become dependent on it. This dependence leads to poor test performance when the augmented feedback is not available.

### Theoretical implications of the frequency effect.

The challenge for those interested in developing motor learning theory is to establish why giving augmented feedback less than 100 percent of the time during practice is better for skill learning. One possible reason is that when people receive augmented feedback after every trial, they eventually experience an attention-capacity "overload." After several trials, the cumulative effect is that there is more information available than the person can handle.

A more likely possibility is that giving augmented feedback on every trial leads to engaging the learner in a fundamentally different type of learning processing than he or she would experience if it were not given on every trial. Schmidt and his colleagues (e.g., Salmoni, Schmidt, and Walter 1984; Schmidt 1988; Winstein and Schmidt 1990) held this view, which is called the **guidance hypothesis.** According to this view, if the learner receives augmented feedback on every trial (i.e., at 100 percent frequency), then it will effectively "guide" the learner to perform the movement correctly. However, there is a negative aspect to this guidance process. By using augmented feedback as the guidance source, the learner develops a dependency on the availability of augmented feedback, so that when he or she must perform the skill without it, performance will be poorer than if augmented feedback were provided. In effect, augmented feedback becomes a crutch for the learner that is essential for performing the skill.

The hypothesis further proposes that receiving augmented feedback less frequently during practice encourages the learner to engage in more beneficial learning processes during practice. For example, active problem-solving activities increase during trials with no augmented feedback. The learner does not become dependent on the availability of augmented feedback, and therefore can perform the skill well, even in its absence.

Two experiments represent two of the more interesting approaches that have produced empirical support for the guidance hypothesis. One approach was to analyze the no-KR practice trials for the conditions using less than 100 percent KR frequency. Sparrow and Summers (1992) reported evidence that performance on these trials indicated a dissipation of guidance, but no significant reduction in learners' accuracy in performing the skill. These results are consistent with the view that beneficial learning processes are active during the trials when learners do not receive augmented feedback.

In the other notable approach taken to test the guidance hypothesis, Winstein, Pohl, and Lewthwaite (1994) compared different levels of performance guidance during practice with different frequencies of KR. Participants practiced rapidly extending their forearms to move a lever to a target location. People who received physical guidance to the target on each trial showed very poor retention test performance compared to people who experienced physical guidance but had it systematically removed during practice, following the fading technique, so that they were guided on only 33 percent of the trials. When these conditions were compared to conditions of 100 percent KR frequency and faded 33 percent KR frequency, the condition of high physical guidance produced results like those of the condition of 100 percent KR, while the condition of faded 33 percent physical guidance produced results like those of the condition of faded 33 percent KR. When experimenters provided strong guidance during practice, either by physically guiding performance or by providing KR on every trial, learning was poorer than when people had opportunities to explore and make errors and were able to correct those errors with minimal guidance.

*A performance-based bandwidth approach to determining frequency.* While the fading technique used by Winstein and Schmidt (1990) can be an effective means of reducing the frequency of augmented feedback, other means also can be effective. One of these is related to the practice of basing augmented feedback on performance-based bandwidth criteria, which we described in the discussion of Concept 5.3. Recall that augmented feedback enhances learning only when performance is *not* within a preestablished tolerance limit, or bandwidth. If we consider the bandwidth technique from the perspective of augmented feedback frequency, then, we can see easily that a bandwidth approach influences frequency.

Lee and Carnahan (1990) concluded that the bandwidth approach to giving augmented feedback is beneficial for greater reasons than a simple reduction in frequency. However, the use of this approach to reduce frequency has merit. If, as Winstein and Schmidt (1990) suggested, weaning individuals from the need for augmented feedback has a positive effect on learning, the provision of augmented feedback on the basis of performance-based bandwidths should be effective as well, because it naturally reduces the frequency with which learners receive augmented feedback. Because the bandwidth is related to individual performance, the weaning process is also specific to each person's performance.

*Learner-regulated frequency.* An option for determining augmented frequency feedback that professionals commonly overlook is to give a person augmented feedback only when he or she asks for it. This approach allows the learner to participate more actively in determining characteristics of the practice conditions by self-regulating the presentation of augmented feedback. An experiment by Janelle, Kim, and Singer (1995) provided evidence that this strategy can enhance the learning of motor skills. College students practiced an underhand golf ball toss to a 10-cm-diameter target on the ground 183 cm away. The students received KP about ball force, ball loft, and arm swing during practice. Compared to groups that received KP according to experimenter-determined frequencies (all of which received it less frequently than on every trial), the groups whose members controlled frequency themselves performed more accurately on the no-KP retention test.

An interesting outcome of the learner-request strategy is the discovery that people do not request augmented feedback very frequently. In the Janelle et al. experiment, people requested KP on only 7 percent of the 40 practice trials. It is also worth noting that the benefit of this strategy relates to more than a frequency effect. In the Janelle et al. experiment, experimenters yoked each participant in a third group to a person in the participant-controlled KP condition, according to when the person received KP. Those in this yoked condition did not perform as well as those in the participant-controlled KP condition on the retention test. In addition to providing benefits from reducing augmented feedback frequency, the request strategy more actively engages the learner in the learning process.

*Summary augmented feedback.* The motor learning research literature refers to the practice of providing a summary of performance information after a certain number of practice trials as **summary augmented feedback.** This reduces the feedback frequency while providing the same amount of information as if augmented feedback were given after every trial.

The summary technique could be advantageous in several types of skill-learning situations. For example, suppose that a therapy patient must do a series of ten leg extensions in relatively rapid succession. To give augmented feedback after every extension may not be possible, if time limits restrict access to performance information after each attempt. A summary of all ten attempts could help overcome this limitation. Or, suppose that a person is practicing a shooting skill for which he or she cannot see the target because of the distance involved. Efficiency of practice could be increased if that person did not receive augmented feedback after each shot, but received information about each shot after every ten shots.

### A CLOSER LOOK

## Practical Implications of the Frequency Effect

The conclusion that augmented feedback does not need to be given after every practice trial

- reduces the demand on the instructor or therapist to provide augmented feedback all the time. This should be especially comforting for those who work with groups, because research evidence shows that they typically do not provide augmented feedback with 100 percent frequency. In fact, in group practice situations, the teacher or therapist provides augmented feedback about one or two times per minute, with the same student rarely receiving more than a few feedback

statements throughout a class session or practice period (e.g., see Eghan 1988; Fishman and Tobey 1978; Silverman, Tyson, and Krampitz 1991).

- is based on the use of augmented feedback to provide error correction information. However, it is important not to ignore the role of augmented feedback as a source of motivation when considering the frequency question. While learners do not need externally presented error correction information after every trial, they may benefit from feedback statements that are motivation oriented on some intervening trials.

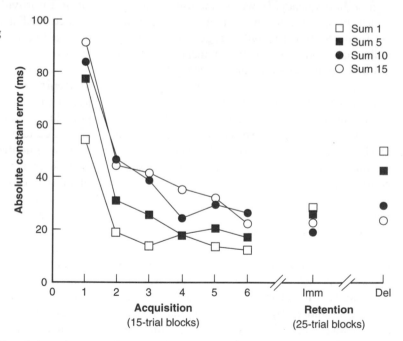

**FIGURE 5.4–7** Results of the experiment by Schmidt et al., showing the effects of learning a timing movement with different summary KR conditions. (Sum 1 = KR after every trial; Sum 5 = KR for 5 trials presented every 5 trials, etc.) (From R.A Schmidt, et al., "Summary Knowledge of Results for Skill Acquisition: Support for the Guidance Hypothesis" in *Journal of Experimental Psychology: Learning, Memory and Cognition,* 1989, 15:352–359. Copyright © 1989 American Psychological Association. Reprinted by permission.)

Both laboratory and sport skill training situations have provided evidence that a summary approach can be effective for administering augmented feedback. For example, in a laboratory-based experiment by Schmidt, Young, Swinnen, and Shapiro (1989), people practiced moving a

lever along a trackway to achieve a goal movement time. During the 90 practice trials, participants received KR after every trial or in summary form after 5, 10, or 15 trials. The results of this experiment (see figure 5.4–7) showed that on a retention test 2 days later, the group that had received KR after every trial performed the worst, while the group that had received summary KR after every 15 trials performed the best.

In an experiment by Boyce (1991), the summary method was successful in an actual university class situation in which students were learning target shooting with rifles. One group received KP after every shot, while another group received KP about every shot after each fifth shot. The results showed no difference in eventual shooting performance by these groups. Although the summary method did not yield better performance than the method giving KP after every shot, its effectiveness as an instructional technique was established, since it was just as effective for improving performance as the other method.

Why is the summary method effective? Its effectiveness is undoubtedly due in part to the same factors that lead to the benefit of reducing augmented feedback frequency, as explained by the guidance hypothesis. During practice trials on which they receive no augmented feedback, people engage in beneficial learning activities that are not characteristic of people who receive augmented feedback after every trial. The explanation of the summary effect as a type of reduced frequency effect has appeal when we consider experiments such as one by Weeks and Sherwood (1994). They compared summary KR with average KR for learning an isometric force production task. The summary condition involved receiving KR for five trials after every fifth trial, while those in the average condition received only the average for the five trials. The results showed that both forms of KR were better for learning than receiving KR after every trial, but that the summary and average conditions did not differ.

An interesting question arises about the summary method: What is the optimal number of performance attempts to include in a summary? Logically, we would expect that when more trials are included than people can attend to, they likely would not concentrate on the complete summary, but on either the general trend of their performance over the summarized trials, or the most recent trials provided (see the discussion in the report of an experiment by Sidaway, Moore, and Schoenfelder-Zohdi 1991). The rule of thumb to guide the use of the summary method is to keep the summary within the limits of the person's attention capacity.

## Summary

Three issues related to the timing aspects of augmented feedback are important to consider if we seek to understand the influence of augmented feedback on skill learning. One of these concerns whether a learner should receive augmented feedback during or after the performance of a skill. Evidence indicates that terminal augmented feedback is generally preferable, although concurrent augmented feedback can be beneficial when it is difficult for a person to determine what to do to achieve a task based on the task-intrinsic feedback. Another timing issue addresses the time intervals involved for terminal augmented feedback. Both the KR-delay and the post-KR intervals are important time periods for skill learning. Both intervals have minimum lengths, but appear to have no maximum effective lengths. Also, engaging in activity during these intervals typically has no effect on skill learning, although engaging in certain types of activities can either hinder or benefit learning. The third timing issue concerns how frequently the therapist or teacher should give augmented feedback to facilitate skill learning. Research evidence shows that giving augmented feedback after every practice attempt is not the optimal condition, and that some relative frequency of less than 100 percent is desirable. Methods for reducing frequency include the fading technique, the error bandwidth technique, and the summary method. One reason to investigate issues related to the timing of providing augmented feedback is that this is a means of addressing questions about the learning processes involved between trials during practice. Evidence shows that attention to processing task-intrinsic feedback is critical for effective skill learning. In fact, when practice conditions create a dependence on augmented feedback by shifting a learner's attention away from task-intrinsic feedback, learning is impeded.

## Related Readings

Adams, J. A. 1971. A closed-loop theory of motor learning. *Journal of Motor Behavior* 3: 111–49. (Read pp. 132–36.)

Bilodeau, E. A., and I. M. Bilodeau. 1958. Variation of temporal intervals among critical events in five studies of knowledge of results. *Journal of Experimental Psychology* 55: 603–12.

Lee, T. D., and R. A. Magill. 1983. Activity during the post-KR interval: Effects upon performance or learning? *Research Quarterly for Exercise and Sport* 54: 340–45.

Schmidt, R. A. 1991. Frequent augmented feedback can degrade learning: Evidence and interpretations (pp. 59–75). In J. Requin and G. E. Stelmach (Eds.), *Tutorials in motor neuroscience* (pp. 59–75). Dordrecht, The Netherlands: Kluwer.

---

# STUDY QUESTIONS FOR CHAPTER 5

1. What are two types of research evidence that show that observing a skilled demonstration of a motor skill influences the acquisition of the coordination characteristics of the skill?

2. How would observing an unskilled person learning a skill help a beginner learn that skill?

3. What are the main features of the two predominant theories about how observing a demonstration helps a person to learn that skill? How do these theories differ?

4. How can verbal cues be used to help overcome some of the problems often associated with giving verbal instructions?

5. What are the two types of information referred to by the terms KR and KP? Give two examples of each.

6. Describe skill-learning conditions where augmented feedback would (a) be necessary for learning, (b) not be necessary for learning, and (c) be a hindrance to learning.

7. Explain how a skill that was dependent on the availability of augmented feedback early in learning can be performed later in learning without augmented feedback.

8. How do quantitative and qualitative augmented feedback differ, and how do they influence the learning of motor skills?

9. What two important points must a therapist or teacher strongly consider when deciding on augmented feedback content? Give an example of a motor skill situation that illustrates these two points.

10. What are two important guidelines for the effective use of videotape as a form of augmented feedback?

11. (a) What do we currently know about the use and benefit of kinematic information as augmented feedback to help someone learn a motor skill? (b) When do you think this type of information would be most helpful?

12. What is the difference between concurrent and terminal augmented feedback? Give two examples of each.

13. Name the two time intervals associated with the giving of terminal augmented feedback during practice. Discuss why researchers are interested in investigating these intervals.

14. (a) What are two types of activity during the KR-delay interval that have been shown to benefit skill learning? (b) Why does this benefit occur?

15. (a) What seems to be the most appropriate conclusion to draw regarding the frequency with which an instructor should give augmented feedback during learning? (b) How does the guidance hypothesis relate to the issue of augmented feedback frequency?

16. Describe a skill-learning situation in which giving summary augmented feedback would be a beneficial technique.

# PRACTICE CONDITIONS

---

## CONCEPT 6.1

Variability in practice experiences is important for learning motor skills

## CONCEPT 6.2

The spacing or distribution of practice can affect both practice performance and learning of motor skills

## CONCEPT 6.3

The amount of practice influences the amount of learning, although the
benefit is not always proportional to the time required

## CONCEPT 6.4

Base decisions about practicing skills as wholes or in parts on
the complexity and organization characteristics of the skills

## CONCEPT 6.5

Mental practice can be effective for learning skills, especially when combined with physical practice

# CONCEPT 6.1

Variability in practice experiences is important for learning motor skills

## Key Terms

practice
  variability

contextual
  interference
  effect

contextual
  interference

## Application

The reason a person practices a skill is to increase his or her capability of performing it in future situations that will require the skill. For example, some people will need to perform sport skills successfully in skills tests, games, and matches. Dancers need to perform in recitals, performances, and competitions. And rehab patients practice skills in the clinic so that they can perform them as needed in the everyday environment. Because of this future performance requirement, teachers, coaches, and therapists must design and establish practice conditions that will lead to the greatest probability of successful performance in the situations that will require the skills being learned.

One practice characteristic that increases the chances for future performance success is variability in the learner's experiences while he or she practices. This includes variations of the characteristics of the context in which the learner performs the skill, as well as variations of the skill he or she is practicing. The teacher, coach, or therapist must address several important questions to determine how to optimize the types and amount of variation to include in practice experiences. First, what aspects of performing the skill should he or she vary? Second, how much variety of experiences is optimal? Third, how should the variety of experiences be organized in the practice sessions? We consider these questions in the discussion that follows.

## Discussion

A consistent characteristic of theories of motor skill learning is their emphasis on the learning benefits derived from practice variability. In these theories, **practice variability** refers to the variety of movement and context characteristics the learner experiences while practicing a skill. For example, in Schmidt's (1975a) schema theory, a key prediction is that successful future performance of a skill depends on the amount of variability the learner experiences during practice. Similarly, Gentile (1972, 1987) emphasized the learner's need during practice to experience variations of regulatory and nonregulatory context characteristics. And more recently, dynamical systems views of skill learning have stressed the learner's need to explore the perceptual-motor workspace and to discover optimal solutions to the degrees of freedom problem posed by the skill (e.g., McDonald, Oliver, and Newell 1995; Vereijken and Whiting 1990).

### The Future Performance Benefit of Practice Variability

The primary benefit a learner derives from practice experiences that promote movement and context variability is an increased capability to perform the skill in a future test situation. This means that the person has acquired an increased capability to perform the practiced skill, as well as to adapt to novel conditions that might characterize the test situation.

An interesting irony here is that an increased amount of practice variability usually is associated with an increased amount of performance error during practice. However, research evidence shows that more performance error can be better than less error for skill learning, when it occurs in the initial learning stage. A good example of this evidence is an experiment by Edwards and Lee (1985). Each participant had to learn to move his or her arm through a specified pattern in 1200 msec. Members of one group, called the prompted group, were told that if they moved according to a "ready, and, 1, 2, 3, 4, 5" count on a tape, they would complete the movement in the criterion time. Each person practiced until he or she could do three trials in a row correctly at 1200 msec. Members of the second group, called the trial-and-error group, were told the goal movement time and received KR about their timing error after each trial.

The results (figure 6.1–1) indicated that the two groups performed similarly on the retention test, and that the trial-and-error group performed the 1800-msec novel transfer task more accurately. What is particularly interesting about these results is how much the two groups differed in the amount of error each produced during practice. The prompted group performed with very little error during practice, while the trial-and-error group experienced much error, especially during the first 15 trials. Yet, experiencing less error during practice was no more beneficial for retention test performance, and it was detrimental for transfer to a novel variation of the practiced movement.

## Implementing Practice Variability

The first step in determining how to provide an appropriate amount of practice variability is to assess the characteristics of the future situations in which the learner will perform a skill. Of particular relevance here are the *characteristics of the physical context* in which he or she will perform the skill and the *skill characteristics* that the performance situation will require. If you regard this situation as a transfer of learning situation, then you will see the value of using the test conditions to determine what the practice environment should be like. As we discussed in Concept 4.2, effective transfer is a function of the similarities between skill, context, and information-processing characteristics of the practice and test situations. A high degree of similarity between these characteristics in the two situations enhances transfer between practice and the test.

*Varying practice contexts.* It is important to keep in mind that when people perform skills, they do so in contexts that have identifiable characteristics. As Gentile (1987) pointed out, some features of the performance context are critical for determining the movement characteristics of an action (which she called *regulatory conditions*), while other features (*nonregulatory conditions*) have no influence.

We find examples of *regulatory context characteristics* in conditions that influence a person's walking behavior. Certain walking characteristics will be different when you walk on a concrete sidewalk from when you walk on ice or on sand. Also, you walk differently on a busy sidewalk that is cluttered with other people than on a sidewalk empty of people. When regulatory conditions like these may vary from one performance context to another, it is important that practice conditions include a variety of similar conditions.

*Nonregulatory context characteristics* also play a role in influencing transfer between practice and test. For the walking skill, some nonregulatory context characteristics could include the physical environment around the walking pathway, such as buildings, trees, and open space. Although these features do not influence the pattern of movement directly, they nonetheless can influence the degree of success a person may achieve in carrying out the action in a unique context. Again, when nonregulatory conditions will vary from one performance context to another, practice conditions should provide opportunities for the learner to experience these characteristics.

*Varying practice conditions for closed skills.* Future performance conditions for closed skills include regulatory conditions that are stable and relatively predictable. However, nonregulatory characteristics are likely to be novel. According to Gentile's model, learners must incorporate two

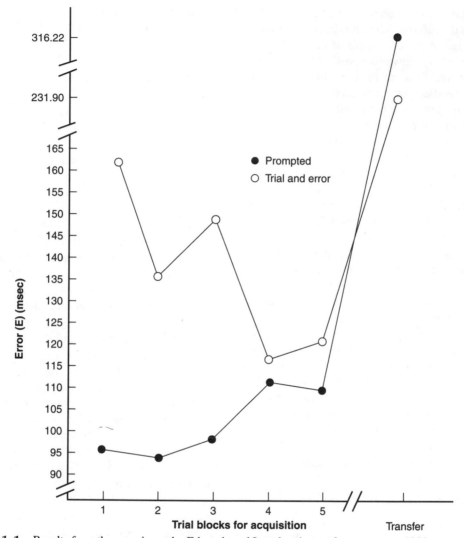

**FIGURE 6.1–1**  Results from the experiment by Edwards and Lee showing performance on a 1200-msec movement-time goal task during the acquisition trials and on an 1800-msec goal for the transfer task for two types of practice conditions: prompted by a tone lasting 1200 msec or practicing with KR (trial and error). (From R.V. Edwards and A.M. Lee, "The Relationship of Cognitive Style and Instructional Strategy to Learning and Transfer of Motor Skills," in *Research Quarterly for Exercise and Sport*, 1985, Vol. 56, pp. 286–290. Copyright © 1985 American Alliance for Health, Physical Education, Recreation, and Dance. Reprinted by permission.)

conditions into practice to enhance their future performance success for closed skills. First, practice should occur under the conditions that will prevail in the test situation. Second, the instructor should hold regulatory characteristics constant while varying the nonregulatory characteristics during practice.

For closed skills, instructors must develop variable practice experiences around the nonregulatory characteristics, while providing similarity rather than variety in trial-to-trial experiences for the regulatory characteristics. To develop appropriate practice conditions, the teacher or therapist first must determine those characteristics of the skill

---

| A CLOSER LOOK |

### An Example of Varying Practice Conditions for a Closed Skill

**BASKETBALL FREE THROW**

The goal is to shoot free throws successfully in games.

**REGULATORY CONTEXT CONDITIONS THAT REMAIN CONSTANT IN GAMES**

- basket height
- basket distance from shooting line
- ball characteristics

**NONREGULATORY CONTEXT CONDITIONS THAT CAN VARY IN GAMES**

- number of free throws to be taken
- importance to game outcome of making free throws
- crowd noise
- time of game

**Practice conditions** should incorporate as many nonregulatory context conditions as possible to match the conditions that players may confront in a game.

---

and the performance context that he or she can classify as regulatory or nonregulatory. Then the instructor can develop an appropriate variety of practice experiences, according to which characteristics should be as similar as possible from one practice attempt to another, and which ones need to vary from one practice attempt to another.

*Varying practice conditions for open skills.* Each performance of an open skill is unique, since in each performance of it, certain characteristics are novel to the performer. That is, the performer must produce certain movements that he or she has not made before in the manner this situation requires. The performer needs to modify previous movements in order to achieve the goal of the skill. For example, if you are preparing to return a serve in tennis, it is likely that certain characteristics of the ball action will be unique to this particular serve. Thus, practice of open skills needs to include experiences with regulatory characteristics that will change from one attempt to another.

An experiment by Wrisberg and Ragsdale (1979) illustrates the benefit of varying regulatory characteristics during the practice of an open skill. Participants practiced an anticipation-timing task requiring them to push a button at the exact moment the last of a series of lights was illuminated along a runway. Different amounts of regulatory conditions variability were present: each participant experienced 40 trials of 4 different stimulus velocities or only 1 velocity, and had to either make or not make an overt response. The test involved performing an overt response for a novel stimulus speed. Results, which we present in figure 6.1–2, showed that participants who experienced a variety of regulatory conditions during practice achieved more accurate test performance.

## Organizing Variable Practice

Having established that practice variability benefits skill learning, we next must consider how the therapist or teacher should organize the variable experiences within a practice session or unit of instruction. The following example illustrates how this practice organization question is involved as the motor skills professional develops practice conditions.

Suppose you are an elementary school physical education teacher organizing a teaching unit on throwing for your classes. You have determined that you will devote six classes to this unit. You want the students to experience three variations of the throwing pattern: the overhand, underhand, and sidearm throws. How should you arrange these three different throws for practice during the six classes? Figure 6.1–3 shows three

**FIGURE 6.1–2**  Results of the experiment by Wrisberg and Ragsdale showing anticipation-timing performance for high and low levels of stimulus variability and response requirements (HRR = high response requirements; LRR = low response requirements). (From C. A. Wrisberg, and M. R. Ragsdale, "Further Tests of Schmidt's Schema Theory: Development of a Schema Rule for a Coincident Timing Task" in *Journal of Motor Behavior*, 1979, 11:159–166. Copyright © 1979 Heldref Publications, Inc., Washington, DC. Reprinted by permission.)

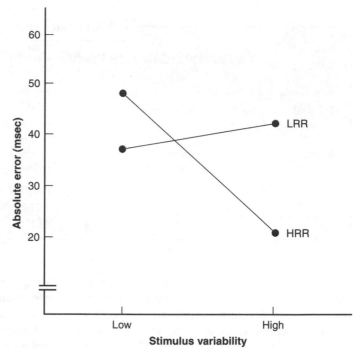

possible arrangements. One is to practice each throw in blocks of two days each (blocked practice). Another possibility is to practice each throw in some random arrangement with ten-minute blocks devoted to each particular pattern (random practice). Thus, each day students would experience three ten-minute blocks, with no specified order of occurrence for the three patterns; the only stipulation would be that they practice all three an equal amount over the course of the unit. The third arrangement, serial practice, also involves a ten-minute block for each pattern. However, in this approach students practice each pattern every day in the same order.

This organization problem is not unique to the teaching of physical education activities. It is characteristic of any situation in which learners must practice several variations of a skill. In a therapy situation, a patient may need to practice grasping objects of different sizes, weights, and shapes. Or a patient who has had a knee joint replacement may need to practice walking on different types of surfaces. In a dance setting, a learner would need to

practice tempo variations in a routine or other variations of particular components of a routine. All of these situations involve the same organization problem: How should the instructor schedule the practice of these variations within the practice time available to help the patient or student learn to perform successfully in various situations?

***The contextual interference approach to organizing practice.***  One way to schedule variable practice is by applying the learning phenomenon known as the **contextual interference effect.** Battig (1979) introduced the term **contextual interference** to label the interference that results from practicing a task within the context of the practice situation. A high degree of contextual interference can occur when a learner practices several different but related skills during the same practice session. On the other hand, when a learner practices only one skill during a practice session, a low-contextual-interference condition exists. Most people tend to see interference as a negative factor, and therefore might expect that a low-contextual-interference

| | | Class day | | | | | |
|---|---|---|---|---|---|---|---|
| | | 1 | 2 | 3 | 4 | 5 | 6 |
| **Blocked practice** | 10 min<br>10 min<br>10 min | All overhand | All overhand | All underhand | All underhand | All sidearm | All sidearm |
| **Random practice** | 10 min<br>10 min<br>10 min | Underhand<br>Overhand<br>Underhand | Sidearm<br>Underhand<br>Overhand | Overhand<br>Sidearm<br>Sidearm | Underhand<br>Overhand<br>Overhand | Sidearm<br>Overhand<br>Sidearm | Underhand<br>Underhand<br>Sidearm |
| **Serial practice** | 10 min<br>10 min<br>10 min | Overhand<br>Underhand<br>Sidearm | Overhand<br>Underhand<br>Sidearm | Overhand<br>Underhand<br>Sidearm | Overhand<br>Underhand<br>Sidearm | Overhand<br>Underhand<br>Sidearm | Overhand<br>Underhand<br>Sidearm |

**FIGURE 6.1–3**  A six-day unit plan demonstrating three different practice structures (blocked, random, and serial) for teaching three different throwing patterns (overhand, underhand, and sidearm). All classes are 30 minutes long and are divided into 10-min segments. Each practice condition provides an equal amount of practice for each throwing pattern.

situation would lead to superior learning. However, Battig proposed that while the low-contextual-interference practice situation often leads to superior practice performance, it is high-contextual-interference practice that results in much higher retention and transfer performance.

Shea and Morgan (1979) reported the first test of Battig's prediction using motor skills. Participants practiced three movement patterns in which the goal was to move one arm through a series of small wooden barriers as rapidly as possible. The blocked practice group, representing a low-contextual-interference condition, practiced each of the three patterns separately, in a series of 18 trials. The high-contextual-interference practice group practiced the patterns in random arrangement, so that the 18 trials of practice for each pattern were distributed randomly throughout the practice trials. Results supported Battig's prediction. The blocked practice group performed better during practice trials, while the random practice group showed superior performance during retention trials and transfer trials, where they encountered a new arrangement of barriers.

In an attempt to uncover possible reasons for the Shea and Morgan results, Lee and Magill (1983b) added a serial practice condition. They arranged the practice trials for this group so that movement pattern 1 always was followed by pattern 2, which always

was followed by pattern 3. This condition combined features of the blocked practice condition (perfect predictability of the upcoming pattern to be practiced) with those of the random practice condition (interference created by practicing other patterns between repetitions of any one pattern). The results (figure 6.1–4) indicated that the random and serial practice conditions performed similarly during both practice and retention. These results showed that the key to understanding the contextual interference effect lies in determining the role played by the activity intervening between practice repetitions of a movement.

Perhaps the most striking negative effect of low-contextual-interference practice is that it inhibits performance of the practiced skills in novel performance contexts. Contextual interference experiments commonly show this. Although blocked practice sometimes leads to blocked retention test performance that is similar to performance following random practice, a large decrement in retention performance is typical when researchers test the skills under random conditions (e.g., Shea, Kohl, and Indermill 1990). On the other hand, high-contextual-interference practice does not show the same transfer problem. Thus, low-contextual-interference practice appears to develop a practice context dependency that decreases a person's capability to adapt to novel test contexts.

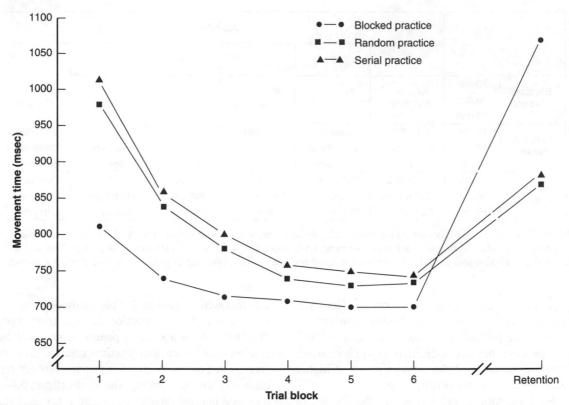

**FIGURE 6.1–4**   Results from the experiment by Lee and Magill showing mean movement time for completing three movement patterns using three different practice structures (blocked, random, and serial). Trial blocks (3 trials per block) 1 through 6 were with KR. The retention block was without KR. (From T. D. Lee and R. A. Magill, "The Locus of Contextual Interference in Motor Skill Acquisition," in *Journal of Experimental Psychology: Learning, Memory, and Cognition,* 1983, 9:730–746. Copyright © 1983. American Psychological Association. Reprinted by permission.)

***The contextual interference effect outside the laboratory.***   It is important to discover whether learning phenomena demonstrated under laboratory conditions also exist in real-world environments. Since the initial experiment by Shea and Morgan (1979), many laboratory-based experiments have demonstrated the contextual interference effect (see Magill and Hall 1990, for a review of these experiments). But evidence has demonstrated the contextual interference effect for real-world skills as well.

We find an example of this evidence in an experiment by Goode and Magill (1986) involving the learning of badminton serves. In this experiment, college women with no prior badminton experience practiced the short, long, and drive

serves from the right service court. They practiced these serves three days a week for three weeks with 36 trials in each practice session, for a total of 324 trials (108 trials per serve) during the practice period. The low-contextual-interference condition was a modification of the blocked condition used in previous studies; in this study, the blocked practice group practiced one serve each day of each week. The group on a random practice schedule practiced each serve randomly in every practice session. In this condition, the experimenter told each learner which serve she should perform next.

As you can see in figure 6.1–5, the authors found the contextual interference effect. The group that practiced with the random schedule outperformed

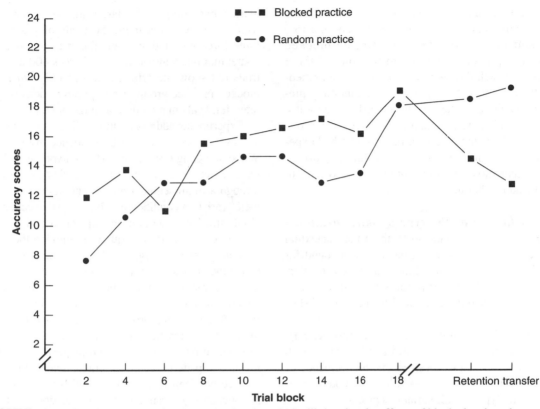

**FIGURE 6.1–5** Results from the experiment by Goode and Magill showing the effects of blocked and random structured practice for three types of badminton serves on acquisition, one-day retention, and transfer. (From S.L. Goode and R.A. Magill, "Contextual Interference Effects in Learning Three Badminton Serves," in *Research Quarterly for Exercise and Sport,* 1987, Vol. 57. pp. 308–314. Copyright © 1987 American Alliance for Health, Physical Education, Recreation, and Dance. Reprinted by permission.)

the blocked practice group on the retention and transfer tests. What is especially remarkable is that on the transfer test, which involved serving from the left service court, the random group showed no deterioration in performance. On the other hand, members of the group that had practiced in a blocked schedule were not able to adapt well to this new performance context. In fact, learners in this group performed in the new context about as well as they had when they had begun practicing the serves from the right court three weeks earlier.

The Goode and Magill study showed the benefit of high contextual interference for beginners learning an actual sport skill (the badminton serve). However, although their experiment used a sport skill, the authors carried it out in controlled experimental conditions. Those who seek even more real-world validity should note that Wrisberg and Liu (1991) attained the same results as Goode and Magill, but in an actual class setting. In that study, students learned the serves in a unit of instruction in an actual physical education class.

One other experiment is worth noting because it demonstrates that the contextual interference effect for real-world skills exists not only for beginners, but also for skilled individuals. Hall, Domingues, and Cavazos (1994) had skilled baseball players practice hitting different types of pitches to improve their batting performance. The experiment engaged the players in 45 extra pitches of batting practice three days a week for five weeks. Batters hit fastballs, curves, or change-ups according to a blocked or random schedule. On the blocked schedule, players practiced hitting one of these pitches on each day, whereas on the random schedule, they hit all three types of pitch, randomly presented, each day. The results showed that on a test involving a random sequence of pitches, like one that would occur in a game, players who had experienced the random practice schedule performed better than those who had practiced according to the blocked schedule.

***The influence of the type of skill variations learned.*** An important point about the contextual interference effect is that it has not been found for learning variations of all skills. To account for this, Magill and Hall (1990) proposed that the effect's presence or absence is related to the type of skill variations that learners are practicing. Based on their synthesis of the results of more than forty experiments published since the Shea and Morgan (1979) experiment, they hypothesized that the influence of contextual interference on skill learning could be related to the type of skill variations practiced.

The Magill and Hall (1990) hypothesis has two parts. First, if the skill variations a person is practicing require different generalized motor programs, various practice schedules create different levels of contextual interference, which in turn lead to different retention and transfer effects. That is, practice schedules that create higher levels of contextual interference lead to better retention and transfer performance than those creating lower levels. Second, if the skill variations a learner is practicing involve parameter modifications of the same generalized motor program, the contextual interference effect typically will not result from a comparison of practice schedules consisting of only random versus blocked conditions.

In the latter case, we could expect that some type of mixed schedule, such as blocked followed by random practice, would be better than blocked or random practice only. Or, as evidence by Shea, Kohl, and Indermill (1990) showed, random practice will be superior to blocked practice after the

learner has completed a large number of practice trials. In their experiment, 50 trials of practicing three force production levels failed to produce the contextual interference effect, whereas 400 practice trials did show the effect, and then only when the blocked practice group was required to perform the retention trials in a random arrangement.

Experiments addressing this skill-related hypothesis have yielded mixed results. Evidence from one by Wood and Ging (1991) supports the hypothesis. People practiced moving an arm as quickly as possible through a multi-segment movement pattern. A parameter variation condition involved a group, called the "high-similarity" condition, that practiced tracing three size variations of a pattern resembling the letter *N* (note patterns in figure 6.1–6). A second group, called the "low-similarity" condition, practiced forming three variations of different shapes of movement patterns, thereby practicing variations of skills requiring different motor programs. Figure 6.1–6 shows the results of this experiment in terms of the velocities participants produced while performing the movement patterns. From the graph, note that the difference between random and blocked practice was statistically significant only for the situation involving "low-similarity" pattern variations. In this case, the random practice led to better retention performance. However, there was no difference between random and blocked practice schedules for learning the three size variations of the same movement pattern.

In general, then, research evidence supports the view that the learning of related skills that are variations of a coordination pattern is more susceptible to the contextual interference effect than the learning of related skills that are parameter variations of the same pattern. But some researchers have reported exceptions to this limitation (e.g., Shea, Kohl, and Indermill 1990; Wulf and Lee 1993; Sekiya et al. 1994). These experimental results demonstrate that we do not yet understand the exact skill characteristics limits of the contextual interference effect. We know that there are situations in which we do not find the effect, but we must await further research to identify the specific characteristics of skill-learning situations in which we will and will not find it.

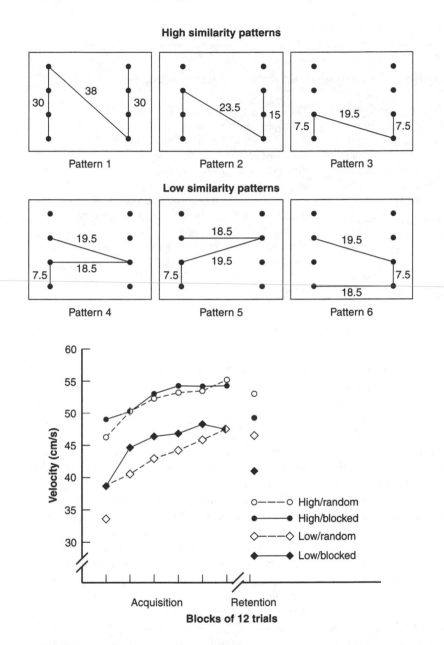

**High similarity patterns**

Pattern 1  Pattern 2  Pattern 3

**Low similarity patterns**

Pattern 4  Pattern 5  Pattern 6

**FIGURE 6.1–6** The movement patterns used in the experiment by Wood and Ging (top) and the results of random and blocked practice schedules for these patterns during acquisition and retention trials. Note numbers in patterns indicate distances in cm. (Reprinted with permission from *Research Quarterly for Exercise and Sport,* Volume 62, pp. 18–26. Copyright © 1991 by the American Alliance for Health, Physical Education, Recreation, and Dance, 1900 Association Drive, Reston, VA 20191.)

## Accounting for the Contextual Interference Effect

An important question that remains unsolved is this: *Why* does the contextual interference effect occur? Two hypotheses predominate in researchers' attempts to account for this effect. One is the *elaboration hypothesis;* the other is known as the *action plan reconstruction hypothesis.* Although we will not debate these two hypotheses at length, we will consider each briefly.

***The elaboration hypothesis.*** In their experiment that first showed the contextual interference effect for learning motor skills, Shea and Morgan (1979)

### A CLOSER LOOK

## Implementing High-Contextual-Interference Practice Schedules

Researchers have compared a variety of types of practice schedules to investigate the contextual interference effect. Keep in mind that blocked and random schedules simply represent the low and high ends of the contextual interference continuum. Many other schedules fall in between these two extremes. Consider the following two examples:

- **modified blocked practice schedule**   A learner practices a skill variation for an entire practice session, but practices a different variation for the next session, and so on.
- **serial practice schedule**   A learner practices the skill variations in a 1-2-3 arrangement of trials within each practice session.

One way to implement either of these two practice schedules is to engage people in practicing different variations of a skill at different stations. For the modified blocked schedule, people remain at one station for one practice session, but rotate to another station at the next session. For the serial schedule, people spend a certain amount of time at each station, where they practice one specific variation. They then move on to another station, so that during one practice session, they experience all variations.

argued that the effect is related to the elaboration of the memory representation of the skill variations that a learner is practicing.[1] During random practice, the person engages in more strategies, as well as more different strategies, than individuals do who practice according to a blocked schedule. Also, because in a random practice schedule the person retains in working memory all the skill variations he or she is practicing, the person can compare and contrast the variations so that each becomes distinct from the other. The result of engaging in these cognitive activities during practice is that the learner develops a memory representation for the skills that he or she then can access more readily during a test.

*The action plan reconstruction hypothesis.*   A hypothesis forwarded by Lee and Magill (1985) argues that high contextual interference benefits learning because the interference requires a person to reconstruct an action plan on the next practice trial for a particular skill variation. This is neces-

sary because the person has partially or completely forgotten the action plan he or she developed on the previous practice trial for that skill variation, due to the interference of the intervening practice trials of the other skill variations. In contrast, the person following a blocked practice schedule can use the same action plan he or she used on the previous trial, or a slightly modified one.

Consider the following illustration of how these different practice schedules would require different types of action plan activity. If you must add a long set of numbers and then you are immediately asked to do the same problem again, you probably will not re-add the numbers, but will remember and repeat only the answer. In contrast, if you are required to add several additional lists of numbers and then are given the first list again, you probably will have forgotten the solution to that problem, and therefore will have to add the same numbers again. The intervening problem-solving activity requires you to re-solve a problem you have solved already.

Lee and Magill hypothesized that the high-contextual-interference practice condition is like the addition situation in which there are several other problems to solve before you see the first

1. Shea and Zimny (1983) developed a more formal version of the elaboration hypotheses.

problem again. When a learner practices a motor skill, the interference created by the practice trials between two trials of the same skill variation causes the person to forget much of the action plan he or she has developed for the first trial. As a result, the learner must reconstruct and modify that plan to attempt the skill on the next trial. On the other hand, the blocked practice schedule is like the addition problem in which the next trial follows immediately, and it is easy to remember the solution and therefore be successful on the next trial.

In the motor learning context, high-contextual-interference conditions require subjects to engage more actively in problem-solving activity during practice. While this activity typically leads learners to perform more poorly during practice than they would with a low-contextual-interference schedule, this short-term performance deficit becomes a long-term benefit, because it leads to better retention and transfer test performance.

***Research supports both hypotheses.***   Much research is needed to establish which of the two hypotheses best accounts for the contextual interference effect. In their review of the research literature, Magill and Hall (1990) indicated that conclusive evidence supporting one view over the other does not exist. Research done since that review shows that both views have supportive empirical evidence. It is possible that there are several reasons for the effect. While this inconclusive state of affairs is troublesome, it should not detract from researchers' general agreement that this effect is an established learning phenomenon. Clearly, we need to know more about it. In addition to needing to know why it occurs, we need to know about the conditions that affect when it will occur and when it will not. And we need to determine why different practice schedules lead to different learning effects.

## Summary

A variety of movement and context experiences is an important ingredient for practice conditions. The benefit of this practice characteristic is that it increases a person's capability to perform the prac-

ticed skill successfully and to adapt to conditions he or she has not experienced previously. To determine an appropriate type and amount of practice variability, the teacher or therapist first must assess the performance characteristics of future situations in which the learner will perform the skill. The specific characteristics of the performance context that instructors need to vary in practice are regulatory and nonregulatory conditions. The specific aspects of these conditions that need to be varied depend on whether the skill the learner is practicing is an open or closed skill.

A related practice condition concern is how the teacher or therapist should organize the variety of experiences within a practice session, unit of instruction, or treatment regime. Researchers have gained insight into the best type of organization by implementing the contextual interference effect into practice scheduling. They have found that increasing the amount of interference created by practicing several skill variations within each practice session is preferable. For example, following a blocked practice schedule, such as practicing only one skill variation during a practice session, leads to poorer learning than following a random practice schedule in which the learner practices several skill variations randomly during each session. The contextual interference effect is a robust learning phenomenon; researchers have found it to apply to beginners as well as skilled performers, and to laboratory as well as real-world motor skills. However, they cannot reach a definitive conclusion concerning why the effect occurs. Two hypotheses are most prominent. The first asserts that higher levels of contextual interference increase the elaborateness of the memory representation of the skills the learner is practicing. The second holds that the learner must reconstruct the action plan for a preceding trial of a skill more actively when trials of a different skill have intervened.

## Related Readings

Horak, M. 1992. The utility of connectionism for motor learning: A reinterpretation of contextual interference in movement schemas. *Journal of Motor Behavior* 24: 58–66.

Lee, T. D., L. R. Swanson, and A. L. Hall. 1991. What is repeated in a repetition? Effects of practice conditions on motor skill acquisition. *Physical Therapy* 71: 150–56.

Proteau, L., Y. Blandin, C. Alain, and A. Dorion. 1994. The effects of the amount and variability of practice on the learning of a multi-segmented motor task. *Acta Psychologica* 85: 61–74.

Shea, C. H., and R. M. Kohl. 1990. Specificity and variability of practice. *Research Quarterly for Exercise and Sport* 61: 169–77.

Wrisberg, C. A. 1991. A field test of the effect of contextual variety during skill acquisition. *Journal of Teaching Physical Education* 11: 21–30.

---

■

---

# CONCEPT 6.2

The spacing or distribution of practice can affect
both practice performance and learning of motor skills

---

## Key Terms

massed          distributed
  practice        practice

## Application

The professional who schedules instruction or rehabilitation sessions must make several decisions regarding how much time to devote to various activities within and across sessions. He or she must determine the amount of time to devote to each activity in a session, the amount of rest between activities within a session, the length of each session, and the amount of time between sessions.

For example, if you are a physical education teacher organizing a volleyball unit, you need to determine how much time you should devote in each class period to working on the various skills, drills, and other activities that you plan to include. If you have determined the total amount of practice time you want to devote to a given activity in the unit, and you know how many class periods you will have in the unit, you will know how much time you need to spend in each class period on that activity.

Similarly, if you are a physical or occupational therapist, you need to determine how much time a patient will spend on each activity within a session, how much rest time you should allow between activities in a session, when the next session should be, and so on. You also may need to instruct the patient concerning how to arrange his or her time schedule to do prescribed activities at home.

These examples illustrate two important practice scheduling decisions that are necessary next steps to the content schedule decisions we discussed in the previous Concept. These two decisions concern how to distribute the time available for practicing a skill. As we discuss them, we will assume that you have determined the total amount of practice or therapy time needed for or available to this person. The first decision concerns how much time the person should spend performing a particular activity in a given practice or therapy session. In order to address this problem, you first must decide whether it is better to perform the activity for shorter or longer periods each day. Your answer will influence the number of days the person needs to achieve the total amount of practice or therapy time. The second scheduling concern is determining the optimal amount of rest between practice trials.

---

■

---

## Discussion

Practice distribution, or the spacing of practice, as researchers sometimes call it, has been a popular topic for research in motor learning for many years. The most popular era for this study extended from the 1930s through the 1950s. A controversy related to the amount of rest people need between practice trials to ensure an optimal learning environment brought widespread attention to this topic. At issue

was the question of whether *massed* or *distributed* practice trials provided for better learning of motor skills. Some researchers argued that distributed practice was better, while others maintained that it did not make much difference which spacing strategy an instructor followed.

While this early controversy focused on between-trial rest intervals, it is important to understand that the study of practice distribution also concerns the amount of practice during each session of practice and the amount of rest between sessions. In this second practice distribution issue, the question of concern is whether it is better to have fewer but longer sessions, or more but shorter sessions.

## Defining Massed and Distributed Practice

When researchers use the terms **massed practice** and **distributed practice** to describe practice distribution across sessions, they generally agree that they are using the terms in a relative way. That is, a massed practice schedule will have fewer practice sessions than a distributed schedule, with each massed practice session requiring more and/or longer practice. A distributed schedule, on the other hand, will distribute the same amount of practice time across more sessions, so that each session is shorter than each session in the massed schedule; the distributed practice sessions must be extended over a longer period to achieve the same total amount of practice.

## The Length and Distribution of Practice Sessions

For most instruction and rehabilitation situations, the primary practice distribution concern is how to use an allotted amount of time within and between practice sessions. An important consideration here is that many instruction and rehabilitation situations have specified limits for the amount of time available. For most clinical applications, a patient can receive treatment for only a limited number of sessions, due to insurance restrictions. Also, in teaching and coaching situations, there is often little flexibility in the number of days available for classes or practice sessions. For example, if a teacher has only ten days for a unit of instruction, then the practice schedule must fit that limit. Similarly, if a dancer must perform in a concert that is one month away, then the rehearsal schedule must adjust accordingly. Thus, outside limitations may determine how many days a person should devote to practice. However, the instructor, coach, or therapist still decides the number of practice sessions and the length of each one.

*The benefit of more and shorter sessions.*    While there is not an abundance of research addressing the optimal number and length of practice sessions, the available evidence points to *the benefit of distributed practice*. The general result of experiments comparing a few long practice sessions with more and shorter sessions is that practicing skills during shorter sessions leads to better learning.

An excellent example of research supporting this general conclusion is a study published by Baddely and Longman (1978). They were attempting to determine the best way to schedule training sessions for postal workers on a mail-sorting machine, which required operating a typewriter-like keyboard. All trainees received 60 hours of practice time and practiced 5 days each week. However, the researchers distributed this practice time in four different ways, according to two lengths and two frequencies of training sessions. Two groups practiced for 1 hour in each session. One of these groups practiced for only one session each day, which resulted in a total training time of 12 weeks, while the second group had two sessions each day, thereby reducing the number of weeks in training to 6. Two other groups practiced for 2 hours in each session. One of these groups had only one session each day, while the other had two sessions per day. These latter two groups therefore had 6 weeks and 3 weeks of training, respectively. As this situation demonstrates, there are a variety of ways to distribute 60 hours of practice. The most distributed schedule required workers to train for 12 weeks, while the most massed schedule allowed them to complete their training in only 3 weeks. The difference lay in how long each session was and how many sessions occurred each day.

The researchers used numerous performance measures to determine the effectiveness of the different practice schedules on workers' learning of the typing task. Table 6.2–1 describes two of these. One was the amount of time the trainees needed to learn the keyboard. The shortest time was 34.9 hours, while the longest was 49.7 hours; these figures represent the most distributed and the most massed schedules, respectively. Thus, for learning the keyboard, keeping practice sessions short and having only one session a day led to faster learning.

**TABLE 6.2–1** Results of the Baddeley and Longman Experiment with Practice Distribution Schedules for Training Postal Workers

| Practice Schedule | Number of Hours to Learn Keyboard | Number of Hours to Type 80 Keystrokes/Minute |
| --- | --- | --- |
| 1 hr/session–<br>1 session/day<br>(12 wks. training) | 34.9 | 55 |
| 1 hr/session–<br>2 sessions/day<br>(6 wks. training) | 43 | 75 |
| 2 hrs/session–<br>1 session/day<br>(6 wks. training) | 43 | 67 |
| 2 hrs/session–<br>2 session/day<br>(3 wks. training) | 49.7 | 80+ |

*Source:* Data from Baddeley, A. D., and D. J. A. Longman. 1978. The influence of length and frequency training session on the rate of learning to type. *Ergonomics* 21: 627–35.

A motor performance measure was typing speed. The workers' goal was to learn to type 80 keystrokes per minute. Only those in the most distributed schedule group attained this goal in the originally allotted training time of 60 hours (they did it in 55 hours). All of the other groups required additional practice time. It is interesting that those in the most massed schedule group, which practiced two 2-hour sessions each day, never achieved this goal. After 80 hours of practice they were still doing only a little better than 70 keystrokes per minute. Retention tests were given 1, 3, and 9 months after the workers had finished training. After 9 months, the most massed group performed worst on the typing speed test; the other groups performed about equally. Finally, the researchers obtained a very revealing result from the trainees' own ratings of the training schedules. Although most workers preferred their own schedule, members of the most massed group preferred theirs the most, whereas members of the most distributed liked theirs the least.

The results of this experiment indicate that fitting 60 hours of training into 3 weeks, where there had to be two 2-hour practice sessions each day, was a poor practice schedule. While those in the most distributed schedule generally attained performance goals in the shortest time, they did not perform any better than two of the other groups on the retention tests. Given all the results, the authors concluded that the 1-hour training sessions were more desirable than the 2-hour sessions, and that one session per day was only slightly more effective than two sessions per day. However, having two 2-hour sessions each day was not a good training regime.

Other studies have shown similar distributed practice superiority effects. For example, Annett and Piech (1985) found that two 5-trial training sessions separated by one day led to better learning of a computer target-shooting game than one 10-trial session. One trial involved shooting at 10 singly-presented moving targets. The authors assessed learning by a performance test given one day after the end of the training session. The distributed group not only had more "hits" on the test but also had less error in the shooting attempts. Bouzid and Crawshaw (1987) reported similar results for the learning of word processing skills. Typists who practiced twelve skills during two sessions of 35 and 25 min each, separated by a 10-min break, required less time to learn the skills and had fewer errors on a test than typists who practiced the skills during one 60-min session.

## The Intertrial Interval and Practice Distribution

By far the greatest amount of research on the distribution of practice has investigated the length of the intertrial interval. An immediate problem that we must overcome when looking at this research is that there is no general agreement about operational definitions for the terms *massed* and *distributed.* For example, some researchers have defined massed practice rather narrowly, to mean practice without any appreciable pauses between trials, and distributed practice to mean including rest intervals between trials. Other researchers have defined massed practice more broadly, to mean practice in

---

### A CLOSER LOOK

## Implications from Research on Massed versus Distributed Practice for Scheduling Practice or Rehabilitation Sessions

- **Practice sessions can be too long.** When in doubt about how long a session should be, opt for a shorter rather than a longer amount of time. If learners need more time, add more sessions.
- **More frequent practice sessions are preferable** to fewer sessions.
- **Time saved in terms of the number of days of practice can be a false savings,** because massing sessions too close together can lead to poorer long-term results.

- **The length and number of sessions desired by students, trainees, or patients may not represent the best schedule** for learning the skill. In the Baddeley and Longman study, if the postal trainees had been given their choice, they would have chosen the schedule that allowed them to complete their training in the fewest days, but that was the poorest schedule for learning the skill.

---

which the time spent on a practice trial is greater than the amount of rest between trials, and distributed practice to mean practice in which the amount of rest between trials equals or exceeds the amount of time in a trial.

For our purposes, we shall define *massed practice* when it relates to between-trial rest as practice in which the amount of rest between trials is either very short or nonexistent, so that practice is relatively continuous. *Distributed practice* is practice in which the amount of rest between trials or groups of trials is relatively large. While the terms "very short" and "relatively large" in these definitions are somewhat ambiguous, we use them here so that we can generalize as much as possible from the research literature on massed versus distributed practice to motor skill learning situations. The precise meanings of these terms will vary with the skill and learning situation to which we apply them.

*A history of controversy.* Although a great deal of research literature exists concerning the distribution of practice as it relates to the length of the intertrial interval, it is filled with controversy about which schedule leads to better learning. The controversy is evident in reviews of this literature as well as motor learning textbooks; both provide a variety of answers to the practice distribution ques-

tion. For example, Ellis (1978) stated that "distributed practice facilitates the acquisition of motor skills" (p. 236). However, in another review of practice distribution research, Adams (1987) concluded that "massed practice influences how well you perform, not how well you learn" (p. 50), indicating that although the massing of practice depresses practice performance, it does not affect the amount of learning. Thus, Adams contended that the practice distribution schedule is of little consequence for skill learning, whereas Ellis held that it is an important learning variable.

Two problems underlie the controversy surrounding this issue. The first is related to the issue of practice performance versus learning effects. The problem is that many of the experiments on massed versus distributed practice reported in the research literature did not include retention or transfer trials. Thus, we must base any conclusions on the results during practice trial performance only. Schmidt (1975b) pointed out the second problem, which Lee and Genovese (1988, 1989) further developed. They indicated that researchers generally have failed to consider that the two practice distribution schedules may have different learning effects on different types of skills.

On the basis of the work reported by Lee and Genovese, we can move toward resolving the historical controversy about which practice distribution schedule is better for skill learning. We can do so by distinguishing between continuous and discrete skills. When we consider the research investigating this issue from this perspective, we find that researchers studying continuous skills have arrived at a conclusion different from that of researchers studying the learning of discrete skills.

*Intertrial practice distribution for continuous skills.* Continuous skills have been the most common type of motor skills used to investigate the effects of massed versus distributed practice between trials. And the most popular continuous task has been the rotary pursuit task, in which a person must keep a hand-held stylus in contact with a small disk on a rotating turntable for as long as possible. A trial is usually a specified length of time, such as 20 or 30 sec. What makes this type of task useful for investigating the issue of massed versus distributed practice is that it is quite easy to specify massed and distributed intertrial interval lengths. Massed practice schedules typically have few, if any, seconds of rest between trials, whereas the intervals in distributed schedules are as long as or longer than the trials themselves. Because of this, researchers can establish intertrial interval lengths that are readily identifiable as distinctly massed or distributed.

The consistent result for continuous skills has been that at the end of the practice trials, the massed practice schedule leads to worse performance than the distributed schedule. Thus, if an experiment includes no retention or transfer trials, the authors conclude that a distributed schedule is better. However, when researchers add a retention or transfer test, performance trials difference goes away and the two conditions show no differences, indicating no learning advantage or disadvantage for either schedule.

Adams and Reynolds (1954) performed the classic experiment commonly cited to support the conclusion that massing practice leads to a performance but not a learning decrement. Participants practiced the pursuit rotor task for 40 trials. All of them began practicing the task under a massed schedule in which they had no rest between trials. Then one

group of participants transferred to a distributed schedule after 5 trials. This switch in schedule occurred following a 5-min rest. A second group of people transferred to the distributed schedule after 10 trials, a third group after 15 trials, and a fourth group after 20 trials of massed practice. A fifth group was a control group that practiced all 40 trials in a distributed schedule. The results of this experiment (figure 6.2–1) showed that after switching to a distributed schedule, participants showed immediate improvement and soon were performing similarly to the control group. These results led to the conclusion that massed practice schedules only depressed practice performance and did not influence the learning of this skill.

*Intertrial practice distribution for discrete skills.* When researchers use discrete skills to investigate the issue of intertrial massed versus distributed practice, a problem arises that is directly related to the definition problem we discussed earlier. If a massed schedule allows no rest between trials, whereas a distributed schedule involves a rest interval that is the same length as the practice trial, then the two contrasted intertrial intervals will be essentially the same length, because a discrete response is typically very short. For example, if people are practicing a rapid-aiming task that has a duration of approximately 150 msec, the distributed practice condition could, by definition, have a 150-msec intertrial interval. But if the massed condition had no rest between trials, only 150 msec would separate the two practice schedules. Thus, the operational definition of the terms *massed* and *distributed* becomes important in experiments using discrete tasks. Probably one reason this has not troubled researchers is that discrete tasks seldom have been used for comparing massed to distributed practice. In fact, in compiling a comprehensive review, Lee and Genovese (1988) found only one study in the research literature that used a discrete task (Carron 1969).

In an experiment that sought to replicate and extend the Carron (1969) experiment, Lee and Genovese (1989) compared massed and distributed schedules during practice and the retention test. In

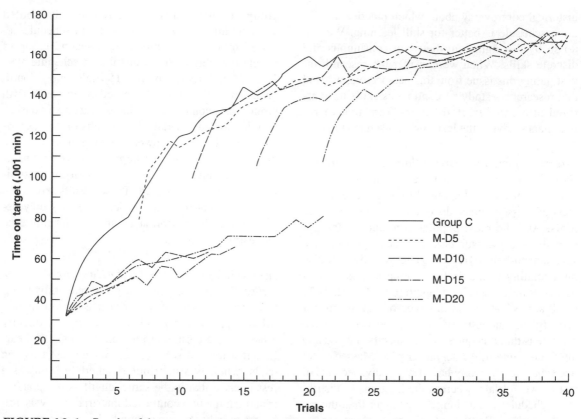

**FIGURE 6.2–1**    Results of the experiment by Adams and Reynolds showing rotary pursuit performance curves for the control group (Group C) and the four experimental groups that practiced under massed practice conditions for different numbers of trials before shifting to a distributed practice condition such as that of the control group. (Source: From J. A. Adams and B. Reynolds, figure from p. 34 in *Journal of Experimental Psychology,* 1954, Vol. 47, American Psychological Association, Washington, DC.)

---

### A CLOSER LOOK

## The Benefit of Massed Practice for Learning a Discrete Hand-Eye Coordination Task

In the experiment by Carron (1969), participants practiced a discrete hand-eye coordination task that required them to pick up a small dowel from a hole, turn it end-for-end, and reinsert it in the hole as quickly as possible. One attempt equalled one trial, which lasted on the average between 1.3 and 1.7 sec. People in the massed practice condition had a maximum 300-msec intertrial interval, whereas those in the distributed group had 5 sec between trials. The results of this experiment showed that the massed practice schedule led to better performance during both the practice trials and the retention test, which participants performed two days after completing the practice trials.

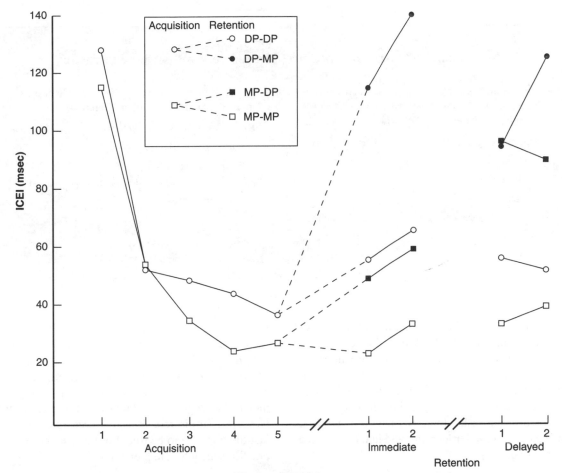

**FIGURE 6.2–2** Results of the experiment by Lee and Genovese showing the effects of massed practice (MP) and distributed practice (DP) on the acquisition and retention performance for the discrete time-based tapping task. Note that during retention trials, the DP and MP practice groups were subdivided into MP and DP groups. (From T. D. Lee and E. D. Genovese, "Distribution of Practice in Motor Skill Acquisition: Different Effects for Discrete and Continuous Tasks," in *Research Quarterly for Exercise and Sport,* in press. Copyright © American Alliance for Health, Physical Education, Recreation, and Dance. Reprinted by permission.)

this experiment, people performed a discrete aiming task that required them to learn to move a hand-held stylus from one small metal plate to another in 500 msec. The massed practice group had 0.5 sec between trials whereas the distributed group had 25 sec between trials. Both groups practiced this task for 50 trials, with KR given on each trial. They performed two retention tests, one 10 min after completing the practice trials, and the other a week later. For these tests, the authors split

each practice group into two groups, a massed and a distributed group.

The results of this experiment (Figure 6.2–2) were, as predicted, that the massed practice group performed better than the distributed group at the end of the practice trials. But then, an unexpected result occurred on the retention tests. The authors saw a strong practice-test context effect. For immediate retention (10 min after practice ended), the massed practice condition led to better retention

---

### A CLOSER LOOK

### Implementing Intertrial Schedules: Massed versus Distributed Practice

- For continuous skills (those that last a reasonably long time and require relatively repetitive actions), a more **distributed practice schedule** is preferable.

  *Examples:* gross motor skills, such as

    walking

    swimming

    bicycling

  repetitive, more precision-oriented skills, such as

    typing

    piano playing

- For skills in which the action is relatively brief, a **massed practice schedule** is preferable.

  *Examples:* sport skills, such as

    hitting golf balls

    hitting tennis balls

  many of the discrete skills used in occupational therapy situations

---

performance only when the test involved a massed schedule. Then, for the 1-wk retention test, the two groups that performed the retention test under the same schedule they followed in practice performed comparably, and better than both groups that were switched to an opposite schedule.

For discrete tasks, then, massing practice trials appears not to hinder learning and in fact can benefit learning.

## Summary

An important decision teachers, coaches, and therapists must make is how to distribute the time that they have been allotted for practicing specific skills. Researchers investigating this issue have compared massed and distributed schedules of practice. Two types of practice schedule concerns are relevant to this issue. One involves the length and frequency of practice sessions. Research evidence is consistent in showing that practice sessions can be too long and too infrequent to lead to optimal learning. Generally, people learn skills better in larger numbers of shorter sessions of practice than in sessions that are long and fewer in number. The second practice schedule issue is the length of the intertrial interval,

which is the rest period between trials. Researchers have found that the optimum intertrial interval length depends on the type of skill being learned. For continuous skills, distributed schedules are generally better than massed ones for learning, although the degree of difference is not a large one. However, for discrete skills, researchers have found just the opposite to be true. For these tasks, massed practice schedules are preferable.

## Related Readings

Adams, J. A. 1987. Historical review and appraisal of research on the learning, retention, and transfer of human motor skills. *Psychological Bulletin* 101: 41–74.

Ammons, R. B. 1988. Distribution of practice in motor skill acquisition: A few questions and comments. *Research Quarterly for Exercise and Sport* 59: 288–90.

Chamberlin, C., and T. Lee. 1993. Arranging practice conditions and designing instruction. In R. N. Singer, M. Murphey, and K. Tennant (Eds.), *Handbook of research on sport psychology* (pp. 213–41). New York: Macmillan. (Read section on "Distribution of Practice," pp. 219–21.)

Singer, R. N. 1965. Massed and distributed practice effects on the acquisition and retention of a novel basketball skill. *Research Quarterly* 36: 68–77.

# CONCEPT 6.3

The amount of practice influences the amount of learning, although the benefit is not always proportional to the time required

## Key Term

overlearning

## Application

It seems reasonable to assume that the more practice a person has, the better his or her performance will be in some future situation. In fact, the conventional wisdom about skills seems to be that how well a person will perform a skill is directly related to the amount of practice the person has had. Let us consider some examples. A dance teacher would encourage a dancer who was a bit tentative in certain parts of a routine to spend as much time as possible going over the routine repeatedly in practice. A golf instructor would try to help a person be more successful when putting in golf by encouraging the person to spend as much time as possible on the practice putting green. And a therapist would encourage a rehabilitation patient to practice the skill he or she was relearning as often as possible. Our experiences in situations like these lead us to accept the "more practice" approach that is so common. But ironically, while this approach seems logical and undoubtedly will work, research evidence indicates that it is not always the best alternative.

The potential problem is that when a person practices a motor skill, he or she may reach a point of "diminishing returns" in terms of the benefits derived from the practice in proportion to the amount of time the practice takes. More simply stated, this means that the performance benefit the person gains is less than the cost in time he or she must spend practicing. This "benefits versus time" trade-off is an important consideration that professionals should not overlook when they design instruction or therapy sessions.

## Discussion

The amount of practice a person devotes to a skill is critical for learning motor skills. This is especially the case when the person has the attaining of expertise as a goal. As the impressive work by Ericsson has shown, expertise in any field is the result of intense practice for a minimum of ten years (Ericsson et al. 1993). Clearly, for achieving expertise, more practice is better than less. However, the amount of practice required to attain expertise is not our focus here (see Concept 4.2 for a discussion of expertise and practice). Instead, we will focus on the amount of practice a person needs to ensure achieving a specific learning goal associated with a specific period of practice.

There are many situations in which it is important to determine the amount of practice people should experience to achieve specific performance goals. For example, a person might need to prepare for a skills test in a physical education activity during the unit of instruction covering that activity. As we address the issue of optimal amounts of practice, we will limit our discussion to this type of situation, and establish some guidelines for the effective and efficient use of available practice time. This limited focus is particularly relevant to those involved in instructional or rehabilitation settings, which place strict practice time limitations on teachers, coaches, and therapists.

## Overlearning and Learning Motor Skills

Researchers historically have investigated the relationship between the amount of practice and the achievement of specific performance goals within the topic of *overlearning*. **Overlearning** is the continuation of practice beyond the amount needed to achieve a certain performance criterion. A teacher, coach, or therapist implements overlearning by establishing a performance criterion, determining the amount of practice time the learner needs to spend in attaining that criterion, and then requiring extra practice time over what is necessary.

When we view it from a theoretical perspective, the idea of assigning extra practice has merit. Those who hold a motor-program-based view of motor learning would say that extra practice helps strengthen the generalized motor program and response schema for the skill a person is learning, so that the person can call it into action more readily when necessary. From a dynamical systems perspective, extra practice is a means by which a learner increases the stability of the coordination and control characterizing the performance of the skill.

***The overlearning strategy for learning procedural skills.*** *Procedural skills* constitute one type of motor skill particularly well suited to deriving benefits from an overlearning practice strategy. A procedural skill typically requires a person to perform a series of discrete movements, which individually are relatively easy to execute. However, to accomplish the total task, the performer must know which movements to make, and in what order. These types of skills are especially common in occupational, industrial, and military settings. For example, people are performing procedural skills when their jobs require them to sort mail into appropriate bins, put together the components of a circuit board for a computer, or type from a written text.

A problem with some procedural skills is that people tend to forget what to do to carry out the entire procedure. This is particularly characteristic of procedural skills that they do not perform routinely every day. For example, several years ago, the U.S. Army was interested in improving the performance of soldiers in assembling and disassembling a machine gun. This skill is especially interesting to study, because soldiers typically learn it in a short training period, but do not perform it again until some time after training; it is not a routine part of their daily duties. The problem was that when they performed a later test on this skill, the soldiers typically showed a large decrement in performance, compared to how they had performed at the end of training. To overcome this problem, researchers for the U.S. Army Research Institute (Schendel and Hagman 1982) proposed that an overlearning training strategy (which they referred to as *overtraining*) would be effective for decreasing the amount the soldiers forgot about the procedure.

The researchers compared two forms of overtraining with a no-overtraining situation. An "immediate" overtraining condition required soldiers to perform 100 percent more trials than were necessary to achieve a performance criterion of one correct assembly/disassembly trial. The second overtraining condition also involved an additional 100 percent more practice trials, but these trials were administered as "refresher" training midway through the 8-week retention interval used for all subjects. Results showed that both of these overtraining groups performed better than the no-overtraining control group on the retention test, which required the soldiers to practice until they were again able to assemble and disassemble the gun correctly on a trial. However, the two overtraining groups did not differ from each other in the number of trials it took to retrain to the criterion performance of one correct trial.

Based on the results of this experiment, the authors recommended the immediate overtraining procedure, because it was more cost- and time-effective. Because the trainees were already in the training session, it would take less time and money to have them engage in additional practice there than to bring them back several weeks later for a refresher training session.

***The overlearning strategy for learning dynamic balance skills.*** In an experiment that involved learning a skill that could be considered more of a "motor" skill than the gun disassembly/assembly skill, Melnick (1971) investigated the use of over-learning for a dynamic balance skill. In addition to addressing the question of whether practice beyond what the learner needed to achieve a performance criterion was beneficial, Melnick asked whether there was an optimal amount of extra practice. In this experiment, people practiced balancing on a stabilometer until they were able to achieve a performance criterion of 28 out of 50 seconds. After achieving this criterion, each group was required to perform further trials in one of the following amounts: 0 percent (none), 50 percent, 100 percent, or 200 percent of the initial number of trials of practice. Then, all participants performed a retention test twice, one week and then one month after practice.

The results showed that extra practice was beneficial. All the groups that engaged in practice beyond what they needed to achieve performance criterion performed better on the retention tests. More interesting, however, was the result that there appeared to be a point of "diminishing returns" for the amount of retention performance benefit in relation to the amount of extra practice. The group that had 50 percent additional practice did as well on the retention tests as the groups that had 100 percent and 200 percent extra practice. So, although additional practice was beneficial, increasing the amount of additional practice beyond a certain amount was not proportionally more beneficial to retention performance.

***The overlearning strategy in a physical education class.*** Researchers have demonstrated the presence of this phenomenon of "diminishing returns" from increases in the amount of practice for learning skills in physical education classes. A good example of this is an experiment by Goldberger and Gerney (1990). In a unit of instruction, fifth-grade boys and girls practiced several football skills. The goal of this unit was to help students improve their performance of these skills. To simplify matters, we will look only at the two-step football punt. One group practiced these skills according to a teacher-rotated format, in which the teacher divided the class into 5 subgroups and assigned each to one of 5 stations where they practiced the skills for 5 min. At the end of every 5 min, students rotated to a new station. Another group of students practiced according to a learner-rotated format: they received index cards describing what they needed to do at each station and then were told to use their 25 min efficiently to practice each skill. Everyone practiced like this for 2 class periods on 2 days. The next week, the students performed the skills in a test.

The results showed that the two groups differed in terms of the number of practice trials for this skill, but not in test performance. The teacher-rotated format group actually practiced the skill an average of 7 more trials than the learner-rotated format group. Students in the learner-rotated format group performed from 0 to 67 trials, whereas students in the teacher-rotated group performed from 0 to 87 trials. But there was no difference between the groups in the amount of improvement in their punting performance scores. The additional practice time induced by the teacher-rotated format did not yield an additional skill improvement benefit. Thus, given the time constraints of the unit of instruction, the learner-rotated format was superior, because it provided more efficient use of that time.

## The Overlearning Strategy Can Lead to Poor Test Performance

Some evidence shows that an overlearning strategy can have another drawback in addition to the diminishing returns effect: learning deficits also may result from providing too many extra practice trials. An experiment by Shea and Kohl (1990) provides an example of this effect. Participants learned to push a handle with a specified amount of force (175N). One group practiced this skill for 85 trials. Another group also practiced this skill for 85 trials, but in addition practiced the same skill at four other force goals (125N, 150N, 200N, and 225N) for 51 trials each, for a total of 289 practice trials. A third group practiced the skill with the 175N goal force for 289 trials. One day later, all participants performed the skill with the goal force of 175N for 10 trials.

The results showed that the group that practiced the 175N goal force for 289 trials did worst on the initial 5 trials of the retention test. In contrast, the group that practiced the variable goals performed

### A CLOSER LOOK

### Implementing the Overlearning Strategy

- The overlearning practice strategy works best when the teacher, coach, or therapist knows how much practice a learner needs to achieve a certain performance level.
- Overlearning practice is effective for skills that a learner will practice during a specified period only, but will not perform for some time after that. The task in the Schendel and Hagman (1982) experiment of disassembling and assembling the machine gun is a good example. Although the soldiers did not need to perform this task every day, they needed to know how to do so in case a situation arose in which they were required to follow those procedures. The most effective practice procedure required the soldiers to engage in 100 percent more practice trials than the number they required to perform the skill correctly one time.
- The instructor should *not* base the amount of extra practice on the notion that "more is better." There can be a point of diminishing returns, and it is even possible that the additional practice can lead to negative test performance. Although the instructor needs to determine the actual amount of extra practice that is best for each situation, a good place to start is to require 100 percent additional practice trials beyond the number the learner requires to achieve the specified performance criterion.
- Practice trials requiring the performance of variations of skill characteristics can be an effective means of establishing an overlearning practice situation.

best. Results for the group that practiced only 85 trials of the 175N goal fell between those of the two other groups. The differences between these groups were most distinct on the first retention trial. However, on the final 5 trials of the retention test, all three groups performed similarly. These results were replicated in another experiment by the same authors (Shea and Kohl 1991).

The significance of the results reported in the Shea and Kohl experiments is that they run counter to what most people would expect. First, adding more practice beyond a certain amount did not improve retention performance. Second, practice of variations of the criterion skill in addition to practice of the criterion skill itself resulted in retention performance better than that following practice of only the criterion skill. Third, additional practice beyond a certain amount was detrimental for initial performance trials on a test given some time after practice ended.

## Overlearning and Other Practice Variables

It can be useful for a learner to continue to practice a skill even though he or she can perform it correctly; such practice increases the permanence of the person's capability to perform the skill at some future time. However, the research investigating the overlearning strategy has shown rather conclusively that *the amount of practice is not the critical variable influencing motor skill acquisition.* The amount of practice invariably interacts with some other variable to influence learning. You have seen this interaction with such variables as the type of KR or the variability of practice. From this perspective, then, the typical overlearning research study indicates that a particular condition of practice is beneficial to a point. However, for continued performance improvement that is more proportionate to the time and effort given to the practice, the instructor and/or learner also must take other practice conditions into account. This does not mean that the question of the amount of practice is unimportant. It does mean that current researchers studying motor learning are aware that they cannot study this issue in isolation, but must consider it as it interacts with other important instructional variables.

## Summary

Research investigating the practice strategy of engaging in extra practice demonstrates that the view that "more is better" is not always true for the learning of motor skills, at least in terms of the benefits derived in relation to the amount of practice experienced. There appears to be a point of "diminishing returns" for amount of practice. While the amount of practice is an important concern for the instructor, it is more important to consider how the amount of practice interacts with other variables influencing motor skill learning. As the amount of time a person spends in practicing a skill increases, the value of certain conditions of practice decreases. However, the person's need to incorporate other variables into the practice routines does increase.

## Related Readings

Chamberlin, C., and T. Lee. 1993. Arranging practice conditions and designing instruction. In R. N. Singer, M. Murphey, and K. Tennant (Eds.), *Handbook of research on sport psychology* (pp. 213–41). New York: Macmillan. (Read section on "Amount of Practice," pp. 236–37.)

Goldberger, M., and P. Gerney. 1990. Effects of learner use of practice time on skill acquisition of fifth grade children. *Journal of Teaching Physical Education* 10: 84–95.

Croce, R. V., and W. H. Jacobson. 1986. The application of two-point touch cane technique to theories of motor control and learning: Implications for orientation and mobility training. *Journal of Visual Impairment and Blindness* 80: 790–93.

Schmidt, R. A. 1971. Retroactive interference and level of original learning in verbal and motor tasks. *Research Quarterly* 42: 314–26.

Shea, C. H., and R. M. Kohl. 1990. Specificity and variability of practice. *Research Quarterly for Exercise and Sport* 61: 169–77.

---

# CONCEPT 6.4

Base decisions about practicing skills as wholes or in parts on the complexity and organization characteristics of the skills

---

## Key Terms

organization     segmentation     progressive
fractionization  simplification   part method

## Application

An important decision you must make when you teach any motor skill concerns whether it is better to have the learner practice the skill in its entirety or by parts. An argument in favor of practicing a skill as a whole is that this experience would help a learner get a better feel for the flow and timing of all the component movements of the skill. The opposing argument is that practicing the skill by parts reduces the complexity of the skill and allows the learner to emphasize performing each part correctly before putting the whole skill together.

One of the reasons this decision is important is that it affects efficiency of instruction. For many skills, both methods of practicing the skill—as a whole and in parts—will be effective in helping the students learn the skill. However, it is not likely that both methods will help the student to attain the same level of competency in the same amount of time. One method generally will be more efficient than the other as a means of attaining competent performance.

Consider the following sport skill instruction situation as an example of the significance of the decision to use whole versus part practice. Suppose you are teaching a beginning tennis class. You are preparing to teach the serve. Most tennis instruction books break down the serve into six or seven parts: the grip, stance, backswing, ball toss, forward swing, ball contact, and follow-through. You must decide whether to have the students practice all of these parts together as a whole or to have them practice each component or group of components separately.

The question of whether to use whole or part practice also confronts professionals in a rehabilitation setting. For example, when a patient needs to relearn the task of getting out of bed, this decision comes into play. This task has distinct identifiable parts, such as moving from the supine position to lying on the side, pushing up to a sitting position, and then rising to a standing position. The therapist must determine whether to have the patient practice each part separately or to have him or her practice the whole sequence at once.

---

## Discussion

The issue of whether to use whole or part practice has been a topic of discussion in the motor learning literature since the early part of this century. Unfortunately, the research generated has led to confusion rather than to understanding. One of the reasons for this confusion is that researchers have tended to investigate the issue in terms of whether one or the other type of practice is better for learning specific skills, without concern for observing skill-related characteristics that could help them make useful generalizations about which practice scheme would be preferable for certain skills. For example, the question of whole versus part practice was investigated by Barton (1921) for learning a maze task; Brown (1928) for learning a piano score; Knapp and Dixon (1952) for learning to juggle; and Wickstrom (1958) for learning gymnastic skills. While this research provided useful information about teaching these specific skills, it did little to establish a guiding principle for decisions about whether to use whole or part practice.

## Skill Complexity and Organization

A breakthrough in understanding the issue of whole versus part practice occurred when James Naylor and George Briggs (1963) hypothesized that the organization and complexity characteristics of a skill could provide the basis for a decision to use either whole or part practice. This hypothesis made it possible for instructors to predict for any skill which method of practice would be preferable.

Naylor and Briggs defined *complexity* in a way that is consistent with the term's use in this text. They stated that *complexity* refers to the number of parts or components in a skill, as well as the information-processing demands of the task. This means that a highly complex skill would have many components and demand much attention, especially from a beginner. Performing a dance routine, serving a tennis ball, and getting from the floor into a wheelchair are examples of highly complex skills. Low-complexity skills have few component parts and demand relatively limited attention. For example, the skills of shooting an arrow and picking up a cup are low in complexity. It is important to keep the term *complexity* distinct from *difficulty*. A low-complexity skill can be difficult to perform.

The **organization** of a skill refers to the relationship among the components of a skill. When the parts are very interdependent—when the way one part is performed depends on the way the previous part is performed—then the skill has a high degree of organization. Shooting a jump shot in basketball and walking are examples. On the other hand, when the parts of a skill are rather independent of one another, the skill is considered to be low in organization. Examples here include many dance routines and handwriting certain words.

***Skill characteristics and the decision to use whole or part practice.*** Based on the Naylor and Briggs hypothesis, assessing the degrees of complexity and organization of a skill and determining how

these two characteristics relate helps a teacher, coach, or therapist decide whether to use whole or part practice. If the skill is *low in complexity and high in organization,* practice of the whole skill is the better choice. This means that people learn relatively simple skills in which the few component parts are highly related most efficiently using the whole practice method. For example, the skills of buttoning a button, throwing a ball, and putting a golf ball have this combination of characteristics. On the other hand, people learn skills that are *high in complexity and low in organization* most efficiently by the part method. For example, the skills of serving a tennis ball; reaching for, grasping, and drinking from a cup; and shifting gears on a car have these characteristics.

To determine effectively which of these complexity and organization combinations describe a particular skill, first analyze the skill. This analysis needs to focus on identifying the skill's component parts and the extent to which those parts are interdependent. When performance of one part of a skill depends on what precedes or follows that part, the skill is higher in organization. Next, it is necessary to decide which part of the continuum of skill complexity and organization best represents the skill.

## Practicing Parts of a Skill

The decision to use a part practice strategy unfortunately solves only part of the problem, because there are several different ways to implement a part practice approach to the practice of a skill. Three different part-task training methods, identified by Wightman and Lintern (1985) in their review of training methods, are most common. One, called **fractionization,** involves practicing separate components of the whole skill. A second method, called **segmentation,** involves separating the skill into parts and then practicing the parts so that after the learner practices one part, he or she then practices that part together with the next part, and so on. Researchers also have called this method the *progressive part method* and the chaining method. A third method of part practice is called **simplification.** This method is actually a variation of a

## A CLOSER LOOK

### An Example of Making the Decision Regarding Use of Whole or Part Practice

Use skill analysis to determine whether to practice juggling three balls as a whole or in parts:

#### SKILL ANALYSIS

**Complexity characteristics**
1. hold the three balls in two hands
2. toss ball 1 from hand 1
3. catch ball 1 in hand 2 while tossing ball 2 with hand 2
4. catch ball 2 in hand 1 while tossing ball 3 with hand 2
5. catch ball 3 in hand 1 while tossing ball 1 with hand 2
6. repeat steps 2 and 5
7. between-component timing: critical for performance

**Organization characteristics**
Doing any one part without doing the part that precedes or follows it does not allow the learner to experience critical between-component timing aspects.

#### Conclusion
Three-ball juggling involves several component parts that are highly interdependent. Therefore, juggling three balls is relatively high in complexity and in organization. **Practicing the whole skill** is the predicted appropriate method.

#### EMPIRICAL EVIDENCE SUPPORTING THE WHOLE PRACTICE PREDICTION
Knapp and Dixon (1952) told university students who had no previous juggling experience to practice until they could make 100 consecutive catches while juggling 3 paddle tennis balls. Results showed that students who followed a whole practice approach achieved this goal in 65 trials, while those who followed a part practice regime needed 77 trials.

---

whole practice strategy and involves reducing the difficulty of the whole skill or of different parts of the skill.

***Fractionization: Practicing separate parts of a skill.*** An important aspect of part practice is determining which component parts of a skill to practice separately. A general rule of thumb is this: practice separately those parts of the skill that do not depend on other parts, and combine as a unit for practice those parts that are dependent on each other. This guideline emphasizes the need to combine as single units those parts of a skill that have critical relationships with each other. Some motor learning scholars have referred to these units as "natural units of coordinated activity" and emphasize the need to establish such units of a skill for instruction or practice (e.g., Holding 1965; Newell et al. 1989).

Consider a couple of examples of how teachers, coaches, or therapists would implement this rule of thumb in practice situations. A sport skill example is the tennis serve. Most would agree that the grip, stance, backswing, and toss are relatively independent, and that the learner therefore could practice each of these parts separately. However, the forward swing, ball contact, and follow-through form a "natural unit," and should not be separated for practice.

A clinical example is the skill of reaching for, grasping, and picking up a cup to drink from it. Research investigating the control of reaching and grasping has shown that the act of grasping is closely related to the reaching phase. Because of this relationship, the therapist should consider these two parts as a natural unit and not have someone practice them separately. However, as we discussed in chapter 2, research has shown that the picking up and drinking parts of this skill are relatively independent of each other and of the reach-grasp parts, indicating that a patient could practice picking up and drinking separately.

In addition to providing a practice method for acquiring a new skill, the part method also is helpful for practicing trouble spots. Consider again the example of the tennis serve. If the source of a person's problems is the toss, for example, it is helpful to know that because the toss is a relatively independent part of the serve, the person can practice it separately. However, if the problem is the follow-through, then the practice should include the forward swing, ball contact, *and* follow-through as one unit. Practice may or may not include the ball toss as well, depending on whether the instructor wants to keep that variable out of the practice. A helpful strategy here is to suspend a ball at the proper height from a string attached to an overhanging pole to provide a ball for contact.

***The practice order for part practice of bimanual skills.*** In the examples we have just described of implementing part practice, the order in which parts are practiced follows the chronological schedule of each part in the skill. However, some skills do not have a built-in order of events. Most notable are bimanual skills, such as piano playing. People have used part practice successfully to facilitate learning these types of skills by practicing each hand separately.

When each hand does the same thing spatially and temporally and the two hands must do these things simultaneously in performance, it does not matter which hand practices first. However, when the bimanual task requires the two hands simultaneously to do two different things spatially and/or temporally, the order in which the hands practice is a concern. The playing of many musical instruments, such as the piano, violin, and drums, can involve this type of two-hand activity. The side-stroke in swimming and the tennis serve are examples of sport skills involving this second bimanual situation.

Sherwood (1994), provided experimental evidence illustrating the effect of practice order on learning these types of bimanual skills. Participants had to learn a two-hand aiming task in which one hand made a short movement while the other made a longer movement. Each hand had to make a reversal movement at a different location (20° and 60°) but at the same time (200 msec). Some people practiced the short movement first, then the long movement, and finally both together. Others did the long movement first. Results showed that those who practiced the short movement first typically overshot the reversal location for the short movement when they performed the two-handed whole task. Those who practiced the long movement first did not have this problem.

This effect of practice order on part practice alerts us to consider the importance of movement control biases for the practice of bimanual skills in which the two hands do something different at the same time. One of these biases (discussed in Concept 2.3) is that the hand that performs the more difficult task will influence the timing of the other hand's movement to be in synchrony with it. In Sherwood's experiment, making the longer movement in 200 msec was very difficult. And when participants practiced that movement second, just prior to practicing with the two hands together, it negatively influenced the hand performing the short movement. But when they practiced this more difficult movement first, the negative bias was not evident for the whole task. We conclude that practice should begin with the hand that must perform the more difficult task.

***Segmentation: The progressive part method.*** Although practicing individual parts can be helpful in learning a skill, the learner can experience difficulty later, when he or she has to put the part back together with the whole skill. One way to overcome this problem is to use the **progressive part method.** Rather than practicing all parts separately before putting them together as a whole skill, the learner practices the first part as an independent unit, then practices the second part—first separately, and then together with the first part. In this way, each independent part progressively joins a larger part. As practice continues, the learner eventually practices the entire skill as a whole.

A common example of the progressive part method is a frequently used practice scheme for learning the breaststroke in swimming. The breaststroke is easily subdivided into two relatively independent parts, the leg kick and the arm action. Because a difficult aspect of learning the breaststroke is the timing of the coordination of these two parts, it is helpful for the learner to reduce the attention demands of the whole skill by practicing each part independently first. This enables the student to devote his or her attention to just the limb action requirements, because he or she can learn each part without attending to how to coordinate the two parts as a unit. After practicing each part independently, the swimmer can put them together to practice them as a whole unit, with his or her attention now directed toward the temporal and spatial coordination demands of the arm and leg actions.

Skills that involve learning movement sequences lend themselves particularly well to the progressive part method. Researchers have demonstrated this for both laboratory and real-world skills. For example, Watters (1992) reported that the progressive part method was beneficial for learning to type an eight-key sequence on a computer keyboard. And Ash and Holding (1990) found that people learning a musical score on a piano benefited from a progressive part practice approach. In this experiment, participants learned a musical score of 24 quarter notes, grouped into 3 sets of 8 notes. The first two segments were easy and the third segment was difficult. Two types of the progressive part method were better than the whole method for learning to perform this musical score, for which performance was based on errors made, rhythmic accuracy, and rhythmic consistency. Of the two progressive part methods, the one that prescribed an easy-to-difficult progression tended to be better than the one stipulating a difficult-to-easy progression.

A key characteristic of the progressive part method is that it takes advantage of the benefits of both part and whole methods of practice. The part method offers the advantage of reducing the attention demands of performing the whole skill, so that the person can focus attention on specific aspects of a part of the skill. The whole method, on the other hand, has the advantage of requiring important spatial and temporal coordination of the parts to be practiced together. The progressive part method combines both of these qualities. Thus, the attention demands of performing the skill are under control, while the parts are put together progressively so that the learner can practice important spatial and temporal coordination requirements of performing the parts as a whole.

***Simplification: Four ways to reduce difficulty.***
For a complex skill, simplification makes either the whole skill or certain parts of the skill less difficult for people to perform. There are several ways to implement a simplification approach to skill practice. We will discuss four of these here. Each is specific to learning a certain type of skill. All of them involve practicing the whole skill, but simplify certain parts of the skill in various ways.

When a person is learning an object manipulation skill, one way to simplify learning the skill involves *reducing the difficulty of the objects.* For example, someone learning to juggle three balls can practice with scarves or bean bags. This reduces the difficulty of the task by involving objects that move more slowly and are therefore easier to catch. Because these objects move more slowly, the person has more time to make the appropriate movements at the right moments. However, the person still must follow the principles of juggling while learning to juggle the easier objects. We would expect early practice using easier objects to enable the person to learn these juggling principles, and then easily transfer them to juggling with more difficult objects. In fact, research evidence supports this approach to learning to juggle three balls (Hautala 1988).

A related simplification method is useful specifically in the learning of skills requiring bimanual polyrhythms, in which the two hands produce separate rhythms simultaneously. Skilled musicians who play instruments such as piano, guitar, and drums acquire this capability. The simplification method involves *reducing the difficulty of the polyrhythm for each hand.* In an experiment by

---

**A CLOSER LOOK**

## The Simplification Method for Learning Three-Ball Juggling

An experiment reported by Hautala (1988) demonstrated that beginning juggling practice by using easier objects is beneficial for learning to juggle three balls.

The participants were boys and girls 10 to 12 years old with no previous juggling experience. All of them practiced 5 min per day for 14 days and then were tested for 1 min with the juggling balls.

The experiment included four practice conditions:

1. Learners began practice using three "juggling balls" of three different colors.
2. Learners began practice using cube-shaped beanbags.

3. Learners followed a progressive simplification scheme:
   a. scarves of different colors
   b. beanbags
   c. juggling balls
4. Learners began practice using weighted scarves and then switched to the balls.

The results of the three-ball juggling test showed this:

• The beanbags practice condition led to the best test performance.

*Note:* The ball-juggling score for subjects in the beanbag practice group was over 50 percent higher than those for the juggling balls group and the progression group, and over 100 percent higher than that of the group that practiced with weighted scarves and then beanbags before using the balls.

---

Summers and Kennedy (1992), participants learned a 5:3 polyrhythm, which involved tapping five beats with one hand while tapping three beats with the other. In the best practice sequence, participants first practiced a 5:1 rhythm with both hands and then practiced a 3:1 rhythm with both hands, before practicing the 5:3 combination with both hands. The advantage of this type of part practice is that it incorporates the integration of the two hands, which is an important component of the whole task. This approach is preferred over practicing separately the beat for each hand.

Third, for skills having a distinct rhythmical characteristic, *providing auditory accompaniment* that cues the appropriate rhythm works well as an aid to facilitate a person's learning of the activity. This approach is especially interesting because it actually simplifies a task by adding an additional component to it. For example, added musical accompaniment can assist people with gait disorders while they practice walking. An experiment by Staum (1983) provided evidence for this involving gait rehabilitation of adults and children who had a variety of gait disorders. The patients wore headphones to hear music

or rhythmic pulses. They received direction to step on the first beat, on the first and third beats, or on all four beats, depending on their individual ability. One practice condition involved marches that maintained consistent tempo. Another condition involved rhythmic pulses produced by tapping two tone blocks together. These pulses kept the same tempi as the marches. After three weeks of rehabilitation, both conditions led to rhythmic and/or consistent walking improvement for all patients in whom arrhythmia had been prevalent.

A fourth simplification method is useful for the learning of complex skills requiring both speed and accuracy. *Reducing the speed* at which a learner first practices a skill can simplify practice. This approach places emphasis on the relative-timing relationships among the skill components and on the spatial characteristics of performing the whole skill. Because a characteristic such as relative time is an invariant feature of a well-established coordination pattern and because people can readily vary overall speed, we would expect that a person could learn a relative-timing pattern at a variety of overall speeds. By practicing at a slower speed, the learner would establish the essential relative-timing characteristics of a coordination pattern.

Researchers have reported evidence for the benefit of reducing overall speed during initial practice for several skills. For example, people's learning of the laboratory task known as rotary pursuit improved when experimenters reduced the speed of the rotating target for initial practice (Leonard et al. 1970). And anecdotal evidence shows that it is standard practice for dance instructors to slow down the tempo initially when they teach their students to perform a new dance routine. The benefit to the dancer is that he or she can focus attention on learning the sequence of steps, as well as on the rhythmical structure of that sequence, before having to perform the sequence at the normal tempo.

***A caution against using miming as a simplification method.*** A common practice in occupational therapy is to have patients mime task performance, or pretend they are performing a task. For example, rather than have a person reach for and grasp a glass of water and drink from it, the therapist asks the person to mime this complete action without the glass present. The problem with this approach is that different patterns of movement characterize the mimed and the real actions.

Mathiowetz and Wade (1995) clearly demonstrated these movement pattern differences for three different tasks for normal adults and adults with multiple sclerosis (MS). The three tasks were eating applesauce from a spoon, drinking from a glass, and turning pages of a book. The authors compared two different types of miming: with and without the object. For both the normal and the MS participants, the kinematic profiles for the three tasks revealed uniquely different characteristics for the real and the mimed situations.

Although this experiment and situation relate specifically to a therapy environment, the message is not limited to that environment. The results have implications for all skill-learning situations. When simplifying practice of a skill, a therapist, teacher, or coach should have the person perform the natural skill. In each of the four simplification methods we recommend here, this is always the case.

## An Attention Approach to Involving Part Practice in Whole Practice

Sometimes it is not advisable or practical to separate the parts of a skill physically for practice. This, however, does not mean that a learner cannot practice parts of the whole skill. It is possible to practice the whole skill, but focus attention on specific parts that need work. This approach provides both the advantage of part practice, where emphasis on specific parts of the skill facilitates improvement of these parts, and the advantage of whole practice, in which the emphasis is on how the parts of the skill relate to one another to produce skilled performance.

Both attention theory and empirical evidence support this attention approach. In Kahneman's model of attention (Concept 3.2), an important factor in attention allocation policy is called *momentary intentions*. When applied to a performance situation, this factor comes into play when a person focuses his or her attention on a specific aspect of the performance. Because we can manipulate our attention resources in this way, we can direct attention to a specific part of a skill while performing the whole skill.

An example of empirical evidence supporting the use of this attention-directing strategy for part practice is an experiment by Gopher, Weil, and Siegel (1989). Participants learned a complex computer game, known as the Space Fortress Game, that requires a person to master perceptual, cognitive, and motor skills as well as to acquire specific knowledge of the rules and game strategy. The player must shoot missiles at and destroy a space fortress. He or she fires the missiles from a movable spaceship, controlling spaceship movement and firing using a joystick and a trigger. To destroy the fortress, the player must overcome several obstacles, such as the fortress's rotating to face the spaceship to defend itself, protection of the fortress by mines that appear on the screen periodically and can destroy the spaceship if it runs into them, and so on (see Mané and Donchin 1989, for a complete description of this computer game).

In the experiment by Gopher, Weil, and Siegel, three groups received instructions during the first six

**FIGURE 6.4–1** Results of the experiment by Gopher, Weil, and Siegel showing the change in performance on the computer game Space Fortress for attention-directing instructions related to specific parts of the skill. (Reprinted from *Acta Physiologica,* Volume 71, D. Gopher, et al., "Practice Under Changing Priorities: An Approach to the Training of Complex Skills," pp. 147–177, 1989, with kind permission of Elsevier Science-NL, Sara Burgerharstraat 25, 1055 KV Amsterdam, The Netherlands.)

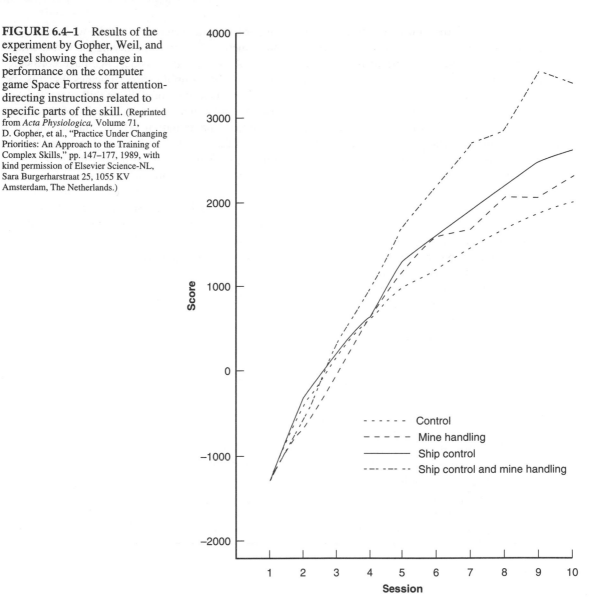

practice sessions that emphasized a strategy requiring them to direct attention to one specific component of the skill. One group's instructions emphasized focusing attention on controlling the spaceship. The second group's instructions emphasized focusing attention on handling the mines around the fortress. The third group received spaceship control instructions for the first three practice sessions and then mine-handling instructions for the

next three sessions. When the researchers compared the performance of these three groups against that of a control group that had not received any strategic instructions, the effectiveness of the attention-directing instructions was evident. As you can see in figure 6.4–1, the control group improved with practice, but not as much as the three instruction groups did. And the group that received two different strategies outperformed those that received only one.

These results provide empirical evidence that attention-directing instructions can serve to establish a part practice environment while allowing the person to practice the whole skill. And these instructions are more effective than having the person practice the skill without providing such strategies. Neither the motor learning nor the teaching methods literature has addressed this type of part practice with any degree of intensity. It clearly deserves more consideration and investigation.

## Summary

An important practice conditions decision is whether to have a person practice a skill as a whole or in parts. The instructor should make the initial decision according to the complexity and organization of the skill. Whole practice is advisable when the skill to be learned is low in complexity and high in organization. Part practice is advisable when the skill is more complex and involves less organization. When a teacher or therapist makes the decision to follow a part practice method, it is important that he or she have the learner practice those components of the skill that are spatially and temporally interdependent together, as a "natural unit." The learner can practice separately those parts of the skill that are relatively independent. At least three different methods can be effective for part practice. The fractionization method involves practicing the parts of the skill separately. The segmentation method is a progressive part method that allows the learner to practice parts, but provides for a building of parts toward performance of the whole skill. The third method involves simplifying the whole skill or parts of the skill for practice. We have considered four different simplification strategies. Each is specific to certain types of skills or skill characteristics. These include reducing the difficulty of the objects for object manipulation skills, reducing the difficulty of the polyrhythm for each hand for skills requiring difficult bimanual polyrhythms, providing acoustical accompaniment for skills characterized by a specific rhythm, and reducing the speed of complex skills requiring speed and accuracy. Additionally, learners can use attention focus strategies when practicing the whole skills, to obtain a part practice type of experience.

## Related Readings

Chamberlin, C., and T. Lee. 1993. Arranging practice conditions and designing instruction. In R. N. Singer, M. Murphey, and K. Tennant (Eds.), *Handbook of research on sport psychology* (pp. 213–41). New York: Macmillan. (Read section on "Part Versus Whole Task Practice," pp. 229–32.)

Holding, D. H. 1987. Concepts of training. In G. Salvendy (Ed.). *Handbook of human factors.* New York: Wiley.

Klapp, S. T., Z. E. Martin, G. G. McMillan, and D. T. Brock. 1987. Whole-task and part-task training in dual motor tasks. In L. S. Mark, J. S. Warm, and R. L. Huston (Eds.), *Ergonomics and human factors* (pp. 125–30). New York: Springer-Verlag.

Wightman, D. C., and G. Lintern. 1985. Part-task training strategies for tracking and manual control. *Human Factors* 27: 267–83.

# CONCEPT 6.5

Mental practice can be effective for learning skills,
especially when combined with physical practice

## Key Terms

mental      external      imagery ability
  practice     imagery
internal
  imagery

## Application

Situations abound in which teachers, coaches, and therapists can apply mental practice to the learning and performing of motor skills. These situations range from helping a patient employ mental practice to learn a new skill to aiding a world-class athlete in performance in a major competitive event. Consider a few examples of situations in which people can use mental practice to their benefit.

A gymnast is standing beside the floor exercise mat waiting to begin his or her routine. Before actually beginning that routine, the gymnast goes through the entire routine mentally, visualizing the performance of each part of the routine, from beginning to end. Following this, the gymnast steps onto the mat and begins the routine.

A paraplegic patient is having difficulty learning how to get into his or her wheelchair from the floor. After several demonstrations by the therapist and several practice attempts, the patient still has trouble performing this skill. The therapist tells the patient to stop practicing and instead to sit down on the floor and mentally practice getting into the chair. The therapist advises the patient to do this by imaging himself or herself getting into the chair perfectly 10 times in a row. The patient goes through the entire sequence mentally, from being on the floor to actually sitting in the chair, on each practice attempt. Following this procedure, the therapist has the patient go back to physically practicing this skill.

Think about a situation in which you have just performed a skill very well and you would like to perform it the same way the next time. But because of the nature of the activity, you cannot physically practice what you have just done. Golf is a good example of this type of situation. If you have just hit a beautiful drive right down the middle of the fairway, you would like to be able to hit a few more practice drives just to try to reproduce and reinforce the swing that produced such a beautiful result. Although you can't do that, you *can* practice that swing mentally as you walk down the fairway to your next shot.

Notice that each of these three situations had a different goal for mental practice. The gymnast used mental practice to prepare for an immediate performance of a well-learned routine. The rehabilitation patient used mental practice to acquire a new skill. Finally, the golfer used a mental practice procedure to reinforce an appropriate action and thereby aid an upcoming performance of that action.

## Discussion

In the skill learning and performance literature, the term **mental practice** refers to the cognitive rehearsal of a physical skill in the absence of overt physical movements. We should not confuse this type of mental practice with meditation, which generally connotes an individual's engagement of his or her mind in deep thought in a way that blocks out awareness of what is happening to or around him or her. We can think of meditation as a form of mental practice; in fact, it seems to be a potentially effective means for enhancing physical performance. However, in this discussion, we limit the term *mental practice* to mean active cognitive or mental rehearsal of a skill, where a person is *imaging* a skill or part of a skill. During this process, an observer would notice no involvement of the body's musculature. This imaging may occur while the learner is observing another person live, another person on film or videotape, or the learner himself or herself on film or videotape. Or it may occur without any visual observation at all.

The act of imaging can involve internal or external forms of imagery (Mahoney and Avener 1977). In **internal imagery,** the individual approximates the real-life situation in such a way that the person actually "images being inside his/her body and experiencing those sensations which might be expected in the actual situation" (p. 137). During **external imagery,** on the other hand, the person views himself or herself from the perspective of an observer, as in watching a movie. We will not compare the efficacy of these two types of imagery conditions in this discussion.

## Two Roles for Mental Practice

The study of mental practice as it relates to the learning and performance of motor skills follows two distinct research directions. One concerns the role of mental practice in the *acquisition* of motor skills. Here the critical question is how effective mental practice is for a person in the initial stages of learning or relearning a skill. The other research direction addresses how mental practice can aid in the *performance* of a well-learned skill.

People use mental practice as a performance aid in two ways. We presented the first in the gymnast example in the Application section. The gymnast use mental practice to prepare for the immediately upcoming performance. When used this way, mental practice is a means of action preparation. We saw the second approach in the example of the golfer mentally imaging a successful swing as he or she walked down the fairway. Here mental practice combines characteristics of both acquisition

and performance situations by providing a person with a means of facilitating the storage and retrieval from memory of an appropriate action.

Beginning as early as the 1890s, research literature is replete with mental practice studies. Several excellent reviews of this research literature can be consulted for more specific information than will be discussed here (see Richardson 1967a, 1967b; Corbin 1972; Feltz and Landers 1983; Feltz, Landers, and Becker 1988). These reviews describe the convincing evidence that is available to support the point that mental practice is an effective strategy for aiding both skill acquisition and performance preparation.

## Mental Practice Aids Skill Acquisition

Investigations of the effectiveness of mental practice in motor skill acquisition typically compare mental and physical practice conditions with a no-practice control condition. In general, research results show that physical practice is better than the other conditions. However, mental practice is typically better than no practice. This finding alone is important, because it demonstrates the effectiveness of mental practice in aiding acquisition. Even more impressive is the effect of using a combination of physical and mental practice.

One of the more extensive comparisons of combinations of mental and physical practice was an experiment by Hird et al (1991). The authors compared six different physical and mental practice conditions. At one extreme was 100 percent physical practice, while at the other extreme was 100 percent mental practice. In between were practice routines requiring 75 percent physical and 25 percent mental practice, 50 percent physical and 50 percent mental practice, and 25 percent physical and 75 percent mental practice. The sixth condition required neither physical nor mental practice, but had participants doing a different type of activity during the practice sessions. Participants practiced two tasks. One required them to place as many round and square pegs in appropriately marked places in the pegboard as they could in 60 sec. The other was a rotary pursuit task in which the target moved in a circular pattern at 45 rpm for 15 sec.

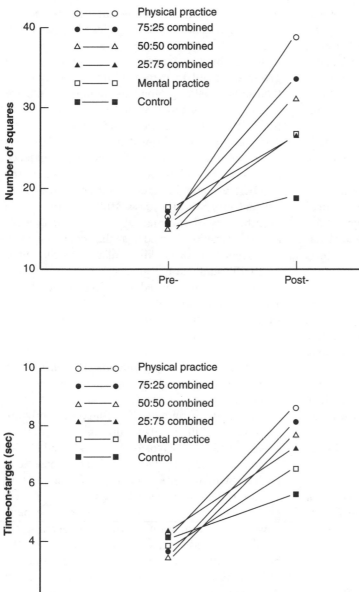

**FIGURE 6.5–1** Results of the experiment by Hird et al. The top graph shows the pre- and posttest results for the different practice conditions for the pegboard task. The bottom graph shows results for the pursuit rotor task. (Reprinted by permission from J. S. Hird, D. M. Landers, J. R. Thomas, and J. J. Horan, 1991. "Physical Practice is Superior to Mental Practice in Enhancing Cognitive and Motor Task Performance," *Journal of Sport and Exercise Psychology,* Vol. 13(No. 3) p. 288. Human Kinetics, Champaign, IL.)

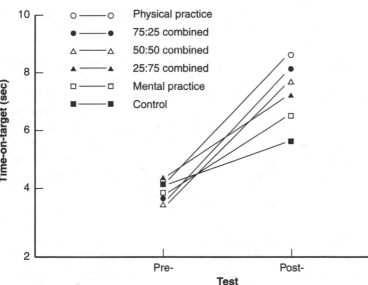

Results of this experiment (figure 6.5–1) showed three noteworthy effects. First, consistent with other research findings was the result that mental practice alone was better than no practice for both tasks. Second, as the proportion of physical practice increased for both tasks, the level of posttest performance rose. Third, although physical practice alone was better than combinations of mental and physical practice, the differences were small.

The similarity in learning effects for combinations of physical and mental practice has been found elsewhere. In fact, some researchers even have shown combinations of these types of practice to be equivalent to physical practice alone. For example, McBride and Rothstein (1979) showed that for learning both an open and a closed skill (involving hitting a moving or a stationary ball), the combination of mental and physical practice trials was superior to a physical-practice-only condition. What was especially notable about their results was that the group using a combination of physical and mental practice had only half as many physical practice trials as the physical practice group.

Why would a combination of mental and physical practice trials lead to learning effects that are as good as or even better than physical practice only? We can derive one answer to this question by considering some points discussed throughout this text about the need to engage in effective practice strategies. An important characteristic of effective strategies for optimizing skill acquisition is active problem-solving activity. Physical practice appears not to be the only means of establishing these beneficial conditions. Mental practice can invoke them as well, although not to the same extent. However, the combination of physical and mental practice appears to establish a learning condition that optimizes these important characteristics.

***Mental practice benefits in rehabilitation settings.***    In addition to being beneficial for the acquiring of new skills, mental practice can be effective for the relearning of skills, as well as for the improvement of skill performance, in rehabilitation contexts. A research example that demonstrates this is an experiment by Linden et al. (1989). They examined the effects of using mental practice on improving walking balance for women aged 67 to 90 years. The task required the women to perform several actions at designated places along an activity course. They began by standing on two footprints and then walked along a simulated balance beam, which was actually a strip of masking tape 4 in. (10.16 cm) wide placed down the center of a carpeted walkway. Then they walked up a ramp

that had a 4° slope, stepped off the ramp, and walked to a table, where they picked up juice and cookies.

For eight days women in the mental practice group engaged in 6 min of mentally imaging themselves walking along the simulated balance beam. A control group spent the same amount of time sitting, playing word and memory games. The participants performed pretests and posttests for the equilibrium task on the simulated balance beam and for walking the activity course on the day before beginning the mental practice or control activity, and the days after the fourth and eighth days of the mental practice or control activity. Results showed that the mental practice was beneficial for walking balance, as measured by equilibrium and foot placement measures, only when participants carried an object in each hand. Thus, while the mental practice routine was not as successful as the researchers had hoped, it was clinically beneficial.

***Mental practice benefits for power training.***    A characteristic of many motor skills is the need to generate speed over relatively short distances. Sprint events in running, bicycling, and crew are examples of skills involving this characteristic. An experiment by Van Gyn, Wenger, and Gaul (1990) demonstrated that mental practice can be beneficial for improving power for people learning a 40-m bicycle sprint. After being pretested on a bicycle ergometer (stationary bicycle) to determine peak power for a 40-m sprint, participants began three training sessions each week for six weeks on the bicycle ergometer to improve power performance. This training involved physical practice in which they had to maintain maximum speed for 10 sec.

Two groups of subjects imaged themselves performing the sprint eight times. One of these groups did only the mental practice, while the other imagery group did imagery practice while they practiced physically. A third group received only the power training. A fourth group served as a control group by receiving neither the imagery nor the power training. The results showed the benefits of combining mental and physical practice. Only the group that received

---

## A CLOSER LOOK

### Imagery Training as a Posture Development Technique

Two experiments by Fairweather and Sidaway (1993) showed that imagery training can help people diagnosed with postural problems related to abnormal curvature of the spinal column. In one of these experiments, participants were 17-year-old males who regularly experienced low back pain and were assessed as having varying degrees of lordosis and kyphosis. The authors compared two different treatments. One involved flexibility and abdominal exercises; the other involved deep muscular relaxation exercises prior to kinesthetic awareness

exercises and visualization practice. The visualization technique consisted of creating images of four different action situations involving trunk, buttocks, pelvis, and thighs. For example, participants were told to visualize their buttocks as unbaked loaves of dough and watch them slide downward toward their heels. Results showed that following a three-week training period during which participants engaged in their respective techniques, both techniques led to improved postural form, as measured by spinal angles, and a reduction in back pain.

both the imagery and the power training showed an improvement in sprint times at the end of the six-week training period. An interesting result was that only the imagery training group and the imagery and power training group improved their peak power scores between the pre- and post-tests.

***Mental practice as a preparation strategy that aids learning.*** We see an interesting example of incorporating mental practice into a practice routine in some work from Singer (1986). First, the author proposed a five-step general learning strategy that involves elements of mental practice in three of the steps. The first step is to get ready physically, mentally, and emotionally. The second step involves mentally imaging performing the action, both visually and kinesthetically. The third step involves concentrating intensely on only one relevant cue related to the action, such as the seams of a tennis ball. The fourth step is to execute the action. Finally, the fifth step is to evaluate the performance outcome.

To test the effectiveness of this general strategy for learning a specific skill, Singer and Suwanthada (1986) compared people who used this strategy with those who did not. The authors compared a group using the five-step general strategy to a group using task-specific strategies and to a condition with no imposed strategy. The task involved throwing a dart underhanded at a rifle target that was on a

wall 3 m from the thrower. After completing 50 practice trials, all participants performed two related tasks: a lawn-dart-throwing task and a type of basketball foul-shooting task. The lawn dart task involved throwing a lawn dart underhand to the rifle target that was on the ground 6 m from the person. The foul-shooting task involved shooting a soccer ball one-handed at a target attached to a basketball backboard from a distance of 4.5 m.

Figure 6.5–2 shows that the five-step general preparation strategy was effective. Those who used the general strategy performed as well as those who used task-specific strategies. It is also notable that those who used some type of preparation strategy performed better than those in the no-strategy group. More importantly, people who used the general five-step strategy during practice performed better on both transfer tasks than members of the other groups. Thus, the authors showed mental practice to be an effective component of a general strategy for preparing for each practice attempt while learning a skill.

## Mental Practice Aids Optimal Performance Preparation

In the field of sport psychology, a popular topic of interest is the benefit of having elite athletes image themselves performing skills prior to actually

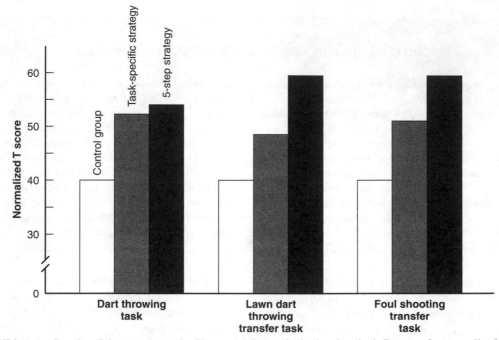

**FIGURE 6.5–2** Results of the experiment by Singer and Suwanthada showing the influence of a generalized learning strategy (5-step strategy), a task-specific strategy, and no strategy for initial practice with a dart-throwing task and for transfer performance with a lawn-dart-throwing task and a foul-shooting task. (Source: Data from R. N. Singer and S. Suwanthada, in "The Generalizability Effectiveness of a Learning Strategy on Achievement in Related Closed Motor Skills," in *Research Quarterly for Sport and Exercise,* Vol. 57, 1986:205–214.)

performing them. While there is ample anecdotal evidence from newspaper and sport magazine stories that athletes engage in this type of preparation (e.g., Hall, Rodgers, and Barr 1990), little empirical evidence exists to help us determine whether this form of preparation is better than any other form. However, some evidence does suggest that mental rehearsal is an effective means of preparation.

Gould, Weinberg, and Jackson (1980) performed an experiment that provided an example of encouraging results. They compared three different preparation techniques for performing a leg strength task. One technique involved focusing participants' attention on the task at hand by having them concentrate on the feelings in the specific muscles that would be associated with maximum performance. Another technique involved increasing participants' arousal levels by having them "psych" themselves up for maximum performance. They accomplished

this by either getting participants angry or "pumping them up" to perform as well as possible. The third technique involved engaging participants in visualizing themselves performing the task and setting a personal best score. The results showed that the imagery and arousal preparation techniques produced higher scores than the attention focus technique and the two control conditions.

The results of this study demonstrate that certain mental preparation strategies are better than others for producing maximum or peak performance. While imagery was not better than arousal preparation, it was better than the attentional focus strategy and than doing nothing at all. Because the task was an explosive strength task, it is not surprising to find that the emotional arousal strategy was effective. Our understanding of the way these different preparation strategies would compare for the performance of a more complex task awaits further research.

---

### A CLOSER LOOK

#### The Use of Mental Imagery by Skilled Athletes

A survey by Hall, Rodgers, and Barr (1990) provided insight into the use of mental imagery as an aid for performing sport skills. They administered a 37-item questionnaire to 381 male and female athletes involved in six sports in Canada. Results showed that athletes use mental imagery as a preparation technique much more commonly during competitions than during practice. This result suggests that athletes see mental imagery more as a technique for enhancing performance than as an aid for learning, and indicates that coaches need to instruct and remind athletes to use mental imagery in their regular practice sessions.

The athletes saw several benefits from using mental imagery during competitions; it helped them keep focused on an event; it helped them remain self-confident about an upcoming performance; and it was a means of controlling their emotions and arousal level. Most of the athletes used mental imagery to image themselves winning rather than losing a competition. Most of the athletes indicated that they did not have structured sessions for using mental imagery. And the higher the level of competition was (e.g., international as opposed to local), the more the athletes used mental imagery.

---

### Why Is Mental Practice Effective?

The two most plausible explanations for why mental practice is effective as both a learning and a performance aid are a neuromuscular explanation and a cognitive explanation.

*A neuromuscular explanation.* We can trace the notion that the benefit of mental practice to learning or performance preparation has a neuromuscular basis to the work of Jacobson (1931) many years ago. When he asked people to visualize bending the right arm, Jacobson observed EMG activity in the ocular muscle, but not in the biceps brachii. However, when he asked them to imagine bending the right arm or lifting a 10-lb weight, he noted EMG activity in the biceps brachii on more than 90 percent of the trials. Since Jacobson's early study, many other researchers have provided evidence for this type of electrical activity in the muscles of people asked to imagine movement (e.g., Hale 1982; Lang et al. 1980).

The creation of electrical activity in the musculature involved in a movement as a result of the performer's imaging of an action suggests that the appropriate neuromotor pathways involved in the action are activated during mental practice.

This activation aids skill learning by helping to establish and reinforce the appropriate coordination patterns that are so essential to develop. For someone performing a well-learned skill, this activation tunes or primes the neuromotor pathways that will be activated when the person performs the skill. This tuning process increases the likelihood that the person will perform the action appropriately and reduces the demands on the motor control system as it prepares to perform the skill.

*A cognitive explanation.* Researchers generally agree that the first stage of learning a motor skill involves a high degree of cognitive activity. Much of this activity is related to questions about "what to do" with this new task. It should not be surprising, then, that mental practice is an effective strategy for people acquiring a new skill or relearning an old one. Mental practice can help the person answer many performance-related questions without the pressure that accompanies physical performance of the skill. In the later stages of learning, mental practice can be beneficial in assisting the person to consolidate strategies as well as to correct errors.

An experiment by Ryan and Simons (1983) provides an example of empirical evidence supporting a cognitive basis for the effectiveness of mental

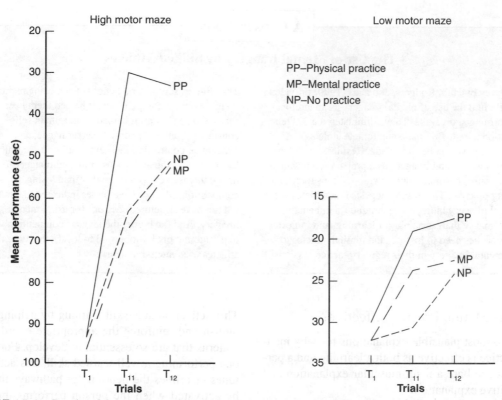

**FIGURE 6.5–3**   Results of the experiment by Ryan and Simons showing performance on two Dial-A-Maze tasks before (T₁) and after (T₁₁ and T₁₂) practice sessions in which subjects engaged in physical, mental, or no practice.
(From E. D. Ryan and J. Simons, "What is Learned in Mental Practice of Motor Skills? A Test of the Cognitive-Motor Hypothesis" in *Journal of Sport Psychology,* 1983, 5:419–426. Copyright © 1983 Human Kinetics Press, Champaign, Illinois. Reprinted by permission.)

practice in aiding skill learning. The authors reasoned that if mental practice is essentially a cognitive phenomenon, then learning of a task that is heavily cognitively oriented should benefit more from mental practice than learning of a task that is more motor oriented. To test this, Ryan and Simons compared acquisition on two motor tasks, one low in motor demands and the other high in motor demands. Participants practiced these tasks under conditions of physical practice, mental practice, and no practice. The task, called a Dial-A-Maze, resembles a child's Etch-A-Sketch toy. The performer moves a stylus through a maze pattern by rotating two handles, one controlling horizontal movement and the other controlling vertical movement. The-low-motor-demand task consisted of moving the stylus through the maze in only hori-

zontal and vertical directions. Motor coordination demands were minimal, because the two hands did not have to work together. The high-motor-demand task required the two hands to work together to move the stylus in a diagonal direction. Figure 6.5–3 provides the results. Notice that, as predicted, the mental practice was superior to the no-practice condition for the low-motor-demands maze. That is, mental practice benefited the task that was heavily cognitively demanding.

## Mental Practice and Imagery Ability

Although researchers have proposed both physiological and psychological reasons for the effectiveness of mental practice for learning and performing motor skills, a related factor also might be operating.

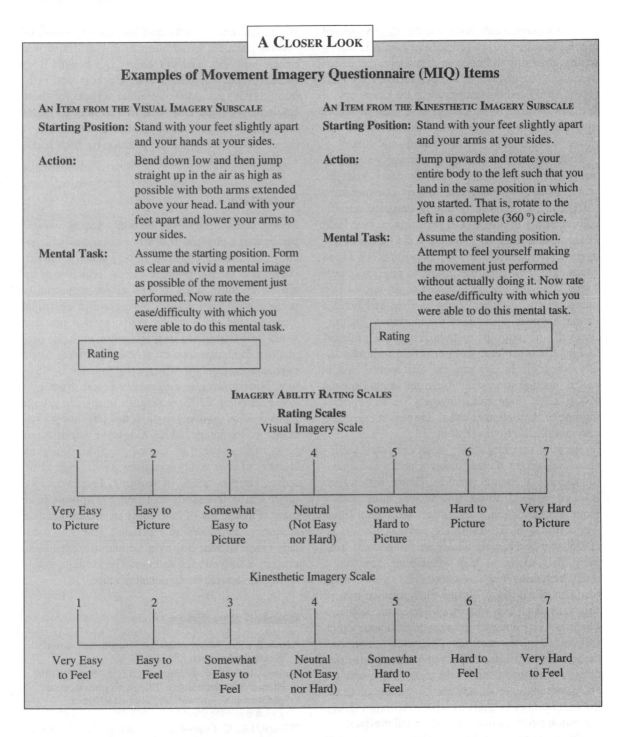

## A CLOSER LOOK

### Examples of Movement Imagery Questionnaire (MIQ) Items

**AN ITEM FROM THE VISUAL IMAGERY SUBSCALE**

**Starting Position:** Stand with your feet slightly apart and your hands at your sides.

**Action:** Bend down low and then jump straight up in the air as high as possible with both arms extended above your head. Land with your feet apart and lower your arms to your sides.

**Mental Task:** Assume the starting position. Form as clear and vivid a mental image as possible of the movement just performed. Now rate the ease/difficulty with which you were able to do this mental task.

Rating

**AN ITEM FROM THE KINESTHETIC IMAGERY SUBSCALE**

**Starting Position:** Stand with your feet slightly apart and your arms at your sides.

**Action:** Jump upwards and rotate your entire body to the left such that you land in the same position in which you started. That is, rotate to the left in a complete (360°) circle.

**Mental Task:** Assume the standing position. Attempt to feel yourself making the movement just performed without actually doing it. Now rate the ease/difficulty with which you were able to do this mental task.

Rating

#### IMAGERY ABILITY RATING SCALES

**Rating Scales**
Visual Imagery Scale

| 1 | 2 | 3 | 4 | 5 | 6 | 7 |
|---|---|---|---|---|---|---|
| Very Easy to Picture | Easy to Picture | Somewhat Easy to Picture | Neutral (Not Easy nor Hard) | Somewhat Hard to Picture | Hard to Picture | Very Hard to Picture |

Kinesthetic Imagery Scale

| 1 | 2 | 3 | 4 | 5 | 6 | 7 |
|---|---|---|---|---|---|---|
| Very Easy to Feel | Easy to Feel | Somewhat Easy to Feel | Neutral (Not Easy nor Hard) | Somewhat Hard to Feel | Hard to Feel | Very Hard to Feel |

There is evidence indicating that the effectiveness of mental practice is related to a person's **imagery ability,** or ability to image an action when requested to do so. According to extensive work by Hall (1980, 1985) and his colleagues at the University of Western Ontario, some people have great difficulty imaging a described action, whereas others can image with a high degree of vividness and control.

Evidence demonstrating that imagery ability is an individual-difference variable came from research using the Movement Imagery Questionnaire (MIQ), a test of imagery ability designed specifically to apply to motor skill performance (see Hall, Pongrac, and Buckolz 1985, for a discussion of imagery ability tests). The MIQ consists of 18 action situations that a person is asked to physically perform. Then the person is asked to do one of two mental tasks, to either "form as clear and vivid a mental image as possible of the movement just performed" or "attempt to positively feel yourself making the movement just performed without actually doing it." In this test, the first mental task is called "mental imagery," while the second mental task is called "kinesthetic imagery." After performing one of these mental tasks, the person rates how easy or difficult it was to do it.

Because imagery ability is an individual difference, Hall proposed that imagery ability influences the success of mental practice. People with a high level of imagery ability will benefit more readily from mental practice of motor skills than those with a low level. To test this hypothesis, Goss et al. (1986) selected people who were categorized from their MIQ scores as high visual/high kinesthetic (HH), high visual/low kinesthetic (HL), or low visual/low kinesthetic (LL). Before each practice trial of four complex arm-movement patterns, subjects kinesthetically imaged the movement about which they received instructions. The results supported the hypotheses, as the HH group performed the patterns to criterion in the fewest trials (11.0), with the HL group next (15.4), and the LL group taking the greatest number of trials to achieve criterion (23.7). Retention performance showed a similar effect.

The importance of this experiment is that it supports the hypothesis that a relationship exists between imagery ability and the effectiveness of mental practice. In addition, it demonstrates that people with low imagery ability can benefit from mental practice. Although Hall, Buckolz, and Fishburne (1989) provided additional support for these findings, we need more research to help us better understand imagery ability and its relationship to the effectiveness of mental practice for both learning and performing motor skills.

## Summary

Mental practice involves mentally seeing oneself performing a physical skill while not actually physically performing the skill. Experimental evidence shows that mental practice can be effective as an aid for learning skills as well as for preparing to perform well-learned skills. As a practice technique when people are learning skills, mental practice works best when used in combination with physical practice. Both neuromuscular and cognitively based explanations exist for why mental practice is effective. Neuromuscular explanations stem from evidence showing EMG recordings in muscle groups that would be involved in the actual physical performance of the imaged skills. Cognitive explanations point to the benefit of mental practice in helping learners answer many questions about what to do during the first stage of learning. Empirical evidence exists indicating that both viewpoints have merit. Finally, the effectiveness of mental practice appears to be related to a person's ability to mentally image action. However, people who are low in imagery ability as well as those who are high in this ability can benefit from mental practice.

## Related Readings

Annett, J. 1995. Motor imagery: Perception or action? *Neuropsychologica* 33: 1395–417.

Burhans, R. S., C. L. Richman, and D. B. Bergey. 1988. Mental imagery training: Effects on running speed performance. *International Journal of Sport Psychology* 19: 26–37.

Driskell, J.E., C. Copper, and A. Moran. 1994. Does mental practice enhance performance? *Journal of Applied Psychology* 79: 481–92.

Kohl, R. M., S. D. Ellis, and D. L. Roenker. 1992. Alternating actual and imagery practice: Preliminary theoretical considerations. *Research Quarterly for Exercise and Sport* 63: 162–70.

Singer, R. N., and J. H. Cauraugh. 1985. The generalizability effect of learning strategies for categories of psychomotor skills. *Quest* 37: 103–19.

Warner, L., and M. E. McNeil. 1988. Mental imagery and its potential for physical therapy. *Physical Therapy* 68: 516–21.

Weinberg, R. S. 1982. The relationship of mental preparation strategies and motor performance: A review and critique. *Quest* 33: 195–213.

# STUDY QUESTIONS FOR CHAPTER 6

1. What is meant by the term *practice variability* and why is it important for skill learning?

2. Give an example of how you would implement practice variability for a closed motor skill and an open skill.

3. (a) How is contextual interference related to the issue of organizing practice for learning a motor skill? (b) Describe how blocked and random practice schedules represent the extreme ends of a contextual interference continuum.

4. Describe how you would implement an appropriate amount of contextual interference into the practice schedule for (a) a novice learning a skill; (b) a skilled person.

5. What are two reasons researchers have proposed for why contextual interference benefits motor skill learning?

6. Describe how the concept of practice distribution is related to the intertrial interval and to the length and distribution of practice sessions. Describe a motor skill learning situation for each.

7. (a) How do massed and distributed intertrial interval schedules differentially influence the learning of discrete and continuous motor skills? (b) Why do you think there is a difference in how these two schedules influence the learning of these skills?

8. (a) What is meant by the term *overlearning* as it relates to learning motor skills? (b) Describe a skill-learning situation in which an overlearning practice strategy would help a person learn that skill.

9. (a) How can you decide whether people would learn a skill best if they practiced it as a whole or in parts? (b) Give a motor skill example to show how to apply these rules.

10. (a) Describe examples of how instructors can apply the part practice methods of fractionization and segmentation to the practice of skills. (b) Describe three ways they can apply the simplification method to the practice of skills.

11. (a) What is *mental practice?* (b) Describe an example of how you would implement mental practice procedures to aid the learning of a new skill and the preparation to perform a well-learned skill.

12. What are three reasons researchers have proposed to explain why mental practice aids motor skill learning and performance?

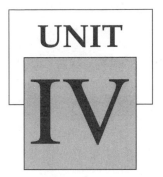
# INDIVIDUAL
# DIFFERENCES

# CHAPTER

# 7

# ABILITIES

---

## CONCEPT 7.1
A variety of abilities underlie motor skill learning and performance success

## CONCEPT 7.2
Identification of levels of motor abilities can help the professional predict a person's potential for successful learning and performance of motor skills

# CONCEPT 7.1

A variety of abilities underlie motor skill learning and performance success

## Key Terms

differential
    psychology
ability
general motor
    ability
    hypothesis

specificity
    of motor
    abilities
    hypothesis
perceptual-
    motor
    abilities

physical
    proficiency
    abilities
psychomotor
    ability

## Application

Some people are good at many different physical activities. Why is this the case? Are they born with some special "motor ability" that enables them to be successful at all they do? Have they had an abundance of good training and practice in a wide variety of activities? Are they really good at everything, or only at certain activities?

Also, people differ in how quickly and successfully they learn motor skills. If you observe a physical activity class for beginners, you will see various degrees of success and failure during the first few days. For example, in a beginning golf class, when the students first start to hit the ball, some will spend an inordinate amount of time simply trying to make contact with the ball. But some will be at the other extreme, able to hit the ball rather well. The remainder of the class usually will be distributed somewhere along the continuum of success between these two extremes.

We can observe parallel differences in other physical activity situations, such as dance classes, driving instruction classes, and physical therapy sessions. People enter these situations with a wide variety of what some refer to as "entry behaviors." These entry behaviors reflect the very real behavioral phenomenon that individuals differ in their capability to perform motor skills. The differences continue as people progress at different rates.

## Discussion

Before addressing the issue of individual differences, we must call attention to a dramatic shift in our orientation with this discussion. In each of the preceding chapters, we have concentrated on what we can call the "average learner." We have focused on people in general as they deal with certain information-processing limitations or motor control limits, or with the influences of certain environmental features. The principles or tendencies we have described represent norms for people in general. By contrast, in this chapter, we are interested in *how individuals differ,* rather than in "average behavior."

**Differential psychology** is the study of individual differences in psychology, as opposed to the study of normative or average behavior. Those who study individual differences are concerned with identifying and measuring individual abilities or traits. The study of intelligence is a prime example of this type of investigation. The study of intelligence led to the identification of the components of intelligence, which led in turn to the formulation of tests to quantify an individual's level of these components, or of a general intelligence.

In motor behavior, the study of individual differences has followed a similar pattern. Research has focused on the identification and measurement of motor abilities. Identification of motor abilities has not been an easy task; as a result, very few researchers have ventured into this area of study. Of those who have investigated human motor abilities, one of the most successful has been Edwin Fleishman (see Fleishman and Quaintance 1984, for a complete description of this work). Fleishman's work on the identification and measurement of motor abilities has been going on for many years and must be considered the major source of information for any scientific discussion of motor abilities.

## Abilities as Individual-Difference Variables

*Ability* is a word commonly used interchangeably in conversation with the word *skill.* We often hear people say, "That person has lots of ability" when they are indicating that the person has a high degree of skill. However, when used in the context of individual differences, **ability** means *a general trait or capacity of the individual* that is related to his or her performance of a variety of skills or tasks. Many different motor abilities underlie the performance of motor skills. The level of success a person can achieve for a specific motor skill depends in large part on the degree to which that person has the abilities related to performing that skill. That is, people with differing degrees of the abilities required to play tennis will have differing achievement potentials in that activity.

*The controversy over general versus specific abilities.* Researchers generally agree that a variety of motor abilities underlie motor skill performance, and that people have various levels of these motor abilities. However, they have been debating for many years over the way these abilities relate to one another in the same individual. One group has argued that abilities are highly related. Those who hold the opposite view say that abilities are relatively independent of one another.

The **general motor ability hypothesis** maintains that there exists in each individual a singular, global motor ability. It holds that the level of that ability in an individual influences the ultimate success that person can expect in performing any motor skill. This notion has been in existence for quite some time. This hypothesis predicts that if a person is good at one motor skill, then he or she has the potential to be good at all motor skills. The

reasoning behind this prediction is that there is *one* general motor ability.

Such well-known figures in physical education as C. H. McCloy, David Brace, and Harold Barrow are generally credited with advancing this. They developed tests that purportedly assessed individuals' present motor ability, and asserted that these tests also would predict their success in athletic endeavors. For example, McCloy (1934; McCloy and Young 1954) developed the General Motor Capacity Test as a general motor ability test. Because McCloy considered *motor capacity* to comprise a person's inborn, hereditary potentialities for general motor performance, he believed that this test provided a means of predicting potential achievement levels for a person.

But contrary to the expectations of proponents of the general motor ability hypothesis, there has been very little research evidence to support this viewpoint.[1] One suspects that the basis for the continued existence of this hypothesis is its intuitive appeal. Tests of general motor ability are convenient, appealing to those who seek an easy explanation for why certain people are successful or unsuccessful at performing motor skills. The fact that these tests are poor predictors of specific motor skill performance has not diminished the appeal of the general motor ability hypothesis.

An alternative perspective, for which there has been substantial support, is the **specificity of motor abilities hypothesis.** This view suggests that individuals have many motor abilities and that these abilities are relatively independent. This means, for example, that if a person exhibited a high degree of balancing ability, we could not predict how well that person would do on a test of reaction time.

Support for the specificity hypothesis has come from experiments based on the common assumption that if motor abilities are specific and independent, then the relationship between any two abilities will be very low. Thus, in the simplest of cases,

1. The tests and measurements text by Johnson and Nelson (1985) provides an excellent review of research investigating the validity of tests assessing general motor ability.

the relationship would be very low between two abilities such as balance and reaction time, or between reaction time and speed of movement, or even between static balance and dynamic balance.

Franklin Henry and many of his students have published the great bulk of the research based on this rationale. The focus of this work was to compare performance on two motor abilities, reaction time (RT) and speed of movement, or movement time (MT). As predicted by the specificity hypothesis, these researchers consistently have found the relationship between RT and MT to be very low.

Experiments comparing other abilities have produced similar results. A good example is one by Drowatzky and Zuccato (1967) that examined balance as an ability. Their results (table 7.1–1) showed that there is no one balancing ability. Rather, there are several specific types of balance. In this experiment, participants performed six different balancing tasks that generally have been regarded as measures of either static or dynamic balancing ability. The results of the correlations among all the tests showed that the highest correlation was .31, between the sideward stand and the bass stand. Most of the correlations ranged between 0.12 and 0.19. On the basis of these results, it would be difficult to conclude that one test exists that we can consider a valid measure of balancing ability. Obviously, we should subdivide even the

ability we generally call "balance" into various types of balance.

It is interesting to note that the specificity notion can be extended to include fundamental motor skills as well. For example, when Singer (1966) examined the relationship between the two basic, or fundamental, motor skills of throwing and kicking, he found a very low relationship between an individual's performance on one test and his or her performance on the other.

*The "all-around athlete."* If motor abilities are numerous and independent, then how can we explain the so-called "all-around athlete," the person who is very proficient at a variety of physical activities? According to the specificity view, abilities fall somewhere along a range containing low, average, and high amounts within individuals. Because people differ, it seems reasonable to expect that some people have a large number of abilities at an average level, and other people have a majority of abilities at either the high or the low end of the scale.

According to the specificity hypothesis, the person who excels in a large number of physical activities has high levels of a large number of abilities. We would expect that a person would do very well in those activities for which the underlying abilities required for successful performance matched the

**TABLE 7.1–1**   Results from the Experiment by Drowatzky and Zuccato (1967) Showing the Correlations Among Six Different Tests of Static and Dynamic Balance

| Test | 1 Stork Stand | 2 Diver's Stand | 3 Stick Stand | 4 Sideward Stand | 5 Bass Stand | 6 Balance Stand |
|---|---|---|---|---|---|---|
| 1 | — | 0.14 | −0.12 | 0.26 | 0.20 | 0.03 |
| 2 | | — | −0.12 | −0.03 | −0.07 | −0.14 |
| 3 | | | — | −0.04 | 0.22 | −0.19 |
| 4 | | | | — | 0.31 | 0.19 |
| 5 | | | | | — | 0.18 |
| 6 | | | | | | — |

*Source:* From Drowatzky, J. N. and F. C. Zuccato, 1967. Interrelationships between selected measures of static and dynamic balance. *Research Quarterly for Exercise and Sport* 38: 509–10. Copyright © 1967 American Alliance for Health, Physical Education, Recreation, and Dance. Reprinted by permission.

abilities for which the person was at the high end of the scale.

In actual fact, the true all-around athlete is a rare individual. Typically, when a person shows high performance levels in a variety of physical activities, a close inspection of those activities reveals many foundational motor abilities in common. We would expect a person exhibiting high levels for a variety of abilities to do well in activities for which those abilities were foundational to performance. However, we would expect average performance if this person engaged in activities for which those abilities were less important, activities based on other abilities, of which the person possessed only average levels.

## Identifying Motor Abilities

As a capacity, an ability is a relatively enduring attribute of an individual. Researchers who study individual differences assume that we can describe the skills involved in complex motor activities in terms of the abilities that underlie their performance. Fleishman (1972) found, for example, that the ability called spatial visualization is related to the performance of such diverse tasks as aerial navigation, blueprint reading, and dentistry. An important step in understanding how abilities and skill performance are related is identifying abilities and matching them with the skills involved. To accomplish this, Fleishman undertook not to identify as many abilities as possible, but to identify the fewest possible ability categories and apply them to the performance of the widest variety of tasks.

*A taxonomy of motor abilities.* From the results of extensive batteries of perceptual-motor tests given to many people, Fleishman developed a "taxonomy of human perceptual-motor abilities" (Fleishman 1972; Fleishman and Quaintance 1984). He proposed that there seem to be eleven identifiable and measurable **perceptual-motor abilities.** He identified these abilities as follows: (1) *multi-limb coordination,* the ability to coordinate the movement of a number of limbs simultaneously; (2) *control precision,* the ability to make

highly controlled and precise muscular adjustments where larger muscle groups are involved, as in the rotary pursuit task; (3) *response orientation,* the ability to select rapidly where a response should be made, as in a choice-reaction-time situation; (4) *reaction time,* the ability to respond rapidly to a stimulus when it appears; (5) *speed of arm movement,* the ability to make a gross rapid-arm movement; (6) *rate control,* the ability to change speed and direction of responses with precise timing, as in following a continuously moving target; (7) *manual dexterity,* the ability to make the skillful, well-directed arm-hand movements that are involved in manipulating objects under speed conditions; (8) *finger dexterity,* the ability to perform skillful, controlled manipulations of tiny objects involving primarily the fingers; (9) *arm-hand steadiness,* the ability to make precise arm-hand positioning movements where strength and speed are minimally involved; (10) *wrist, finger speed,* the ability to move the wrist and fingers rapidly, as in a tapping task; and (11) *aiming,* the ability to aim precisely at a small object in space.

In addition to perceptual-motor abilities, Fleishman also identified nine abilities that he designated as **physical proficiency abilities.** These abilities differ from the perceptual-motor abilities in that they are more generally related to athletic and gross physical performance. Most people would consider these abilities physical fitness abilities. The physical proficiency abilities identified by Fleishman are as follows: (1) *static strength,* the maximum force that a person can exert against external objects; (2) *dynamic strength,* the muscular endurance used in exerting force repeatedly, as in a series of pull-ups; (3) *explosive strength,* the ability to mobilize energy effectively for bursts of muscular effort, as in a high jump; (4) *trunk strength,* the strength of the trunk muscles; (5) *extent flexibility,* the ability to flex or stretch the trunk and back muscles; (6) *dynamic flexibility,* the ability to make repeated, rapid trunk-flexing movements, as in a series of toe touches; (7) *gross body coordination,* the ability to coordinate the action of several parts of the body while the body is in motion; (8) *gross* *body equilibrium,* the ability to maintain balance without visual cues; and (9) *stamina,* the capacity to sustain maximum effort requiring cardiovascular effort, as in a distance run.

We should not consider Fleishman's lists to be exhaustive inventories of all the abilities related to motor skill performance, because Fleishman wanted to identify the smallest number of abilities that would describe the tasks performed in the test battery. While he used hundreds of tasks to identify those abilities, the inclusion of additional types of tasks besides those Fleishman used could lead to the identification of other motor abilities. For example, Fleishman did not include the following abilities in his two lists: *static balance,* the ability to balance on a stable surface when no locomotor movement is required; *dynamic balance,* the ability to balance on a moving surface or to balance while involved in locomotion; *visual acuity,* the ability to see clearly and precisely; *visual tracking,* the ability to follow a moving object visually; and *eye-hand* or *eye-foot coordination,* the ability to perform skills requiring vision and the precise use of the hands or feet.

An important assumption of this view of human abilities is that all individuals possess these motor abilities. Another is that because it is possible to measure these motor abilities, it is also possible to determine a quantified measure of the level of each ability in a person. People differ in the amount of each ability they possess. Their motor abilities indicate limits that influence their potential for achievement in skills.

## Relating Motor Abilities to Motor Skill Performance

An approach presented by Ackerman (1988) helps us to see where motor abilities fit into the broader issue of motor skill performance. He described motor abilities as one of three categories of human abilities that affect motor skill performance. One category is general intelligence, or general ability. Included are cognitively oriented abilities and memory-related processes, such as acquiring, storing, retrieving, combining, and comparing memory-based information, as well as using it in new contexts. The second category is perceptual speed ability. This category includes abilities associated with a person's facility for solving problems of increasing complexity, and with the person's speed at processing information he or she must use to solve problems. Tests of such tasks as finding the $X$s in an array of letters and transcribing symbols on a

---

### A CLOSER LOOK

#### The Value of Identifying Motor Abilities

Identifying and assessing motor abilities can allow a teacher, coach, or therapist to

- identify the source of problems or difficulties in performing a skill. Often a person has difficulty learning a new skill because he or she lacks adequate experience involving the motor ability essential to performing that particular skill.

*Example:* A child may be having difficulty catching a thrown ball because of a poorly developed ability to visually track a moving object.

- develop appropriate physical activities to improve performance in a variety of skills involving the same motor ability.

*Example:* Balance is a foundational ability to many different skills. As a result, movement experiences that provide people the opportunity to develop their balance ability in a variety of movement situations should benefit learning skills requiring balance.

- predict a person's potential for success in a specific skill. (*Note:* this point is the basis for the discussion in Concept 7.2.)

list assess these abilities. Finally, **psychomotor ability** (i.e., motor ability) is the third category. Abilities in this category, which is the focus of our discussion, are related to speed and accuracy of movements that place little or no cognitive demand on the person. To fully understand individual differences, we must see performance of all types of skills in terms of these three foundational categories of abilities. However, for the purposes of the present discussion, we will limit our attention to motor abilities.

Figure 7.1–1 illustrates the view that motor abilities are underlying, foundational components of motor skill performance. This figure shows how we can analyze complex motor skills by a process known as *task analysis* in order to identify the abilities that underlie any motor skill. For example, to serve a tennis ball successfully, a player must perform certain components of that skill properly. Figure 7.1-1 identifies these components, which are the first level of analysis of the tennis serve, in the middle tier of the diagram. Identification of these components helps us to identify more readily the underlying motor abilities that are involved in the successful performance of this task. The bottom tier of the diagram presents these abilities. Based on Fleishman's lists, they include such abilities as multi-limb coordination, control precision, speed of arm movement, rate control, aiming, and static strength. You undoubtedly could add others. However, these few examples should serve to illustrate the foundational role perceptual-motor and physical proficiency abilities play in the performance of motor skills.

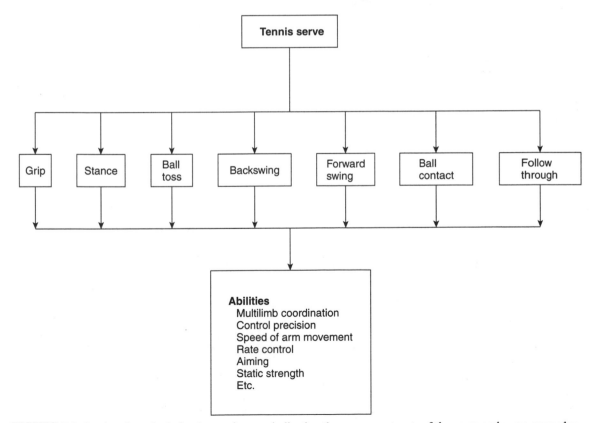

**FIGURE 7.1–1** A task analysis for the tennis serve indicating the component parts of the serve and some examples of perceptual-motor abilities underlying performance of the serve.

## Summary

Individual-difference research in motor behavior is concerned with the study of motor abilities. In this context, *ability* refers to a general trait or capacity of the individual that is related to the performance of a variety of skills or tasks. A variety of motor abilities underlie motor skill performance. Different people have different levels of these abilities. An important question that researchers have debated for many years concerns how these abilities relate to one another in the same individual. The general motor ability hypothesis proposes that abilities are highly related, whereas the specificity hypothesis argues that abilities are relatively independent of one another. Research evidence consistently has supported the specificity hypothesis.

One approach to identifying motor abilities is Fleishman's taxonomy of perceptual-motor and physical proficiency abilities. These abilities play a foundational role in the performance of motor skills. Because it is possible to measure these abilities, a motor skills professional can make an assessment of a person's level of each ability. Research evidence shows that people differ in the amounts of each ability they possess. Levels of motor abilities indicate limits that influence a person's potential for skill achievement.

## Related Readings

Cronbach, L. 1957. The two disciplines of scientific psychology. *American Psychologist* 12: 671–84.

Fleishman, E. A. 1978. Relating individual differences to the dimensions of human tasks. *Ergonomics* 21: 1007–19.

Fleishman, E. A. 1982. Systems for describing human tasks. *American Psychologist* 37: 821–34.

Thomas, J. R., and W. Halliwell. 1976. Individual differences in motor skill acquisition. *Journal of Motor Behavior* 8: 89–99.

■

# CONCEPT 7.2

Identification of levels of motor abilities can help the professional predict a person's potential for successful learning and performance of motor skills

## Key Terms

variance
accounted for

superdiagonal
form

## Application

One of the characteristics that is common to industry, sport, and the military is that those in authority must select people to do specific jobs requiring motor skill performance. This selection process involves *predicting* that a person selected for a job will do that job better than some other job. This predicting process also assumes that the individual selected for that job will perform it better than those not selected. If the right people are doing the right jobs, then much time and money is saved, and the people performing the jobs are more satisfied with what they are doing. A key part of the prediction process in these situations is developing appropriate ways to assess the motor abilities of candidates for the jobs and then directing people who show potential for success at specific jobs into training for those jobs.

An event that occurs every four years brings about interesting concerns for prediction of future performance. During preparation for the Olympic Games, the selection and development of the best athletes in a country becomes a major issue. Certain countries appear to have well-developed selection processes, while others appear to have less-than-desirable selection processes. The common view is that the country that can most accurately predict those who will be world-class athletes at the earliest possible age will have an advantage in competitions such as the Olympic Games.

A prediction situation in physical activity classes occurs when an instructor wants to subdivide a large class into smaller, more homogeneous groups. It is common to place people who exhibit high initial performance levels into one group, people who exhibit poor initial performance levels into another group, and so on. The instructor might justify this procedure on the basis of the relationship between initial performance levels and later success in the activity. But does a person who begins an activity by performing it poorly have any chance for later success? Or, conversely, is a person who begins an activity by performing it well effectively guaranteed a high level of future success?

■

## Discussion

The focus of this discussion is on predicting a person's *potential* for future success rather than a person's actual future success. Whether or not an individual actually achieves his or her potential will depend on many factors, such as motivation, training, opportunities, etc. Thus, those who make predictions on the basis of motor abilities must limit each judgment to the assessment of a person's potential for success, given the appropriate opportunities to develop that potential.

### Prediction Accuracy

Before considering how an instructor can use motor abilities information for prediction purposes, we must consider some of the limitations on the accuracy of such a prediction. While prediction accuracy depends on several factors, two are particularly critical.

First, predicting the potential for success in a motor skill depends on an accurate identification and assessment of the essential abilities the person needs to perform the skill successfully. We will refer to this skill as the *target skill.* The first step is to develop a task analysis for the target skill, as we discussed in Concept 7.1. This analysis should identify the abilities that seem to underlie the successful performance of the skill. The next step is to administer to a large sample of people a battery of tests of the abilities identified in the task analysis. Finally, the instructor must compare the scores on the abilities tests to the actual performance of the target skill by the sample of people, using an appropriate performance measure.

A statistic that is very useful in this prediction process is known as the **variance accounted for.** This simply refers to the percentage of the statistical variance of the performance scores for the target skill that is accounted for by the scores on the abilities tests. If the target skill performance variance accounted for by the tests is high (i.e., 70 percent or better), you can be confident that you have identified the essential abilities underlying performance of the target skill. If, on the other hand, the variance accounted for is below 70 percent, then other abilities remain to be identified.

The second factor critical to the accuracy of the success prediction is *the validity and reliability of the abilities tests* used. If these tests are not valid and reliable measures, there is little basis for expecting reasonable prediction accuracy for motor skill performance.

Much work remains to be done in both identifying the important abilities underlying successful performance of skills and developing valid and reliable ability tests. However, as you will see, researchers have had sufficient success in many situations to warrant the consideration of the use of motor abilities testing to predict future success potential.

## Relating Initial and Later Achievement

An important factor involved in using motor abilities to predict future skill achievement is the relationship between skill performance during early learning and its performance at a later stage of learning. A low relationship between performance in early and late stages of learning would indicate that abilities underlying performance at each stage of learning may differ. On the other hand, a high relationship simplifies matters by allowing the identification of critical abilities without regard for the stage of learning.

*Correlating initial and later performance scores.* One way to determine the relationship between initial skill performance and later achievement is to correlate performance scores of a person as he or she progresses across the stages of learning. The simplest method is to correlate early performance scores with later performance scores. This correlation will, in most cases, be low, indicating a low relationship between initial and later achievement.

A classic experiment by Ella Trussell (1965) provides an example of research evidence with this typical result. College women practiced juggling three tennis balls for 27 practice sessions (3 sessions per week for 9 weeks). Each session included 75 tosses. The author defined juggling performance as the number of errors or dropped balls. As expected, the women's performance improved with practice. As the top panel of figure 7.2–1 shows, error scores dropped from 50 errors per 75 tosses in the first practice period to 20 errors per 75 tosses in the final session. More important, however, is the bottom graph of this figure, which shows the extent to which the author could predict final scores (the last 4 practice sessions) on the basis of the error scores for each practice period. During the first 5 practice sessions, such a prediction of final scores would be correct only 50 to 60 percent of the time. These odds are about the same as those involved in flipping a coin. But this prediction capability

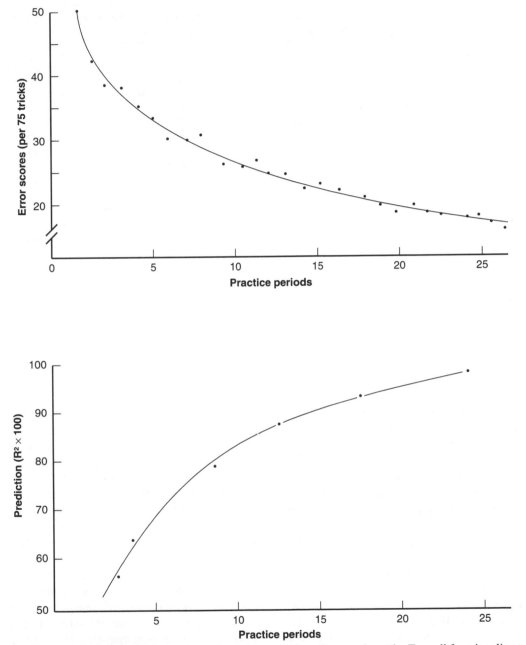

**FIGURE 7.2–1** The top graph shows the performance curve from the experiment by Trussell for a juggling task. The numbers of errors are indicated for the practice periods. The bottom graph indicates the accuracy of prediction of final performance in the juggling task as a function of the amount of practice used for prediction. (From E. Trussell, "Prediction of Success in a Motor Skill on the Basis of Early Learning Achievement," in *Research Quarterly for Exercise and Sport*, 1965. Vol. 36, pp. 342–347. Copyright © 1965 American Alliance for Health, Physical Education, Rrecreation, and Dance. Reprinted by permission.)

**TABLE 7.2–1**   The Intertrial Correlation Matrix from Performance on a Rhythmic Arm-Movement Task Reported by Thomas and Halliwell (The correlations are based on the spatial error scores from the task.)

| Trial | 1 | 2 | 3 | 4 | 5 | 6 | 7 | 8 | 9 | 10 | 11 | 12 | 13 | 14 | 15 |
|-------|---|---|---|---|---|---|---|---|---|----|----|----|----|----|----|
| 1 | — | 27 | −.05 | .33 | .23 | .08 | .27 | .15 | .00 | −.04 | −.09 | .11 | −.05 | .13 | −.12 |
| 2 | | — | .63 | .71 | .57 | .57 | .64 | .54 | .57 | .38 | .54 | .29 | .15 | .67 | .25 |
| 3 | | | — | .60 | .46 | .18 | .56 | .50 | .45 | .53 | .48 | .12 | .09 | .37 | .24 |
| 4 | | | | — | .73 | .45 | .61 | .62 | .45 | .29 | .51 | .15 | .17 | .49 | .12 |
| 5 | | | | | — | .37 | .67 | .57 | .59 | .32 | .52 | .22 | .28 | .52 | .21 |
| 6 | | | | | | — | .53 | .54 | .50 | .39 | .68 | .52 | .41 | .61 | .35 |
| 7 | | | | | | | — | .71 | .67 | .70 | .65 | .51 | .57 | .80 | .50 |
| 8 | | | | | | | | — | .67 | .67 | .65 | .52 | .43 | .59 | .48 |
| 9 | | | | | | | | | — | .47 | .73 | .54 | .61 | .78 | .41 |
| 10 | | | | | | | | | | — | .56 | .59 | .63 | .62 | .64 |
| 11 | | | | | | | | | | | — | .49 | .57 | .72 | .62 |
| 12 | | | | | | | | | | | | — | .63 | .58 | .47 |
| 13 | | | | | | | | | | | | | — | .71 | .63 |
| 14 | | | | | | | | | | | | | | — | .53 |
| 15 | | | | | | | | | | | | | | | — |

increased with more practice sessions. After 15 sessions, or 1,025 tosses, the author predicted final session performance with about 85 percent accuracy.

*Intertrial correlations.*   A more complex correlation procedure involves correlating practice trials with each other. This approach provides information about the relationship between the performance scores of any two trials. The common finding from this analysis has been that trials that are close to each other in time are more highly correlated than trials that are farther from each other. This between-trials relationship follows what has been called a **superdiagonal form.** This term describes the way the trial-to-trial correlations appear on a correlation matrix that compares all trials against each other, with the same trials located on both the vertical and the horizontal axes of the matrix. The correlation of a trial with the trial that succeeds it, such as that of trial 2 with trial 3, is found just above the diagonal of the matrix, where a trial would be correlated with itself. According to the superdiagonal form, the highest correlations in the matrix should be along the diagonal that is just above the main diagonal of the matrix.

We find an example of this approach in an experiment by Thomas and Halliwell (1976). In this experiment, participants learned three motor skills: the rotary pursuit task, the stabilometer task, and a rhythmic arm-movement task. The correlation matrix in table 7.2–1 comes from the results of participants' initial 15 trials of practice on the rhythmic arm-movement task. This task involved learning to move a lever held at the side of the body to a visual target in time with a metronome. Both spatial and temporal error  constituted the performance score. As you can see in table 7.2–1, the highest between-trial correlations for spatial error performance on the practice trials for this task are typically along the diagonal located just above the main diagonal

---

> ## A CLOSER LOOK
>
> ### Individual Differences in Skill Learning from a Dynamical Systems Perspective
>
> According to a dynamical systems view of skill learning (e.g., Zanone and Kelso 1994), a person initiates practice to learn a new skill by using a coordination pattern that is familiar to him or her yet is similar in some way to the pattern that the person must learn. The pattern the person uses on the initial practice trial spontaneously results from his or her attempt to achieve the action goal of the new skill.
>
> Because of previous skill performance experiences and certain physiological and biomechanical constraints, the person has developed distinct coordination-pattern preferences (called *attractor states*). These preferences represent stable patterns that the person can repeat with little variation and that involve optimal efficiency of energy use. Examples include preferred walking and running gaits and speeds, as well as rhythmical bimanual limb movements that are both in-phase (with simultaneous activation of homologous muscles) and anti-phase (with alternate activation of homologous muscles).
>
> Learning a new skill involves a transition between the preferred, stable coordination pattern and the new pattern. If the coordination dynamics of the new skill are similar to those characterizing the preferred pattern, competition between attractor states will lead to slower learning of the new skill than if the patterns were dissimilar. Thus, the professional must consider the individual's coordination-pattern tendencies at the time he or she begins practice for learning a new skill. These tendencies constitute an individual-difference factor that influences the rate of skill learning.

---

of the correlation matrix. As you can see by looking to your right to compare a particular trial to other trials, the correlation between trials farther away is generally lower. For example, the correlation between trials 4 and 5 is 0.73, while the correlation between trials 4 and 12 drops to 0.15. Thus, these results provide additional evidence that performance early in practice is a poor predictor of performance later in practice.

***Accounting for poor prediction.*** A question arises from the finding that early practice performance poorly predicts later achievement: What accounts for this poor prediction? Although there is some debate among individual-difference psychologists (see Ackerman 1989; Henry and Hulin 1987, for good discussions of both sides of this debate), a prevalent view is that *the repertoire of abilities a person needs to perform a skill changes as the person practices the skill.* This means that the abilities related to performance early in practice are not the same abilities related to performance later in practice.

Ackerman (1988) provided insight into these changes when he proposed three principles describing the abilities that account for performance in each of the three learning stages of the Fitts and Posner model (discussed in Concept 4.2). *Principle 1* is that in the first stage of learning, the cognitive stage, general abilities are most critical for performance. General abilities relate primarily to general intelligence, or cognitive ability. *Principle 2* states that in the second stage of learning, the associative stage, perceptual speed ability accounts for performance. This ability is the facility to solve problems, especially problems requiring visual search and memory use, quickly. Finally, *Principle 3* indicates that in the third stage of learning, the autonomous stage, task-specific, noncognitive motor abilities predominate to allow successful performance of the skill. Speed and accuracy while performing the movement components of a skill are the most common of these abilities.

According to these three principles, we should expect cognitive abilities to correlate more highly with early skill practice than with later practice. Conversely, task-specific motor abilities should

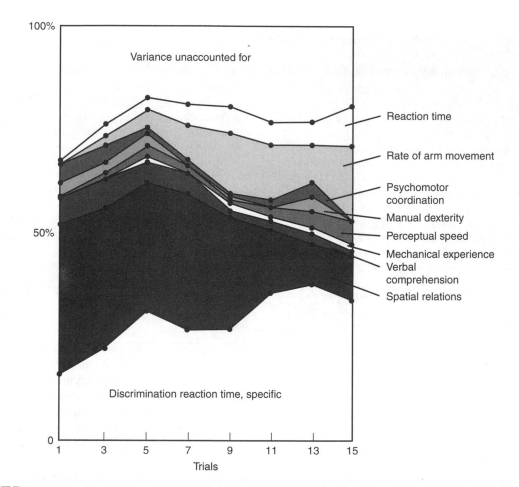

**FIGURE 7.2–2** Results of the experiment by Fleishman and Hempel showing the percentage of variance accounted for by different abilities at different stages of practice on a complex discrimination reaction-time task. Percentage of variance is represented by the size of the shaded areas for each ability. (Source: E. A. Fleishman and W. E. Hempel, "The Relationship Between Abilities and Improvement with Practice in a Visual Discrimination Reaction Task," in *Journal of Experimental Psychology*, 1955, Vol. 49, American Psychological Association.)

yield lower correlations during early practice than during later practice. A number of different experiments have provided support for these expectations. Fleishman and Hempel (1955) reported one of the classic experiments providing evidence of these types of stages-of-learning relationships.

Participants performed a battery of nine motor abilities tests. Then they practiced the complex discrimination and coordination motor skill of pushing toggle switches as quickly as possible in response to a pattern of signal lights. The authors established the complexity of this task by requiring certain movement responses to different patterns of

signal lights. The participants had to learn the appropriate combination of signal light pattern and response as they practiced the task. Practice involved 16 sessions of 20 trials each. Participants improved their response times from almost 500 msec during the first practice session to under 250 msec during the final practice session.

Figure 7.2–2 presents the results indicating the relationship between the nine abilities and the performance levels across the practice sessions. The figure shows the percentage of variance accounted for by each of the nine abilities. In this graph, a marked area indicates the percentage of the total

---

**A CLOSER LOOK**

### Teaching and Rehab Implications of the Influence of Changes in Motor Abilities from Early to Later Practice

- A person eventually may perform better than his or her initial performance indicates. This means that you should not "give up" on a person because of such undependable evidence as early performance alone.
- Awareness of the coordination characteristics of a person's initial practice attempts can help a teacher or therapist to determine the ease or difficulty the person will have learning the new skill. A change in the coordination pattern itself is more difficult to achieve than are changes in parameter components of the pattern.

- Skill analyses are important in helping the teacher or therapist distinguish between individual-ability factors that will contribute to more or less successful skill performance during early and later practice trials.
- Screening tests to assess potential for future performance success should emphasize assessing in novices the specific abilities that are related to successful performance by people who are skillful performers.

---

variance accounted for by a particular ability. The greater the percentage of the total variance accounted for by an ability is, the more important that ability is to performance of the task.

During the first practice session, spatial relations (36 percent), discrimination reaction time (17 percent), verbal comprehension (6 percent), and psychomotor coordination (5 percent) accounted for 64 percent of the total variance for the performance on the complex task. The right-hand side of the graph, which records the abilities accounting for performance variance during the last session of practice shows that the relative importance of the various abilities had changed in many cases from what it was earlier in practice. In the last practice session, the most significant abilities related to task performance were discrimination reaction time (35 percent), rate of arm movement (17 percent), spatial relations (11 percent), reaction time (9 percent), and perceptual speed (5 percent).

These results supported Ackerman's principles by showing that early in practice, more general abilities, such as spatial relations, are important factors accounting for task performance. As a person progresses through the stages of learning, these general abilities decrease in importance as more task-specific abilities increase in importance. Note how the Fleishman and Hempel experiment supported this prediction. By the last practice

session, the importance of the spatial relations ability had decreased significantly (from 36 percent to 11 percent). However, the rate of arm movement, which was of negligible importance early in practice, accounted for over 30 percent of the variance of the task performance.

The key point is that it is very difficult to predict future achievement in learning a motor skill when we base the prediction on early performance only. Abilities that account for a person's level of performance change in importance as the person moves from the early stage of learning to later stages. Those abilities that are important in accounting for a person's performance score early in practice are typically not as important later in practice. However, prediction of future performance improves if the teacher, coach, or therapist is aware of both the specific abilities that are essential to performance in the different stages of learning, and also the corresponding abilities within the learner.

## Using Abilities Tests to Predict Performance Potential

Although there are problems associated with predicting an individual's potential for success in a motor skill, abilities testing does play a role in the prediction process. We see this role in industry, for example, in what is called "screening." Tests developed for screening purposes are usually batteries of specific tests designed to determine the potential for success of candidates for specific jobs. We will consider three studies, each from a different type of performance context, to exemplify how screening can be successful.

To predict pole-climbing performance for telephone company trainees, Reilly, Zedeck, and Tenopyr (1979) used a battery of fourteen physical and motor ability measures such as height, weight, body density, leg strength, reaction time, arm strength, balance, and static strength. From this battery, the authors found three measures to predict pole-climbing performance successfully: body density, balance, and static strength. As a result, they suggested that training course applicants take three tests as an initial screening device to determine who should be permitted to enroll in the course. That is, a person achieving a score above a specified score on the test battery would have a 90 percent chance of passing the training course.

The U. S. Air Force has been interested in predicting the success of pilot trainees for many years. The Air Force has estimated that it loses approximately $65,000 for each trainee who does not graduate from the training program. Thus, a valid screening program that is simple and provides good prediction of success could save the Air Force significant amounts of money. Cox (1988) reported on a good example of a successful screening effort. Researchers analyzed the performance of 320 prospective pilots in the Air Force Undergraduate Pilot Training Program, which lasts approximately 49 weeks. The two major ability tests used were the Two-Hand Coordination Task and the Complex Coordination Test. Each of these tests demands coordinating movement of both hands to track moving targets on a computer screen. By analyzing performance on these tasks, Cox was able to predict success in the training program with significant accuracy.

In a sport setting, a study by Landers, Boutcher, and Wang (1986) provides an example of the use of ability testing. They showed that for people involved in training programs in archery, certain physical, perceptual-motor and psychological characteristics accurately predicted archery performance. The results of several batteries of physical and psychological tests given to 188 amateur archers showed that individuals with greater relative leg strength, lower percentages of body fat, faster reaction times, better depth perception, greater imagery ability, more confidence, and better use of past mistakes achieved higher archery performance scores. In fact, the characteristics of leg strength, percentage of body fat, reaction time, depth perception, and use of past mistakes, taken together, correctly predicted how 81 percent of the archers would be classified (i.e., as average or above average). Clearly, people require certain abilities and characteristics to achieve different levels of sport performance.

## A Developmental Caveat to Predicting Future Success

When children are involved in assessments designed to predict future success, those assessing them must give close attention to a critical individual-difference feature of child development. Of particular importance is the fact that children mature at different rates. That is, a child of 12 may be physically more like the typical 8- or 9-year-old or more like the typical 12- or 13-year-old. Early maturers are physically advanced for their age, and may be successful because of their physical advantage rather than their skill advantage. When the late maturers, those who are physically behind for their age, catch up, the apparent difference in skill levels often disappears. Thus, future success predictions for preadolescents and adolescents are tenuous at best. Because of this, it is essential that those who work with children and youth provide optimal skill development experiences and opportunities for all, not just for those who look as if they will be successful because of their current success.

## Summary

The assessment of motor abilities can be a useful aid in predicting a person's potential for success in specific motor skills. Predicting success potential depends on the accuracy of the identification of the essential abilities related to successfully performing the motor skill of interest, and on the development and use of valid and reliable tests of motor abilities. Abilities related to performance of a skill in the early stages of learning are often different from those that are important for performance of the skill later in learning. Researchers have specified the types of abilities related to performance according to the stage of learning: more general abilities account for performance early in learning, while more task-specific motor abilities are related to success in later stages. For a professional to predict future success, he or she must identify which abilities within the task relate to successful performance of the task, and also identify levels of abilities within the individual that are essential to successful task performance. Screening tests to make this type of prediction have been used successfully in industrial, military, and sport settings.

## Related Readings

Ackerman, P. L. 1987. Individual differences in skill learning: An integration of psychometric and information processing perspectives. *Psychological Bulletin* 102: 3–27.

Fleishman, E. A. 1982. Systems for describing human tasks. *American Psychologist* 37: 821–24.

Henry, R. A., and C. L. Hulin. 1987. Stability of skilled performance across time: Some generalizations and limitations on utilities. *Journal of Applied Psychology* 72: 457–62.

Levine, E. L., P. E. Spector, S. Menon, L. Narayanan, and J. Cannon-Bowers. 1996. Validity generalization for cognitive, psychomotor, and perceptual tests for craft jobs in the utility industry. *Human Performance* 9: 1–22.

Malina, R. M. 1984. Physical growth and maturation. In J. R. Thomas (Ed.), *Motor development during childhood and adolescence* (pp. 2–26). Minneapolis: Burgess.

---

# STUDY QUESTIONS FOR CHAPTER 7

1. How does the study of individual differences differ from the study of normative or average behavior?

2. (a) How do people who study individual differences define the term *abilities?* (b) Distinguish the meaning of *abilities* from the term *skill.*

3. (a) What is the difference between the general motor ability hypothesis and the specificity of motor abilities hypothesis? (b) Give an example of research evidence indicating which of these hypotheses is more valid.

4. How can a specificity view of motor abilities explain how a person can be very successful at performing a lot of different motor skills?

5. (a) Name and describe five perceptual-motor abilities identified by Fleishman. (b) What other motor abilities can you identify?

6. Describe how Ackerman presented motor abilities as one category of abilities involved in motor skill performance.

7. How successfully can how well a person performs a motor skill in early practice predict that person's eventual success in the performance of that skill?

8. (a) What is the *superdiagonal form* that characterizes the relationships between practice trials of many motor skills? (b) What does this correlation pattern tell us about the relationship between early and later practice performance?

9. What are Ackerman's three principles that relate motor abilities to performance and three different stages of skill learning?

10. Describe how the Fleishman and Hempel study provides evidence showing that abilities that account for successful skill performance early in learning a skill typically differ from those accounting for successful performance later in learning.

11. (a) Describe how a motor skills professional can assess a person's motor abilities to provide useful information for predicting that person's potential for success in a specific motor skill. (b) Give an example.

12. Why is cutting a 10-year-old from a sports team because of poor performance a bad policy? Consider this in terms of differences in maturation rates in children and relate it to predicting future success in motor skill performance.

# REFERENCES

Abernethy, B., and D. G. Russell. 1987. Expert-novice differences in an applied selective attention task. *Journal of Sport Psychology* 9: 326–45.

Ackerman, P. L. 1988. Determinants of individual differences during skill acquisition: Cognitive abilities and information processing. *Journal of Experimental Psychology: General* 117: 288–318.

Ackerman, P. L. 1989. Within-task intercorrelations of skilled performance: Implications for predicting individual differences? (A comment on Henry & Hulin, 1987). *Journal of Applied Psychology* 74: 360–64.

Ada, L., N. J. O'Dwyer, and P. D. Neilson. 1993. Improvement in kinematic characteristics and coordination following stroke quantified by linear systems analysis. *Human Movement Science* 12: 137–53.

Adam, J. J. 1992. The effects of objectives and constraints on motor control strategy in reciprocal aiming movements. *Journal of Motor Behavior* 24: 173–85.

Adams, J. A. 1978. Theoretical issues for knowledge of results. In G. E. Stelmach (Ed.), *Information processing in motor control and learning* (pp. 87–107). New York: Academic Press.

Adams, J. A. 1986. Use of the model's knowledge of results to increase the observer's performance. *Journal of Human Movement Studies* 12: 89–98.

Adams, J. A. 1987. Historical review and appraisal of research on the learning, retention, and transfer of human motor skills. *Psychological Bulletin* 101: 41–74.

Adams, J. A., and B. Reynolds. 1954. Effects of shift of distribution of practice conditions following interpolated rest. *Journal of Experimental Psychology,* 47: 32–36.

Allport, D. A. 1980. Attention and performance. In G. Claxton (Ed.), *Cognitive psychology: New directions* (pp. 112–53). London: Routledge & Kegan Paul.

Anderson, D. I., R. A. Magill, and H. Sekiya. 1994. A reconsideration of the trials-delay of knowledge of results paradigm in motor skill learning. *Research Quarterly for Exercise and Sport* 65: 286–90.

Anderson, D. I., and B. Sidaway. 1994. Coordination changes associated with practice of a soccer kick. *Research Quarterly Exercise and Sport* 65: 93–99.

Annett, J. 1959. Learning a pressure under conditions of immediate and delayed knowledge of results. *Quarterly Journal of Experimental Psychology* 11: 3–15.

Annett, J., and J. Piech. 1985. The retention of a skill following distributed training. *Programmed Learning and Educational Technology* 22: 182–86.

Annett, J., and J. Sparrow. 1985. Transfer of training: A review of research and practical implications. *Programmed Learning and Educational Technology* 22: 116–24.

Anson, J. G. 1982. Memory drum theory: Alternative tests and explanations for the complexity effects on simple reaction time. *Journal of Motor Behavior* 14: 228–46.

Ash, D. W., and D. H. Holding. 1990. Backward versus forward chaining in the acquisition of a keyboard skill. *Human Factors* 32: 139–46.

Assaiante, C., A. R. Marchand, and B. Amblard. 1989. Discrete visual samples may control locomotor equilibrium and foot positioning in man. *Journal of Motor Behavior* 21: 72–91.

Baddeley, A. D., and D. J. A. Longman. 1978. The influence of length and frequency of training session on the rate of learning to type. *Ergonomics* 21: 627–35.

Bahill, A. T., and T. LaRitz. 1984. Why can't batters keep their eyes on the ball? *American Scientist* 72: 249–52.

Bandura, A. 1984. *Social foundations of thought and action: A social cognitive theory.* Englewood Cliffs, NJ: Prentice-Hall.

Bard, C., J. Paillard, Y. Lajoie, M. Fleury, N. Teasdale, R. Forget, and Y. Lamarre. 1992. Role of afferent information in the timing of motor commands: A comparative study with a deafferented patient. *Neuropsychologia* 30: 201–6.

Bartlett, F. C. 1932. *Remembering: A study in experimental and social psychology.* Cambridge: Cambridge University Press.

Barton, J. W. 1921. Smaller versus larger units in learning the maze. *Journal of Experimental Psychology* 4: 414–24.

Battig, W. F. 1979. The flexibility of human memory. In L. S. Cermak and F. I. M. Craik (Eds.), *Levels of processing in human memory* (pp. 23–44). Hillsdale, NJ: Erlbaum.

Beek, P. J., C. E. Peper, and D. F. Stegeman. 1995. Dynamical models of movement coordination. *Human Movement Science* 14: 573–608.

Beek, P. J., and M. T. Turvey. 1992. Temporal patterning in cascade juggling. *Journal of Experimental Psychology: Human Perception and Performance* 18: 934–47.

Beek, P. J., and P. C. W. van Wieringen. 1994. Perspectives on the relation between information and dynamics: An epilogue. *Human Movement Science* 13: 519–33.

Benedetti, C., and P. McCullagh. 1987. Post-knowledge of results delay: Effects of interpolated activity on learning and performance. *Research Quarterly for Exercise and Sport* 58: 375–81.

Berg, W. P., M. G. Wade, and N. L. Greer. 1994. Visual regulation of gait in bipedal locomotion: Revisiting Lee, Lishman, and Thomson (1982). *Journal of Experimental Psychology: Human Perception and Performance* 20: 854–63.

Bernstein, N. 1967. *The co-ordination and regulation of movement.* Oxford: Pergamon Press.

Bilodeau, E. A., and I. M. Bilodeau. 1958a. Variation of temporal intervals among critical events in five studies of knowledge of results. *Journal of Experimental Psychology* 55: 603–12.

Bilodeau, E. A., and I. M. Bilodeau. 1958b. Variable frequency of knowledge of results and the learning of a simple skill. *Journal of Experimental Psychology* 55: 379–83.

Bilodeau, E. A., I. M. Bilodeau, and D. A. Schumsky. 1959. Some effects of introducing and withdrawing knowledge of results early and late in practice. *Journal of Experimental Psychology* 58: 142–44.

Bilodeau, I. M. 1969. Information feedback. In E. A. Bilodeau (Ed.), *Principles of skill acquisition* (pp. 225–85). New York: Academic Press.

Bizzi, E., and A. Polit. 1979. Processes controlling visually evoked movements. *Neuropsychologia* 17: 203–13.

Blais, C. 1991. Instructions as constraints on psychomotor performance. *Journal of Human Movement Studies* 21: 217–31.

Blouin, J., C. Bard, N. Teasdale, J. Paillard, M. Fleury, R. Forget, and Y. Lamarre. 1993. Reference systems for coding spatial information in normal subjects and a deafferented patient. *Experimental Brain Research* 93: 324–31.

Bootsma, R. J., and P. C. W. van Wieringen. 1990. Timing an attacking forehand drive in table tennis. *Journal of Experimental Psychology: Human Perception and Performance* 16: 21–29.

Boulter, L. R. 1964. Evaluations of mechanisms in delay of knowledge of results. *Canadian Journal of Psychology* 18: 281–91.

Bouzid, N., and C. M. Crawshaw. 1987. Massed versus distributed wordprocessor training. *Applied Ergonomics* 18: 220–22.

Boyce, B. A. 1991. The effects of an instructional strategy with two schedules of augmented KP feedback upon skill acquisition of a selected shooting task. *Journal of Teaching in Physical Education* 11: 47–58.

Brady, J. I., Jr. 1979. Surface practice, level of manual dexterity, and performance of an assembly task. *Human Factors* 21: 25–33.

Bransford, J. D., J. J. Franks, C. D. Morris, and B. S. Stein. 1979. Some general constraints on learning and memory research. In L. S. Cermak and F. I. M. Craik (Eds.), *Levels of processing in human memory* (pp. 331–54). Hillsdale, NJ: Erlbaum.

Broadbent, D. E. 1958. *Perception and communication.* Oxford: Pergamon Press.

Brown, R. W. 1928. A comparison of the whole, part, and combination methods for learning piano music. *Journal of Experimental Psychology* 11: 235–47.

Brown, T. G. 1911. The intrinsic factors in the act of progression in the mammal. *Proceedings of the Royal Society of London (Biology)* 84: 308–19.

Bryan, W. L., and N. Harter. 1897. Studies in the physiology and psychology of the telegraphic language. *Psychological Review* 4: 27–53.

Buekers, M. J., R. A. Magill, and K. G. Hall. 1992. The effect of erroneous knowledge of results on skill acquisition when augmented information is redundant. *Quarterly Journal of Experimental Psychology* 44A: 105–17.

Bullock, D., and S. Grossberg. 1991. Adaptive neural networks for control of movement trajectories invariant under speed and force rescaling. *Human Movement Science* 10: 3–53.

Campbell, K. C., and R. W. Proctor. 1993. Repetition effects with categorizable stimulus and response sets. *Journal of Experimental Psychology: Learning, Memory, and Cognition* 19: 1345–62.

Carlton, L. G., M. J. Carlton, and K. M. Newell. 1987. Reaction time and response dynamics. *Quarterly Journal of Experimental Psychology* 39A: 337–60.

Carroll, W. R., and A. Bandura. 1987. Translating cognition into action: The role of visual guidance in observational learning. *Journal of Motor Behavior* 19: 385–98.

Carroll, W. R., and A. Bandura. 1990. Representational guidance of action production in observational learning: A causal analysis. *Journal of Motor Behavior* 22: 85–97.

Carron, A. V. 1969. Performance and learning in a discrete motor task under massed vs. distributed practice. *Research Quarterly* 40: 481–89.

Cauraugh, J. H., D. Chen, and S. J. Radlo. 1993. Effects of traditional and reversed bandwidth knowledge of results on motor learning. *Research Quarterly for Exercise and Sport* 64: 413–17.

Cavanagh, P. R., and R. Kram. 1985. The efficiency of human movement—A statement of the problem. *Medicine and Science in Sports and Exercise* 17: 304–8.

Chieffi, S., and M. Gentilucci. 1993. Coordination between the transport and the grasp components during prehension movement. *Experimental Brain Research* 50: 7–15.

Chollet, D., J. P. Micallef, and P. Rabischong. 1988. Biomechanical signals for external biofeedback to improve swimming techniques. In B. E. Ungerechts, K. Wilke, and K. Reichle (Eds.), *Swimming science V* (pp. 389–96). Champaign, IL: Human Kinetics.

Christina, R. W. 1973. Influence of enforced motor and sensory sets on reaction latency and movement speed. *Research Quarterly* 44: 483–87.

Christina, R. W., M. G. Fischman, A. L. Lambert, and J. F. Moore. 1985. Simple reaction time as a function of response complexity: Christina et al. (1982) revisited. *Research Quarterly for Exercise and Sport* 56: 316–22.

Christina, R. W., M. G. Fischman, M. J. P. Vercruyssen, and J. G. Anson. 1982. Simple reaction time as a function of response complexity: Memory drum theory revisited. *Journal of Motor Behavior* 14: 301–21.

Christina, R. W., and D. J. Rose. 1985. Premotor and motor response time as a function of response complexity. *Research Quarterly for Exercise and Sport* 56: 306–15.

Cockrell, D. L., H. Carnahan, and B. J. McFayden. 1995. A preliminary analysis of the coordination of reaching, grasping, and walking. *Perceptual and Motor Skills* 81: 515–19.

Cook, T. 1936. Studies in cross education. V. Theoretical. *Psychological Review* 43: 149–78.

Corbin, C. 1972. Mental practice. In W. P. Morgan (Ed.), *Ergogenic aids and muscular performance* (pp. 93–118). New York: Academic Press.

Cox, R. H. 1988. Utilization of psychomotor screening for USAF pilot candidates: Enhancing prediction validity. *Aviation, Space, and Environmental Medicine* 59: 640–45.

Crossman, E. R. F. W. 1959. A theory of the acquisition of speed skill. *Ergonomics* 2: 153–66.

Crossman, E. R. F. W., and P. J. Goodeve. 1983. Feedback control of hand movements and Fitts' Law. *Quarterly Journal of Experimental Psychology* 35A: 251–78. (Original work published in 1963.)

Cutting, J. E. 1986. *Perception with an eye for motion.* Cambridge, MA: MIT Press.

Cutting, J. E., and L. T. Kozlowski. 1977. Recognizing friends by their walk: Gait perception without familiarity cues. *Bulletin of the Psychonomic Society* 9: 353–56.

Cutting, J. E., P. M. Vishton, and P. A. Braren. 1995. How we avoid collisions with stationary and moving objects. *Psychological Review* 102: 627–51.

Cutton, D. M., and D. Landin. 1994. *The effects of two cognitive learning strategies on learning the tennis forehand.* Paper presented at the annual meeting of the Southern District American Alliance for Health, Physical Education, Recreation, and Dance, Nashville, TN.

Czerwinski, M., N. Lightfoot, and R. A. Shiffrin. 1992. Automatization and training in visual search. *American Journal of Psychology* 105: 271–315.

Damos, D., and C. D. Wickens. 1980. The identification and transfer of timesharing skills. *Acta Psychologica* 46: 15–39.

Daniels, F. S., and D. M. Landers. 1981. Biofeedback and shooting performance: A test of disregulation and systems theory. *Journal of Sport Psychology* 3: 271–82.

Davids, K. 1988. Developmental differences in the use of peripheral vision during catching performance. *Journal of Motor Behavior* 20: 39–51.

Davis, R. C. 1942. The pattern of muscular action in simple voluntary movements. *Journal of Experimental Psychology* 31: 437–66.

den Brinker, B. P. L. M., J. R. L. W. Stabler, H. T. A. Whiting, and P. C. van Wieringen. 1986. The effect of manipulating knowledge of results in the learning of slalom-ski type ski movements. *Ergonomics* 29: 31–40.

Doody, S. G., A. M. Bird, and D. Ross. 1985. The effect of auditory and visual models on acquisition of a timing task. *Human Movement Science* 4: 271–81.

Drowatzky, J. N., and F. C. Zuccato. 1967. Interrelationships between selected measures of static and dynamic balance. *Research Quarterly* 38: 509–10.

Duncan, J. 1977. Response selection rules in spatial choice reaction tasks. In S. Dornic (Ed.), *Attention and performance VI* (pp. 49–61). Hillsdale, NJ: Erlbaum.

Durand, M., V. Geoffroi, A. Varray, and C. Préfaut. 1994. Study of the energy correlates in the learning of a complex self-paced cyclical skill. *Human Movement Science* 13: 785–99.

Eason, R. G., A. Beardshall, and S. Jaffee. 1965. Performance and physiological indicants of activation in a vigilance situation. *Perceptual and Motor Skills* 20: 3–13.

Edwards, R. V., and A. M. Lee. 1985. The relationship of cognitive style and instructional strategy to learning and transfer of motor skills. *Research Quarterly for Exercise and Sport* 56: 286–90.

Eghan, T. 1988. *The relation of teacher feedback to student achievement.* Unpublished doctoral dissertation. Louisiana State University.

Elliott, D. 1985. Manual asymmetries in the performance of sequential movements by adolescents and adults with Down Syndrome. *American Journal of Mental Deficiency* 90: 90–97.

Elliott, D., and F. Allard. 1985. The utilization of visual information and feedback information during rapid pointing movements. *Quarterly Journal of Experimental Psychology* 37A: 407–25.

Elliott, D., S. Zuberec, and P. Milgram. 1994. The effects of periodic visual occlusion on ball catching. *Journal of Motor Behavior* 26: 113–22.

Ellis, H. C. 1978. *Fundamentals of human learning, memory, and cognition* 2d ed. Dubuque, IA: Wm. C. Brown.

Ericsson, K. A., R. T. Krampe, and C. Tesch-Romer. 1993. The role of deliberate practice in the acquisition of expert performance. *Psychological Review* 100: 363–406.

Ericsson, K. A., and J. Smith. 1991. Prospects and limits of the empirical study of expertise: An introduction. In K. A. Ericcson and J. Smith (Eds.), *Toward a general theory of expertise: Prospects and limits* (pp. 1–38). Cambridge: Cambridge University Press.

Fairweather, M. M., and B. Sidaway. 1993. Ideokinetic imagery as a postural development technique. *Research Quarterly for Exercise and Sport* 64: 385–92.

Feltz, D. L. 1992. Understanding motivation in sport: A self-efficacy perspective. In G. C. Roberts (Ed.), *Motivation in sport and exercise* (pp. 93–127). Champaign, IL: Human Kinetics.

Feltz, D. L., and D. M. Landers. 1983. The effects of mental practice on motor skill learning and performance: A meta-analysis. *Journal of Sport Psychology* 5: 25–57.

Feltz, D. L., D. M. Landers, and B. J. Becker. 1988. A revised meta-analysis of the mental practice literature on motor skill learning. In D. Druckman and J. Swets (Eds.), *Enhancing human performance: Issues, theories, and techniques* (pp. 1–65). Washington, DC: National Academy Press.

Fischman, M. G. 1984. Programming time as a function of number of movement parts and changes in movement direction. *Journal of Motor Behavior* 16: 405–23.

Fischman, M. G., and T. Schneider. 1985. Skill level, vision, and proprioception in simple one-hand catching. *Journal of Motor Behavior* 17: 219–29.

Fishman, S., and C. Tobey. 1978. Augmented feedback. In W. Anderson and G. Barrette (Eds.), *What's going on in gym: Descriptive studies of physical education classes* (pp. 51–62). Monograph 1 in *Motor Skills: Theory into Practice.*

Fitts, P. M. 1954. The information capacity of the human motor system in controlling the amplitude of movement. *Journal of Experimental Psychology* 47: 381–91.

Fitts, P. M., and M. I. Posner. 1967. *Human performance.* Belmont, CA: Brooks/Cole.

Fitts, P. M., and C. M. Seeger. 1953. S-R compatibility: Spatial characteristics of stimulus and response codes. *Journal of Experimental Psychology* 46: 199–210.

Fleishman, E. A. 1972. On the relationship between abilities, learning, and human performance. *American Psychologist* 27: 1017–32.

Fleishman, E. A., and W. E. Hempel. 1955. The relationship between abilities and improvement with practice in a visual discrimination reaction task. *Journal of Experimental Psychology* 49: 301–11.

Fleishman, E. A., and M. K. Quaintance. 1984. *Taxonomies of human performance.* Orlando, FL: Academic Press.

Flinn, N. 1995. A task-oriented approach to the treatment of a client with hemiplegia. *American Journal of Occupational Therapy* 49: 560–69.

Forssberg, H., B. Johnels, and G. Steg. 1984. Is parkinsonian gait caused by a regression to an immature walking pattern? *Advances in Neurology* 40: 375–79.

Franks, I. M., and R. W. Wilberg. 1982. The generation of movement patterns during the acquisition of a pursuit tracking task. *Human Movement Science* 1: 251–72.

Franks, I. M., R. B. Wilberg, and G. J. Fishburne. 1982. Consistency and error in motor performance. *Human Movement Science* 1: 109–24.

Gallagher, J. D., and J. R. Thomas. 1980. Effects of varying post-KR intervals upon children's motor performance. *Journal of Motor Behavior* 12: 41–46.

Gentile, A. M. 1972. A working model of skill acquisition with application to teaching. *Quest,* Monograph 17: 3–23.

Gentile, A. M. 1987. Skill acquisition: Action, movement, and the neuromotor processes. In J. H. Carr, R. B. Shepherd, J. Gordon, A. M. Gentile, and J. M. Hind (Eds.), *Movement science: Foundations for physical therapy in rehabilitation* (pp. 93–154). Rockville, MD: Aspen.

Gentner, D. 1987. Timing of skilled motor performance: Tests of the proportional duration model. *Psychological Review* 94: 255–76.

Geurts, A. C. H., and T. W. Mulder. 1994. Attention demands in balance recovery following lower limb amputation. *Journal of Motor Behavior* 26: 162–70.

Gibson, J. J. 1966. *The senses considered as perceptual systems.* Boston: Houghton Mifflin.

Gibson, J. J. 1979. *The ecological approach to visual perception.* Boston: Houghton Mifflin.

Glass, L., and M. C. Mackey. 1988. *From clock to chaos: The rhythms of life.* Princeton, NJ: Princeton University Press.

Gleick, J. 1987. *Chaos: Making a new science.* New York: Viking Penguin.

Glencross, D. J. 1973. Response complexity and latency of different movement patterns. *Journal of Motor Behavior* 5: 95–104.

Godwin, M. A., and R. A. Schmidt. 1971. Muscular fatigue and discrete motor learning. *Research Quarterly* 42: 374–83.

Goldberger, M., and P. Gerney. 1990. Effects of learner use of practice time on skill acquisition of fifth grade children. *Journal of Teaching Physical Education* 10: 84–95.

Goode, S. L., and R. A. Magill. 1986. The contextual interference effect in learning three badminton serves. *Research Quarterly for Exercise and Sport* 57: 308–14.

Gopher, D., M. Weil, and D. Siegel. 1989. Practice under changing priorities: An approach to the training of complex skills. *Acta Psychologica* 71: 147–77.

Goss, S., C. Hall, E. Buckolz, and G. Fishburne. 1986. Imagery ability and the acquisition and retention of motor skills. *Memory and Cognition* 14: 469–77.

Gould, D., R. Weinberg, and A. Jackson. 1980. Mental preparation strategies, cognitions, and strength performance. *Journal of Sport Psychology* 2: 329–35.

Goulet, C., C. Bard, and M. Fleury. 1989. Expertise differences in preparing to return a tennis serve: A visual information processing approach. *Journal of Sport and Exercise Psychology* 11: 382–98.

Green, T. D., and J. H. Flowers. 1991. Implicit versus explicit learning processes in a probabilistic, continuous fine-motor catching task. *Journal of Motor Behavior* 23: 293–300.

Grillner, S., and P. Zangger. 1979. On the central generation of locomotion in the low spinal cat. *Experimental Brain Research* 34: 241–61.

Hadden, C. M., R. A. Magill, and B. Sidaway. 1995, June. Concurrent vs. terminal augmented feedback in the acquisition and retention of a discrete bimanual motor task. Presented at the annual meeting of the North American Society for the Psychology of Sport and Physical Activity, Asilomar, CA. [Abstract published: *Journal of Sport & Exercise Psychology* 17 (1995), Supplement, p. S54].

Hale, B. D. 1982. The effects of internal and external imagery on muscular and ocular concomitants. *Journal of Sport Psychology* 4: 379–87.

Hall, C. R. 1980. Imagery for movement. *Journal of Human Movement Studies* 6: 252–64.

Hall, C. R. 1985. Individual differences in the mental practice and imagery of motor skill performance. *Canadian Journal of Applied Sport Sciences* 10: 17S–21S.

Hall, C. R., E. Buckolz, and G. Fishburne. 1989. Searching for a relationship between imagery ability and memory for movements. *Journal of Human Movement Studies* 17: 89–100.

Hall, C. R., and J. Pongrac. 1983. *Movement Imagery Questionnaire*. London, Ontario, Canada: University of Western Ontario.

Hall, C. R., J. Pongrac, and E. Buckolz. 1985. The measurement of imagery ability. *Human Movement Science* 4: 107–18.

Hall, C. R., W. M. Rodgers, and K. A. Barr. 1990. The use of imagery by athletes in selected sports. *The Sport Psychologist,* 4: 1–10.

Hall, K. G., D. A. Domingues, and R. Cavazos. 1994. Contextual interference effects with skilled baseball players. *Perceptual and Motor Skills* 78: 835–41.

Hamilton, W. 1859. *Lectures on metaphysics and logic.* Edinburgh, Scotland: Blackwood.

Hancock, G. R., M. S. Butler, and M. G. Fischman. 1995. On the problem of two-dimensional error scores: Measures and analyses of accuracy, bias, and consistency. *Journal of Motor Behavior* 27: 241–50.

Hand, J., and B. Sidaway. 1993. Relative frequency of modeling effects on the performance and retention of a motor skill. *Research Quarterly for Exercise and Sport* 65: 250–57.

Hatze, H. 1976. Biomechanical aspects of successful motion optimization. In P. V. Komi (Ed.), *Biomechanics V-B* (pp. 5–12). Baltimore: University Park Press.

Hautala, R. M. 1988. Does transfer of training help children learn juggling? *Perceptual and Motor Skills* 67: 563–67.

Hautala, R. M., and J. H. Conn. 1993. A test of Magill's closed-to-open continuum for skill development. *Perceptual and Motor Skills* 77: 219–26.

Hebert, E. P., and D. Landin. 1994. Effects of a learning model and augmented feedback on tennis skill acquisition. *Research Quarterly for Exercise and Sport* 65: 250–57.

Heise, G. D. 1995. EMG changes in agonist muscles during practice of a multijoint throwing skill. *Journal of Electromyography and Kinesiology* 5: 81–94.

Helsen, W., and J. M. Pauwels. 1990. Analysis of visual search activity in solving tactical game problems. In D. Brogan (Ed.), *Visual search* (pp. 177–84). London: Taylor & Francis.

Henry, F. M. (1960). Influence of motor and sensory sets on reaction latency and speed of discrete movements. *Research Quarterly* 31: 459–68.

Henry, F. M. 1961. Stimulus complexity, movement complexity, age, and sex in relation to reaction latency and speed in limb movements. *Research Quarterly* 32: 353–66.

Henry, F. M., and D. E. Rogers. 1960. Increased response latency for complicated movements and the "memory drum" theory of neuromotor reaction. *Research Quarterly* 31: 448–58.

Henry, R. A., and C. L. Hulin. 1987. Stability of skilled performance across time: Some generalizations and limitations on utilities. *Journal of Applied Psychology* 72: 457–62.

Heuer, H. 1991. Invariant relative timing in motor-program theory. In J. Fagard and P. H. Wolff (Eds.), *The development of timing control and temporal organization in coordinated action* (pp. 37–68). Amsterdam: Elsevier.

Hick, W. E. 1952. On the rate of gain of information. *Quarterly Journal of Experimental Psychology* 4: 11–26.

Hicks, R. E., J. M. Frank, and M. Kinsbourne. 1982. The locus of bimanual skill transfer. *Journal of General Psychology* 107: 277–81.

Hicks, R. E., T. C. Gualtieri, and S. R. Schroeder. 1983. Cognitive and motor components of bilateral transfer. *American Journal of Psychology* 96: 223–28.

Higgins, J. R., and R. A. Spaeth. 1972. Relationship between consistency of movement and environmental conditions. *Quest* 17: 61–69.

Hird, J. S., D. M. Landers, J. R. Thomas, and J. J. Horan. 1991. Physical practice is superior to mental practice in enhancing cognitive and motor task performance. *Journal of Sport & Exercise Psychology* 13: 281–93.

Hoenkamp, H. 1978. Perceptual cues that determine the labeling of human gait. *Journal of Human Movement Studies* 4: 59–69.

Hogan, J., and B. Yanowitz. 1978. The role of verbal estimates of movement error in ballistic skill acquisition. *Journal of Motor Behavior* 10: 133–38.

Holding, D. H. 1965. *The principles of training.* Oxford: Pergamon Press.

Holding, D. H. 1976. An approximate transfer surface. *Journal of Motor Behavior* 8: 1–9.

Holding, D. H. 1987. Concepts of training. In G. Salvendry (Ed.), *Handbook of human factors* (pp. 939–62). New York: Wiley.

Hubbard, A. W., and C. N. Seng. 1954. Visual movements of batters. *Research Quarterly* 25: 42–57.

Jacobson, E. 1931. Electrical measurement of neuromuscular states during mental activities: VI. A note on mental activities concerning an amputated limb. *American Journal of Physiology* 43: 122–25.

Jaegers, S. M. H. J., R. F. Peterson, R. Dantuma, B. Hillen, R. Geuze, and J. Schellekens. 1989. Kinesiologic aspects of motor learning in dart throwing. *Journal of Human Movement Studies* 16: 161–71.

Jakobson, L. S., and M. A. Goodale. 1991. Factors influencing higher-order movement planning: A kinematic analysis of human prehension. *Experimental Brain Research* 86: 199–208.

James, W. 1890. *Principles of psychology.* New York: Holt.

Janelle, C. M., J. Kim, and R. N. Singer. 1995. Subject-controlled performance feedback and learning of a closed motor skill. *Perceptual and Motor Skills* 81: 627–34.

Jeannerod, M. 1981. Intersegmental coordination during reaching at natural visual objects. In J. Long and A. Baddeley (Eds.), *Attention and Performance IX* (pp. 153–68). Hillsdale, NJ: Erlbaum.

Jeannerod, M. 1984. The timing of natural prehension. *Journal of Motor Behavior* 16: 235–54.

Johansson, G. 1973. Visual perception of biological motion and a model for its analysis. *Perception and Psychophysics* 14: 201–11.

Johnson, B., and J. K. Nelson. 1985. *Practical measurement for evaluation in physical education.* 4th ed. Minneapolis: Burgess.

Jongsma, D. M., D. Elliott, and T. D. Lee. 1987. Experience and set in the running sprint start. *Perceptual and Motor Skills* 64: 547–50.

Kahneman, D. 1973. *Attention and effort.* Englewood Cliffs, NJ: Prentice-Hall.

Kamon, E., and J. Gormley. 1968. Muscular activity pattern for skilled performance and during learning of a horizontal bar exercise. *Ergonomics* 11: 345–57.

Kantowitz, B. H., and J. L. Knight, Jr. 1976. Testing tapping timesharing: II. Auditory secondary task. *Acta Psychologica* 40: 343–62.

Karlin, L., and R. G. Mortimer. 1963. Effect of verbal, visual, and auditory augmenting cues on learning a complex skill. *Journal of Experimental Psychology* 65: 75–79.

Keele, S. W. 1968. Movement control in skilled motor performance. *Psychological Bulletin* 70: 387–403.

Keele, S. W., and M. I. Posner. 1968. Processing of visual feedback in rapid movements. *Journal of Experimental Psychology* 77: 153–58.

Kelso, J. A. S. 1977. Motor control mechanisms underlying human movement reproduction. *Journal of Experimental Psychology: Human Perception and Performance* 3: 529–43.

Kelso, J. A. S. 1984. Phase transitions and critical behavior in human bimanual coordination. *American Journal of Physiology: Regulatory, Integrative, & Comparative Physiology* 15: R1000–4.

Kelso, J. A. S., and K. G. Holt. 1980. Exploring a vibratory systems analysis of human movement production. *Journal of Neurophysiology* 43: 1183–96.

Kelso, J. A. S., K. G. Holt, and A. E. Flatt. 1980. The role of proprioception in the perception and control of human movement: Toward a theoretical reassessment. *Perception and Psychophysics* 28: 45–52.

Kelso, J. A. S., and J. P. Scholz. 1985. Cooperative phenomena in biological motion. In H. Haken (Ed.), *Complex systems: Operational approaches in neurobiology, physical systems, and computers* (pp. 124–49). Berlin: Springer-Verlag.

Kelso, J. A. S., and G. Schöner. 1988. Self-organization of coordinative movement patterns. *Human Movement Science* 7: 27–46.

Kelso, J. A. S., D. L. Southard, and D. Goodman. 1979. On the coordination of two-handed movements. *Journal of Experimental Psychology: Human Perception and Performance* 5: 229–38.

Kelso, J. A. S., B. H. Tuller, E. Vatikiotis-Bateson, and C. A. Fowler. 1984. Functionally specific articulatory cooperation following jaw perturbations during speech: Evidence for coordinative structures. *Journal of Experimental Psychology: Human Perception and Performance* 10: 812–32.

Kernodle, M. W., and L. G. Carlton. 1992. Information feedback and the learning of multiple-degree-of-freedom activities. *Journal of Motor Behavior* 24: 187–96.

Knapp, C. G., and W. R. Dixon. 1952. Learning to juggle: II. A study of whole and part methods. *Research Quarterly* 23: 398–401.

Kohl, R. M., and D. L. Roenker. 1980. Bilateral transfer as a function of mental imagery. *Journal of Motor Behavior* 12: 197–206.

Kugler, P. N., J. A. S. Kelso, and M. T. Turvey. 1980. On the concept of coordinative structures as dissipative structures: I. Theoretical lines of convergence. In G. E. Stelmach and J. E. Requin (Eds.), *Tutorials in motor behavior* (3–47). Amsterdam: North-Holland.

Landers, D. M., S. H. Boutcher, and M. Q. Wang. 1986. A psychobiological study of archery performance. *Research Quarterly for Exercise and Sport* 57: 236–44.

Landers, D. M., and D. M. Landers. 1973. Teacher versus peer models: Effect of model's presence and performance level on motor behavior. *Journal of Motor Behavior* 5: 129–39.

Landin, D. 1994. The role of verbal cues in skill learning. *Quest* 46: 299–313.

Landin, D., and E. Hebert. 1995. *Investigating the impact of attention-focusing cues on collegiate tennis players' volleying.* Paper presented at the annual meeting of the Association for the Advancement of Applied Sport Psychology, New Orleans.

Lang, P. J., M. J. Kozak, G. A. Miller, D. M. Levin, and A. McLean, Jr. 1980. Emotional imagery: Conceptual structure and pattern of somato-visceral response. *Psychophysiology* 17: 179–92.

Larish, D. D., and G. E. Stelmach. 1982. Preprogramming, programming, and reprogramming of aimed hand movements as a function of age. *Journal of Motor Behavior* 14: 322–40.

Lashley, K. S. 1917. The accuracy of movement in the absence of excitation from the moving organ. *American Journal of Physiology* 43: 169–94.

Lashley, K. S. 1951. The problem of serial order in behavior. In L. A. Jeffress (Ed.), *Cerebral mechanisms in behavior* (pp. 112–36). New York: John Wiley.

Laszlo, J. L. 1966. The performance of a single motor task with kinesthetic sense loss. *Quarterly Journal of Experimental Psychology* 18: 1–8.

Laszlo, J. L. 1967. Training of fast tapping with reduction of kinesthetic, tactile, visual, and auditory sensation. *Quarterly Journal of Experimental Psychology* 19: 344–49.

Laurent, M., and J. A. Thomson. 1988. The role of visual information in control of a constrained locomotor task. *Journal of Motor Behavior* 20: 17–38.

Leavitt, J. L. 1979. Cognitive demands of skating and stickhandling in ice hockey. *Canadian Journal of Applied Sport Sciences* 4: 46–55.

Lee, D. N. 1974. Visual information during locomotion. In R. B. MacLeod and H. Pick (Eds.), *Perception: Essays in honor of J. J. Gibson* (pp. 250–67). Ithaca, NY: Cornell University Press.

Lee, D. N. 1976. A theory of visual control of braking based on information about time-to-collision. *Perception* 5: 437–59.

Lee, D. N. 1980. Visuo-motor coordination in space-time. In G. E. Stelmach and J. Requin (Eds.), *Tutorials in motor behavior* (pp. 281–95). Amsterdam: North-Holland.

Lee, D. N., and E. Aronson. 1974. Visual proprioceptive control of standing in human infants. *Perception & Psychophysics* 15: 527–32.

Lee, D. N., J. R. Lishman, and J. A. Thomson. 1982. Regulation of gait in long jumping. *Journal of Experimental Psychology: Human Perception and Performance* 8: 448–59.

Lee, T. D. 1988. Testing for motor learning: A focus on transfer-appropriate-processing. In O. G. Meijer and K. Roth (Eds.), *Complex motor behaviour: 'The' motor-action controversy* (pp. 210–15). Amsterdam: Elsevier.

Lee, T. D., and H. Carnahan. 1990. Bandwidth knowledge of results and motor learning: More than just a relative frequency effect. *Quarterly Journal of Experimental Psychology* 42A: 777–89.

Lee, T. D., and E. D. Genovese. 1988. Distribution of practice in motor skill acquisition: Learning and performance effects reconsidered. *Research Quarterly for Exercise and Sport* 59: 59–67.

Lee, T. D., and E. D. Genovese. 1989. Distribution of practice in motor skill acquisition: Different effects for discrete and continuous tasks. *Research Quarterly for Exercise and Sport* 59: 277–87.

Lee, T. D., and R. A. Magill. 1983a. Activity during the post-KR interval: Effects upon performance or learning. *Research Quarterly for Exercise and Sport,* 54: 340–45.

Lee, T. D., and R. A. Magill. 1983b. The locus of contextual interference in motor skill acquisition. *Journal of Experimental Psychology: Learning, Memory, and Cognition* 9: 730–46.

Lee, T. D., and R. A. Magill. 1985. Can forgetting facilitate skill acquisition? In D. Goodman, R. B. Wilberg, and I. M. Franks (Eds.), *Differing perspectives in motor learning, memory and control* (pp. 3–22). Amsterdam: North-Holland.

Lee, T. D., S. P. Swinnen, and S. Verschueren. 1995. Relative phase alterations during bimanual skill acquisition. *Journal of Motor Behavior* 27: 263–74.

Lee, T. D., M. A. White, and H. Carnahan. 1990. On the role of knowledge of results in motor learning: Exploring the guidance hypothesis. *Journal of Motor Behavior* 22: 191–208.

Leonard, S. D., E. W. Karnes, J. Oxendine, and J. Hesson. 1970. Effects of task difficulty on transfer performance on rotary pursuit. *Perceptual and Motor Skills* 30: 731–36.

Lindahl, L. G. 1945. Movement analysis as an industrial training method. *Journal of Applied Psychology,* 29: 420–36.

Linden, C. A., J. E. Uhley, D. Smith, and M. A. Bush. 1989. The effects of mental practice on walking balance in an elderly population. *Occupational Therapy Journal of Research* 9: 155–69.

Lintern, G., and S. N. Roscoe. 1980. Visual cue augmentation in contact flight simulation. In S. N. Roscoe (Ed.), *Aviation psychology* (pp. 227–38). Ames, IA: Iowa State University Press.

Lintern, G., S. N. Roscoe, and J. Sivier. 1990. Display principles, control dynamics, and environmental factors in pilot training and transfer. *Human Factors* 32: 299–317.

Little, W. S., and P. M. McCullagh. 1989. Motivation orientation and modeled instruction strategies: The effects on form and accuracy. *Journal of Sport and Exercise Psychology* 11: 41–53.

Locke, E. A., N. Cartledge, and J. Koeppel. 1968. Motivational effects of knowledge of results: A goal-setting phenomenon. *Psychological Bulletin* 70: 474–85.

Loeb, J. 1890. Untersuchungen uber die Orientirung im Fuhlraum der Hand und im Blickraum. *Pflueger Archives of General Physiology* 46: 1–46.

Logan, G. D. 1982. On the ability to inhibit complex movements: A stop-signal study of typewriting. *Journal of Experimental Psychology: Human Perception and Performance* 8: 778–92.

Logan, G. D. 1985. Skill and automaticity: Relations, implications, and future directions. *Canadian Journal of Psychology* 39: 367–86.

Loken, W. J., A. E. Thornton, R. L. Otto, and C. J. Long. 1995. Sustained attention after severe closed head injury. *Neuropsychology* 9: 592–98.

Mackworth, N. H. 1956. Vigilance. *Nature* 178: 1375–77.

Magill, R. A. 1977. The processing of knowledge of results for a serial motor task. *Journal of Motor Behavior* 9: 113–18.

Magill, R. A. 1988. Activity during the post-knowledge of results interval can benefit motor skill learning. In O. G. Meijer and K. Roth (Eds.), *Complex motor behavior: 'The' motor-action controversy* (pp. 231–46). Amsterdam: Elsevier.

Magill, R. A., C. J. Chamberlin, and K. G. Hall. 1991. Verbal knowledge of results as redundant information

for learning an anticipation timing skill. *Human Movement Science* 10: 485–507.

Magill, R. A., and M. N. Dowell. 1977. Serial position effects in motor short-term memory. *Journal of Motor Behavior* 9: 319–23.

Magill, R. A., and K. G. Hall. 1989. *Implicit and explicit learning in a complex tracking task.* Paper presented at the annual meeting of the Psychonomics Society, Atlanta, Georgia.

Magill, R. A., and K. G. Hall. 1990. A review of the contextual interference effect in motor skill acquisition. *Human Movement Science* 9: 241–89.

Magill, R. A., and P. F. Parks. 1983. The psychophysics of kinesthesis for positioning responses: The physical stimulus-psychological response relationship. *Research Quarterly for Exercise and Sport* 54: 346–51.

Magill, R. A., and B. Schoenfelder-Zohdi. 1996. A visual model and knowledge of performance as sources of information for learning a rhythmic gymnastics skill. *International Journal of Sport Psychology* 27: 7–22.

Magill, R. A., B. Schoenfelder-Zohdi, and K. G. Hall. 1990. *Further evidence for implicit learning in a complex tracking task.* Paper presented at the annual meeting of the Psychonomics Society, New Orleans, LA.

Magill, R. A., and C. A. Wood. 1986. Knowledge of results precision as a learning variable in motor skill acquisition. *Research Quarterly for Exercise and Sport* 57: 170–73.

Mahoney, M. J., and A. Avener. 1977. Psychology of the elite athlete: An exploratory study. *Cognitive Therapy and Research* 1: 135–41.

Mané, A., and E. Donchin. 1989. The Space Fortress game. *Acta Psychologica* 71: 17–22.

Mark, L. S. 1987. Eyeheight-scaled information about affordances: A study of sitting and stair climbing. *Journal of Experimental Psychology: Human Perception and Performance* 13: 361–70.

Marteniuk, R. G. 1986. Information processes in movement learning: Capacity and structural interference. *Journal of Motor Behavior* 5: 249–59.

Marteniuk, R. G., and S. K. E. Romanow. 1983. Human movement organization and learning as revealed by variability of movement, use of kinematic information and Fourier analysis. In R. A. Magill (Ed.), *Memory and control of action* (pp. 167–97). Amsterdam: North-Holland.

Martens, R., L. Burwitz, and J. Zuckerman. 1976. Modeling effects on motor performance. *Research Quarterly* 47: 277–91.

Masser, L. S. 1993. Critical cues help first-grade students' achievement in handstands and forward rolls. *Journal of Teaching in Physical Education* 12: 301–12.

Mathiowetz, V., and M. G. Wade. 1995. Task constraints and functional motor performance of individuals with and without multiple sclerosis. *Ecological Psychology* 7: 99–123.

McBride, E., and A. Rothstein. 1979. Mental and physical practice and the learning and retention of open and closed skills. *Perceptual and Motor Skills* 49: 359–65.

McCloy, C. H. 1934. The measurement of general motor capacity and general motor ability. *Research Quarterly* 5, Supplement: 46–61.

McCloy, C. H., and N. D. Young. 1954. *Tests and measurements in health and physical education.* 3d ed. New York: Appleton-Century-Crofts.

McCullagh, P., and J. K. Caird. 1990. Correct and learning models and the use of model knowledge of results in the acquisition and retention of a motor skill. *Journal of Human Movement Studies* 18: 107–16.

McCullagh, P., J. Stiehl, and M. R. Weiss. 1990. Developmental modeling effects on the quantitative and qualitative aspects of motor performance. *Research Quarterly for Exercise and Sport* 61: 344–50.

McCullagh, P., M. R. Weiss, and D. Ross. 1989. Modeling considerations in motor skill acquisition and performance: An integrated approach. In K. B. Pandolf (Ed.), *Exercise and sport science reviews* (Vol. 17, pp. 475–513). Baltimore: Williams & Wilkins.

McDonald, P. V., S. K. Oliver, and K. M. Newell. 1995. Perceptual-motor exploration as a function of biomechanical and task constraints. *Acta Psychologica* 88: 127–65.

Meeuwsen, H., and R. A. Magill. 1987. The role of vision in gait control during gymnastics vaulting. In T. B. Hoshizaki, J. Salmela, and B. Petiot (Eds.), *Diagnostics, treatment, and analysis of gymnastic talent.* (pp. 137–55). Montreal: Sport Psyche Editions.

Melnick, M. J. 1971. Effects of overlearning on the retention of a gross motor skill. *Research Quarterly* 42: 60–69.

Meyer, D. E., R. A. Abrams, S. Kornblum, C. E. Wright, and J. E. K. Smith. 1988. Optimality in human motor performance: Ideal control of rapid aimed movements. *Psychological Review* 95: 340–70.

Meyer, D. E., A. M. Osman, D. E. Irwin, and S. Yantis. 1988. Modern mental chronometry. *Biological Psychology* 26: 3–67.

Miller, G. A., E. Galanter, and K. H. Pribram. 1960. *Plans and the structure of behavior.* New York: Holt, Rinehart, and Winston.

Montes, R., M. Bedmar, and M. Martin, 1993. EMG biofeedback of the abductor pollicis brevis in piano performance. *Biofeedback and Self-Regulation* 18: 67–77.

Moore, S. P., and R. G. Marteniuk. 1986. Kinematic and electromyographic changes that occur as a function of learning a time-constrained aiming task. *Journal of Motor Behavior* 18: 397–426.

Mourant, R. R., and T. H. Rockwell. 1972. Strategies of visual search by novice and experienced drivers. *Human Factors* 14: 325–35.

Mowbray, G. H. 1960. Choice reaction times for skilled responses. *Quarterly Journal of Experimental Psychology* 12: 193–202.

Mowbray, G. H., and M. U. Rhoades. 1959. On the reduction of choice reaction times with practice. *Quarterly Journal of Experimental Psychology* 11: 16–23.

Mulder, T., and W. Hulstijn. 1985. Delayed sensory feedback in the learning of a novel motor skill. *Psychological Record* 47: 203–9.

Navon, D., and D. Gopher. 1979. On the economy of the human processing system. *Psychological Review* 86: 214–55.

Naylor, J., and G. Briggs. 1963. Effects of task complexity and task organization on the relative efficiency of part and whole training methods. *Journal of Experimental Psychology* 65: 217–44.

Newell, K. M. 1974. Knowledge of results and motor learning. *Journal of Motor Behavior* 6: 235–44.

Newell, K. M. 1985. Coordination, control, and skill. In D. Goodman, R. B. Wilberg, and I. M. Franks (Eds.), *Differing perspectives in motor learning, memory and control* (pp. 295–317). Amsterdam: North-Holland.

Newell, K. M. 1986. Constraints on the development of coordination. In M. G. Wade and H. T. A. Whiting (Eds.), *Motor development in children: Aspects of coordination and control* (pp. 341–60). The Hague, The Netherlands: Nijhoff.

Newell, K. M., M. J. Carlton, A. T. Fisher, and B. G. Rutter. 1989. Whole-part training strategies for learning the response dynamics of microprocessor driven simulators. *Acta Psychologica* 71: 197–216.

Newell, K. M., J. T. Quinn, Jr., W. A. Sparrow, and C. B. Walter. 1983. Kinematic information feedback for learning a rapid arm movement. *Human Movement Science* 2: 255–69.

Newell, K. M., and R. E. A. van Emmerik. 1989. The acquisition of coordination: Preliminary analysis of learning to write. *Human Movement Science* 8: 17–32.

Nideffer, R. M. 1993. Attention control training. In R. N. Singer, M. Murphey, and L. K. Tennant (Eds.), *Handbook of research on sport psychology* (pp. 542–56). New York: Macmillan.

Norman, D. A. 1968. Toward a theory of memory and attention. *Psychological Review* 75: 522–36.

Norrie, M. L. 1967. Practice effects on reaction latency for simple and complex movements. *Research Quarterly* 38: 79–85.

Paulignan, Y., M. Jeannerod, C. MacKenzie, and R. Marteniuk. 1991. Selective perturbation of visual input during prehension movements. 2: The effects of changing object size. *Experimental Brain Research* 87: 407–20.

Peper, C. E., P. J. Beek, and P. C. W. van Wieringen. 1995. Multifrequency coordination in bimanual tapping: Asymmetrical coupling and signs of supercriticality. *Journal of Experimental Psychology: Human Perception and Performance* 21: 1117–38.

Peters, M. 1977. Simultaneous performance of two motor activities: The factor of timing. *Neuropsychologia* 15: 461–65.

Peters, M. 1985. Performance of a rubato-like task: When two things cannot be done at the same time. *Music Perception* 2: 471–82.

Pew, R. W. 1974. Levels of analysis in motor control. *Brain Research* 71: 393–400.

Pieron, M. 1982. Effectiveness of teaching a psychomotor task: Study in a micro-teaching setting. In M. Pieron and J. Cheffers (Eds.), *Studying the teaching in physical education* (pp. 79–89). Liege, Belgium: Association Internationale des Supérieures d'Education Physique.

Polit, A., and E. Bizzi. 1978. Processes controlling arm movements in monkeys. *Science* 201: 1235–37.

Polit, A., and E. Bizzi. 1979. Characteristics of motor programs underlying arm movements in monkeys. *Journal of Neurophysiology* 42: 183–94.

Pollock, B. J., and T. D. Lee. 1992. Effects of the model's skill level on observational learning. *Research Quarterly for Exercise and Sport* 63: 25–29.

Posner, M. I., and S. W. Keele. 1969. Attention demands of movements. *Proceedings of the 16th Congress of Applied Psychology.* Amsterdam: Swets & Zeitlinger.

Poulton, E. C. 1957. On prediction in skilled movements. *Psychological Bulletin* 54: 467–78.

Proctor, R. W., and T. G. Reeve. 1988. The acquisition of task-specific productions and modification of declarative representations in spatial precuing tasks. *Journal of Experimental Psychology: General* 117: 182–96.

Proctor, R., and T. G. Reeve (Eds.), 1990. *Stimulus-response compatibility: An integrated perspective.* Amsterdam: North-Holland.

Proteau, L., and L. Cournoyer. 1990. Vision of the stylus in a manual aiming task: The effects of practice. *Quarterly Journal of Experimental Psychology* 42B: 811–28.

Proteau, L., R. G. Marteniuk, Y. Girouard, and C. Dugas. 1987. On the type of information used to control and learn an aiming movement after moderate and extensive training. *Human Movement Science* 6: 181–99.

Queseda, D. C., and R. A. Schmidt. 1970. A test of the Adams-Creamer decay hypothesis for the timing of motor responses. *Journal of Motor Behavior* 2: 273–83.

Rabbitt, P. M. A., and S. M. Vyas. 1979. Signal recency effects can be distinguished from signal repetition in serial CRT tasks. *Canadian Journal of Psychology* 33: 88–95.

Raibert, M. 1977. *Motor control and learning by the state-space model.* Technical Report, Artificial Intelligence Laboratory, Massachusetts Institute of Technology (AI-TR-439).

Reeve, T. G. 1976. *Processing demands during the acquisition of motor skills requiring different feedback cues.* Unpublished doctoral dissertation, Texas A&M University.

Reilly, R. R., S. Zedeck, and M. L. Tenopyr. 1979. Validity and fairness of physical ability tests for predicting performance in craft jobs. *Journal of Applied Psychology* 64: 262–74.

Richardson, A. 1967a. Mental practice: A review and discussion. Part I. *Research Quarterly* 38: 95–107.

Richardson, A. 1967b. Mental practice: A review and discussion. Part II. *Research Quarterly* 38: 263–73.

Roberts, W. H. 1930. The effect of delayed feeding on white rats in a problem cage. *Journal of Genetic Psychology* 37: 35–38.

Rogers, C. A. 1974. Feedback precision and post-feedback interval duration. *Journal of Experimental Psychology* 102: 604–8.

Rosenbaum, D. A. 1980. Human movement initiation: Specification of arm, direction, and extent. *Journal of Experimental Psychology: General* 109: 444–74.

Rosenbaum, D. A. 1983. The movement precuing technique: Assumptions, applications, and extensions.

In R. A. Magill (Ed.), *Memory and control of action* (pp. 251–74). Amsterdam: North-Holland.

Rosenbaum, D. A. 1991. *Human motor control.* San Diego, Academic Press.

Rosenbaum, D. A., and M. J. Jorgensen. 1992. Planning macroscopic aspects of manual control. *Human Movement Science* 11: 61–69.

Rosenberg, K. S., H. L. Pick, and C. von Hofsten. 1988. Role of visual information in catching. *Journal of Motor Behavior* 20: 150–64.

Rothstein, A. L., and R. K. Arnold. 1976. Bridging the gap: Application of research on videotape feedback and bowling. *Motor Skills: Theory Into Practice* 1: 36–61.

Roy, E. A., and D. Elliott. 1986. Manual asymmetries in visually directed aiming. *Canadian Journal of Psychology* 40: 109–21.

Ryan, E. D., and J. Simons. 1983. What is learned in mental practice of motor skills? A test of the cognitive-motor hypothesis. *Journal of Sport Psychology* 5: 419–26.

Salmoni, A. W., R. A. Schmidt, and C. B. Walter. 1984. Knowledge of results and motor learning: A review and reappraisal. *Psychological Bulletin* 95: 355–86.

Sanders, R. H., and J. B. Allen. 1993. Changes in net torques during accommodation to change in surface compliance in a drop jumping task. *Human Movement Science* 12: 299–326.

Schendel, J. D., and J. D. Hagman. 1982. On sustaining procedural skills over a prolonged retention interval. *Journal of Applied Psychology* 67: 605–10.

Schmidt, R. A. 1975a. A schema theory of discrete motor skill learning theory. *Psychological Review* 82: 225–60.

Schmidt, R. A. 1975b. *Motor skills.* New York: Harper & Row.

Schmidt, R. A. (1985). The search for invariance in skilled movement behavior. *Research Quarterly for Exercise and Sport* 56: 188–200.

Schmidt, R. A. 1987. *Motor control and learning: A behavioral emphasis* 2d ed. Champaign, IL: Human Kinetics.

Schmidt, R. A. 1988. Motor and action perspectives on motor behavior. In O. G. Meijer and K. Roth (Eds.), *Complex motor behaviour: 'The' motor-action controversy* (pp. 3–44). Amsterdam: Elsevier.

Schmidt, R. A., and J. L. White. 1972. Evidence for an error detection mechanism in motor skills: A test of Adams' closed-loop theory. *Journal of Motor Behavior* 4: 143–53.

Schmidt, R. A., and D. E. Young. 1987. Transfer of movement control in motor skill learning. In S. M.

Cormier and J. D. Hagman (Eds.), *Transfer of learning* (pp. 47–79). Orlando, FL: Academic Press.

Schmidt, R. A., D. E. Young, S. Swinnen, and D. C. Shapiro. 1989. Summary knowledge of results for skill acquisition: Support for the guidance hypothesis. *Journal of Experimental Psychology: Learning, Memory, and Cognition* 15: 352–59.

Schmidt, R. A., H. N. Zelaznik, B. Hawkins, J. S. Frank, and J. T. Quinn, Jr. 1979. Motor output variability: A theory for the accuracy of rapid motor acts. *Psychological Review* 86: 415–51.

Schmidt, R. C., and M. T. Turvey. 1992. Long-term consistencies in assembling coordinated rhythmic movements. *Human Movement Science* 11: 349–76.

Schneider, K., R. F. Zernicke, R. A. Schmidt, and T. J. Hart. 1989. Changes in limb dynamics during the practice of rapid arm movement. *Journal of Biomechanics* 22: 805–17.

Schoenfelder-Zohdi, B. G. 1992. *Investigating the informational nature of a modeled visual demonstration.* Ph.D. Dissertation, Louisiana State University.

Scully, D. M., and K. M. Newell. 1985. Observational learning and the acquisition of motor skills: Toward a visual perception perspective. *Journal of Human Movement Studies* 11: 169–86.

Sekiya, H., R. A. Magill, B. Sidaway, and D. I. Anderson. 1994. The contextual interference effect for skill variations from the same and different generalized motor programs. *Research Quarterly for Exercise and Sport* 65: 330–38.

Selder, D. J., and N. Del Rolan. 1979. Knowledge of performance, skill level and performance on the balance beam. *Canadian Journal of Applied Sport Sciences* 4: 226–29.

Shaffer, L. H. 1981. Performances of Chopin, Bach, and Beethoven: Studies in motor programming. *Cognitive Psychology* 13: 326–76.

Shank, M. D., and K. M. Haywood. 1987. Eye movements while viewing a baseball pitch. *Perceptual and Motor Skills,* 64: 1191–97.

Shapiro, D. C., R. F. Zernicke, R. J. Gregor, and J. D. Diestel. 1981. Evidence for generalized motor programs using gait-pattern analysis. *Journal of Motor Behavior* 13: 33–47.

Shea, C. H., and R. M. Kohl. 1990. Specificity and variability of practice. *Research Quarterly for Exercise and Sport* 61: 169–77.

Shea, C. H., and R. M. Kohl. 1991. Composition of practice: Influence on the retention of motor skills. *Research Quarterly for Exercise and Sport* 62: 187–95.

Shea, C. H., R. Kohl, and C. Indermill. 1990. Contextual interference contributions of practice. *Acta Psychologica* 73: 145–57.

Shea, J. B., and R. L. Morgan. 1979. Contextual interference effects on the acquisition, retention, and transfer of a motor skill. *Journal of Experimental Psychology: Human Learning and Memory* 5: 179–87.

Shea, J. B., and S. T. Zimny. 1983. Context effects in memory and learning in movement information. In R. A. Magill (Ed.), *Memory and control of action* (pp. 345–66). Amsterdam: North-Holland.

Shepherd, M., J. M. Findlay, and R. J. Hockley. 1986. The relationship between eye movements and spatial attention. *Quarterly Journal of Experimental Psychology* 38A: 475–91.

Shepherd, R. B., and A. M. Gentile. 1994. Sit-to-stand: Functional relationship between upper and lower body limb segments. *Human Movement Science* 13: 817–40.

Sheridan, M. R. 1984. Response programming, response production, and fractionated reaction time. *Psychological Research* 46: 33–47.

Sherrington, C. S. 1906. *Integrative action of the nervous system.* New York: Scribner.

Sherwood, D. E. 1988. Effect of bandwidth knowledge of results on movement consistency. *Perceptual and Motor Skills* 66: 535–42.

Sherwood, D. E. 1994. Hand preference, practice order, and spatial assimilation in rapid bimanual movement. *Journal of Motor Behavior* 26: 123–34.

Shumway-Cook, A., and M. Woollacott. 1995. *Motor control: Theory and practical applications.* Baltimore: Williams & Wilkins.

Sidaway, B., G. Heise, and B. Schoenfelder-Zohdi. 1995. Quantifying the variability of angle-angle plots. *Journal of Human Movement Studies* 29: 181–97.

Sidaway, B., J. McNitt-Gray, and G. Davis. 1989. Visual timing of muscle preactivation in preparation for landing. *Ecological Psychology* 1: 253–64.

Sidaway, B., B. Moore, and B. Schoenfelder-Zohdi. 1991. Summary and frequency of KR presentation effects on retention of a motor skill. *Research Quarterly for Exercise and Sport* 62: 27–32.

Sidaway, B., H. Sekiya, and M. Fairweather. 1995. Movement variability as a function of accuracy demands in programmed aiming responses. *Journal of Motor Behavior* 27: 67–76.

Siedentop, D. 1983. *Developing teaching skills in physical education.* 2d ed. Boston: Houghton Mifflin.

Siegel, D. 1986. Movement duration, fractionated reaction time, and response programming. *Research Quarterly for Exercise and Sport* 57: 128–31.

Silverman, S., L. A. Tyson, and J. Krampitz. 1991. *Teacher feedback and achievement in physical education: Interaction with student practice.* Paper presented at the annual meeting of the American Educational Research Association, Chicago, Illinois.

Singer, R. N. 1966. Comparison of inter-limb skill achievement in performing a motor skill. *Research Quarterly* 37: 406–10.

Singer, R. N. 1986. Sports performance: A five-step mental approach. *Journal of Physical Education and Recreation* 57: 82–84.

Singer, R. N., J. Cauraugh, L. K. Tennant, M. Murphey, R. Chen, and R. Lidor. 1991. Attention and distractors: Considerations for enhancing sport performances. *International Journal of Sport Psychology* 22: 95–114.

Singer, R. N., and S. Suwanthada. 1986. The generalizability effectiveness of a learning strategy on achievement in related closed motor skills. *Research Quarterly for Exercise and Sport* 57: 205–14.

Slater-Hammel, A. T. 1960. Reliability, accuracy, and refractoriness of a transit reaction. *Research Quarterly* 31: 217–28.

Smyth, M. M., and A. M. Marriott. 1982. Vision and proprioception in simple catching. *Journal of Motor Behavior* 14: 143–52.

Smyth, M. M., and G. Silvers. 1987. Functions of vision in the control of handwriting. *Acta Psychologica* 65: 47–64.

Solmon, M. A., and J. Boone. 1993. The impact of student goal orientation in physical education classes. *Research Quarterly for Exercise and Sport* 64: 418–24.

Solmon, M. A., and Lee, A. M. 1996. Entry characteristics, practice variables, and cognition: Student mediation of instruction. *Journal of Teaching in Physical Education* 15: 136–50.

Southard, D., and T. Higgins. 1987. Changing movement patterns: Effects of demonstration and practice. *Research Quarterly for Exercise and Sport* 58: 77–80.

Southard, D., and A. Miracle. 1993. Rhythmicity, ritual, and motor performance: A study of free throw shooting in basketball. *Research Quarterly for Exercise and Sport* 64: 284–90.

Sparrow, W. A., E. Donovan, R. E. A. van Emmerik, and E. B. Barry. 1987. Using relative motion plots to measure changes in intra-limb and inter-limb coordination. *Journal of Motor Behavior* 19: 115–19.

Sparrow, W. A., and V. W. Irizarry-Lopez. 1987. Mechanical efficiency and metabolic cost as measures of learning a novel gross motor task. *Journal of Motor Behavior* 19: 240–64.

Sparrow, W. A., and J. J. Summers. 1992. Performance on trials without knowledge of results (KR) in reduced relative frequency presentations of KR. *Journal of Motor Behavior* 24: 197–209.

Staum, M. J. 1983. Music and rhythmic stimuli in the rehabilitation of gait disorders. *Journal of Music Therapy* 20: 69–87.

Steenbergen, B., R. G. Marteniuk, and L. E. Kalbfleisch. 1995. Achieving coordination in prehension: Joint freezing and postural contributions. *Journal of Motor Behavior* 27: 333–48.

Stelmach, G. E. 1970. Learning and response consistency with augmented feedback. *Ergonomics* 13: 421–25.

Summers, J. J. 1975. The role of timing in motor program representation. *Journal of Motor Behavior* 7: 229–42.

Summers, J. J., and T. M. Kennedy. 1992. Strategies in the production of a 5:3 polyrhythm. *Human Movement Science* 11: 101–12.

Summers, J. J., D. A. Rosenbaum, B. D. Burns, and S. K. Ford. 1993. Production of polyrhythms. *Journal of Experimental Psychology: Human Perception and Performance* 19: 416–28.

Swinnen, S. P. 1990. Interpolated activities during the knowledge of results delay and post-knowledge of results interval: Effects of performance and learning. *Journal of Experimental Psychology: Learning, Memory, and Cognition* 16: 692–705.

Swinnen, S. P., R. A. Schmidt, D. E. Nicholson, and D. C. Shapiro. 1990. Information feedback for skill acquisition: Instantaneous knowledge of results degrades learning. *Journal of Experimental Psychology: Learning, Memory, and Cognition* 16: 706–16.

Swinnen, S. P., C. B. Walter, J. M. Pauwels, P. F. Meugens, and M. B. Beirinckx. 1990. The dissociation of interlimb constraints. *Human Performance* 3: 187–215.

Taub, E., and A. J. Berman. 1963. Avoidance conditioning in the absence of relevant proprioceptive and exteroceptive feedback. *Journal of Comparative and Physiological Psychology* 56: 1012–16.

Taub, E., and A. J. Berman. 1968. Movement and learning in the absence of sensory feedback. In S. J. Freedman (Ed.), *The neuropsychology of spatially oriented behavior* (pp. 173–92). Homewood, IL: Dorsey Press.

Taylor, H. G., and K. M. Heilman. 1980. Left-hemisphere motor dominance in righthanders. *Cortex* 16: 587–603.

Teichner, W. H. 1954. Recent studies of simple reaction time. *Psychological Bulletin* 51: 128–49.

Terzuolo, C., and P. Viviani. 1980. Determinants and characteristics of patterns used for typing. *Neuroscience* 5: 1085–103.

Thomas, J. R., and W. Halliwell. 1976. Individual differences in motor skill acquisition. *Journal of Motor Behavior* 8: 89–100.

Thorndike, E. L. 1914. *Educational psychology: Briefer course.* New York: Columbia University Press.

Treisman, A. 1988. Features and objects: The fourteenth Bartlett Memorial Lecture. *Quarterly Journal of Experimental Psychology* 40A: 201–37.

Treisman, A., and G. Gelade. 1980. A feature integration theory of attention. *Cognitive Psychology* 12: 97–136.

Tresilian, J. R. 1994. Approximate information sources and perceptual variables in interceptive timing. *Journal of Experimental Psychology: Human Perception and Performance* 20: 154–73.

Trowbridge, M. H., and H. Cason. 1932. An experimental study of Thorndike's theory of learning. *Journal of General Psychology* 7: 245–58.

Trussell, E. 1965. Prediction of success in a motor skill on the basis of early learning achievement. *Research Quarterly* 39: 342–47.

Turvey, M. T. 1977. Preliminaries to a theory of action with reference to vision. In R. Shaw and J. Bransford (Eds.), *Perceiving, acting, and knowing* (pp. 211–65). Hillsdale, NJ: Erlbaum.

Turvey, M. T. 1990. Coordination. *American Psychologist* 45: 938–53.

Twitmeyer, E. M. 1931. Visual guidance in motor learning. *American Journal of Psychology* 43: 165–87.

van Galen, G. P. 1991. Handwriting: Issues for a psychomotor theory. *Human Movement Science* 10: 165–91.

Van Gyn, G. H., H. A. Wenger, and C. A. Gaul. 1990. Imagery as a method of enhancing transfer from training to performance. *Journal of Sport & Exercise Psychology* 12: 366–75.

Vander Linden, D. W., J. H. Cauraugh, and T. A. Greene. 1993. The effect of frequency of kinetic feedback on learning an isometric force production task in nondisabled subjects. *Physical Therapy* 73: 79–87.

Vereijken, B., R. E. A. van Emmerik, H. T. A. Whiting, and K. M. Newell. 1992. Free(z)ing degrees of freedom in skill acquisition. *Journal of Motor Behavior* 24: 133–42.

Vereijken, B., and H. T. A. Whiting. 1990. In defence of discovery learning. *Canadian Journal of Sport Science* 15: 99–106.

Vishton, P. M., and J. E. Cutting. 1995. Wayfinding, displacements, and mental maps: Velocity fields are not typically used to determine one's aimpoint. *Journal of Experimental Psychology: Human Perception and Performance* 21: 978–95.

Vorro, J., F. R. Wilson, and A. Dainis. 1978. Multivariate analysis of biomechanical profiles for the coracobrachialis and biceps brachii (caput breve) muscles in humans. *Ergonomics* 21: 407–18.

Wadman, W. J., J. J. Dernier van der Gon, R. H. Geuze, and C. R. Mol. 1979. Control of fast goal-directed arm movements. *Journal of Human Movement Studies* 5: 3–17.

Wagenaar, R. C., and W. J. Beek. 1992. Hemiplegic gait: A kinematic analysis using walking speed as a basis. *Journal of Biomechanics* 25: 1007–15.

Wagenaar, R. C., and R. E. A. Van Emmerik. 1994. Dynamics of pathological gait. *Human Movement Science* 13: 441–71.

Wallace, S. A., and R. W. Hagler. 1979. Knowledge of performance and the learning of a closed motor skill. *Research Quarterly* 50: 265–71.

Wallace, S. A., E. Stevenson, D. L. Weeks, and J. A. S. Kelso. 1992. The perceptual guidance of grasping a moving object. *Human Movement Science* 11: 691–715.

Wallace, S. A., and D. L. Weeks. 1988. Temporal constraints in the control of prehensile movement. *Journal of Motor Behavior* 20: 81–105.

Walter, C. B., and S. P. Swinnen. 1992. Adaptive tuning of interlimb attraction to facilitate bimanual coupling. *Journal of Motor Behavior* 24: 95–104.

Wann, J. P., and I. Nimmo-Smith. 1991. The control of pen pressure in handwriting: A subtle point. *Human Movement Science* 10: 223–46.

Warren, W. H., Jr. 1987. An ecological conception of action. *European Journal of Cognitive Psychology* 7: 199–203.

Warren, W. H., Jr., D. S. Young, and D. N. Lee. 1986. Visual control of step length during running over irregular terrain. *Journal of Experimental Psychology: Human Perception and Performance* 12: 259–66.

Watters, R. G. 1992. Retention of human sequenced behavior following forward chaining, backward chaining, and whole task training procedures. *Journal of Human Movement Studies* 22: 117–29.

Weeks, D. J., and R. W. Proctor. 1990. Salient-features coding in the translation between orthogonal stimulus and response dimensions. *Journal of Experimental Psychology: General* 119: 355–66.

Weeks, D. L., and D. E. Sherwood. 1994. A comparison of knowledge of results scheduling methods for promoting motor skill acquisition and retention. *Research Quarterly for Exercise and Sport* 65: 136–42.

Weeks, D. L., and S. A. Wallace. 1992. Premovement posture and focal movement velocity effects on postural responses accompanying rapid arm movement. *Human Movement Science* 11: 717–34.

Weinberg, D. R., D. E. Guy, and R. W. Tupper. 1964. Variations of post-feedback interval in simple motor learning. *Journal of Experimental Psychology* 67: 98–99.

Weir, P. L., and J. L. Leavitt. 1990. The effects of model's skill level and model's knowledge of results on the acquisition of an aiming task. *Human Movement Science* 9: 369–83.

Weir, P. L., C. L. Mackenzie, R. G. Marteniuk, and S. L. Cargoe. 1990. Is object texture a constraint on human prehension kinematic evidence? *Journal of Motor Behavior* 23: 205–10.

Welford, A. T. 1952. The psychological refractory period and the timing of high-speed performance—A review and a theory. *British Journal of Psychology* 43: 2–19.

Welford, A. T. 1967. Single channel operations in the brain. *Acta Psychologica* 27: 5–22.

Whiting, H. T. A. 1988. Imitation and the learning of complex cyclical actions. In O. G. Meijer and K. Roth (Eds.), *Complex motor behaviour: 'The' motor-action controversy* (pp. 381–401). Amsterdam: North-Holland.

Whiting, H. T. A., E. B. Gill., and J. M. Stephenson. 1970. Critical time intervals for taking in-flight information in a ball-catching task. *Ergonomics* 13: 265–72.

Wickens, C. D. 1980. The structure of processing resources. In R. Nickerson (Ed.), *Attention and performance VII* (pp. 239–57). Hillsdale, NJ: Erlbaum.

Wickens, C. D. 1984. Processing resources in attention. In R. Parasuraman and D. R. Davies (Eds.), *Varieties of attention* (pp. 63–102). Orlando, FL: Academic Press.

Wickens, C. D., D. L. Sandry, and M. Vidulich. 1983. Compatibility and resource competition between modalities of input, control processing, and output: Testing a model of complex performance. *Human Factors* 25: 227–48.

Wickstrom, R. L. 1958. Comparative study of methodologies for teaching gymnastics and tumbling stunts. *Research Quarterly* 29: 109–15.

Wiese-Bjornstal, D. M., and M. R. Weiss. 1992. Modeling effects on children's form kinematics, performance outcome, and cognitive recognition of a sport skill. *Research Quarterly for Exercise and Sport* 63: 67–75.

Wightman, D. C., and G. Lintern. 1985. Part-task training strategies for tracking and manual control. *Human Factors* 27: 267–83.

Williams, A. M., K. Davids, L. Burwitz, and J. G. Williams. 1994. Visual search strategies in experienced and inexperienced soccer players. *Research Quarterly for Exercise and Sport* 65: 127–35.

Williams, J. G. 1988. Perception of a throwing action from point-light demonstrations. *Perceptual and Motor Skills* 67: 273–74.

Williams, J. G. 1989. Throwing action from full-cue and motion-only video-models of an arm movement sequence. *Perceptual and Motor Skills* 68: 259–66.

Williams, J. G., and N. McCririe. 1988. Control of arm and fingers during ball catching. *Journal of Human Movement Studies,* 14: 241–47.

Winstein, C. J., P. S. Pohl, and R. Lewthwaite. 1994. Effects of physical guidance and knowledge of results on motor learning: Support for the guidance hypothesis. *Research Quarterly for Exercise and Sport* 65: 316–23.

Winstein, C. J., and R. A. Schmidt. 1990. Reduced frequency of knowledge of results enhances motor skill learning. *Journal of Experimental Psychology: Learning, Memory, and Cognition* 16: 677–91.

Wood, C. A., J. D. Gallagher, P. V. Martino, and M. Ross. 1992. Alternate forms of knowledge of results: Interaction of augmented feedback modality on learning. *Journal of Human Movement Studies* 22: 213–30.

Wood, C. A., and C. A. Ging. 1991. The role of interference and task similarity on the acquisition, retention, and transfer of simple motor skills. *Research Quarterly for Exercise and Sport* 62: 18–26.

Woodrow, H. 1914. The measurement of attention. *Psychological Monographs* (No. 76).

Wrisberg, C. A., and Z. Liu. 1991. The effect of contextual variety on the practice, retention, and transfer of an applied motor skill. *Research Quarterly for Exercise and Sport* 62: 406–12.

Wrisberg, C. A., and M. R. Ragsdale. 1979. Further tests of Schmidt's schema theory: Development of a schema rule for a coincident timing task. *Journal of Motor Behavior* 11: 159–66.

Wrisberg, C. A., and C. H. Shea. 1978. Shifts in attention demands and motor program utilization during motor learning. *Journal of Motor Behavior* 10: 149–58.

Wulf, G., and T. D. Lee. 1993. Contextual interference in movements of the same class: Differential effects on program and parameter learning. *Journal of Motor Behavior* 25: 254–63.

Wuyts, I. J., and M. J. Buekers. 1995. The effects of visual and auditory models on the learning of a rhythmical synchronization dance skill. *Research Quarterly for Exercise and Sport* 66: 105–15.

Young, D. E., R. A. Magill, R. A. Schmidt, and D. C. Shapiro. 1988. *Motor programs as control structures for reversal movements: An examination of rapid movements and unexpected perturbations.* Paper presented at the annual meeting of the North American Society for the Psychology of Sport and Physical Activity, Knoxville, Tennessee.

Zanone, P. G., and J. A. S. Kelso. 1994. The coordination dynamics of learning: Theoretical structure and experimental agenda. In S. Swinnen, H. Heuer, J. Massion, and P. Casaer (Eds.), *Interlimb coordination: Neural, dynamical, and cognitive constraints* (pp. 461–90). San Diego: Academic Press.

Zelaznik, H. N., and E. Franz. 1990. Stimulus-response compatibility and the programming of motor activity: Pitfalls and possible new directions. In R. Proctor and T. G. Reeve (Eds.), *Stimulus-response compatibility: An integrated perspective* (pp. 279–95). Amsterdam: North-Holland.

Zelaznik, H. N., B. Hawkins, and L. Kisselburgh. 1983. Rapid visual feedback processing in single-aiming movements. *Journal of Motor Behavior* 15: 217–36.

# GLOSSARY

**Ability**   A general trait or capacity of an individual that is a foundational element for the performance of a variety of motor skills.

**Absolute error (AE)**   The unsigned deviation from the target or criterion, representing amount of error. A measure of the magnitude of response error without regard to the direction of the deviation.

**Acceleration**   A kinematic measure that describes change in velocity during movement. We derive it from velocity by dividing change in velocity by change in time.

**Action**   A goal-directed response that consists of body and/or limb movements.

**Arousal**   The general state of excitability of a person, involving physiological, emotional, and mental systems.

**Associative stage**   The second stage of learning in the Fitts and Posner model. An intermediate stage on the learning stages continuum.

**Asymmetric transfer**   Bilateral transfer in which there is a greater amount of transfer from one limb than from the other limb.

**Attention**   In human performance, conscious or non-conscious engagement in perceptual, cognitive, and/or motor activities before, during, and after performing skills. The human information-processing system includes limitations to the number of these activities that can be performed simultaneously.

**Attentional focus**   The directing of attention to specific characteristics or cues in a performance situation to enhance performance by maintaining attention demands within capacity limits.

**Attractors**   The stable behavioral steady states of systems. In terms of human coordinated movement, attractors characterize preferred behavioral states, such as the in-phase and out-of-phase states for rhythmic bimanual finger movements.

**Augmented feedback**   Information about performing a skill that is added to sensory feedback and comes from a source external to the person performing the skill.

**Automaticity**   A characteristic of skilled performance; indicates that a person uses knowledge and procedures automatically, without requiring attention resources.

**Autonomous stage**   The third stage of learning in the Fitts and Posner model. The final stage on the learning continuum. Also called the *automatic stage*.

■

**Bilateral transfer**    Transfer of learning that occurs between limbs.

**Bimanual coordination**    A skill performance requirement when success depends on the simultaneous use of the two arms. The skill may require the two arms to have the same or different spatial and/or temporal characteristics while performing.

**Biofeedback**    A type of augmented feedback that provides information about physiological processes through the use of instrumentation.

■

**Central-resource theories**    Attention-capacity theories that propose one central reserve of attention resources for which all activities compete.

**Closed-loop control system**    A system of control in which feedback is compared against a standard or reference to enable a specified action to be carried out as planned.

**Closed motor skill**    A skill performed in a stable or predictable environment where the performer determines when to begin the action.

**Cognitive mediation theory**    A theory for explaining the benefit of modeling proposing that when a person observes a model, the person translates the observed movement information into a cognitive code that the person stores in memory and uses when the observer performs the skill.

**Cognitive stage**    The first stage of learning in the Fitts and Posner model. The beginning or initial stage on the learning continuum.

**Collective variables**    Functionally specific and abstract variables that define the overall behavior of a system. They enable a coordinated pattern of movement to be reproduced and distinguished from other patterns. Known also as order parameters.

**Concurrent augmented feedback**    Augmented feedback that is provided while a person is performing a skill or making a movement.

**Constant error (CE)**    The signed (+/−) deviation from the target or criterion. It represents amount and direction of error and is also a measure of response bias.

**Contextual interference**    The interference that results from practicing variations of a skill within the context of a practice situation.

**Contextual interference effect**    The learning benefit resulting from practicing multiple skills in a high-contextual-interference practice schedule (as in random practice), rather than practicing the skills in a low-contextual-interference schedule (as in blocked practice).

**Continuous motor skill**    A skill with arbitrary beginning and end points.

**Control parameters**    Coordinated movement control variables (e.g., tempo, or speed, and force) that freely change according to the characteristics of an action situation. According to the dynamical systems view of motor control, when a control parameter is systematically varied (e.g., speed is increased from slow to fast), a collective variable may remain stable or change its stable state characteristic at a certain level of change of the control parameter.

**Coordination**    The patterning of body and limb motions relative to the patterning of environmental objects and events.

**Coordinative structures**    Functionally specific collectives of muscles and joints that are constrained by the nervous system to act cooperatively to produce an action.

**Cost-benefit trade-off**    The cost (in terms of slower RT), and benefit (in terms of faster RT) that occur as a result of biasing the preparation of a response in favor of one of several possible responses (as opposed to preparing as if each possible response is equally probable).

■

**Deafferentation**    A procedure that researchers use to make proprioceptive feedback unavailable (through surgically severing or removing afferent neural pathways involved in the movement). It also can result from injury or surgery to afferent neural pathways involved in proprioception.

**Degrees of freedom**    The number of independent elements or components in a control system and the number of ways each component can act.

**Degrees of freedom problem**    A control problem that occurs in the designing of a complex system that must produce a specific result. The design problem involves determining how to constrain the system's many degrees of freedom so that it can produce the specific result.

**Descriptive KP**    A verbal knowledge of performance (KP) statement that only describes the error a person has made during the performance of a skill.

**Differential psychology**    The study of individual differences in psychology.

**Discrete motor skill**    A skill with clearly defined beginning and end points, usually requiring a simple movement.

**Displacement**    A kinematic measure describing changes in the spatial locations of a limb or joint during the time course of the movement.

**Distributed practice**    A practice schedule in which the amount of rest between trials or groups of trials is relatively large.

**Dual-task procedure**    An experimental procedure used in the study of attention to determine the degree of interference caused by one task when the subject is simultaneously performing another task.

**Dynamical systems theory**    An approach to describing the control of coordinated movement that emphasizes the role of information in the environment and the dynamical properties of the body and limbs.

**Dynamic view of modeling**    A theoretical view explaining the benefit of visually observing a model. It proposes that the visual system is capable of processing the observed movement in a way that constrains the motor control system to act accordingly, so that the person does not need to engage in cognitive mediation.

□

**Electromyography (EMG)**    A technique for recording the electrical activity of a muscle or group of muscles.

**External imagery**    A form of mental practice in which a person imagines viewing himself or herself performing a skill from the perspective of an observer.

□

**Fading technique**    A method of decreasing the frequency of augmented feedback by systematically reducing the frequency during the course of practice so that the person is effectively "weaned" from depending on its availability.

**Fine motor skill**    A skill that requires control of the small muscles of the body to achieve the goal of the skill, and typically involves eye-hand coordination.

**Fitts' Law**    The law specifying the movement time for an aiming response when the distance to be moved and the target size are known. It is quantified as $MT = a + b \log_2(2 D/W)$, where $a$ and $b$ are constants and $W$ = target width, and $D$ = distance from the starting point to the target.

**Fixation/diversification**    The second stage of learning in Gentile's model. *Fixation* refers to closed skills in which learners refine movement patterns so that they can produce them correctly, consistently, and efficiently from response to response. *Diversification* refers to open skills in which learners develop large repertoires of motor patterns.

**Foreperiod**    In a reaction time paradigm, the time interval between a warning signal and the go signal, or stimulus.

**Fractionization**    A part-task training method that involves practicing separate components of a whole skill.

**Freezing the degrees of freedom**    A common initial strategy of beginning learners when a skill requires the coordination of various segments of a limb. To control the many degrees of freedom of the limb segments, the person holds some joints rigid (i.e., "freezes" them) while performing the skill.

□

**General motor ability hypothesis**    A hypothesis that maintains that there exists in an individual a singular, global motor ability.

**Generalized motor program**    The general memory representation of a class of actions that share common invariant characteristics. It provides the basis for controlling an action.

**"Getting the idea of the movement"**    The first stage of learning in Gentile's model. It refers to the need for the learner to establish an appropriate movement pattern to accomplish the goal of the skill.

**Gross motor skill**    A skill involving large musculature to achieve the goal of the skill.

**Guidance hypothesis**    Hypothesis indicating that the role of augmented feedback in learning is to guide performance to be correct during practice. However, if it is provided too frequently, it can cause the learner to develop a dependency on its availability and therefore to perform poorly when it is not available.

■

**Hick's Law**    A law of human performance stating that RT will increase logarithmically as the number of stimulus-response choices increases.

■

**Identical elements theory**    An explanation of positive transfer proposing that transfer is due to the degree of similarity between the component parts or characteristics of two skills or two performance situations.

**Imagery ability**    An individual-difference characteristic that differentiates people who can image an action with a high degree of vividness and control from people who have difficulty imaging an action.

**Index of difficulty (ID)**    According to Fitts' Law, a quantitative measure of the difficulty of performing a skill involving both speed and accuracy requirements. It is calculated as the $\log_2(2\ D/W)$, where $W$ = target width, and $D$ = distance from the starting point to the target.

**Internal imagery**    A form of mental practice in which a person imagines being inside his or her own body while performing a skill and experiencing the sensations that are expected in the actual situation.

**Intertask transfer**    Transfer between tasks or skills.

**Intertrial variability**    An environmental characteristic in Gentile's taxonomy of motor skills. The term refers to whether the regulatory conditions that exist for the performance of a skill in one situation or for one trial are present or absent in the next situation or trial.

**Intratask transfer**    Transfer occurring within one task or skill as a result of an intervening experience.

**Invariant features**    A unique set of characteristics that defines a generalized motor program. Fixed characteristics of a motor program that do not vary from one performance of the action to another.

■

**Kinematics**    The description of movement without regard to force or mass. It includes displacement, velocity, and acceleration.

**Kinetics**    The study of the role of force as a cause of motion.

**Knowledge of performance (KP)**    A type of augmented feedback that gives information about the movement characteristics that led to the outcome of the movement or skill performance.

**Knowledge of results (KR)**    A type of augmented feedback that gives information about the outcome of a movement or skill performance.

**KR-delay interval**    The interval of time between the completion of a movement and the presentation of augmented feedback.

■

**Learning**    A change in the capability of a person to perform a skill. It must be inferred from a relatively permanent improvement in performance as a result of practice or experience.

■

**Massed practice**    A practice schedule in which the amount of rest between trials or groups of trials is either very short or nonexistent, so that practice is relatively continuous.

**Mental practice**    The cognitive rehearsal of a physical skill in the absence of overt physical movements. It usually involves imaging oneself performing a skill.

**Modeling**    The use of demonstration as a means of conveying information about how to perform a skill.

**Motor program**    A memory representation that stores information needed to perform motor skills. It provides the basis for giving commands to the motor system so that the person can perform these skills in a way that will allow him or her to achieve their action goals. It also has been referred to as a *generalized motor program.*

**Motor skill**    A skill that requires the coordination of body and/or limb movement to achieve its goal.

**Movement preparation**    The activity that occurs between the intention to perform and the initiation of an action. Sometimes, the term *motor programming* is used to refer to this activity.

**Movements**    Behavior characteristics of specific limbs or a combination of limbs that are component parts of an action or motor skill.

**Movement time (MT)**    The interval of time between the initiation of a movement and the completion of the movement.

**Multiple-resource theories**    Theories of attention proposing that there are several information-processing mechanisms, each of which is limited in how much information it can process simultaneously during performance and learning.

◼

**Negative transfer**    The negative effect of prior experience on performance of a skill, so that a person performs the skill less well than he or she would have without prior experience.

**Nonregulatory conditions**    Characteristics of the performance environment that do not influence the movement characteristics of an action.

◼

**Observational learning**    Learning a skill by observing a person performing the skill. Also known as *modeling*.

**Open-loop control system**    A control system in which all the information needed to initiate and carry out an action as planned is contained in the initial commands to the effectors.

**Open motor skill**    A skill that involves a changing, unpredictable environment where the environment determines when to begin the action.

**Organization**    When applied to a complex motor skill, the relationship among the components of the skill.

**Overlearning**    Practice that continues beyond the amount needed to achieve a certain performance criterion.

◼

**Parameters**    Features of the generalized motor program that can be varied from one performance of a skill to another. The features of a skill that must be added to the invariant features of a generalized motor program before a person can perform a skill to meet the specific demands of a situation.

**Percentage of transfer**    A measure of the amount of transfer indicating the percentage of improvement in the transfer situation due to the previous experience.

**Perceptual-motor abilities**    Abilities of an individual that include such things as multi-limb coordination, manual dexterity, etc.

**Performance**    The behavioral act of performing a skill.

**Performance bandwidth**    In the context of providing augmented feedback, a tolerance limit for performance error that specifies when augmented feedback will or will not be given.

**Performance curve**    A line graph illustrating performance in which the level of achievement of a performance measure is plotted for a specific sequence of time (e.g., sec, min, days) or trials. The levels of the performance measure are on the Y-axis (vertical axis) and the time units or trials are on the X-axis (horizontal axis).

**Performance outcome measures**    Measures of movement that indicate the outcome or result of a motor skill performance. E.g., how far a person walked, how fast a person ran a certain distance, or how many degrees a person flexed a knee.

**Performance plateau**    While learning a skill, a period of time in which the learner experiences no improvement after having experienced consistent improvement. Typically, the learner then experiences further improvement with continued practice.

**Performance production measures**    Measures of movement that concern how various aspects of the motor control system are functioning during the performance of an action. E.g., limb kinematics, force, EEG, EMG, etc.

**Physical proficiency abilities**    Physical and athletic abilities of an individual, including things such as static strength, dynamic strength, stamina, etc.

**Point-light technique**    A research procedure used to determine the relative information people use to perceive and identify coordinated human actions. It involves placing LEDs or light-reflecting material on certain joints of a person, then filming or videotaping the person performing an action. When a research project participant views the film or video, he or she sees only the bright spots, i.e., only the joints, in action.

**Positive transfer**    Enhancement in performance of a skill due to prior experience.

**Post-KR interval**    The interval of time between the presentation of augmented feedback and the beginning of the next trial.

**Power law of practice**    A mathematical law describing the change in rate of performance improvement during skill learning. Large amounts of improvement occur rapidly during early practice and smaller improvement rates characterize further practice.

**Practice variability**   The variety of movement and context characteristics a person experiences while practicing a skill.

**Prehension**   The action of reaching for and grasping an object that may be stationary or moving.

**Prescriptive KP**   A verbal statement of knowledge of performance (KP) that describes errors made during the performance of a skill and states (i.e., prescribes) what needs to be done to correct them.

**Progressive part method**   A part-task training method that involves practicing the parts of a skill in the order in which each part occurs in performing the skill, and practicing the parts progressively together.

**Proprioception**   The perception of limb and body movement characteristics. Afferent neural pathways send to the central nervous system proprioceptive information about characteristics such as limb and/or body movement direction, location in space, velocity, and muscle activation.

**Psychological refractory period (PRP)**   A delay period during which a person seems to put planned response "on hold" while executing a previously initiated response.

**Psychomotor ability**   A category of human abilities related to speed and accuracy of movements where little or no cognitive demand is placed on the person.

□

**Qualitative augmented feedback**   Augmented feedback that is descriptive in nature (e.g., using such terms as *good, long*), and indicates the quality of performance.

**Quantitative augmented feedback**   Augmented feedback that indicates a performance quantity, such as the amount of error made in the performance.

□

**Reaction time (RT)**   The interval of time between the onset of a signal (stimulus) and the initiation of a response.

**Regulatory conditions**   Characteristic of the skill performance environmental context that determine (i.e., "regulate") the required action and the movement characteristics needed to perform the action.

**Relative timing**   The proportion of time required by the various components of a skill during the performance of that skill.

**Response time**   The time interval involving both reaction time and movement time; that is, the time from the onset of a signal (stimulus) to the completion of a response.

**Retention test**   A test of a practiced skill that a learner performs following an interval of time after practice has ceased.

**Root-mean-squared error (RMSE)**   An error measure indicating the amount of error between the displacement curve produced and the criterion displacement curve.

□

**Savings score**   A measure of the amount of transfer indicating the amount of practice time a person saves in learning a particular skill because of previous experience.

**Schema**   A rule or set of rules that serves to provide the basis for a decision. In Schmidt's schema theory, an abstract representation of rules governing movement.

**Segmentation**   A part-task training method that involves separating the skill into parts and then practicing the parts so that after one part is practiced, it is then practiced together with the next part, and so on. *See also* progressive part method.

**Self-organization**   The emergence of a specific stable pattern of behavior due to certain conditions characterizing a situation rather than to a specific control mechanism organizing the behavior; e.g., in the physical world hurricanes self-organize when certain wind and water temperature conditions exist.

**Serial motor skill**   A skill involving a series of discrete skills.

**Serial position effect**   An effect seen when a learner must remember a series of items in sequence. The first few and last few items are remembered best, whereas the middle items are remembered worst.

**Simplification**   A part-task training method that involves reducing the difficulty of different parts of a skill.

**Skill**   (a) An action or task that has a specific goal to achieve. (b) An indicator of quality of performance.

**Specificity of motor abilities hypothesis**   A hypothesis that maintains that the many motor abilities in an individual are relatively independent.

**Speed-accuracy trade-off**   A characteristic of motor skill performance in which speed of performing the skill is influenced by movement accuracy demands. The trade-off is that increasing speed yields decreasing accuracy, and vice versa.

**Stability**    In the dynamical systems view of the control of coordinated movement, a behavioral steady state of a system. It represents a preferred behavioral state and incorporates the notion of invariance by noting that a stable system will spontaneously return to a stable state after it is slightly perturbed.

**Stimulus-response compatibility**    A characteristic of the spatial arrangement relationship between a stimulus and a response. This relationship will influence the amount of preparation time in a reaction time task involving stimulus and response choices.

**Subjective error estimation**    Indication by the person performing a skill of what he or she thinks was wrong with the performance.

**Summary augmented feedback**    A method of reducing the frequency of augmented feedback by giving a person augmented feedback for a certain number of trials at the completion of those trials (e.g., KR for each of five trials after the completion of every fifth trial).

**Superdiagonal form**    A term describing the way the trial-to-trial correlations appear in a correlation matrix where all trials are correlated with each other. Trials that are closer to each other have scores more highly correlated. The correlation decreases as trials become farther apart.

**Symmetric transfer**    Bilateral transfer in which the amount of transfer is similar from one limb to another, no matter which limb is used first.

■

**Task-intrinsic feedback**    The sensory feedback available while performing a skill that is a naturally occurring part of the skill performance situation itself.

**Terminal augmented feedback**    Augmented feedback that is provided after a person has completed the performance of a skill or the making of a movement.

**Transfer of learning**    The influence of having previously practiced or performed a skill or skills on the learning of a new skill.

**Transfer-appropriate processing**    An explanation of positive transfer proposing that transfer is due to the similarity in the cognitive processing characteristics required by the two skills or two performance situations.

**Transfer test**    A test in which a person must perform a skill that is different from the skill that he or she practiced, or must perform the practiced skill in a situation different from the practice situation.

**Trials-delay procedure**    An experimental procedure used in the study of augmented feedback. It involves giving augmented feedback for a trial not after a person completes that trial, but following completion of a later trial. E.g., for a two-trial delay, an experimenter gives augmented feedback about trials 1, 2, and 3 after trials 3, 4, and 5 respectively.

■

**Variable error (VE)**    An error score representing the variability (or conversely, the consistency) of responses by a person.

**Variance accounted for**    The amount, as designated by a percentage, of the statistical variance of a performance score accounted for by some factor, such as an ability test score.

**Velocity**    A kinematic measure describing the rate of change of a movement's position with respect to time. It is derived by dividing displacement by time.

**Verbal cues**    Short, concise phrases that direct a performer's attention to important environmental regulatory characteristics, or that prompt the person to perform key movement pattern elements, while performing a skill.

**Vigilance**    Maintaining attention in a performance situation in which the frequency of stimuli requiring a response is low.

**Visual search**    Actively engaging vision in seeking information in the environment that will enable the performer to determine what to do in a situation.

# NAME INDEX

# SUBJECT INDEX